Schriften des Instituts für Migrationsforschung
und Interkulturelle Studien (IMIS), Bd. 13

SCHRIFTEN DES INSTITUTS FÜR
MIGRATIONSFORSCHUNG
UND INTERKULTURELLE STUDIEN (IMIS)
DER UNIVERSITÄT OSNABRÜCK

IMIS-SCHRIFTEN

herausgegeben vom Vorstand des Instituts

Bd. 13

Wissenschaftlicher Beirat:
Leo Lucassen, Werner Schiffauer, Thomas Straubhaar,
Dietrich Thränhardt, Andreas Wimmer

National Paradigms
of Migration Research

edited by
Dietrich Thränhardt and Michael Bommes

V&R unipress
Universitätsverlag Osnabrück

Redaktionsanschrift:
Universität Osnabrück
Institut für Migrationsforschung
und Interkulturelle Studien (IMIS)
FB 2, Neuer Graben 19/21
49069 Osnabrück

Tel.:   05 41/9 69-43 84
Fax: 05 41/9 69-43 80
e-mail: imis@uni-osnabrueck.de
internet: http://www.imis.uni-osnabrueck.de

„Dieses Hardcover wurde auf FSC-zertifiziertem Papier gedruckt. FSC (Forest Stewardship Council) ist eine nichtstaatliche, gemeinnützige Organisation, die sich für eine ökologische und sozialverantwortliche Nutzung der Wälder unserer Erde einsetzt."

Bibliographische Information Der Deutschen Bibliothek

Die Deutsche Bibliothek verzeichnet diese Publikation in der Deutschen Nationalbibliographie; detaillierte bibliographische Daten sind im Internet über <http://dnb.ddb.de> abrufbar

1. Aufl. 2010
© 2010 Göttingen, V&R unipress GmbH
mit Universitätsverlag Osnabrück
Alle Rechte vorbehalten

Gedruckt auf säurefreiem, total chlorfrei gebleichtem Werkdruckpapier. Alterungsbeständig.
Printed in Germany

ISBN 978-3-89971-223-0

Contents

Preface. 7

Introduction: National Paradigms of Migration Research.
By Michael Bommes and Dietrich Thränhardt 9

Part I:
Immigration as a Part of National Identity:
Two Traditional Immigration Countries

Canadian Multiculturalism as an Ethos, Policy and Conceptual Lens
for Immigration Research. *By Oliver Schmidtke* 41

Aborigines, Anglos and Asians – Discourses on Multiculturalism
and National Identity in Australian Migration Research.
By Sigrid Baringhorst 61

Part II:
How to Integrate Migration into Old Nation State Narratives

How to Face Reality. Genres of Discourse within Dutch Minorities Research.
By Baukje Prins 81

Beyond the Race Relations Model: Old Patterns and New Trends in Britain.
By Karen Schönwälder 109

Migration Research in Germany: The Emergence of a Generalised Research
Field in a Reluctant Immigration Country. *By Michael Bommes* 127

Migration Studies in Austria – Research at the Margins?
By Bernhard Perchinig 187

Part III:
Emerging Research in New Migration Countries

Italy – Migration Research Coming of Age. *By Tiziana Caponio* 207

Japan: A Non-Immigration Country Discusses Migration.
By Takashi Kibe and Dietrich Thränhardt 233

Migration Research in a Transformation Country: The Polish Case.
By *Krystyna Iglicka* 259

Part IV:
New Nation States:
Defining Nations and Their Migration Contexts

India and its Diaspora. Changing Research and Policy Paradigms.
By *Daniel Naujoks* 269

The National Context of Migration Research in Malaysia.
Which Nation, What State, Whose Migration? *By Diana Wong* 301

A Paradigm for Nigerian Migration Research? *By Dirk van den Boom* 315

The Autors 323

Preface

Migration is a world-wide phenomenon these days, evoking high hopes, deep anxieties, bringing people together, as the American motto *e pluribus unum* suggests, and enabling political entrepreneurs to find ever new objects of antagonism and exclusion. Not only in traditional immigration countries but also in many other places research on immigration has emerged, as well as in many academic disciplines like sociology, history, anthropology, political science, geography, economics and education. Despite the overwhelming influence of the American academia and media and despite the status of English as the *lingua franca* of today's scientific world, research approaches vary strongly between countries.

»Methodological nationalism« cannot only be understood in the sense Andreas Wimmer coined the term, the nation state being the only frame of reference but also the ever-present repetition of national research outlooks to the traditional concepts and construction ideas of the given nation states, including their historic fears and idiosyncracies, with an affirmative or a critical intention. Our aim was to represent, discuss and compare these different research traditions, not only in the Western world but also in some Asian and African countries. We thank all the participants of the conference in Osnabrück where the first versions of the papers were discussed, and the contributors of the volume for their patience during the long editing process. We are grateful to the Friedrich-Ebert-Stiftung for the gratious funding of the conference. As ever with these series, Jutta Tiemeyer precisely and carefully prepared the manuscripts for publication. Simone Rehrs controlled and adjusted the bibliographical data. We hope that the volume will encourage ever more international exchange and debate.

Münster and Osnabrück, November 2009

Dietrich Thränhardt and Michael Bommes

Introduction:
National Paradigms of Migration Research

By Michael Bommes and Dietrich Thränhardt

Migrations are an inherent part of current processes of globalisation and internationalisation, which provide undoubtedly the foundation for the increasing call for more international and comparative research. Accordingly, the number of international research projects and networks in the research area of migration has grown considerably over the last two decades.[1] Scholars participating in this endeavour, however, soon discover that the academic modes of conceptualising, defining and recording problems depend to a large extent on the respective national histories of science. This applies particularly to academic research into international migration and the ensuing problems in the regions where migration begins and ends. Research questions and approaches are frequently designed along the lines of national traditions and patterns of state reactions towards international migration and its societal effects. Seen in this way, migration research seems itself to be rather a part of the complex of problems that it claims to describe and explain. This context dependency becomes certainly more visible in international research projects, since here researchers are more often compelled to explicate their preconceptions.

Systematically, this leads to a number of questions: To which extent and how is migration research shaped by ›national paradigms‹ or ›hidden national agendas‹ like ›race relations‹ in the UK, ›ethnic minority policies‹ in the Netherlands, ›assimilation into a French citizenry‹ in France or ›integration into a welfare state‹ in Germany? These paradigms are perhaps even present in critical efforts of scholars who strive to overcome their very boundaries.[2] How do these national patterns influence the way in which international research and scientific modes conceptualise their research questions? What are the consequences of this for the claim of scientific validity with regard to propositions and applied theories? These questions have hardly been addressed systematically in migration studies (Lavenex 2005; Vasta and Vasoo 2006) yet their investigation is an essential precondition for adequately reflexive international research.

The assumption that research may be imbued with ›national paradigms‹ is intentionally constructed in a paradoxical manner. Put in this way, we focus on one

---

1   One exceptional example is the research funding of the EU. Within the Sixth Framework Programme, the Network of Excellence (IMISCOE) has been funded since 2004 (project period: 5 years). This network comprises over 20 established European research institutes.
2   Like in the work of Robert Miles (1993; 1994), who is clearly as fascinated with the frame of race relations as he tries to move away from it.

characteristic of the field of research, i.e. the indexing of the paradigms of migration research as ›national‹. This may refer, on the one hand, to a quite unproblematic matter of fact: Migration research takes on different national shapes, since migration and the resulting societal constellations differ in each country. As a consequence, different research questions need to be asked, and correspondingly, different theories and methodological approaches need to be applied. Seen in this way, the heterogeneous appearance of migration research and concomitant problems of mutual understanding may be simply the result of a lack of sufficient joint explication and translation of approaches as well as their implicit context dependency. This would, however, not principally foreclose scientific claims of generalisability made by propositions on the basis of theories and methodologies applied in nationally confined migration research. It seems that the apparent paradox can be rectified easily and that it concerns a rather unproblematic case: Internationalisation of research would simply imply that nationally established approaches in migration research become more explicit about their generalisability claims and enable a process in which these claims are tested in an extended context of research, involving comparative research designs and competition among alternative scientific approaches. This will certainly be linked with the failure of research approaches and theories, i.e. we would just observe the normal and unspectacular course of science not really worth specific mentioning.

However, we approach the issue of ›national research paradigms‹ inspired by a more far-ranging assumption: The paradigms of migration research are ›national paradigms‹ not just because of their context dependency and insufficient clarification of the conditions of generalisability; they are ›national‹ because the modes of presenting problems and questions are politically constituted by the nation states for which migration becomes a problem or a challenge. This assumption finds initial evidence in the fact that migration research is usually perceived as part of the applied social sciences: This type of research emerged as a response to ›social problems‹ with the claim to contribute to their solution. This holds true for early American sociology, whose first chair was established in Chicago at the end of the nineteenth century, linked with the political expectation that it would generate useful practical knowledge able to contribute to the practical solution of those social problems stemming from immigration.[3] This similarly applies to Australia (Vasta 2006) and to migration research in different European countries since the Second World War (Vuddamalay and Withol de Wenden 2006; Scholten 2007; Favell 2001; 2005; Boswell 2009). These practical conditions during the emergence of migration research do not necessarily prove that its different traditions

---

3 In the introduction to their monumental work *The Polish Peasant in Europe and America* Thomas and Znaniecki (1958) criticise this line of thought as an inadequate basis for scientific analysis as early as 1918 (first publication 1918). In principle, they see the migration and integration of Poles as a theoretically interesting case for the constitution of social order – but in the substantial parts of the book, they fail to follow their own line of thought, i.e. to detach themselves from practical normative issues.

create ›national paradigms‹ in the political sense introduced above, since no initial condition determines the structure of research programmes.

We take this point only as a first indicator for the validity of our assumption, and it turns out that it is easy to find others: 1) Up to the present, migration researchers tend to be rather ›committed‹ and less ›distanced‹ researchers.[4] In many countries, they play a major role in conceptualising migration and integration policies, either directly or as government advisors. Much research is embedded in such activities, and ›policy relevance‹ is seen as an important criterion for migration research. 2) During the last decades, migration research has gained prominence in the relevant disciplines[5], although it did not contribute significantly to the theoretical or methodological progress of these disciplines. Central and paradigmatically relevant theoretical and methodological debates in the various disciplines have only to a minor extent influenced migration research and vice versa: the findings of migration research had and still have a rather low impact on these (sub-) disciplines. The general (political) consensus about the societal relevance of international migration – linked with the willingness to provide more resources for research – has created a climate of reputation and recognition for migration research, which is not substantiated by scientific achievement. Research may be confronted with increasing expectations, but the research questions and answers as well as research approaches remain largely the same – certainly permitting differences in scientific preferences mainly dependent on the orientations of researchers.

Before this backdrop, we suspect that the paradigms of migration research are national in the sense that they are hybrids resulting from the handling and redesign of politically constituted problems by means of scientific research. We want to clarify if and to what extent the tension between the national constitution of the migration problem and its scientific treatment affects the scientific claim of universality. Do aspects external to science penetrate the internal conceptualisation of problems, theory building and research design in migration research in a way that leads to the emergence of ›national paradigms‹ of migration research?

In order to answer these questions, we need to clarify first to what extent the problem of migration is constituted by the organisational form of the nation state, and how different nation states frame the specific modes of raising problems, which in turn define the subject of research (I). Second, we discuss how the relation between practical relevance and scientific claim, between »commitment and distance« (Elias 1956) is moderated in migration research, and what kind of ›national paradigms‹ emerge out of this process. *The challenge is to identify the relation between politics/policies and science in different traditions of migration*

---

4 Following a concept by Norbert Elias (1956) which was taken up by Treibel (1988) for a sociological overview of the *Ausländerforschung* in Germany during the 1970s and 1980s; see also Bommes in this volume.
5 Especially sociology, political science, ethnology, history, geography, linguistics, education and economics. This multi- or interdisciplinary profile of migration research will be discussed in more detail below.

research. We assume that in each case a specific relation of mutual enablement and restriction provides the ground for different national paradigms (II.). Finally, we discuss to what extent these paradigms and their foundations remain relevant for a more and more internationally and comparatively oriented migration research.

I. Nation States as Constitutive Frame for the Problem of International Migration

In all nation states, international migration and migrants become periodically a political issue, yet in varying ways and with a focus on different topics. Therefore, an analytical framework of analysis is required that allows to account for commonalities and differences between nation states in dealing with international migration (1). Based on this framework, we provide some arguments for the assumption that nation states conceptualise international migration based on their structural constitution (2). In a third step, we discuss the extent to which these conceptualisations are mirrored in the different national traditions of migration research (3).

(1) Migration is usually defined as the movement across borders, from one nation state to the other – or from one society to another (Treibel 1990, 21). In contrast, internal migration is evidently considered as normal, unproblematic or even functional and necessary, strengthening national cohesion and opening access to locations where people can work and live most effectively and satisfyingly – the practical realisation of Adam Smith's idea of the invisible hand. In other words, internal migration in national labour markets is not only seen as normal, it also refers to the socially institutionalised expectation of social mobility. Internal migrants are therefore neither perceived nor treated as migrants. Instead, the emergence of conflicts about internal migrations usually indicates that a nation state is in crisis, that processes of political erosion articulate themselves in increasing desires to split up and create new states – be it a most imaginative ›Padania‹ in the North of Italy, an independent Assam in the North East of India, an independent Kurdistan cutting across Turkey, Syria and Iran, or a Kosovo free of Serbian domination.

The field of migration research dealing with international migration is therefore over-determined by a contradiction, which has been prominently labelled ›the liberal paradox‹ (Hollifield 1996): One central assumption of liberalism is that the freedom of movement of people as well as of goods, capital and services does not only refer to a natural right but also provides the basis for the smooth operation of society. Restrictions upon such freedoms are associated with authoritarian governments – pre-modern, colonial, fascist or communist – and are seen as dysfunctional for a modern, i.e. open, economy. On the other hand, national sovereignty, including the right to control access to state territory, remains largely unquestioned. This is taken as a basic principle of international and national law, only slightly modified by the non-refoulement clause of the Geneva Convention. Communitarian philosophers have reaffirmed this position as a legitimate right of closure, based on the operational mode of communities and the requirements for societal cohesion (Taylor 1993; Walzer 1983; 1990)

Only a small minority of political theorists takes a principled stance against the territorial sovereignty of states (Bauböck 1994). On the whole, however, idealist hopes for a borderless world (Soysal 1994; Jacobson 1996) have faded away since the fall of the Berlin wall. Inside the European Union, the liberal paradox seems to be solved: The freedom of movement is largely institutionalised, and despite the recurrent fears accompanying each enlargement round, no serious social tensions have arisen so far. The liberal paradox re-emerges, however, at the external frontier of the EU, and new member states situated at this border have to prove their maturity for full membership by implementing Schengen conditions and by establishing border control capacities according to EU standards.

In more general terms, ›the liberal paradox‹ refers to a structural contradiction of modern world society: On the one hand, international migration is an outcome of the social expectation involved in the institutionalised form of mobility in modern world society, i.e. individuals are expected to move where relevant social chances for participation and resources for an autonomous life are available. International migration means precisely the effort to realise opportunities for a living by means of geographical mobility. This does per se not imply structural problems for the primarily affected social systems, like labour markets, education systems or families – the freedom to move may be rather a precondition for their functioning, as liberals argue.[6] Nevertheless, most international migrations are, on the other hand, confronted with all kinds of legal and political interventions and restrictions.

The structural basis for these regular interventions is the organisational form of politics in modern society, i.e. the nation state. Political and legal interventions in international migration occur regularly and not just by historical chance. They make manifest the internal structural contradiction of world society (Stichweh 1998), i.e. the permanent production of motives for international migration – due mainly to the demand of labour markets and the opportunities of educational systems, the institutionalisation of the nuclear family, the worldwide communication of options by the mass media and the accessibility of transport (just to name the most important factors) – and the constant political effort to control these migrations[7] and to mould motives for migration, according to the specific structure of the political system, i.e. its internal segmentary differentiation into nation states.

---

6 This is why geographical mobility within nation states, due to employment, family reunion or education, is socially not perceived as migration, and those involved are normally not treated as migrants.
7 See Castles and Miller 2009; the Global Commission on International Migration (GCIM) Report (http://www.gcim.org/en/finalreport.html) can be read as an effort to overcome this basic contradiction by means of temporalisation: arguing that international migration will be in the benefit of all ›in the long run‹ – being faced however at present with all kinds of ›short term‹ barriers.

One strong implication of the worldwide institutionalisation of national states has been the partitioning of the world population into state populations (Halfmann 2005). International migrations have always challenged this division by crossing borders in the quest for chances of social participation. The reactions of nation states towards these migrations are mediated by the two constitutive dimensions that define the relation between states and their populations: a) the dimension of *loyalty* refers to the requirement that citizens and all other persons residing in a nation-state territory show obedience and participate in political decisions; it is therefore a fundamental condition for the reproduction of state sovereignty; b) the dimension of *provision* refers to the obligation of the state to provide legal, political and social security in exchange for loyalty coagulating in the concept of the welfare state (Marshall 1950).[8] Nearly all political modes of regulating international migration are geared towards aspects linked to one or both of these *dimensions – loyalty and provision* (Bommes 1999).[9] These two dimensions are deeply interlinked. States shape their take on migration on the ground of patterns based on the conceptualisation of the population as citizens resulting from historical state building processes: How the population is constituted as a national community of citizens and the related design of the welfare state define the common ground for all kinds of political reactions to be found in states dealing with migration. They are, however, differently articulated due to the different course of state building based on different dynamics in the emergence of the state population and the building up of welfare systems.

One major difference between European nation states and the traditional immigration countries (USA, Canada, Australia) has always been the building process of state populations and the related concept of *loyalty*: European state populations are the historical outcome of the efforts of emerging states to establish sovereignty over a territory and a people against competing claims of neighbouring states (Tilly 1990). Nation building in Europe took place as a process by which a population was delineated and transformed into a nation, a people within a politically defined territory (Koselleck 1992). This outlines the historical background for the varying« concepts and meanings of civic community as »the people« (Brubaker 1992) and the specific relevance of the loyalty dimension in dealing with migrants in Europe (Bade 2003). In contrast, in traditional immigration countries immigration has been an integral part of the population building process by conceptualising immigrants in principle as future citizens – despite the exclusion of certain migrants for a long time on racist grounds.

---

8 Not all states achieve to be welfare states, since they are not able to build up the necessary capacity of provision. It is obvious, however, that no state can ignore the demands of its population to care for welfare, and so-called failing states can to a large extent not preserve the loyalty of their population because of their reduced or absent capacity to guarantee security and provision.

9 Current examples are the public association of migration and terrorism, which questioned the loyalty of migrants, on the one hand, and the frequent debates in nearly all European welfare states but also in the US concerning the effects of international migration on the capacity of welfare states in terms of costs and benefits, on the other hand (Bade and Bommes 2004).

The different histories of state building also provide the background for the different meaning of the *welfare dimension* in Europe and in traditional immigration countries in dealing with migration. The emerging modern states in Europe sought to politically mediate the chances of inclusion and exclusion in reaction to the breakdown of pre-modern stratified orders of inclusion (Bommes 1999). The modern nation state can most generally be defined by its successful claim of sovereignty over a territory and a population. From the outset, this was linked with the emergence of the welfare state (Swaan 1988). By providing chances for participation in the social realms of the economy, law, health or education – that is within a welfare state – the nation state created the social preconditions for a process in which former subjects were transformed into political citizens. This was a process in which the inclusion of the whole population into the political system via the individual citizens and the claim of political sovereignty over them could gain political legitimacy and universal validity. The welfare state became the central authority in modern society moderating relations between the principle of universal access[10] to and inclusion in the social realms of the economy, law, education, health or politics and the empirical reality of social exclusion.

The effect was that national welfare states became the worldwide institutionalised organisational model of the political system in world society, and with their emergence, they have evolved as international »thresholds of inequality« (Stichweh 1998). This means that they have guaranteed the *internal loyalty* of their citizens by a welfare policy that promotes chances for inclusion based on *external closure and exclusion*. From its beginning, welfare provided by nation states had a territorial index. The provisions of welfare states initially addressed primarily citizens, i.e. those individuals perceived by states as belonging to their territory. The nation may have been defined in either cultural (e.g., Germany) or republican terms (e.g., France), but in the historical context of competitive state building processes in Europe, the common welfare of the people of the nation – of the community of national citizens – evolved as the general frame of reference for states (Bommes 1999). This involved the political claim for not only formal, but also some substantial equality for all members of the national community; a claim based on the political form of membership, i.e. citizenship (Marshall 1950).

This European model of the national welfare state gained worldwide relevance (Meyer et al. 1997)[11], although in different ways. Again, for our purpose, one major difference between European welfare states and the traditional immigration

---

10 Universalism of inclusion in modern society means that nobody *should be* excluded from claiming economic, legal or educational provisions, if he or she fulfils the social preconditions for these claims (Luhmann 1989). For example, one can participate in education, if one is perceived as educable; one can participate in the economy, if one finds access to monetary means; one can participate in law, if one knows how to act on behalf of one's rights. At the same time, none of these necessarily imply that inclusion always succeeds empirically – on the contrary, it often fails. Yet the valid institutionalisation of social expectations, like the universalism of inclusion, provides the ground for the perception of this failure as a problem in need of remedy, e.g., by means of social policy.

11 See footnote 9.

countries is telling: Welfare in Europe implies a more or less thick notion of ›the people‹ as the original political collective that defines the addressee of welfare; correspondingly, migrants are seen as potentially illegitimate welfare seekers from outside. In contrast, immigration countries conceptualise and recruit immigrants traditionally as potential contributors to welfare – not because these countries do not provide welfare in a privileging manner, addressing primarily citizens, but because immigrants are right from the start expected to become future citizens. In other words, the production of welfare has always been based on immigration, whereas welfare in Europe is still to a large extent perceived as a ›(gross) national product‹ leaving the contribution of outsiders, i.e. migrants, with only limited acknowledgement.[12]

Despite these differences, in a most general sense, all national welfare states try to privilege their citizens (or what they consider to be their core citizens). They try

- to open or facilitate access to the relevant social systems (the economy, law, education, family or health) and to reduce the risks of exclusion;
- to stabilise these systems and their capacities of inclusion (labour markets, families, education, health, etc.);
- to equip individuals so that they fulfil the conditions for social participation;
- to compensate for the social consequences of failing access.

In order to achieve these objectives, states rely fundamentally on law as a means of assigning rights and duties, of the political distribution and redistribution of funds and the symbolic communication of civic duties. These state efforts lead to highly differentiated welfare infrastructures encompassing social security systems, which deal with the modern core risks of accident, health, age and unemployment, with social benefits for families, programmes to increase access to education, social benefit payments for the long-term excluded and poor, various public provisions of social services, etc.

National welfare states differ tremendously, even in Europe, and it seems that this will also remain the case in the near future, despite the advancement of globalisation and European integration and some, although limited, processes of model mixing and assimilation (Obinger et al. 2006). These differences are a result of the varied histories of national state building. Welfare structures are the outcome of the accumulated political decisions in history; they mould welfare in nationally specific ways with regard to concepts of social cohesion, the size and qualities of a constituency, legitimate membership and access to rights as well as notions of social risks and failure, and expectations of mutual obligations constituted by solidarity, which define we-collectives of insiders and complementary outsiders. Different welfare states represent therefore different welfare cultures, i.e. bundles of organisations, regulations and institutions referred to as welfare states are

---

12 As an effect of demographic changes, European countries start to realise the extent to which they do rely on the attraction of immigrants. The recent debates on the integration of migrants articulate some of the fears linked with the realisation of the increasingly fictive character of nationally delimited perceptions.

culturally deeply imbued. Conceptions of security and insecurity, assumptions about responsibilities for the provision of welfare, the limits of welfare and the extent of individual self-responsibility are contingent and not self-evident. There are always alternative ways, and it is certainly – at least in principle – possible to organise welfare differently. Each welfare state is based on different assumptions about what states should do, and to what extent they should intervene, about the meaning and foundations of freedom or solidarity, about the main institutions and foundations of society, etc.[13]

---

13   Different welfare states make therefore use of those institutions in different ways, i.e.
  – individual freedom on markets (liberty and private welfare: liberal individualistic welfare states);
  – families/communities (reproduction of the communitarian foundations of society: conservative corporatist welfare states);
  – the state (social equality in labour market society; social democratic universalist welfare states).
  Based on those distinctions, it is possible to categorise welfare states in different types. According to Esping-Andersen (1990), we find three such types, i.e. the liberal, the conservative and the social democratic type of welfare state in Western society. Accordingly, welfare states differ with regard to
  – their extent of de-commodification, i.e. the extent to which income and social security is made dependent on participation in the labour market;
  – the role and amount of residual spending, i.e. national assistance as a percentage of social spending;
  – their redistributive aims and capacity;
  – their corporatist structure, i.e. the differentiation of social security systems according to different occupational and status groups;
  – the amount of private spending for health and pension systems;
  – their conceptual assumptions about the main provider of welfare, i.e. the market, the family or the state.
  Along these lines, welfare states vary largely according to their orientation, which can be distinguished as individualistic vs. corporatist vs. universalistic. Examples for the liberal individualistic type are the UK and the USA, for the conservative corporatist type Germany, Austria, Italy and France and for the social democratic universalistic type the Scandinavian countries, especially Sweden and Denmark (Esping-Andersen 1990; Schmid 2002; Opielka 2004). Many aspects of this modelling have been criticised. Some argue that there is a fourth type in Europe, the Mediterranean type (Ferrera 1998); some question the empirical applicability of the model (Alber 2000). For a discussion, see also Kaufmann 2004. During the last ten or fifteen years, there have also been extensive discussions about the adaptive capacity of these different welfare state types and their ability to cope with new constellations as a consequence of the challenges of globalisation; see Esping-Andersen 1996; 2002; Ganßmann and Haas 1999; Goodin et al. 1999; Alber 2000; Fligstein 2000; Kaufmann 2003; Leibfried and Zürn 2005); on a most general level, the outcome of this discussion is that those welfare states do best which manage to combine access to labour and the provision of welfare, instead of providing welfare as a substitute for labour – a problem mainly for the conservative corporatist type of welfare states. In many countries, the recent shift to so-called activating welfare policies is a reaction to these problems. Integration policies in many countries belong in this context.
  Typologies of welfare states have been developed in the context of international comparative welfare state research. Certainly, they are to a large extent based on the analyses of leading Western countries; see, however, Esping-Andersen 2002 for more comprehensive comparisons. New immigration countries like Malaysia (an ethnic welfare state), Nigeria (a corrupt state) and Hong Kong (a free market system) do not fit into these schemes.

(2) These considerations on the relation of national welfare states and international migration provide an adequately generalised model in order to account for the different modes in which international, i.e. trans-border, migrations are conceptualised as political issues and handled by states. By adequately generalised, we mean that this model should allow further case-dependent respecifications, e.g. to account for differences between large and small welfare states, the formation problems of new nations in Asia and Africa, the transition of countries, like Turkey, from traditional emigration countries to transit and immigration countries. We assume that these political modes of conceptualising migration resurface in the paradigms of migration research, mirroring country specific constellations. In the following, we summarise the assumptions of this model:

A commonality of different states is defined by the need to solve a bundle of problems, in order to build and maintain a capacity for the production of collectively binding decisions. Essentially, this includes the enforcement of the claim of sovereignty over a territory and its population, i.e. the people. This implies, as elaborated above, the two dimensions of loyalty and provision: What kind of loyalty is expected from whom, and who is suspected to be disloyal (e.g., autochthonous minorities, migrants coming from competing neighbouring states)? Who should be included in civil, political and social provisions, and who should be excluded? What kind of civil, political and social provisions are institutionalised, and how are they related to internal historical conflict constellations and cleavages? Dependent on the historical handling of these constellations by states, international migrants denote groups that stand in many respects in stark contrast to the different demarcations and delineations resulting from state building processes:

a) The relation between international migrants and the group of citizens is precarious. Dependent on how delineations are defined, the conditions for the inclusion of migrants are more or less open or restrictive, linked with expectations concerning cultural similarity, the willingness of acculturation, assimilation and loyalty. These expectations are anchored in notions of the hereditary or acquirable character of cultural patterns, paradigmatically articulated in the opposition of republican and ethnic concepts of citizenship.[14] These distinctions prove to be relevant not only in Europe, but also for migrations in the successor states of the Soviet empire or the postcolonial states of the former Third World. Additional complications face those postcolonial migrants in Europe for whom national citizenships had been open (like in Great Britain, the Netherlands, France and more recently in Spain and Portugal). After closure, however, their social position has been redefined in most of these countries in terms of ethnic or race relations.

b) Notions of (potential) belonging organise not only the formal rules of access to welfare provision, which may in- or exclude different migrants to a different

---

14 Often but misleadingly explicated by the difference between the French and the pre-2000 German concepts of citizenship; see Hagedorn 2001 and Gosewinkel 2003.

extent, but also the social perceptions of the legitimacy to claim benefits and the chance to scandalise it publicly.
c) In different national welfare states, migrants acquire differentiated access to social rights and provisions. This depends on the different mode of construction of welfare states; and fairly often, it is removed from the question whether this access is politically perceived as legitimate: It can be the long-term outcome of participation in the labour market of welfare states which make access to social rights dependent on employment; it can be the effect of welfare provisions that address the legally resident population living in the state territory.
d) Migrations become a political issue in different ways dependent on the internal order and infrastructure of states: in countries with majority voting systems differently from countries with systems of proportional representation; in centralistic systems differently from federalist systems; in democracies differently from dictatorships, etc. That is to say, the forms and dynamics of the reproduction of state power are relevant for the question if and how migrants become an issue under the perspectives of loyalty and provision.

If one regards this approach as an underlying framework of reference, one can immediately notice that international migration and migrants assume in different countries the form of specific problems, which depend on the design of these states, their internal way of reproducing sovereignty and the related conceptualisation of loyalty and power relations. This explains the difference between immigration countries and those countries in Europe that conceive of their form of political organisation by dint of founding myths as the constitution of native populations on ancestral territory. We have already discussed that this leads in each case to different conceptualisations of migrants in their relation to the state population as well as to welfare.

Nevertheless, the ›multiculturalisms‹ of the immigration countries Canada, USA and Australia differ substantially from one another: In Canada, multiculturalism has served since the 1960s as a sort of moderator for the latent tensions between the two founding nations, while at the same time it commits immigrants to this constellation. In Australia, it can be traced back to a changed international situation in which the country repositioned itself politically in the Pacific region under the motto ›populate or perish‹, by opening itself to immigration from Asia since the late 1960s. Australia linked this development with a ›re-description‹ of its state population. As in the United States, this was accompanied by recurring fears, whether on the basis of plural origins living together harmoniously, immigrants can turn into loyal citizens, or, vice versa, whether the foundation of the state, a certain degree of uniformity and coherence among its inhabitants, is at risk. On the basis of the highly selective admission of immigrants, these countries also differ with regard to the access immigrants have to welfare benefits. However, especially their selectivity reduces the likelihood that such benefits are claimed. It is, therefore, hardly accidental that, particularly in the US, public debates arise regularly on the issue of the exclusion from such benefits – yet, these concern in particular illegal immigrants before the backdrop of an economic situation in which the extended employment of such immigrants in certain sectors of the labour market and the continued demand for them is hardly a hot topic. This leads to hypocrisy in public scandalisation and the establishing of harsh control and defence apparatus, in particular along the border with Mexico, while the immigration and employment of such migrants continues (Cornelius et al. 2009).

In Europe, despite processes of adjustment during the last 15 years, differences between the states remain, be it between cultural and political concepts of nations (*Kulturnation* vs. *Staatsnation*), between republican and multicultural-pluralistically oriented policies, or with regard to the constitution of their welfare states. This finds expression in the conceptualisations of migrants in relation to state population and in the variations of what, unlike in the United States, is in most European countries purposely taken as the ›integration‹ and not as the ›assimilation problem‹ of migrants. In France, for instance, republicanism turns out to be a quasi-lens through which all immigrant-related issues are seen, be it the issue of access to citizenship, which as a matter of course is open to migrants conceived as immigrants based on the recognition of the republican order and the assimilatively oriented expectation to become French, the shaping of the inclusion of migrants in the educational system, or the handling of cultural and religious pluralisation. This has the mirror effect that immigrants perceive their actual social marginalisation as withholding the republican promise to be part of the French nation.

In the Netherlands the conceptualisation of immigrants as ethnic minorities was, since the 1970s, based on the pillar model anchored in the specific Dutch state building. Until the 1990s, the corresponding direction of welfare state integration policies allowed the combining of post-colonial immigration and recruited labour migration in a historically proven model. The resulting tension between political, multicultural tolerance and the de facto marginalisation of large sections of the immigrant population in the labour market and in cities under well-developed welfare-state conditions initiated the continuous and increasingly restrictive transformation of migration and integration policies, associated with both increasingly aggressive, publicly expressed expectations of migrants to assimilate and considerable turbulence in the political party system. In Denmark, immigration and its consequences run counter to the country's self-image as a culturally and socially completely homogeneous nation.

In the British case, the conceptualisation of the immigration issue as ›race relations‹ shapes the public debate, which has its basis in the immigration of ›former subjects‹ of the British Crown from the 1950s to the 1970s. Migration and opportunities for social participation of migrants are primarily conceptualised as problems of the equitable cohabitation of ›races‹, of multicultural tolerance and anti-discrimination, which are meant to domestically signal acceptance and equality towards immigrants, given the closure of the British state for their home countries and for former subjects of the Commonwealth in general. Historically rooted in the history of the Empire, this conceptualisation is currently being ›overwritten‹ by a new wave of immigration after the EU enlargement. According to the priorities of New Labour, it is being replaced by a new interest in ›indicators of social integration‹ regarding immigrants from Eastern Europe, also in view of the increasingly apparent limits of the absorption capacity of the ›open labour market‹.

The conceptualisation of migration and migrants in Germany, which has experienced several immigrations encompassing refugees and expellees, ›guest workers‹, asylum seekers, civil war refugees and ethnic Germans (*Aussiedler*) was determined by two reference frames: a) Germany is not an immigration country (*Einwanderungsland*), and therefore immigrants (*Zuwanderer*) are not automatically seen as immigrants (*Einwanderer*); they can and should become Germans only under restrictive conditions; b) permanent immigration (*Zuwanderung*)[15] and the settlement of migrants refer to problems of social integration, which are the responsibility of the welfare state. Into the 1990s, an ethnically founded citizenship barred access to the naturalisation of migrants. Since then, under certain conditions concerning integration, citizenship has become obtainable. On the other hand, since the Second World War, the positive reference to what constitutes a German was eclipsed and cultural difference was primarily conceptualised as a problem for social integration, as a deficit and hurdle for the required adaptation, particularly in education and the labour market. This perspective remains prevalent until the present day and now also includes ethnic Germans (*Aussiedler*) after their reconceptualisation from formerly cultural Germans to culturally and socially different migrants with typical integration problems. On the other hand, the German welfare state proved to be inclusive in the sense that it effectively provided protection not only for large parts of the migrant workers of the 1960s and 1970s due to compulsory social insurance, but it also covers the basic needs (food, clothing, accommodation, health) of all individuals residing in its territory via the welfare state concept. To a limited extent, this also applies to asylum seekers. In Germany, the problem conceptualisation of migration and migrants revolves, therefore, mainly around the question of whether immigrants can provide for themselves and whether they receive social benefits legitimately – in other words, whether in the long run they manage their ›social integration‹ successfully. This finds its most recent expression in the fact that probably in no other country in Europe was a ›national integration plan‹ created with a comparable symbolic effort.

Moreover, the management of immigration by the Mediterranean countries in Europe is embedded in their specific state traditions. The Italian case indicates that the political handling of the significant immigration since the late 1980s, rooted in the demands of an EU increasingly organised in regard to migration questions, can only be explained in the context of a growing demand for services of a familistic welfare state faced with the demographically accelerated ageing process of its

---

15   Migrants who enter the country are not automatically perceived as continuous immigrants. So the question whether they want to remain as immigrants is kept open by the expression *Zuwanderer* whereas the expression *Einwanderer* in German means that the migrant is expected to stay in the country. By choosing the word *Zuwandungsgesetz* in Germany it is connoted that migrants are not automatically seen as immigrants.

population and a tradition of the legal rectification of illegal situations, be it in relation to the building code or residence permits. In this way, as in Spain, illegal migration and its legalisation became de facto migration policy, against the actual backdrop of an official EU-oriented policy.

Discussions about the way in which states conceptualise problems associated with international migration are usually confined to traditional immigration countries and Europe. A look at worldwide migration (Castles and Miller 2009; Massey et al. 1998; Thränhardt and Hunger 2003) shows quickly, however, that the political handling of international migration is also anchored in the structures of statehood in the respective countries and regions. As the contributions on Nigeria and Malaysia in this volume show, both countries debate ›social cohesion‹, the definition of a constituency, of the people constituting the nation, of its delimitation and the claim and testing of the reach of state sovereignty with regard to migrants, who are partly, even by dint of violence, excluded from rights and benefits and expelled from state territory.[16]

Public policy regarding international migration and migrants was and is embedded in international discourses. One can characterise the late nineteenth and the first half of the twentieth century as the era of the prevalence of the nation state. This era is also associated with unquestioned domestic assimilation policies of countries towards their minorities and immigrants as well as related policies, such as the one set forward by the League of Nations, which reacted to the vulnerability of this policy, apparent in forced cultural homogenisation, separatist tendencies and wars, with the redesign of state borders based on the ›right of self-determination of peoples‹ or with the resettlement of ethnic minorities, be it ›voluntarily‹, as in the case of the Greeks and Turks in the Treaty of Lausanne, or coerced, as in the case of the Allied Potsdam Agreement with regard to the Germans in Eastern Europe.

The period since the Second World War was characterised by a decline of nationalism in Western countries, the dominance of liberalism and the increasing differentiation between law and politics as well as decolonisation in the Third World. This was associated with a relative decoupling of state, nation and culture. Since then, cultural differences are seen as legitimate, cultures are considered equal, and cultural pluralism is now regarded as beneficial. An early source is the UNESCO Declaration on the equality of cultures, which emphasised the right to diversity and its value. This has not necessarily been replaced but, rather, has been accompanied by a »return of assimilation« (Brubaker 2001) in discourse and

---

16 The Gulf States are an interesting case, which we can however not cover here in detail. Some of these ›pensioner states‹, which obtain a substantial income from their energy resources, exclude their population from political participation on the basis of providing for them. Associated with this are significant ›modernisation deficits‹ resulting in an insufficient work force, at least with regard to the necessary skills for developing an infrastructure. This work force is increasingly made up of migrants from neighbouring countries (Egyptians, Jordanians, Palestinians, etc.) and since the 1990s from Asia, who are vice versa prepared to do such work under considerable constraints to their private lives in view of the employment opportunities and wages in their home countries.

political expectations in many countries, which does not necessarily constitute a negation of the UNESCO Declaration, but in different ways in different countries, calls into question the benefits and value of cultural pluralism. The need to clarify the relationship between cultural pluralism and the indispensable conditions for the participation in the functional systems of education, the economy, law, health, religion, and the mass media is also brought into focus, such as the tension between human rights, cultural pluralism and relativism, respectively.

International discursive formations impact differently on the political public as well as on policies of individual countries; they are re-articulated against the backdrop of respective national histories. Multiculturalism, concepts of diversity, integration and assimilation denote different things in each case and can therefore not be understood adequately in isolation from their contextual embedding.

(3) International migration and its associated problems are, as shown, substantially constituted by the character of policy and the specific structure of states. They form the filter for international migration, which is essentially caused by the mobility in modern society and thereby lend it a specific shape as a problem. The latter is reflected in the ways of conceptualisation in the various strands of national migration research.

Even a cursory comparative glance shows that the outline in the previous section of individual aspects of concepts of international migration as problems in various countries finds its reflection in the main issues of national migration research, which shall be briefly illustrated in the following:

West German migration research formed itself by means of state-constituted migrant groups. At first, it succeeded as research into refugees and expellees, then as research into guest workers, foreigners and ethnic Germans (*Aussiedler*), before it developed into general migration research. At the centre of its research stands the question of social integration, and the latter, in its different ways of conceptualisation since the 1970s, is evidently geared towards the guiding precepts of the West German welfare state, its guest worker, foreigner policy and later policy concerning ethnic Germans as well as, finally, its current immigration and integration policy.

The issues of French migration research revolve around republicanism and related questions: Which consequences do international migration and the settlement of migrants have, especially for the associated expectations and concepts of assimilation, citizenship and laïcité; whether immigration is inevitably associated with the growing importance of cultural, ethnic and religious differences; whether their public irrelevance should be maintained or instead be replaced with forms of tiered recognition; and finally, the questions of whether such differences can be empirically recorded and whether their relation to other social dynamics within families, at labour and housing markets, or in the school system ought to be and shall be explored.

In the United Kingdom, ›race relations‹ are the constitutive reference point for British research on migration until well into the 1990s. The critics of this approach distance themselves by marking this approach as ›racist‹ (Miles 1994) in a *tu quoque* mode and thus remain performatively tied to the criticised frame of reference in a peculiar way. This constellation, based on the immigrations of the 1950s to 1970s in the context of a disintegrating commonwealth, is increasingly replaced by more recent research, which essentially follows the objectives of New Labour, highlights the potential and benefits migration brings and explores ›indicators of integration‹.[17]

To the present, migration research in the United States is often characterised by the old question of assimilation, starting with Thomas and Znaniecki, Park and Gordon, from Gans, Portes/Rumbault, to Alba/Nee and Waldinger. It places at its centre the constitutive problem of the United States – how social order and coexistence can be guaranteed on the basis of the coming together of so many different nations/regions (*e pluribus unum*). This continuation finds its plausibility in the huge waves of immigration since the civil rights reforms in the mid-1960s, which currently keeps timely the question of whether the ›melting pot‹ still works. Noted processes of differentiation are characteristically discussed as ›segmented assimilation‹.

In Australia, migration research and its concepts were not only shaped by the multicultural orientation of immigration policy since the 1970s, but the latter has also significantly helped to develop this policy – not least because of its close organisational link to politics.

Especially the last example shows that the orientation of different national migration research towards the ways in which different states conceptualised international migration, immigration and settlement as political problems did not hinder the production of solid empirical and theoretical contributions. However, a reflection from a sociology of knowledge perspective of this conceptually narrow focus and the often organisationally close links between science and politics in the field of migration research is still lacking.

II. National Paradigms of Migration Research? The Relationship of Politics and Science in Migration Research

The aim of the following considerations is to develop a framework for such a reflection. The contributions of this volume provide, to some extent, material with which to begin such a project in a comparative perspective. Upon closer inspection, the determination of what could constitute national paradigms of migration research creates, conceptually, more difficulties than the charm of this initially attractive project suggests.

a) In the previous sections, we have highlighted how deeply migration research is imbued by its embeddedness in the respective nation states. This does not

---

17 Moreover, this also expresses the Europeanisation of research, as efforts in the English context, promoted by the Labour government, are at the same time linked to projects funded by the EU.

overlook the fact that migration researchers have in turn a significant influence on the shaping of migration policies and related problem conceptualisations in many countries. The permeation of migration research by politics and statehood is therefore not based on a relationship of instruction. The issue is rather the interplay between the two on the basis – usually, at least – of mutual independence. We assume that this independence constitutes their interdependence[18]: Politics cannot produce scientific, i.e. research-legitimated, knowledge and science, vice versa, has no access to political power and collectively binding decision-making[19], but it remains for central functional conditions – particularly the freedom of science and access to resources – dependent on law and its political enforcement as well as to a significant extent on resources made available politically. This captures the relationship between science and politics in very general terms, yet the issue here is how they are shaped in and impact on the relationship between migration research and politics.

b) Migration research does not match the internal differentiation of science into disciplines, and this justifies the assumption that it is research with an essentially interdisciplinary orientation (Brettell and Hollifield 2000; Bommes and Morawska 2005). In the political and academic discourse, interdisciplinarity is, much like internationality, seen as an indicator of quality, but initially, it primarily constitutes a problem. Migration outlines a field that involves many disciplines and calls for their responsibility: sociology, psychology, economics, political science, pedagogy or law, social geography, ethnology and medicine. This characteristic transverse position of migration as a topic repeats itself within the individual disciplines, as can be easily shown with regard to sociology. Here, migration research operates, on the one hand, as a reference point for sub-disciplinary specialisation, and accordingly there exists a nationally and internationally organised sociological migration research.

On the other hand, according to an established textbook, sociological migration research deals with migration as the »permanent or increasingly permanent move into another society or into another region by an individual or multiple persons« and »with the causes, course and consequences of migration« (Treibel 1990, 21). It can therefore hardly avoid dealing with almost all fields with which sociology is also concerned in its various sub-disciplines. »Causes« refer to the initial socio-structural contexts of migration, which require migration sociologists to have substantial knowledge of developmental and migration sociology as well as anthropology, in order to produce scientifically adequate descriptions. The »consequences« of migration consist in the fact that migrants often appear in all relevant social contexts, i.e. the economy, politics, law, education, health, sports, mass media, or religion of the target region, either individually or as families. Therefore, migration sociologists also have to assume roles as family sociologists, educational

---

18 In such general terms, this point also denotes a commonplace in the sociological theory of differentiation since Marx and Durkheim.
19 This is the reason why it can complain without any risk that its advice is ignored, as it has neither to bring about the necessary decisions nor to take responsibility for them.

sociologists, youth or legal sociologists, labour market researchers, business, industry or organisational sociologists, inequality researchers, conflict sociologists, political scientists or political theorists and so forth.[20] This is almost inevitable, as migrants, like all other individuals, occur in society and its differentiated social structures. They become relevant to political, legal, economic, educational, health or religious issues, or as members of organisations. The manner in which they appear here makes them first visible as migrants.

This leads to the problem of generating a framework of reference for research that tends to repeat every sub-disciplinary specialisation of the discipline and that can therefore determine its identity only in terms of its difference to these specialisations. In a variety of fields, it therefore continually runs the risk of structural amateurism. This constellation recurs for migration research in a similar manner in other disciplines, such as law, political science (Freeman 2005) or linguistics (Maas 2007).

Consequently, migration research does not constitute a discipline, but refers to a multi- and interdisciplinary conglomeration of research which deals with issues of international migration coming from different disciplines. Hitherto, it is unlikely, yet not impossible, that it evolves into a discipline, if disciplines are understood in a preliminary way as »forms of institutionalisation of processes of cognitive differentiation« (Stichweh 1979), including the following elements: 1) a nexus of communication between researchers, 2) a body of scientific knowledge coagulated in textbooks, which is codified, accepted and teachable in the discipline, 3) a common set of problems and questions, 4) a common set of research methods and theoretical frameworks, 5) a career structure and modes of socialising and recruiting young scholars.[21] One can certainly discover elements of an internal differentiation and of the emergence of an (international) migration research; yet, this issue does not have to find its final answer here. Especially, at the organisational level, the founding of research institutes and the establishing of research associations occur. Yet, there are hardly indications for the formation of a discipline. For the international and interdisciplinary research on migration, it can be stated in rather general terms: »Since there [...] is no theoretical integration of disciplines, this form of cooperation is forced to take place at a low theoretical level« (Luhmann 1990, 642). Instead, migration research primarily gains relevance among the differentiated disciplines. However, due to its transverse position among the disciplines and the resulting danger of structural amateurism in view of the specialisations in various sub-disciplines, as mentioned above, it is even more confronted with the problem of defining its constitutive *problematique*.

c) In section I, we argued that the problem of international migration has its foundation in the contradiction of world society, the simultaneous production of

---

20 If one accepts Treibel's definition of the problem constellation, migration research would also urgently require engagement with social theory – this might indeed not be harmful, but would increase the problem of poaching in too many reserves.
21 For a historical approach concerning the relation between disciplines and interdisciplinarity, see Swoboda 1979.

migration motives through its institutionalised form of mobilisation and its restraint through the shape of politics – that national migration research finds its respective issues here and that thereby it mirrors, more or less, the ways in which the respective states conceptualise their policy issues. Due to its peculiar intra-and transdisciplinary mismatch and the resulting problem of how to delimitate those problems defining research, one has to presume that migration research orients itself towards state conceptualisations of migration for structural reasons, namely due to its free-floating nature – not only because the politically explosive nature of the topic guarantees attention and resources, but also because this way of conceptualising offers a moderator, who serves to hold together the rather indefinite and frayed problem field of migration research with reference to two main views: ›integration‹ and ›inequality‹.

These have, strictly speaking, their foundation in the classical nation-state problem of cohesion vs. corrosion (integration vs. disintegration), peace vs. conflict, in modern European terms: social cohesion vs. disintegration. This problematique is rooted in the historical way the modern nation state emerged and differentiated itself. The latter links its claim to have the sovereign right to enforce collectively binding decisions within its territory and for people residing there and constituted as state population with the self-description as an entity, the uppermost and controlling body of nationally conceived society. This claim is based on the argument that the nation state is the legitimate expression and bearer of the national, be it politically or ethnically constituted, will of the community. From the perspective of the state, functionally differentiated society is a state-delimited context in need of integration, which finds unity and cohesion in the nation, visible despite globalisation in the ›national economy‹, in the national education system, or in the nationally constituted welfare systems. From the outset, cohesion and corrosion, integration and disintegration of society are rooted in the notion of the state as an entity, as the national bond of society. With this focus on the state, the claim of the ›rule of the people‹ permeates the community as the promise, however difficult to keep, to steer society. Against this background, loyalty and domestic peace are signs of the integration of society as a community, whereas disloyalty and conflict, vice versa, are signs of disintegration. From this perspective, states have historically viewed ethnic minorities as well as political opposition groups as potentially disloyal and conflictive – in Germany the Social Democrats were, as is well known, seen as an »unpatriotic bunch (*vaterlandslose Gesellen*)« (Groh and Brandt 1992). And in Britain the diverging cultures of the emerging proletariat, on the one hand, and the bourgeoisie, on the other hand, caused Benjamin Disraeli in the nineteenth century to talk of »two nations« before the backdrop of the social upheaval of the industrial revolution, begging the follow-up question of whether this indicates the disintegration of society or casts doubt on its integration.

Cohesion and corrosion, ›integration‹ and ›inequality‹ – the central issue of migration research captured in different terms rehearses this old problematique: the problems of differentiation and inequality, and the question of whether and how the poor or the lower classes come to terms with unequal living opportunities; which potential for conflict it entails and to what extent this is relevant for the integration of society? These questions address recurrently and especially in Europe, with its development into a world immigration region after the Second World War, migrants and the consequences of their settlement, their integration perceived as precarious. And the EU reformulates this problem in tandem with the expansion of its competence claims in terms of inclusion/exclusion and social cohesion.

The main precepts ›integration‹ and ›inequality‹ of migration research are therefore owed to the modern state, as the birth of ›society‹ in the modern social sciences has its roots in the spirit of the nation state (Tenbruck 1981; 1992). In a manner similar to hardly any other sub-discipline in the social sciences until the present, migration research breathes the original spirit of sociology and of social science as a science of crisis (Habermas 1981); they present the problem of political order as the problem of cohesion, ›integration‹ and the threat of internal disintegration through ›differentiation‹ and ›inequality‹, paradigmatically formulated by Durkheim in the late nineteenth century in his question about the possibility of a ›conscience collective‹ in modern differentiated society.[22]

Here, for migration research, the respective terms used are not of importance: in the American context the problem of assimilation concerns the question of how assimilation can be successful and considers cultural and structural assimilation, i.e. the relatively identical socio-structural positioning and the individual and social conditions under which this can succeed, as a prerequisite for the development of unity, whose extent has to be established in each case. In the German context, the same debate revolves primarily around the concepts of integration and inequality. In the Anglo-Saxon context, racial equality, ascertainable through non-discrimination in labour and housing markets, education, health, law and politics, is meant to allow coexistence on the basis of unity in diversity; similar points apply to the various types of multicultural policy. Certain aspects of policy might favour an orientation towards unity as the demand for adjustment or alignment, instead of granting civil and social equality; in a republican context migrants may be confronted with this demand. On the other hand, their principled otherness, defining the state population by its confines, might until the present lead to their expulsion.

In this perspective, terminologies, the ways of conceptualisation in the different states, and the associated migration research rearticulate the problem of ›migration and integration‹ in various ways, rooted in the various histories of nation building. This is the exact reason for the various ways of conceptualisation. Yet, on close inspection, the same kinds of problems recur, and research remains tied to its state-specifically articulated problems, even if it deals with most different areas:

---

22 Durkheim 1977; it is easy to recognise that sociology tried from the outset to distance itself from a Marxian perspective, which however shares with it the assumption that the cohesion of a society can only be conceived of in a ›classless society‹, in which asymmetries, unintended inequalities and, hence, integration problems are absent.

Whether it deals with families, education, health, work, politics, law, mass media, religion, or language, everything is seen in terms of integration and inequality, successful or failed assimilation, the successful or unsuccessful easing of ›race relations‹.

d) Does it make sense to talk of ›paradigms of migration research‹, if they are, as argued here, rather scientific re-articulations of nation-state specific ways to constitute international migration-related problem constellations? To answer this question, we first need to define the meaning, which has until now been left open, of the term ›paradigm‹. Aware of the elaborate discussion following the ›paradigmatic‹ investigation of Thomas Kuhn in *The Structure of Scientific Revolutions* (1970/1976), we generally assume that a paradigm can be recognised by the central distinctions used to determine the subject of scientific research and the accordingly applied theories. The empirical study of science is concerned with the question of how science establishes the very criteria it applies to successful research. In this context, Kuhn (1970) distinguishes in his postscript, in order to clarify what can be called a paradigm in the strict sense, between scientific communities[23] and what constitutes a paradigm in the strict sense as a ›model‹, its productive basic distinctions as starting point and basis for the discovery, differentiation and development of problems. Paradigms describe, therefore, functioning problem/problem-solving constellations, which are unlimited in regard to the number of problems to be discovered yet productive, and at the same time, they allow one to turn them into common forms of describing a problem and solving it (Kuhn 1970, 189).

The emergence of such paradigms requires the differentiation of science. Kuhn speaks of the »unparalleled insulation of mature scientific communities from the demands of the laity and of everyday life« (164). Scientists aim to cater to the expectations of the scientific system, and their primary audience are scientists. Here, Kuhn sees a significant difference between the ›mature‹ paradigm-governed natural sciences and the humanities and social sciences in the fact that scientists of these disciplines have to more or less familiarise themselves with the entire history of problems and problem solutions for the area they work in; they also face a wide range of competing paradigms, whose appropriateness they have to evaluate themselves from case to case. This leads to a much lamented paradigm pluralism in these disciplines with the respective scientific communities as ›camps‹. This might also be the basis for the tendency of social science, recognised by Kuhn, toward the »choice of a research problem – e.g., the effects of racial discrimination or the causes of the business cycle – chiefly in terms of the *social importance* of achieving a solution« (Kuhn 1970, 164; emphasis added, M.B.). Yet, this is far from compelling, and the mentioned pluralism does not exclude scientific introversion in these disciplines and their »insulation [...] from the demands of the laity

---

23 Discernible, for instance, with regard to similar education and career, shared literature, intensity of communication and mutual references in publications, shared standards, conferences, etc.

and of everyday life«. The question is rather, under which conditions these disciplines follow such tendencies, and what their subsequent consequences are.

e) The community of researchers on migration may certainly be considered a peculiar example for the case that the choice of research problems is recurrently justified »chiefly in terms of the *social importance* of achieving a solution«. Migration researchers are also hardly reserved, when it comes to communicating preferred solutions. Their majority advocates the equality of migrants – be it as integration, reduction of barriers to assimilation, inclusion and avoidance of exclusion, incorporation, and so forth – and see this as a condition for the cohesiveness of society, of its integration. Hence, they stand until the present not only in the tradition of the social sciences as a science of crisis and maintain its original spirit in their close link to the state; they also do not aim for the »insulation [...] from the demands of the laity and of everyday life«, but rather continuously emphasise their respective relevance. This applies to the various booms of migration. In times in which migration attracts less attention, migration research follows its daily business, that is it delves into the ramifications of migration and integration processes and warns of the possible negative consequences of reduced attention to the overlooked or insufficiently noted effects of failing integration, indicated by social inequality, social deviation, etc.[24]

However, if migration and integration find attention, migration research is a sought-after science of crisis, as migration and integration then become synonymous with the politically communicated public perceptions of the crisis of cohesion of a society essentially conceived as a national one (Bade and Bommes 2004). The capability to political action is then demonstrated nationally and at the European level by, among other means, the funding of research – and this despite the fact that sufficient experience already exists: »The politician who grants research money, founds new universities, establishes institutions can pride herself immediately, without having to wait, whether and what the results are« (Luhmann 1990, 639).

This leads to a peculiar state of migration research, which is not simply caused, as one can see now, by the fact that it is traditionally rather an applied science, because the term applied science – differently from fundamental research – refers

---

[24] It is striking that migration research in different countries maintains its way of looking at problems by tying itself to politically mediated patterns of conceptualising, in significant isolation from the general and special theoretical debate in related disciplines – it operates only in a limited way with an internal orientation. In German-speaking sociology, this can be seen in the fact that the debate about adequate theoretical concepts for the description and explanation of inequality, conducted for more than twenty years in inequality research, and the question of the relation between inequality research and differentiation theory in migration research were kept at distance – as if migrants were clear cut cases (of inequality), for which these debates are of no significance. This has only started to change in recent years: Bommes 2003a, Weiß 2005 and the latest Sinus study (Sinus Sociovision 2008) demonstrate that this point of view has no reason apart from an established division of labour between nationally oriented inequality research interested in the position of citizens in the social structure and migration research covering the ›rest‹.

to the relation of provision of science[25] to other non-scientific social fields. It points to the provision of scientific valid and specifically required knowledge.[26] This does however not question the fact that applied science remains embedded in fundamental research, it must not contradict it and does also more or less contribute to it.

However, this applies at best to a limited extent to migration research. Instead, one must probably state – pointedly – that migration research is periodically »taken in« by its subject and »allows to be abused« by it, as due to its proximity to politics there »lies in-between« no »sufficient alienation« with the »headstrong ability to discriminate« of a genuine scientifically constituted theory (Luhmann 1990, 645). Inversely, this is illustrated by the fact that migration research claims in Euro-technocratic terms its »policy relevance«, in contrast to what constitutes a modern science and that it increases the »social imposition« of its knowledge and answers political questions all too often: »This is as it is, make it so« (634). The risk here is reflected in the fact that those using this knowledge turn away due to foreseeable frustration. Thus, the permanent effect of damage to the »facade of the security of scientific knowledge« (641) increases in the case of the contact of science with other areas of society. This becomes visible in the recent intense public debate in Europe surrounding the question of whether the integration of immigrants has failed and whether migration research has failed to provide the necessary knowledge and, therefore, in its role as early warning system.[27] Due to its claimed practical relevance, it can hardly refuse this task – and reinforces this point by the repeatedly heightened claim of its policy relevance.

f) Should we, therefore, drop the concept of paradigm for migration research and, hence, also the assumption of national paradigms in migration studies? This is not an inevitable consequence; rather, one has to ask what kind of science migration research is. On the one hand, one can certainly talk about a community of migration researchers in the Kuhnian sense, based on the criteria outlined above, and this applies in recent years not only more and more to the national but also to the international level – remember that this was exactly the starting point for the argument developed here. Furthermore, migration research and most of its scientists are active in organisations of the scientific system, in universities and research institutes. Moreover, a consequence of the previously argued is that one

---

25 In difference to the functional orientation of fundamental research understood as the orientation towards securing the conditions to experience the world in the same manner.
26 Regardless of the fact that the usability of knowledge is decided by its users and not its producers; Wingens and Fuchs 1989.
27 In the Netherlands, there was a strong denunciation of researchers who were accused of having invented multicultural illusions. The public debate which emerged during 2006/07 in German daily and weekly newspapers about the achievements and failures of migration research, about right and wrong science (cf. Bommes 2006), threw glaring light on the awkward situation of migration research, according to Kuhn (1970). He argues that solutions are only seen as sufficient when they are accepted by many. They »may not, however, be drawn at random from society as a whole«, but they have to come from the scientific community. »One of the strongest, if still unwritten, rules of scientific life is the prohibition of appeals to heads of state or to the populace at large in matters scientific.« (168).

can speak of paradigms of migration studies in the sense that they display integration and inequality as central, nation state-specifically re-articulated distinctions with which the subject of migration research and the theories it applies are delimited and defined. In addition, this paradigm was productive, as can be easily seen with regard to the scope and breadth of migration and integration research.

The discussion of the peculiarities of migration research and the pointed formulation that migration studies »allows to be abused« by its subject-matter, as it develops due to its proximity to politics no »sufficient alienness« with a »headstrong ability to discriminate« of a genuine scientifically constituted theory is essentially based on the assertion that migration research is not a case of a differentiated science in the sense introduced. To properly understand this fact, the Kuhnian distinction between mature and immature science is not of much help. Paradigm pluralism and competition does not exclude the differentiation of science, rather the latter requires the former. Therefore, this does not cover the claim that migration research is not a differentiated science.

Rather, we have above suggested that migration research solves the structural problem of its disciplinary and transdisciplinary transverse position with reference to the political constitution of the problems of international migration. In this way, it is and remains (from a systematic perspective), thus far a hidden reflexive theory of the political system by producing descriptions of migration studies in response to the self-descriptions of this system and its environment, here migration and its consequences, as its composition and not as a scientific outside description.[28] The concepts of migration research are based on an understanding of the political system, which in reference to the latter's self-conception, the hypostasis of its function – to produce collectively binding decisions – the primacy of the »integration of society« assigns it a kind of overall responsibility for society and, therefore, with regard to the relevant subject here, for the problems caused by international migration.[29]

---

28 Outside descriptions are not only produced in science: The economy describes politics, education or the law under its premises and so forth. Every time the respective system is seen with its benefits for the describing system in view, whether, for instance, the educational system produces qualified individuals for the economy, families render children educable, science produces usable knowledge for political decisions, etc. Here the relation of the self-description of social systems and outside descriptions by sciences is the topic; cf. in detail Kieserling 2004.

29 The role of migration research as reflexive theory (for this term, see Luhmann and Schorr 1988) becomes apparent, once one compares it to disciplines that became responsible for dealing with modern society in the trajectory of the scientific system: political science for politics, economics for the economy, pedagogy for the educational system, theology for religion, etc. In all these cases, the same tension arises between outside and self-description, formulated as the question of the extent to which they are reflexive theories of the respective social system or scientific theories. Reflexive theories take up the differentiated perspectives and plausibilities of practice, presuppose them, and provide them with justifications: in pedagogy, economy, law, or (normative) political science. The described tension becomes apparent when the societal improbability of education, economy, law, or politics can still also become a topic; this can be checked by the fact that scientific contributions practically still match the problems of the functional systems they deal with.

This policy-centric concept of society is shared by migration research not only with everyday accounts, the mass media, protest movements, and with some of the other social sciences, not least political science. There are several reasons for this fact, which need no further elaboration in our context. However, the difference to political science is revealing: The latter translates the tension between science and reflexive theory of the political system internally in the contrast between normative and descriptive approaches, externally in its difference to political sociology. However, in contrast, migration research turns out to be a quasi-unacknowledged reflexive theory of the political system, resulting from the handling of its disciplinary mismatch and the subsequent scientific exclusion and determination of its problems. The paradigms of migration research are national, as seen, because they constitutively gain their problems from the ways in which its respective reference state conceptualises international migration and its consequences. This similarity is the reason for its diversity, and with regard to these ways of conceptualisation it fleshes out its issues: the problems of integration and inequality in different areas of ›the society‹ and their need to be governed by politics.

From this vantage point, one can also recognise why the systematic nature of migration research as hidden reflexive theory of the political system does not go away through its internationalisation – a notion which we can only touch upon here at the end. The insight that society can hardly be conceived of as national anymore does not need further detailed reasoning – strictly speaking, international comparative research still mostly denotes the comparison of national ›societies‹. Transnationalism takes the criticism of the notion of society as a national container as its starting point, in order, by the way, to continue to assume national societies (Bommes 2003b). All this aside, the continuation of migration research as hidden reflexive theory of the political system seems, above all, to surface where it abandons the (exclusive) reference to the state as the organisational form of the political system. This becomes apparent in two currently important issue areas: In European migration research, the main themes of ›integration‹ and ›social cohesion‹ remain[30]; in the wake of the ›high-level dialogue‹ of the Global Commission, the increasingly important field of research on ›migration and development‹ tries to link problems of migration control with issues of integration, on the one hand, and conditions of a (failed) development policy on the other. Again, problems are here fleshed out in reference to the political system and its conceptualisations, oriented towards policy relevance and practical recommendations, whether they are consequences of the internal freedom of movement within the EU, the handling of illegal immigrants, or migration models as a ›triple-win‹ recommendation.

Due to the outlined reasons, an internationalising migration research should work diligently to ascertain the respective national paradigms, if only to dissolve the preliminary sketched ›I can't understand you‹ (*Kannitverstan*) situations in international research cooperation. In addition, it would suit it well to reflect its

---

30 So the name of the EU-funded Network of Excellence ›Immigration, Integration and Social Cohesion in an Integrating Europe‹ (IMISCOE).

national histories as hidden reflexive theories of the political system, of its nation states, before it starts with enthusiasm to merely repeat old routines in a transformed manner at the international level.

References

Alber, Jens. 2000. Sozialstaat und Arbeitsmarkt: Produzieren kontinentaleuropäische Wohlfahrtsstaaten typische Beschäftigungsmuster? Gleichzeitig eine Abhandlung über einige Probleme komparativer statistischer Analyse. *Leviathan* 28 (4): 535–69.

Bade, Klaus J. 2003. *Migration in European History.* Oxford: Blackwell.

Bade, Klaus J., and Michael Bommes. 2004. Einleitung: Integrationspotentiale in modernen europäischen Wohlfahrtsstaaten – der Fall Deutschland. In *Migrationsreport 2004. Fakten - Analysen – Perspektiven,* ed. idem and Rainer Münz, 11–42. Frankfurt am Main and New York: Campus.

Bauböck, Rainer. 1994. *Transnational Citizenship. Membership and Rights in International Migration.* Aldershot: Edward Elgar.

Bommes, Michael. 1999. *Migration und nationaler Wohlfahrtsstaat. Ein differenzierungstheoretischer Entwurf.* Opladen and Wiesbaden: Westdeutscher Verlag.

Bommes, Michael. 2003a. The Shrinking Inclusive Capacity of the National Welfare State: International Migration and the Deregulation of Identity Formation. In *The Multicultural Challenge (Comparative Social Research, vol. 22),* ed. Grete Brochmann, 43–67. Amsterdam: JAI.

Bommes, Michael. 2003b. Der Mythos des transnationalen Raumes. Oder: Worin besteht die Herausforderung des Transnationalismus für die Migrationsforschung? In *Migration im Spannungsfeld von Globalisierung und Nationalstaat (Leviathan Sonderband 22),* ed. Dietrich Thränhardt and Uwe Hunger, 90–116. Wiesbaden: Westdeutscher Verlag.

Bommes, Michael, and Ewa Morawska. ed. 2005. *International Migration Research: Constructions, Omissions, and the Promises of Interdisciplinarity.* Aldershot: Ashgate.

Bommes, Michael. 2006. Migrations- und Integrationspolitik in Deutschland zwischen institutioneller Anpassung und Abwehr. In *Migrationsreport 2006. Fakten – Analysen – Perspektiven,* ed. idem and Werner Schiffauer, 9–30. Frankfurt am Main and New York: Campus.

Boswell, Christina. 2009. *The Political Uses of Expert Knowledge: Immigration Policy and Social Research.* Cambridge: Cambridge University Press.

Brettell, Caroline, and James Hollifield. 2000. *Migration Theory: Talking about Disciplines.* New York: Routledge 2000.

Brubaker, Rogers. 1992. *Citizenship and Nationhood in France and Germany.* Cambridge, MA: Harvard University Press.

Brubaker, Rogers. 2001. The Return of Assimilation? Changing Perspectives on Immigration and its Sequels in France, Germany, and the United States. *Ethnic and Racial Studies* 24 (4): 531–48.

Castles, Stephen, and Mark J. Miller. 2009. *The Age of Migration. International Population Movements in the Modern World*, 4th ed. Basingstoke: Palgrave Macmillan.

Cornelius, Wayne et al. ed. 2009. *Mexican Migration and the U.S. Economic Crisis: A Transnational Perspective*. Boulder, CA: Lynne Rienner.

Durkheim, Emile. 1977. *Über die Teilung der sozialen Arbeit*. Frankfurt am Main: Suhrkamp.

Elias, Norbert. 1956. Problems of Involvement and Detachment. *British Journal of Sociology* 7: 226–52.

Esping-Andersen, Gøsta. 1990. *The Three Worlds of Welfare Capitalism*. Cambridge: Polity Press.

Esping-Andersen, Gøsta. 1996. *Welfare States in Transition. National Adaptations in Global Economies*. London: Sage.

Esping-Andersen, Gøsta. 2002. *Why We Need a Welfare State*. Oxford: Oxford University Press.

Favell, Adrian. 2001. *Philosophies of Integration: Immigration and the Idea of Citizenship in France and Britain*. 2nd ed. Basingstoke et al.: Palgrave.

Favel, Adrian. 2005. Integration Nations: The Nation-State and Research on Immigrants in Western Europe. In *International Migration Research*, ed. Bommes and Morawska, 41–86.

Ferrera, Maurizio. 1998. ›The Four Social Europes‹: Between Universalism and Selectivity. In *The Future of European Welfare: A New Social Contract*, ed. Martin Rhodes and Yves Meny, 79–96. London and New York: Macmillan.

Fligstein, Neil. 2000. Verursacht Globalisierung die Krise des Wohlfahrtsstaates? *Berliner Journal für Soziologie* 10 (3): 349–79.

Freeman, Gary. 2005. Political Science and Comparative Immigration Politics. In *International Migration Research*, ed. Bommes and Morawska, 111–28.

Ganßmann, Heiner, and Michael Haas. 1999. *Arbeitsmärkte im Vergleich. Rigidität und Flexibilität auf den Arbeitsmärkten der USA, Japans und der BRD*. Marburg: Schüren.

Goodin, Robert E. et al. 1999. *The Real Worlds of Welfare Capitalism*. Cambridge: Cambridge University Press.

Gosewinkel, Dieter. 2003. *Einbürgern und Ausschließen: die Nationalisierung der Staatsangehörigkeit vom Deutschen Bund bis zur Bundesrepublik Deutschland*. Göttingen: Vandenhoeck&Ruprecht.

Groh, Dieter, and Peter Brandt. 1992. *»Vaterlandslose Gesellen«. Sozialdemokratie und Nation 1860–1990*. Munich: C.H. Beck.

Habermas, Jürgen. 1981. *Theorie des kommunikativen Handelns*, 2 vols. Frankfurt am Main: Suhrkamp.

Hagedorn, Heike. 2001. *Wer darf Mitglied werden? Einbürgerung in Deutschland und Frankreich im Vergleich*. Opladen: Leske & Budrich.

Halfmann, Jost. 2005. World Society and Migrations. Challenges to Theoretical Concepts of Political Sociology. In *International Migration Research*, ed. Bommes and Morawska, 129–53.

Hollifield, James F. 1996. The Migration Crisis in Western Europe: The Search for a National Model. In *Migration – Ethnizität – Konflikt. Systemfragen und Fallstudien*, ed. Klaus J. Bade, 367–402. Osnabrück: Universitätsverlag Rasch.

Jacobson, David. 1996. *Rights Across Borders. Immigration and the Decline of Citizenship*. Baltimore and London: Johns Hopkins University Press.

Kaufmann, Franz-Xaver. 2003. *Sozialpolitik und Sozialstaat: Soziologische Analysen*. Opladen: Leske & Budrich.

Kaufmann, Franz-Xaver. 2004. *Varianten des Wohlfahrtsstaats. Der deutsche Sozialstaat im internationalen Vergleich*. Frankfurt am Main: Suhrkamp.

Kieserling, André. 2004. Überschätzte Reflexionstheorien. Die politische Theorie im Vergleich. In idem, *Selbstbeschreibung und Fremdbeschreibung. Beiträge zur Soziologie soziologischen Wissens*, 170–91. Frankfurt am Main: Suhrkamp.

Koselleck, Reinhart. 1992. Volk, Nation. Einleitung. In *Geschichtliche Grundbegriffe. Historisches Lexikon zur politisch-sozialen Sprache in Deutschland, vol. 7*, ed. Otto Brunner, Werner Conze and Reinhart Koselleck, 142–49. Stuttgart: Klett-Cotta.

Kuhn, Thomas S. 1970. *The Structure of Scientific Revolutions (International Encyclopedia of Unified Science, vol. 2.2)*: University of Chicago Press; German: (1976) *Die Struktur wissenschaftlicher Revolutionen*, 2nd revised ed. Frankfurt am Main: Suhrkamp.

Lavenex, Sandra. 2005. National Frames in Migration Research: The Tacit Political Agenda. In *International Migration Research*, ed. Bommes and Morawska, 243–60.

Leibfried, Stephan, and Michael Zürn. 2006. *Transformations of the State?* Cambridge, MA: Cambridge University Press.

Luhmann, Niklas, and Karl Eberhard Schorr. 1988. *Reflexionsprobleme im Erziehungssystem*. 2nd ed. Frankfurt am Main: Suhrkamp.

Luhmann, Niklas. 1989. Individuum, Individualität, Individualismus. In idem, *Gesellschaftsstruktur und Semantik. Studien zur Wissenssoziologie der modernen Gesellschaft, vol. 3*, 149–258. Frankfurt am Main: Suhrkamp.

Luhmann, Niklas. 1990. *Die Wissenschaft der Gesellschaft*. Frankfurt am Main: Suhrkamp.

Maas, Utz. 2007. *Sprache und Sprachen in der Migrationsgesellschaft. Die schriftkulturelle Dimension (IMIS-Schriften, vol. 15)*. Göttingen: V&R unipress.

Marshall, Thomas H. 1950. *Citizenship and Social Class and other Essays*. Cambridge: Cambridge University Press.

Massey, Douglas S. et al. 1998. *Worlds in Motion: Understanding International Migration at the End of the Millenium*. Oxford: Clarendon Press.

Meyer, Jon W. et al. 1997. World Society and the Nation-State. *American Journal of Sociology* 103: 144–81.

Miles, Robert. 1993. *The Articulation of Racism and Nationalism. Reflections on European History*. Oxford et al.: Berg.

Miles, Robert. 1994. *Racism after ›Race Relations‹*. London: Routledge.

Obinger, Herbert, Heinz Rothgang, and Stephan Leibfried. 2006. The State and its Welfare State – How do Welfare State Changes Affect the Make-up of the Nation State. *Social Policy and Administration* 40 (3): 250–66.

Opielka, Michael. 2004. *Sozialpolitik. Grundlagen und vergleichende Perspektiven*. Reinbek bei Hamburg: Rowohlt.

Schmid, Josef. 2002. *Wohlfahrtsstaaten im Vergleich. Soziale Sicherung in Europa: Organisation, Finanzierung, Leistungen und Probleme*. Opladen: Leske & Budrich.

Scholten, Peter. 2007. Constructing Immigrant Policies. Research-policy Relations and Immigrant Integration in the Netherlands, 1970–2004. PhD Thesis, University of Twente, Arnhem: Printpartners Ipskamp.

Sinus Sociovision. 2008. *Migranten-Milieus. Lebenswelten und Werte von Menschen mit Migrationshintergrund in Deutschland. Sozialwissenschaftliche Repräsentativuntersuchung für das Bundesministerium für Familie, Senioren, Frauen und Jugend*. Heidelberg.

Soysal, Yasemin. 1994. *Limits of Citizenship: Migrants and Postnational Membership in Europe*. Chicago and London: University of Chicago Press.

Stichweh, Rudolf. 1979. Differenzierung der Wissenschaft. *Zeitschrift für Soziologie* 8 (1): 82–101.

Stichweh, Rudolf. 1998. Migration, nationale Wohlfahrtsstaaten und die Entstehung der Weltgesellschaft. In *Migration in nationalen Wohlfahrtsstaaten. Theoretische und vergleichende Untersuchungen (IMIS-Schriften, vol. 6)*, ed. Michael Bommes and Jost Halfmann, 49–62. Osnabrück: Universitätsverlag Rasch.

Swaan, Abram de. 1988. *In the Care of the State. Health Care, Education and Welfare in Europe and the USA in the Modern Era*. Cambridge: Polity Press.

Swoboda, Wolfram W. 1979. Disciplines and Interdisciplinarity: A Historical Perspective. In *Interdisciplinarity and Higher Education*, ed. Joseph J. Kockelmans, 49–92. University Park: Pennsylvania State University Press.

Taylor, Charles. 1993. *Multikulturalismus und die Politik der Anerkennung*. Frankfurt am Main: Fischer.

Tenbruck, Friedrich H. 1981. Emile Durkheim oder die Geburt der Gesellschaft aus dem Geist der Soziologie. *Zeitschrift für Soziologie* 10: 333–50.

Tenbruck, Friedrich H. 1992. Was war der Kulturvergleich, ehe es den Kulturvergleich gab? In *Zwischen den Kulturen? (Soziale Welt, Sonderband 8)*, ed. Joachim Matthes, 13–35. Göttingen: Schwartz.

Thomas, William I., and Florian Znaniecki. 1958. *The Polish Peasant in Europe and America* (1st ed. 1918), New York: Dover.

Thränhardt, Dietrich, and Uwe Hunger. 2003. *Migration im Spannungsfeld von Globalisierung und Nationalstaat (Leviathan Sonderheft 22)*. Wiesbaden: Westdeutscher Verlag.

Tilly, Charles. 1990. *Coercion, Capital and European States: AD 990–1990*. Cambridge, MA: Blackwell.

Treibel, Annette. 1988. *Engagement und Distanzierung in der westdeutschen Ausländerforschung. Eine Untersuchung ihrer soziologischen Beiträge*. Stuttgart: Enke.

Treibel, Annette. 1990. *Migration in modernen Gesellschaften. Soziale Folgen von Einwanderung und Gastarbeit*. Weinheim and Munich: Juventa.

Vasta, Ellie, and Vasoodeven Vuddalamay. ed. 2006. *International Migration and the Social Sciences: Confronting National Experiences in Australia, France and Germany*. Basingstoke et al.: Palgrave Macmillan.

Vasta, Ellie. 2006. Migration and Migration Research in Australia. In *International Migration and the Social Sciences*, ed. Vasta and Vuddalamay, 13–78.

Walzer, Michael. 1983. *Spheres of Justice. A Defence of Pluralism and Equality*. New York: Basic Books.

Walzer, Michael. 1990. The Communitarian Critique of Liberalism. *Political Theory* 18: 6–23.

Weiß, Anja. 2005. The Transnationalization of Social Inequality. Conceptualising Social Positions on a World Scale. *Current Sociology* 53 (4): 707–28.

Wingens, Matthias, and Stephan Fuchs. 1989. Ist die Soziologie gesellschaftlich irrelevant? *Zeitschrift für Soziologie* 18 (8): 208–19.

Part I:
Immigration as a Part of National Identity: Two Traditional Immigration Countries

Canadian Multiculturalism as an Ethos, Policy and Conceptual Lens for Immigration Research

By Oliver Schmidtke

Abstract

Canada is portrayed as a country that over the last 30–40 years has undergone a fundamental transformation from a white settler society to one that is characterised by an extraordinary degree of ethno-cultural diversity and a deeply entrenched political commitment to multiculturalism. The resulting structural changes in the fabric of Canadian society and politics have established a distinct environment for public debate and scholarship on migration. First, migration-related issues have become a pervasive part of mainstream policy-making and scholarly debate: In particular in the disciplines of economics, geography, political science, and sociology, migration studies have become firmly established in research and the curriculum at universities. In addition, and mainly due to the salience of migration and integration as political issues, there is a vivid exchange between policy-makers and academics on how to manage immigration and integration successfully. Second, the legacy of multiculturalism as a state initiative and practice in civil society has established an ethos of diversity whose normative expectations of equitable inclusion critically informs research agendas. Given the almost uncontested consensus that properly managed immigration is beneficial and desirable, public as well as scholarly debate largely focuses on issues related to how to improve the integration of newcomers into Canadian society (in particular with view to patterns of social inequality, achievements in the educational system and the labour market, etc.). Third, the experience of sustained immigration and growing ethno-cultural diversity has sparked a theoretically driven debate among prominent Canadian political philosophers about the nature of political community in contemporary society and the need to address group and minority rights more forcefully in liberal democracies.

Introduction:
Canada as an Immigrant Society in Comparative Perspective

In many respects Canada can be seen as the multicultural society par excellence. Not only does an immigration rate of about 250,000 annually shape the character of Canadian society in manifold ways but Canada's major cities also show an exceptional degree of ethnic-cultural and religious diversity. In 2006 immigrants constituted 19.8 per cent of the population, a higher proportion than in any Western country except Australia (where the figure is 22.2 per cent). Most of the newcomers reside in the country's bigger cities. For instance, roughly 46 per cent of Toronto's population is made up of Canadian citizens who were born outside the country. Canada is equally exceptional in terms of the ethnic-cultural diversity of its immigrant communities: Given that Canada's new citizens represent more than 200 ethnic groups, the country has become something of a microcosm of the world's population. In cities like Toronto, Vancouver and Montreal, »visible minorities« are predicted to become the majority of the population by 2017 (Belanger 2005). It is worth noting that in 1960, only about 2 per cent of the country's population could be classified as belonging to a visible minority.

Equally important for the purpose of this essay is that this diversity finds expression in how Canadians see themselves as a nation and the character of the political community to which they belong. Since the 1960s multiculturalism has become a state policy promoted and adopted in all segments of society. Over the past four decades this tendency to view cultural and ethnic diversity as a societal feature worthy of preservation and protection has become an integral part of a Canadian national identity. An ever-increasing cultural heterogeneity has developed into an ethos of plurality widely cherished by the majority of Canadians and deeply institutionalised in state practices.

In order to shed light on the particularities of the Canadian case this contribution will adopt an implicitly comparative perspective. Though a comprehensive analysis of what sets the Canadian case apart from the European case is not possible here, the national paradigm of research in the field of migration will be illustrated by employing an ideal-typical contrast: How can an emerging Canadian approach to migration studies be described in light of its distinctiveness from mainstream European research agendas and analytical perspectives?[1] On the one hand, European and Canadian perspectives are sufficiently similar to allow a comparison. Their patterns of migration are rooted in a genuinely European legacy of nation-building and similar experiences in modern European history. On the other hand, Canadian and European attitudes toward migration have followed different trajectories in recent decades and have developed distinct ways of perceiving immigrants and formulating immigration policy. Canada has gradually separated its immigration policies from any notion of an ethnically rooted national identity and has simultaneously developed an ethos of diversity fundamentally opposed to the exclusive concept of nationhood as it has been cultivated in the European tradition (see Brubaker 1992).

The main hypothesis of this contribution assumes that the Canadian programme of multiculturalism adopted in the late 1960s and early 1970s has dramatically changed political agendas and intellectual reflection on the effects of immigration

---

1 It might be somewhat flawed to speak of a coherent European approach to immigration, as national traditions and legacies vary considerably. For heuristic reasons, however, this article demonstrates that there is something to be learned from such a constructed, ›nationalized‹ dichotomy between established European nation states and North American settler societies.

in Canada. This multiculturalist paradigm has triggered a profound re-evaluation of migrants' contribution to society in popular perception, policy making and scholarship. Although the scholarly community primarily provides critical reflection on the new multiculturalism of modern Canadian society, it is simultaneously an integral part of this reality. Scientific research is not immune to popularised interpretations of social realities and can in fact be an important factor in framing such interpretations; scholars are part of the social fabric they seek to describe. In this respect the main research programs, heuristic approaches and underlying normative agendas of Canadian scholars are shaped by the dominant sociopolitical perceptions of migrants and cultural diversity. From a theoretical, constructivist perspective this paper presupposes that these scientific approaches are modelled on the basis of socially shared perspectives and normatively guided narratives of migration and related topics.

The primary argument is developed in three parts. First, the text will discuss briefly the transformation of Canada from a white settler society with a well-articulated legacy of discriminatory practices aimed at non-European immigrants into a multicultural society that cherishes ethnic and cultural diversity. Next the focus will shift to how the multicultural turn has shaped policies and popular attitudes towards immigrants. This discussion provides the context for the reflection on how this new socio-political reality has come to shape the intellectual and scholarly debate on the issue of migration. Finally, the paper will identify some key framing devices that guide these debates in the Canadian context as compared to those traditionally reproduced in European nation states.

The Historic Roots of Canadian Nation Building and the Emergence of Multiculturalism

Canada is historically founded on immigration and, with respect to its underlying sense of collective identity, strongly shaped by the image of a settler community where the newcomer helps to determine the inner organisation and self-perception of society. At the same time, however, Canada also demonstrates many of those features (or, perhaps more appropriately in this context, pathologies) characteristically attributed to a European sense of nationhood: discriminatory, if not openly racist, practices against those not considered to be legitimate members of the culturally dominant groups; a sense of superiority vis-à-vis minority ethnic groups; and contempt for those who do not fit the white, Anglo-Saxon mould. Anxiety about the imperialist aspirations of Canada's large southern neighbour prompted measures intended to protect Canada's ethnic-cultural composition and its distinct ethnically framed identity as a former British (and French) colony.

This was the environment in which Canada's Immigration Law was developed. The making of Canada is closely linked to the idea of employing immigration as a nation-building device while at the same time imposing severe immigration restrictions on certain national and ethnic groups. In its earliest years Canada portrayed itself as a »white settler society or colony« (Stasiulis and Jhappan 1995); this model was firmly in place until well after the end of the Second World War. Shortly after Confederation in 1867, which saw Canada become a self-governing state, the country adopted provisions designed to maintain the ethnic-cultural composition that the colonial powers had established in this part of North America. Immigration policy at this time explicitly favoured the influx of new citizens from a white, preferably British-Protestant background. The idea of racial purity and civilisational superiority attributed to (Anglo-Saxon) Europeans was a clear component of the English-Canadian approach to nation-state building (Badgley 1998).

A vivid indication of the themes dominating early Canadian immigration policies was the *Chinese Head Tax and Exclusion Act,* which was in place until 1923. The act was designed to discourage permanent settlement of Chinese labourers by preventing female family members and other Chinese women from entering Canada. The distinction between white Anglo-Saxon Protestants and other ethnic groups was driven by a strong image of national identity, characterised by the belief in the insuperable superiority of the »white race« and keenly protected by the state. The results of this legacy were marked inequalities between migrant groups and discriminatory, at times openly racist, state practices in selecting newcomers to the country. After the Second World War the explicitly xenophobic elements of Canadian immigration policies were downplayed and partly replaced by an anti-Communist rhetoric used against applicants from Central and Eastern Europe. The idea of a white European settler community, now framed in terms that reflected the effects of the Cold War, remained the guiding principle for designing immigration policies and settlement programs.

The second determinant of immigration policy in the newly independent Canadian state followed an entirely different logic: Immigration was meant to be an instrument to meet labour-market driven imperatives and thus to reflect the broader socio-economic needs of the country. Yet this economic determinant, fuelled by highly pragmatic and utilitarian concerns, was in many ways in direct competition with the state's desire to effect a particular cultural environment through immigration. Only gradually did the pragmatic, interest-driven approach replace the initially dominant concerns for protecting Canada's cultural identity.

After the Second World War it became increasingly evident that the open discrimination against immigrant communities from certain ethnic or religious backgrounds was at odds with the emerging reality and needs of modern Canadian society. The most important effect that this had on the principles guiding immigration polices was the introduction of a ›point system‹ in 1967.[2] Responding to the needs of a booming economy, the state began to choose immigrants on the basis of their qualifications and abilities rather than on their ethnic and geographic origins

---

2 The Immigration Act of 1967 and its numerous amendments in the following years diversified categories and applications schemes while confirming the same principles, namely the perceived economic benefit resulting from immigration.

(Green and Green 2004; Whitaker 1987, 1991). Also, the move away from encouraging British immigrants exclusively was complemented by new ideas about how to accommodate migrant communities from all parts of the world.[3] This new approach to evaluating and governing pluralism was most apparent in the policies adopted by the government under Pierre Elliot Trudeau. Officially introduced in 1971, the policy of multiculturalism recognised and welcomed the cultural practices, traditions and values of all citizens, regardless of their country of birth, at the same time that it encouraged the integration of newcomers into the social, economic, cultural and political life of the country. This policy reflected the recommendations of the Royal Commission on Bilingualism and Biculturalism, which in 1965 asked for an end to the bicultural, French-British policies that had been in place for much of Canada's history. Multiculturalism was the creed intended to complement the exclusive idea of the »two founding peoples« of Canada (Stasiulis and Jhappan 1995, 110) and to encourage immigration from all parts of the world. Trudeau and the Liberal Party undertook sweeping measures to ensure that the relationship between individuals and the community was not shaped by place of birth but by a new form of societal and political integration, intended to establish a more appropriate balance between Canada's national community and the plurality of its cultural groups (Day 2000).

Although the bilingual character of the country constitutes an important element of the traditional narrative of Canadian national identity, it also became a driving force behind the paradigmatic re-orientation of Canada's immigration policies. From early in its colonial history, Canada's sense of unity and identity has been ambiguous, blurred by the divide between English-speaking Canada and French Quebec. While many politicians of British descent intended to build Canada as a unitary state based on British-style institutions and the English language, Confederation established a federal state in which substantive authority was transferred to the provinces (in particular Quebec) and the use of French was officially acknowledged. In the 1960s and early 1970s, with the ›quiet revolution‹ providing the socio-cultural context for a more politically self-conscious province, Quebec's insistence on cultural and linguistic recognition developed into a major challenge to Canada's integrity as a country. Canada was forced to take the issue of Quebec's linguistic and cultural differences very seriously if it wished to avoid jeopardising its federation. The policy response to this challenge was to decentralise Canadian federalism further and to constitutionally recognise Quebec as a ›distinct society‹, thus formally acknowledging British and French culture as having equal roles in shaping public life in Canada.

With the introduction of issues related to respect for other cultures and equal opportunities for all citizens, regardless of their origin, the 1970s also saw the Canadian Aboriginal peoples start to speak out about the suppression and exploi-

---

3   Prior to 1961, 90 per cent of immigrants came from countries in Europe. Today only 23 per cent of all immigrants come from Europe and the US. Close to 60 per cent of Canada's immigrants now come from Asia.

tation of the Canadian indigenous population. Although this paper does not detail how Canada has sought to address its past (and present) mistreatment of this group, it is important to note that this period in the country's history marked a critical threshold: The question of how issues of cultural diversity should find institutionalised public recognition determined how Canadians reflected on the fundamental values of their society. The meaning of a fair and free society became entwined with the question of how to accommodate minorities and provide them with full opportunities to thrive in Canada. Clearly the strengthening of the multicultural agenda is closely connected with an empowered notion of social citizenship that shaped political demands and mobilisation in this period (Arat-Koc 1999; Jenson and Phillips 1996).[4]

Many factors have contributed to this paradigmatic shift in regulating and integrating immigration, the most important of which are probably related to the overall political and cultural climate during these ›threshold‹ years. Concern for human rights, democratic self-determination and a state-sponsored deepening of the meaning of citizenship rights were now on the agenda for public debate in Canada. There was a dramatic shift in the importance and meaning attributed to issues related to cultural diversity and equal opportunities for minorities. The newly coined term ›multiculturalism‹ was meant to reflect this new consciousness. Multicultural policy was designed to mend the rent between British and French communities (and between these communities and the Aboriginal peoples) and establish a framework of mutual recognition and cultural diversity that included all immigrant communities, while at the same time preserving Canada as a unified society and polity.

The Multiculturalist Turn of Modern Canadian Society

The 1960s and 1970s saw a series of fundamental changes in how Canadian state and society perceived and dealt with immigration. This paper will consider three interconnected elements that also had a major impact on scholarly approaches in the field: a) the presence of the state in promoting diversity and multiculturalism; b) the altered state symbolism of national identity; and c) the active role of civil society and immigrant advocacy groups.

The Presence of the State in Promoting Diversity and Multiculturalism

To a significant extent, the multicultural turn can be attributed to a new approach to migration adopted by state authorities. As indicated above, the liberal Canadian government at the time committed itself to moving away from favouring white Anglo-Saxon immigrants and toward a mode of selecting new citizens that did not place importance on their place of origin. In addition, policies directed at assisting immigrants and at promoting the virtues of diversity complemented this new

---

4 Banting (1999) shows how the multiculturalist agenda and the expansion of the welfare state historically were closely intertwined.

immigration regime. Here the first element, next to a rapid process of naturalisation, was a public policy intended to support integration, fuelled by the idea of turning newcomers into full citizens with equal opportunities as quickly as possible after their arrival in Canada. Key aspects of these so-called ›settlement programs‹ are state-sponsored forms of assistance in finding employment, comprehensive language training, and ensuring improved representation of immigrant groups that have been historically underrepresented in key areas in the labour market as a result of systemic discrimination (most prominently a policy termed Equity Employment). Integrating immigrants into their new host society was deemed to be an overriding duty of all levels of government and, reflecting the mindset of the expanding welfare state of the 1970s, was not simply left to the market or civil society (Foster 1998).

The second element of the new immigration policy was the way in which the Canadian state came to play a more proactive role in policies of integration and was explicitly committed to promoting cultural diversity as an organising principle for modern Canadian society. Under the new multiculturalist creed, the Trudeau government initially used state funding to protect the cultural heritage of ethno-cultural groups and to remove cultural-linguistic barriers to their full participation in Canadian life. This emphasis on support of cultural activities shifted in the 1980s towards addressing wider issues related to racist and discriminatory practices endured by minority communities who came to Canada after 1967 (Harles 1997; Li 2003). The 1988 *Multiculturalism Act* officially acknowledged this focus on concerns for equality, identity and justice and gave it a more solid legal base.[5]

This changed perspective on and commitment to immigrants was reflected in the amended Constitution. In 1982 the new Canadian Charter of Rights and Freedoms aimed to modernise the relationship between individuals and the state. At its core this Charter is a bill of rights, a major achievement of which is to explicitly recognise a sequence of group rights worth protecting.[6] Among these are linguistic minorities, ethno-cultural minorities and Aboriginal peoples; these group rights are meant to complement the list of rights and freedoms assigned to individuals in the first sections of the Charter.

Altered State Symbolism of National Identity

The steps towards implementing multiculturalist policies were accompanied by a decisive shift in defining the national identity of Canada. The new source of a Canadian identity was the diversity of its peoples. This replaced the traditional image of a British or French settler colony. Today, what it means to be Canadian

---

5 The most important provision in the Multiculturalism Act reads as follows: »All federal institutions should promote policies, programs and practices that Canadians of all origins have an equal opportunity to obtain employment and advancement in those institutions.«
6 The rights referred to in these sections of the Charter (16–27) basically give minorities the right to use their language for public and educational purposes and to protect their cultural heritage. The Multiculturalism Act of 1988 complemented the Charter and explicitly granted to all members of Canadian society the right to see their cultures and ancestral languages protected (see Magsino et al. 2000).

is to a large extent defined by the idea that this country is home to a great variety of cultures that are not assimilated into any kind of dominant model (the metaphor of the Canadian salad bowl or the Canadian cultural mosaic is meant to capture this characteristic, in contrast to the American melting pot). The state has become a promoter of this idea and in a way engages in endorsing and selling diversity[7] as a competitive advantage that Canada is alleged to have in social and economic terms. Cultural diversity is thus not simply a defining characteristic of social life; in official language it has also become an important resource in modernising Canadian society and bringing it in line with the reality of a globalised world. This pragmatism in promoting the country's multicultural identity is nicely captured in the following quotation from a Minister of the Canadian government:

> »*Canada has become a post-national multicultural society. It contains the globe within its borders, and Canadians have learned that their two international languages and their diversity are a comparative advantage and a source of continuing creativity and innovation.*« *(Canadian Heritage 2001, 3)*

In a way, diversity has come to be seen not only as compatible with the dominant image of Canada as a society and a political community but also, in a more radical sense, as the virtuous core of a new (post-)national identity. The American motto *e pluribus unum* could be seen as an appropriate description of the Canadian spirit: diversity is the source of its unity, plurality the source of its strength.

In this respect, multiculturalism, beyond being conceptualised in terms of a set of policy initiatives, carries an ethical-philosophical weight that suggests commonly shared social values with regard to how ethnic-cultural diversity is seen normatively. Surveys from the 1990s show that most Canadians (79 per cent) see multiculturalism as fundamental to their self-understanding as a community and their sense of unity (Inglis 1996, 58f.). The concept of multiculturalism shapes significantly the political values of individual Canadians. In spite of the fact that there have been and still are controversial debates about perceived failures of multiculturalism as a state policy, there is an overwhelming consensus that integration into Canadian society is viable only as long as immigrants continue to experience some public recognition of their cultural distinctiveness. Paradoxically, at first glance there is good reason to argue that the democratic debate on this topic itself confirms how deeply ingrained the idea of multiculturalism as a common point of departure has become: The ethos of diversity is rarely challenged. Instead it is the mode of implementation that is contested.

The Role of Civil Society and Immigrant Advocacy Groups

The multicultural project would not have been as successful as it has been if it had been orchestrated as a state-centred, top-down approach. The political elite headed by Trudeau's Liberal Party may have initiated the programme in order to

---

[7] This description is borrowed from Abu-Laban and Gabriel's (2002) book and refers to the way in which, echoing the neoliberal mood of the 1990s, Canada promotes its multicultural identity as an advantage in tackling the challenges of market-driven globalization.

deal more effectively with the cleavages of a pluri-ethnic society or, as some argue, as an opportunistic move to capture the votes of minority groups. Yet the state-centred policies are partly responsible for setting in motion a dynamic that far exceeds the initial motivation of the federal government. Recent decades have demonstrated how groups in civil society have increasingly engaged in defining the reach and boundaries of group-specific rights. In this respect multiculturalism has become a kind of political umbrella under which civil rights activists, immigrant advocacy groups, union organisations and parties as well as business groups have engaged in determining the meaning of abstract principles of fostering cultural diversity in actual socio-political terms. Particularly striking in the Canadian context is how advocacy groups representing different migrant communities have become an articulate and influential voice in the public arena, affecting the political agenda in a way unimaginable within a typical European context. To put this in provocatively candid terms: Issues of migration and related questions of identity and equal integration have become profound political tools of influence in contemporary Canadian society. Underlying normative issues have come to shape much of the social movement sector of the country and party politics, even beyond the activities of migrant lobbying groups (Schmidtke 2007).[8]

The activity of civil society groups has helped to ensure that diversity and cultural pluralism are principal issues in public debate and, from a normative perspective, foundational principles of Canadian society. One example is the social movement sector, in particular the Canadian Women's Movement, which has been strongly affected by issues of diversity. Its anti-discriminatory ethos has made the Canadian Women's Movement especially sensitive to issues of racism and minority rights, though by no means exclusively so among Canadian social movements. The National Action Committee on the Status of Women (NAC), the main organisation for women's groups in Canada, adopted an amendment of its constitution in 1991 that required that one of four vice-presidential and other leading positions be reserved for women of colour, Aboriginal women and women with disabilities. In 1993 Sunera Thobani became the first member of a visible minority to be the president of the NAC. Her leadership was part of a larger step for the organisation that involved re-defining ›women's issues‹ to include such aspects as racism, immigration and refugee policy, and economic and trade policies. Far from being merely a policy guideline, the idea of multiculturalism is now a critical reference point in many political battles. In this regard, multiculturalism shifted away from a celebration of folkloristic differences towards matters of power sharing and political cleavages in Canadian society.

---

8 One illustration of the impact that multiculturalism has had on scholarship about migration is that in the standard text book on Canadian politics the articles on immigration and multiculturalism come under the heading of »Electoral Politics and Social Movements« (Bickerton and Gagnon 1999).

Oliver Schmidtke

Framing the Research Questions on Migration: Towards a Canadian Paradigm?

From these far-reaching changes in Canadian social and political life one can identify some general features that characterise the socially dominant perspective on migration. Distinguishing fundamental shifts in how the issue of migration is framed in public discourse will set the stage for understanding the Canadian scientific approaches and the underlying suppositions guiding research in this field. Presuming that dominant frames in public discourse and perspectives in (social) scientific research are mutually linked, the final section of the paper will identify some of the elementary factors in scholarly debate and reflection. These factors are not meant to suggest in any detail the investigative direction of research in Canada. Rather, they are the »master frames«[9] of a nationally specific agenda that in turn provides the stimuli for formulating questions and theories related to migration.

Mainstreaming of Research on Immigration and Integration

What is most striking about the Canadian context of conducting research in the field of migration is its sheer prominence and breadth, not only in public but also in scholarly discourse. One can describe this development in Canada – borrowing a concept from current debates in feminism and gender politics – as migration mainstreaming. This means that the topic cannot be dealt with in an isolated and highly specialised manner. Rather, the impact of immigration and the task of integrating newcomers into all segments of Canadian society are seen as issues that have a bearing on different sub-fields of the social sciences and humanities. For instance, in a Canadian context, research on policy issues such as welfare, education, employment, health and training would almost unavoidably integrate elements related to migration.[10]

One critical element in this respect is the availability of the data on ethnocultural identity that are part of the census survey. These data allow scholars (and policy makers) to evaluate the role of immigrants in all sectors of Canadian society and the economy. State agencies such as *Statistics Canada* and *Citizenship and Immigration Canada* provide comprehensive data on the socio-structural background of immigrants and minorities on an annual basis. Both agencies have research units that intersect with the scholarly world at Canada's universities. The exchange of data and research findings works both ways: The policy community is open to considering academic research findings and creating venues of exchange between both worlds. A prominent example is the Metropolis Project (An Interna-

---

9   The idea of frames is a sociological concept originally developed by Goffman (1974) to show how individuals orient themselves based on perceptions of reality. Focusing on processes of public communication, Gamson (1992), and Snow and Benford (1992), among others, have used this concept to study the process of political mobilisation.
10 On the breadth and interdisciplinary character of migration research in a North American context, see Brettell and Hollifield 2000.

tional Forum for Research and Policy on Migration, Diversity and Changing Cities).[11] Generously financed by Canada's state funding agency over the past ten years, the Metropolis network has created forums of exchange and debate for scholars, policy makers and front-line service providers. The Metropolis network has notably supported immigration- and integration-related research at Canadian universities, boosted the number of graduate students and ensured that scholars working in this field enjoy greater visibility in public life and greater influence in policy decisions.

This translates into concrete terms for formulating research questions. One example of this is the socio-economic impact of immigration and its underlying normative agenda of equality and colour-blind integration. Asking whether immigration is ›good‹ or ›bad‹ in principle for a country seems an outdated question; there is an almost unchallenged presumption that immigration is an integral part of a country's attempt to manage economy matters. Instead the debate is on how to maximise the economically desirable impact of immigration policies, in a way that adequately reflects the needs of the economy and society at large. In this context the full integration of immigrants into the social and economic life in Canada is a paradigm that steers the interests of many social scientists who critically investigate Canada's social reality in light of this ideal. In more general terms, what we see in the Canadian research agenda on migration is a decisive shift in attention towards the host society itself.[12] Scholars show particular interest in questions related to forms of social inclusion/exclusion and patterns of socio-economic marginalisation. The degree to which Canadian society offers opportunities to its newcomers and allows them to integrate is a critical yardstick for the success of the Canadian immigration regime and thus of considerable interest for the scholarly and policy community (see, for example, Reitz and Banerjee 2007; Frenette and Morissette 2005).

However, it is worth noting that the multiculturalism narrative is somewhat ambivalent: On the one hand, sensitivity for concerns of ethnic-cultural diversity has spurred research and public debate on the actual achievements of recent immigrant groups (for instance, such a report is regularly part of the annual release by Citizenship and Immigration Canada). On the other hand, however, critics of the Canadian multiculturalism model argue that its primary focus on cultural diversity tends to obscure the discriminatory (sometimes even racist) practices that immigrants are exposed to in their daily life and their professional careers (Satzewich 1998). If Canadian society is by definition more multiculturalist in character, then the existence of racism and xenophobia that presuppose a strong sense of a dominant ethnic-cultural group seems almost paradoxical. Yet there are

---

11 http://canada.metropolis.net/index_e.html
12 Dominating the research agenda in Canada are questions such as: What are the contributions of immigrants to the social and economic life of our country? How can we find an appropriate balance between the legitimate claims for cultural diversity and the viability of the broader political community? Does our society do justice to the liberal promise of equal opportunities in light of the different backgrounds that immigrants bring to this country?

many scholarly accounts of racist practices in Canada and the persistence of a highly exclusionary sense of a white Anglo-Saxon cultural elite (Nieguth 1999). Also, research has repeatedly focused on the questionable desirability of the policies adopted under the heading of multiculturalism. One argument presumes that multiculturalism policy often promotes the (unintentional) »ghettoisation« of ethnic minorities. Rather than actively striving for equality of all citizens, regardless of their origin, some argue that such a policy sustains (potentially discriminatory) boundaries between ethnic-cultural communities (Abu-Laban 1999; Bissoondath 1994).

Do these appraisals of applied multiculturalism indicate that a national agenda driven by an ethos of plurality is flawed? At least they suggest that there is indeed a gap between the benevolent self-perception of Canada as a fundamentally multicultural country and the lingering sense of the mentality associated with a white settler community. At the same time, however, scholarly perspectives confirm the paradigmatic normative emphasis on respect for different cultures and the aim of equal and colour-blind integration of immigrants.

Beyond the Us versus Them Dichotomy

The strong pluralist ethos that Canada has developed in perceiving ethnic and cultural diversity as a constitutive part of its collective identity has left a lasting mark on dominant scholarly perspectives on migration. In a way this ethos provides the narrative basis for the development of conceptual tools and normative assumptions. This refers primarily to the normative underpinning of the dominant form of collective identity in Canada. The fact that there is no static and ethnically conceived concept of a national identity against which to measure alleged risks linked to migration shapes the nature of migration research. If the notion of the national community and the assimilation of immigrants become tied to a notion of a national whole that is in a state of continuous historical flux, then traditional ideas about how migrants relate to the host society must be re-examined. In this case, ideas about the process of assimilation and integration need to be reconsidered in terms of a mutual transformation, not a one-way imperative. That is, not only must immigrants adapt to their new reality, but the host society must also adapt to its new immigrants, whose participation in the new environment helps to define the society's ever-evolving identity. The Canadian context throws into question the rationale of the classical model of integration, in which newcomers go through several developmental stages as they adapt to their host society, eventually becoming »incorporated« patterned on a form of assimilation that makes them indistinguishable from the majority.[13]

When we compare the Canadian context to the European context, it becomes clear that in Canadian public discourse, and to a certain extent in Canadian

---

13 The classical definition of integration and its meaning for the field of migration research have been shaped by Robert Park and the studies of the Chicago School (Park 1928; Rauer and Schmidtke 2001).

society as a whole, the non-acceptance of immigrants in principle has ceased to be a relevant force. When I suggest that this notion is still a force in the European context, I am not referring to the incidents of open xenophobia that have become a sad commonplace of Europe's contemporary reality. Rather, I refer to how the myth of cultural homogeneity as a defining mark of an integrated political community guides national thinking about the desirability of diversity. The terms used to describe migrants reflect this deep-rooted symbolic divide between national and alien, the categorical difference that exists between insiders and outsiders in most European societies: ›aliens‹, ›étrangers‹, ›Ausländer‹ and ›guest workers‹ are now common terms. Their meanings reflect an elemental concern for the cultural ›purity‹ of the national community and the underlying sense that the community's cultural integrity is in constant danger of being diluted or compromised. In popular discourse, as in scholarly debate, the idea of a fundamental gap between insiders and outsiders translates into concern that immigration poses an economic and cultural threat. Even the European quality press prominently echoes such concerns over how much ethnic diversity can be tolerated (Eder et al. 2004). Such a mind-frame reproduces the symbolic divide and establishes the resources for what Stolcke (1995) describes as a disturbingly contemporary *rhetoric of exclusion* in Europe.

Although scholarship in the field is often critical of the exclusionary effects of such framing, it still provides a very forceful interpretative tool for looking at issues of integration or assimilation of immigrants in Europe. This has repercussions for the normative underpinning that concepts such as unity, identity and integration receive in scientific discourse on immigration. For instance, in a European discourse there is a tendency to conceptualise homogeneity as an indication of stability, strength and viability, whereas heterogeneity is likely to be associated with instability, weakness and decay. Emphasis normally rests on the perceived threat to the integrity of national society. To conceptualise the cultural heterogeneity of a people as the source of its identity and the defining mark of its political community is still alien to European ways of reflecting on the fate of the nation state. Here the belief that cultural retention is an obstacle to integration and a hazard to society as a whole still underlies scholarly debate.

In the Canadian context, immigration is not something perceived to be potentially threatening that the national society must cope with and protect against. Rather, immigration is critical to the self-organisation and self-perception of Canada as a political community. It is interesting to note that the dichotomy between the national culture and the culture of the newcomer that informs much of the discussion on migrants in Europe is virtually non-existent in the Canadian context. As long as one adheres to the traditional definition of national community (and its integrating sense of identity), one easily falls into the trap of viewing migrants as intruders, aliens that pose a genuine threat to the integrity of the whole. If, however, the sense of the identity of the political community is subject to constant change (partly in response to the constant influx of new migrant communities, as it is in Canada), the dichotomy is deprived of its fundamental rationale. Questions such as whether in principle immigrants are able to assimilate take on a very different meaning if the society that would assimilate them is also subject to a continuous process of re-definition. In this case, the question is de-dramatised and reflects less emotionally driven conflicts of interest, and is thus deprived of the salient culturalist underpinning that implicitly informs scholarly perspectives in Europe.

Towards an Exclusively Political Foundation of National Community

Part of the multiculturalist turn was to radically reconsider what the national community stands for and under what collective identity it should be integrated. Satzewich (1998) speaks with regard to the Canadian context about the »deconstruction of a nation«. Briefly, this refers to the idea that in Canada the European legacy of defining a national community (namely, using features of ethnic or cultural identity as a common denominator for determining membership within this community) was – with some notable exceptions[14] – largely abandoned.[15] Features of national belonging were stripped of their cultural underpinning and reformulated in terms of a strictly legal status and a set of political principles and norms that Canadians could agree on. There are many popular stories and jokes about a Canadian national identity or, rather, the lack thereof. Yet behind this perceived deficiency we might see a far more meaningful reconfiguration of the defining elements of a truly multicultural or ›post-national‹ society.

This does not mean that there are no attempts to foster an understanding of the Canadian collective identity and what political role it should play. One such attempt would be the widely endorsed television series *Canada – A Nation's History*, a deliberate attempt by the state-run Canadian Broadcasting Corporation (CBC) to revive a historically rooted notion of national identity. By the same token, however, the very sense of what it means to be Canadian is mediated by ideas with a distinctly political base (Taras and Rasporich 2001). With respect to the cultural identity of the country, the story about Canada narrated by the television series was very much centred on the issue of diversity and the impact that different immigrant and Aboriginal communities have had on Canada as a national community. Here again scholars were prominently involved in ›constructing‹ a modern collective identity for a highly pluri-ethnic Canadian society.

It does not come as a surprise, then, that the debate on citizenship that started about a decade ago surfaced very prominently in Canada at a very early stage. The challenge to reconsider the standards by which immigrants are made full citizens

---

14 One of these exceptions is Howard-Hassmann (1999), who very forcefully and provocatively argues that for English-speaking, non-Aboriginal Canadians there is something like an »ethnic Canadian identity« (522). This ethnic identity is described as resting on a notion of territory, the English language, European ancestry, Christian religious heritage and a broader Canadian culture.

15 Brubaker (1992) made a forceful argument that, for instance, when defining »nationhood«, the Republican French tradition is categorically different from an ethnically coded German one. Yet even the universalistic French model rests on a notion of a cultural community with notable exclusionary effects (Kastoryano 2002).

and to disassociate the entitlements connected to them from any strong sense of national identity is echoed in the scholarship on citizenship or post-national membership in political communities (Soysal 1994). Citizenship can be described as a status of integration into a political community that transcends principles of race, ethnicity, language, culture and religion as the traditional boundary markers of the nation state (Schmidtke 2001). The rights-based approach in focusing on citizenship seems to be tailor-made for Canada, accommodating the plurality of its migrant communities while at the same time seeking to safeguard egalitarian inclusion on universalistic grounds.

Minority Rights as Political Theory

It is, perhaps, not by accident that the most articulate political theorists advocating multiculturalism and the rights of minority groups are Canadians (Kymlicka 1995, 1998; Taylor 1994; Tully 1995). At the core of their normative theory is an idea that is widely alien in comparable intellectual circles in Europe. This is the far-reaching assumption that our basic theories about freedom, democracy and justice must be reconsidered in light of the endemic weakness that established notions of liberalism demonstrate in terms of accommodating the legitimate rights of minority groups. For instance, according to Kymlicka, liberalism needs to come to terms with the fact that its universalistic principles are compromised by its reliance on a dominant national culture. Without going into the details of his well-articulated plea for reforming the practice of liberal democracies in light of the legitimate claims of minorities, we can summarise Kymlicka's crucial theoretical idea as follows: The formal principles of individual freedom and autonomy are critically dependent on a *societal culture* to make them work. Only by relating in a profound way to their community (defined by sharing a culture, language, a territorial homeland, etc.) can individuals make meaningful choices and take advantage of opportunities. Kymlicka (1995) seeks to remind liberals that questions of political and socio-economic equality cannot be de-coupled from issues of cultural diversity. With this he suggests a sweeping reconceptualisation of liberalism in terms of perceiving minority rights as something that concerns the viability of its fundamental values.

In contrast, in the European context the constitutive links between basic liberal concerns for individual freedom, social justice and the autonomy of national minorities have not entered the debate among political theorists in a meaningful sense (some notable exceptions can be found in the UK; see for instance Modood 2007). The critique of liberalism as naïve in its exclusive notion of national community has been marginalised, accepted only by a highly specialised circle of scholars. This reflects the particularities of a European context in which the universalistic ideas of liberalism are still strongly, if not exclusively, tied to the narrative of (national) political community and its political manifestation, the unitary nation state. The political philosophical debate in Canada has critically challenged this national narrative and the belief in the nation state as the exclusive pre-condition for a universalistic, liberal democracy. It is not by accident that scholars working in the wider field of migration studies have made an important contribution to this debate on the politics of identity, the links between diversity and the changing features of political community (see, for example, Eisenberg 2006; Kymlicka and Opalski 2001).

Conclusions: Towards a Canadian Paradigm?

Is there a hidden agenda driving research on migration in Canada? On the one hand, if there is such a paradigm in Canada, then it would not be appropriate to describe it as hidden in character. Dominant analytical and normative perspectives on migration reflect rather boldly the way in which Canadian society and (immigration) politics have changed in terms of attracting and integrating newcomers into the country. Yet at the same time, the impact is subtler than a crude sociology of knowledge might insinuate. Even though they might share some basic assumptions, scholarly approaches in the social sciences and the humanities are different in their critical approach to the subject of their research. When it comes to issues such as multiculturalism, cultural diversity and social equality between groups, the heated academic debate is anything but a mere reflection of bland governmental policy programs. Yet the debate is informed by narrative structures of unity and diversity, and by a gradual transformation of the social imagery of the national community. These have left a crucial mark on the formulation of research questions in this field. For a scholar socialised in Canadian culture, it might not be so obvious that many of the unexamined assumptions that direct his or her research are intimately linked to his or her social environment. Drawing some broad comparisons to the European context can shed light on what in Canada are often now almost uncontested approaches to migration.

There are deep-rooted differences between the European and Canadian experiences that account for directions in intellectually and politically motivated research in the areas of immigration and integration. One seemingly banal notion (albeit critical in its effect) is that, compared to prevailing European perspectives, research in Canada is strongly shaped by the conviction that issues of integration cannot be separated from issues of migration. When it comes to the motivations of migrants to leave their country of origin and the effects that immigration has on the country of their destination, the mode of incorporating immigrants into their new host society is perceived to be of critical importance. For this reason the issues dealt with in Canadian research on migration tend to be less marginalised in terms of academic fields of specialisation, broader in scope and far more complex than they are in the typical European research setting. Migration is seen to be at the heart of the modernising dynamic shaping current Canadian society and politics, both with respect to key policy domains and political debates about the society's constitutive values.

Related to this notion is the second crucial aspect that accounts for the particularity of the Canadian case. Since the 1960s, the perception of what constitutes a national community, thus providing the rationale for inclusion and exclusion of non-nationals, has been transformed in an essential way. When the sense of national identity is freed from any kind of thick ethnic or cultural description, migration research is significantly affected. This holds true both for the range of topics considered relevant with respect to migration and the way in which research questions and approaches are formulated. A conceptual framework in which migration is seen as a driving force in the transformation of society and politics replaces the dichotomy between the host society and the alien immigrants, who have to be accommodated without compromising the social and political status quo. It is within this framework that such issues as the integration of immigrants into the labour market, the management of cultural diversity and the quest for equality have established themselves as dominant themes of research in Canada.

Canada's approach to regulating immigration has developed into something like a blueprint for how modern states should strive to organise their immigration regimes. The pragmatism that informs the immigration regime in Canada has notable attraction for European politicians and scholars. However, this does not mean that Canada can quasi-naturally claim the role of a historic *avant-garde* in advancing research on migration and formulating promising agendas for dealing with cultural diversity in a productive way. As national paradigms reflect political and societal experiences, they are subject to change determined by new challenges. In the Canadian context, it is evident that the neo-liberal agenda of the 1990s noticeably transformed the role of the state in managing the economy and, related to this, the relations between societal groups. As a result, the commitment of the state to achieving equality of opportunities for immigrants and to establishing state-based programs (Settlement, Employment, Equity Programs) to integrate them into Canadian society have been scaled back to a considerable degree. In this context multiculturalism, as a concept once strongly equipped with a normative vision for what modern Canada should look like, has become subject to a far more utilitarian, economy-driven issue (Abu-Laban 1998; Arat-Koc 1999). Whether this will have a structural effect on the ›Canadian way of seeing things‹, and whether the dynamic driving globalisation and European integration will gradually undermine the differences between the Canadian and European perspectives, remains to be seen.

References

Abu-Laban, Yasmeen. 1998. Welcome/ STAY OUT: The Contradiction of Canadian Integration and Immigration Policies at the Millennium. *Canadian Ethnic Studies* 30 (5): 190–211.

Abu-Laban, Yasmeen. 1999. The Politics of Race, Ethnicity and Immigration. In *Canadian Politics*, ed. James Bickerton and Alain Gagnon, 463–83. Peterborough, ON: Broadview Press.

Abu-Laban, Yasmeen, and Christina Gabriel. 2002. *Selling Diversity. Immigration, Multiculturalism, Employment Equity, and Globalization.* Peterborough, ON: Broadview Press.

Arat-Koc, Sedef. 1999. Neo-liberalism, State Restructuring, and Immigration: Changes in Canadian Policies in the 1990s. *Journal of Canadian Studies* 34 (2): 31–56.

Badgley, Kerry. 1998. »As long as he is an immigrant from the United Kingdom«: Deception, Ethnic Bias and Milestone Commemoration in the Department of Citizenship and Immigration, 1953–1965. *Journal of Canadian Studies* 33 (3): 130–44.

Banting, Keith. 1999. Social Citizenship and the Multicultural Welfare State. In *Citizenship, Diversity and Pluralism*, ed. Alan C. Cairns, 108–36. Montreal and Kingston: McGill-Queen's University Press.

Belanger, Alain. 2005. *Population Projections of Visible Minority Groups. Canada, Provinces and Regions, 2001–2017.* Ottawa: Statistics Canada.

Bickerton, James, and Alain Gagnon, ed. 1999. *Canadian Politics.* Peterborough, ON: Broadview Press.

Bissoondath, Neil. 1994. *Selling Illusions: The Cult of Multiculturalism in Canada.* Toronto: Penguin.

Brettell, Caroline, and James Hollifield, ed. 2000. *Migration Theory. Talking Across Disciplines.* New York and London: Routledge.

Brubaker, Rogers. 1992. *Citizenship and Nationhood in France and Germany.* Cambridge, MA: Harvard University Press.

Canadian Heritage. 2001. *Annual Report on the Operation of the Canadian Multiculturalism Act 1999–2000.* Ottawa: Minister of Public Works and Government Services Canada.

Day, Richard J.F. 2000. *Multiculturalism and the History of Canadian Diversity.* Toronto: University of Toronto Press.

Eder, Klaus, Valentin Rauer, and Oliver Schmidtke. 2004. *Die Einhegung des Anderen. Türkische, polnische und russlanddeutsche Einwanderer in Deutschland.* Opladen: VS Verlag für Sozialwissenschaften.

Eisenberg, Avigail, ed. 2006. *Diversity and Equality: The Changing Framework of Freedom in Canada.* Vancouver: UBC Press.

Foster, Lorne. 1998. *Turnstile Immigration: Multiculturalism, Social Order, and Social Justice in Canada.* Toronto: Thompson Educational Press.

Frenette, Marc, and René Morissette. 2005. Will They Ever Converge? Earnings of Immigrant and Canadian-born Workers over the Last Two Decades. *International Migration Review* 39: 228–57.

Gamson, William. 1992. *Talking Politics.* New York: Cambridge University Press.

Goffman, Erving. 1974. *Frame Analysis.* New York: Harper Row.

Green, Alan, and David Green. 2004. The Goals of Canada's Immigration Policy: A Historical Perspective. *Canadian Journal of Urban Research* 13 (1): 102–39.

Harles, John C. 1997. Integration before Assimilation: Immigration, Multiculturalism and the Canadian Polity. *Canadian Journal of Political Science* 30: 711–36.

Howard-Hassmann, Rhoda. 1999. Canadian as an Ethnic Category: Implications for Multiculturalism and National Unity. *Canadian Public Policy* 25 (4): 523–37.

Inglis, Christine. 1996. *Multiculturalism: New Policy Responses to Diversity*. MOST Policy Papers no. 4. Paris: UNESCO.

Jenson, Jane, and Susan Phillips. 1996. Regime Shift: New Citizenship Practices in Canada. *International Journal of Canadian Studies* 14: 111–35.

Kastoryano, Riva. 2002. *Negotiating Identities. States and Immigrants in France and Germany*. Princeton and Oxford: Princeton University Press.

Kurthen, Hermann. 1997. The Canadian Experience with Multiculturalism and Employment Equity: Lessons for Europe. *New Community* 23 (2): 249–70.

Kymlicka, Will. 1995. *Multicultural Citizenship. A Liberal Theory of Minority Rights*. New York: Oxford University Press.

Kymlicka, Will. 1998. *Finding Our Way: Rethinking Ethnocultural Relations in Canada*. Don Mills, ON: Oxford University Press.

Kymlicka, Will, and Magda Opalski, ed. 2001. *Can Liberal Pluralism Be Exported? Western Political Theory and Ethnic Relations in Eastern Europe*. Oxford: Oxford University Press.

Li, Peter. 2003. The Multiculturalism Debate. In *Race and Ethnic Relations in Canada*, ed. idem, 148–77. Don Mills, ON: Oxford University Press.

Magsino, Romulo, John Long, and Raymond Théberge. 2000. Canadian Pluralism, the Charter, and Citizenship Education. *Canadian Ethnic Studies* 32 (1): 89–110.

Modood, Tariq. 2007. *Multiculturalism: A Civic Idea*. Oxford: Polity.

Nieguth, Tim. 1999. Privilege or Recognition: The Myth of State Neutrality. *Critical Review of International Social and Political Philosophy* 2 (2): 112–31.

Park, Robert. 1928. Human Migration and the Marginal Man. *American Journal of Sociology* 33: 881–93.

Rauer, Valentin, and Oliver Schmidtke. 2001. Integration als Exklusion? Zum medialen und alltagspraktischen Umgang mit einem umstrittenen Konzept. *Berliner Journal für Soziologie* 3: 277–96.

Reitz, Jeffrey G., and Rupa Banerjee. 2007. Racial Inequality, Social Cohesion, and Policy Issues in Canada. In *Belonging? Diversity, Recognition and Shared Citizenship in Canada*, ed. Keith Banting, Thomas J. Courchene, and F. Leslie Seidle, 489–545. Montreal: Institute for Research on Public Policy.

Satzewich, Vic, ed. 1998. *Racism and Inequality in Canada*. Toronto: Thompson.

Schmidtke, Oliver 2001. Trans-national Migration: A Challenge to European Citizenship Regimes. *World Affairs* 164 (1): 3–16.

Schmidtke, Oliver. 2007. (Dis-)Empowering Immigrants: Cultural Diversity in the Health Care Sector and Political Advocacy in Canada. *International Journal of Migration, Health and Social Care* 3 (3): 20–9.

Snow, David, and Robert Benford. 1992. Master Frames and Cycles of Protest. In *Frontiers in Social Movement Theory,* ed. Aldon Morris and Carol Mueller, 133–55. New Haven, CT: Yale University Press.

Soysal, Yasemin N. 1994. *Limits of Citizenship: Migrants and Postnational Membership in Europe.* Chicago: University of Chicago Press.

Stasiulis, Daiva, and Radha Jhappan. 1995. The Fractious Politics of a Settler-Society: Canada. In *Unsettling Settler Societies: Articulations of Gender, Race, Ethnicity and Class,* ed. Daiva Stasiulis and Nira Yuval-Davis, 106–16. London: Sage.

Stolcke, Verena. 1995. Talking Culture. New Boundaries, New Rhetorics of Exclusion in Europe. *Current Anthropology* 36: 1–24.

Taras, David, and Beverly Rasporich. 2001. *A Passion for Identity. Canadian Studies for the 21st Century.* Scarborough, ON: Thompson.

Taylor, Charles. 1994. *Multiculturalism: Examining the Politics of Recognition.* Princeton, NJ: Princeton University Press.

Tully, James. 1995. *Strange Multiplicity: Constitutionalism in an Age of Diversity.* Cambridge, MA: Cambridge University Press.

Whitaker, Reginald. 1987. *Double Standard: The Secret History of Immigration.* Toronto: Lester and Orpen Dennys.

Whitaker, Reginald. 1991. *Canadian Immigration Policy.* Ottawa: Canadian Historical Association.

Aborigines, Anglos and Asians –
Discourses on Multiculturalism and National Identity in Australian Migration Research

By Sigrid Baringhorst

Abstract

The first part of the chapter characterises the historical development and current disciplinary as well as interdisciplinary institutionalisation and core themes of migration and multicultural studies in Australia. Apart from the plethora of disciplines involved the overview shows the dependency of migration-related research on government funding and changing political preferences. In the second part some major strands of argument of the dominant Australian academic discourse on multiculturalism are discussed. A particular emphasis is given to the criticism on multiculturalism put forward by neo-conservative authors, on the one hand, and post-structuralist and post-colonialist authors, on the other hand. In this context, a particular emphasis is given to the role of culture, race and territoriality within the Australian discourse.

Institutionalisation of Research on Immigration, Ethnic and Multicultural Studies

Migration studies comprise a very broad and heterogeneous field within the Australian research community and thus they cannot be summed up as all following merely one particular national frame or hidden agenda. There are different academic disciplines involved, that follow their own methodology and research interests: population research focuses on the impact of migration on the demographic development of Australian society, economics are mainly interested in the economic gains and costs of immigration, education deals especially with the impact of migration processes on educational needs and problems of schools, historians try to reconstruct the history of migration of different groups of migrants, while social scientists analyse processes of political decision-making within the field of migration research and aspects of social inclusion and exclusion. Apart from these traditional disciplines dealing with migration issues, there are trans- and interdisciplinary approaches within the growing field of cultural, communal or area studies. This transdisciplinary approach is particularly reflected in the set-up of various courses, professorships and research centres in the field of cultural studies and area studies like Asian studies, Australian, European or Multicultural studies. Market-orientation and a high degree of self-organisation have rendered university structures in Australia much more flexible than in Germany, and thus facilitated the development of new transdisciplinary course structures.

Since the late 1980s there is a particular public support for Asian studies. Prime Minister Keating's (Australian Labor Party) shift of national orientation, that is the official shift from defining Australia primarily on the basis of its colonial past and links to Britain to defining it as ›part of Asia‹, has led to the creation of comparatively large departments on Asian Area Studies, for instance, at the International Centre of Excellence in Asia-Pacific Studies at the Australian National University, the School of Asian Studies at the University of Western Australia in Perth, the Centre for Asia-Pacific Social Transformation Studies at the University of Newcastle and University of Wollongong, the Monash Asia Institute, the Asia Institute at Melbourne University or the Asian Studies Programmes at the Universities of Sydney and Adelaide. Strong emphasis on Australia's links to Asia is also reflected in the institutionalisation of migration research. In this respect, the Asia-Pacific Migration Research Network, set up by the UNESCO in June 1995, is of particular importance. Its conferences, meetings and working papers expressed the growing research collaboration on issues of multiculturalism and migration in the Asia-Pacific Region. The main focus of this network »is the long-term role of migration and increased ethno-cultural diversity as major factors in the social transformation of societies in the Asia-Pacific Region« (APMRN 2009). Australia is one of the coordinating countries in the network, bringing together partners in Thailand, Indonesia, Fiji, Singapore, PDR China, Korea, New Zealand, Philippines, Malaysia, Hong Kong, and Japan. Major research centres of multicultural and immigration studies have been established at the Australian National University (ANU) in Canberra (Centre for Immigration and Multicultural Studies), at Monash University (Centre for Population and Urban Research), the University of Western Sydney (Centre for Cultural Studies), the University of Adelaide (Centre for Intercultural Studies and Multicultural Education) and especially at universities that have been former Colleges of Adult Education (CAEs) and turned into universities more recently like Royal Melbourne Institute of Technology (RMIT), Victoria University of Technology, University of South Australia, the University of New England and the University of Wollongong.

Due to their specialisation in vocational education the former CAEs encouraged particularly work in such fields as multicultural education, language teaching, welfare work, interpreting or media studies, areas of interest to public agencies and likely to attract public funding. Although there are some departments like History at the University of Melbourne that have developed a particular research interest in this field, the older universities have been much less prominent in migration and multicultural studies. A known exception is the ANU and its Demography Department. Several of the main founders of migration research like Charles Price, Jerzy Zubrzycki and W.D. Borrie as well James Jupp, a leading scholar of immigration research in the last twenty years, were or have been based at ANU. Pioneer studies in this field such as *Southern Europeans in Australia* (Price 1963), *Settlers of the Latrobe Valley* (Zubrzycki 1964) or *Refugee Settlers* (Martin 1965) were all published by ANU Press.

The largest of the university centres was founded in Wollongong in 1978. It flourished under the directorship of Stephen Castles; however, it was formally disbanded by the university in 1997. Its staff and functions are now integrated in the new Institute of Social Change and Critical Inquiry. The vacant space has been filled only partly by the Melbourne based Centre for Population and Urban Research at Monash University. However, while the Wollongong Centre was working within the normative frame of a strong support for multicultural citizenship, the Centre for Population and Urban Research at Monash has made its quarterly ›People and Place‹ to an important publication arena for more sceptical approaches to immigration and multiculturalism.

This shift of influence from Wollongong to Monash reflects the general political shift from migration and multicultural policies under the ALP governments (1982 until 1996) to the neo-conservative Coalition Governments formed by the Liberal and National Party 1996 to 2007. In general, there is a strong dependency on public support and funding in the field of migration and multicultural studies. In his report to the Australian Research Council, James Jupp (ANU) stresses the lack of internal cohesion of research and its strong link to public agencies that goes with a marked variety of disciplines and interests involved: »Unfortunately this variety has also meant a lack of central institutions, conferences, journals and appointments, other than those funded by public agencies for their own non-academic purposes. There is a large body of literature, but it lacks coherence or a central focus and much of it originates in official reports« (Jupp 1998, 113).

After some pioneering research in the 1960s and 1970s, the initiation of research shifted from universities like ANU to government and public agencies. As part of a general political paradigm change from assimilation to multicultural policies, the government established the Australian Institute of Multicultural Affairs in 1979 and thus created a strong government base for research. It directly responded to a need for coordinated and publicly funded research expressed in the influential Galbally report of 1978: »If we are to achieve the benefits of a multicultural society, its development must be guided, supported and given direction by independent experts of high calibre« (Galbally 1978, sec. 9.18). The Institute employed its own staff and focussed its research particularly on issues related to settlement, employment and ageing. Despite its fruitful and productive contribution to research in issues of immigration and multicultural studies, the Institute was closed in 1986. Jupp explains this closure as being mainly due to the difficult non-autonomous status of the Institute and its strained relations to researchers outside the Institute as well as to the Labour government: »It was not essentially an academic body, and its uneasy relationship with other researchers and the federal Labour government led to its abolition in 1986. The field study might have been better served had one or two centres been set up within existing universities, similar to the Institute, immune from political and bureaucratic considerations. This model was not favored by the Labor government« (Jupp 1998, 115).

Two years later, the FitzGerald Committee on immigration criticised a significant lack of professionalism in the Department of Immigration and particularly recommended public funding for research on economic aspects of immigration. The committee report resulted in the set-up of the Bureau of Immigration Research. It was headed by Melbourne University economist John Nieuwenhuysen, and although it was part of the Department of Immigration, it was based in Melbourne. It was subsequently renamed by adding ›Population‹ and ›Multicultural‹ to its title, according to political preferences of Department ministers. The Bureau was highly regarded among the wider academic research community and produced a significant amount of publications on economic aspects of immigration. However, dependency on political will showed its negative implications when the Conservative Coalition Government took over in 1996. The Melbourne-based Bureau was abolished. Together and with it came severe cuts of funding in many areas of multicultural policies. Staff and library of the Bureau were dispersed and the networks it had established over the time through seminars and conferences dissolved. Jupp describes the consequences of the abolition as severely damaging for the whole research on the issue of immigration: »Eventually, like its predecessor the Institute, it fell victim to political and bureaucratic intrigue. Its abolition in 1996 by the Howard government put immigration and ethnic research back to the level of the early 1970s in terms of well-funded institutional support« (Jupp 1998, 116).

On the one hand, the brief overview on the institutionalisation of research on multiculturalism and migration in Australia has shown the plethora of disciplines involved, and on the other hand, it has shown the dependency of research on government funding and its vulnerability regarding changing political preferences. The following chapters highlight some major elements of the dominant academic discourse on multiculturalism and migration in Australian social sciences. The broad consensus on multiculturalism is explained by referring to the particular meaning of multiculturalism in Australia and particular political and ideological contexts that supported the academic success of the concept of multicultural citizenship. The consensus on multiculturalism has been challenged by a neoconservative political backlash and a growing importance of academic criticism of high immigration and multiculturalism, particularly under the Howard governments 1996–2007. However, there is also growing criticism from the political left and authors like Ghassan Hage, Ien Ang, and Jon Stratton, who apply post-structuralist and post-colonialist discourses on whiteness to the Australian context. The paper sums up some of their main arguments, emphasising the particular role of culture, race and territoriality within Australian discourses on multiculturalism and national identity.

Consensus on Multiculturalism

Given the plethora of research areas and disciplines involved, it is rather difficult to single out a national paradigm of research on multiculturalism and migration. Especially since the mid-1990s, issues on these topics have not only become politically highly debated. Academic voices that stress the damaging consequences of high immigration have become more vocal, as the grown importance of the Monash-based Centre for Population and Urban Research and the public resonance of provocative publications by authors like Katherine Betts (1999) show.

Despite of the criticism from the political and academic right and left there is still a broad academic consensus among social scientists in Australia that is strongly supportive of the concept of multiculturalism and basically regards immigration to Australia as necessary and good. The majority of Australian researchers support a universalistic concept of multiculturalism based on the notion of what Will Kymlicka has called »cultural liberalism« (2001, 64). This concept relates especially to two core issues: 1. that there is considerable consent to the demand by national minorities to be entitled to some form of distinctive political status, including self-government. Territorial minorities that were involuntarily incorporated into a nation state should not be forced to adopt the national identity of the majority and be granted the rights and powers to sustain themselves as distinctive national minorities within the larger multi-nation state. Apart from this ›reconciliation‹ between liberalism and nationalism, the concept argues in favour of a liberal multiculturalism and is concerned with the cultural politics of non-national cultural groups like immigrants or refugees, religious minorities or non-ethnic cultural groups such as gays or disabled that seek recognition and accommodation not separate from but within mainstream societies. The overall assumption is that »such groups have a valid claim, not only to tolerance and non-discrimination, but also to explicit accommodation, recognition and representation within the institutions of the larger society« (Kymlicka 2001, 65).

Among Australian experts multiculturalism is conceived as a public policy model based on a »conjunction of *cultural pluralism* and the *universalism of citizenship*« (Jayasuriya 2008, 1). Most scholars generally share the view that the Australian mode of incorporating an ethnically fragmented immigrant society can best be analysed by referring to the concept of multicultural citizenship. This concept has an empirically descriptive as well as a normative and prescriptive dimension. It has been discussed in detail and in numerous publications by Stephen Castles (e.g. 2000, 133ff.) and by Mary Kalantzis (2000, 99ff.).[1] According to Castles the main elements of multicultural citizenship are: equality of citizenship rights, equality of respect, resources, opportunities or welfare, mechanisms for group representation and participation and differential treatment for people with different characteristics (Castles 2000, 144).

---

1 See also Dutton 2002.

The particularity of the Australian approach to multicultural policies as well as of the academic understanding of multiculturalism in Australia only becomes clear if we look at the particular relation between discourses on multiculturalism and discourses on national identity.

Because of its specific history and geography, many social scientists would argue that Australian state and society are more future-oriented and less burdened with problems of ethnic exclusiveness than European nation states and societies. Mary Kalantzis, for instance, argues that Australia differs from other nations as it represents »the nation of the future« and that the country is therefore particularly able to successfully confront the challenges of a globalised economic and political world. »With its weak sense of nationalism and its history of commitment to government policies of cultural and linguistic diversity, Australia has a chance of producing the nation of the future: a nation with a post-nationalist sense of common purpose, a nation without nationalism. Australia is a nation where it is already almost possible to conceptualise the public realm as one that facilitates and negotiates diversity in such a way that groups can self-determine in significant ways at the local and personal level« (Kalantzis 2000, 107f.).

This widely shared interpretation of the Australian nation as a multicultural, post-national nation strikes the external observer, because in statistical terms Australian society is much less culturally diverse than other Anglo-Saxon democracies (Jupp 2009). Depending on the generosity of the definition, the ›ethnic‹ population in Australia is not higher than 18 to 25 per cent. The country is ›multicultural‹ compared with its former self that is compared to Australian society until the 1950s. However, current Australian society does not include very large numbers of well established and regionally based ethnic minorities. This is true in comparison to the United States, Canada, New Zealand or Britain, and even more so compared with India, Indonesia or the late Yugoslav federation (Jupp 1996; 2009). The largest group of new settlers is still derived from the British Isles, or increasingly from British derived immigration from New Zealand, South Africa, Canada and the United States. Britain has been the largest single source of immigrants from 1788 to 1996, when it has for the first time been passed by New Zealand as a source of immigrants. Thus at least one third of all new settlers are still essentially ›British‹ in their origin. This dominance of immigrants born in Britain or in one of its former colonies is expressed in the widely used differentiation of the Australian population into two opposing categories:

All settlers from an English-speaking background – roughly three quarters of the population – are generally classified as Anglo-Celtic. The term has replaced the term Anglo-Saxon which has been used up to the 1980s. However, it has to be mentioned that the term ›Anglo-Celtic‹ is rightly criticised as being an artificial construction of a unity of actually very different fragments of the population – Catholic Irish versus Anglican or Protestant English – and that the term has therefore officially been banned in New South Wales. All other immigrants are classified as NESB, i.e. signified by their origin as coming from a Non-English-Speaking Background. In older academic publications the abbreviation or term

NESB was more clearly linked to what it basically means, i.e. non-British settlers (Lyng 1935).

Given this clear dominance of settlers of British origin, why – it has to be asked – has multiculturalism become such a successful narrative Down Under. Why has it been so widely and easily accepted in academic discourse throughout different disciplines? The widespread support of multiculturalism among Australian academics and the conceptualisation of the Australian nation as a ›multicultural‹ and ›post-national‹ (sometimes also called ›post-modern‹ nation) can be explained by at least three different but interrelated reasons. From the point of view of a sociology of knowledge, discourses on multiculturalism are strongly related to two major factors: On the one hand, they are strongly influenced by national policies and their underlying paradigms – although we should better talk of a mutual interdependence between academic discourse and politics because policy changes have often been evoked and sustained by major research reports. On the other hand, it is the particular relation between the academic discourse on multiculturalism and understandings of national history and notions of national identity that shape the particular Australian approach to migration studies.

1. The bipartisan support of multiculturalism in Australia since the 1970s. Migration and multicultural studies thrived under the ›protective climate‹ of long-term Australian Labor Party (ALP) rule in the 1980s and early 1990s. Until the rise of the right-wing populist party One Nation and the Coalition Government under John Howard (1996–2007), researchers as well as intellectuals in general could rightly assume that multiculturalism had become an »unchallenged fixture in the political firmament« (Burchell 2001, 233). It had been first introduced by a Labour government in 1972, kept and developed according to an ›ethnic group model‹ under the conservative Fraser government 1975–1983 and then further developed under successive ALP governments as a model of ›multicultural citizenship‹ (Castles 1999). The Howard government has officially confirmed the principle consensus expressed in the 1989 National Agenda for a Multicultural Australia (OMA 1989) on multiculturalism and used the term as a programmatic label. However, its contents have been hollowed out in many respects.[2]

---

[2] The Howard Government kept the term because opinion polls had shown that the majority of Australians supported it. In the New Agenda for Multicultural Australia issued in December 1999, the concept was however reinterpreted strongly emphasising the aim of national unity and harmony. »The term Australian multiculturalism summarizes the way we address the challenges and opportunities of our cultural diversity. It is a term which recognizes and celebrates Australia's cultural diversity. It accepts and respects the right of all Australians to express and share their individual cultural heritage within an overriding commitment to Australia and the basic structures and values of Australian democracy. It also refers specifically to the strategies, policies, and programs that are designed to: – make our administrative, social and economic infrastructure more responsive to the rights, obligations and needs of our culturally diverse population; – promote social harmony among the different cultural groups in our society; and – optimize the benefits of our cultural diversity for all Australians.« (Agenda 1999, 4f.)

2. The particular Australian meaning of the term multiculturalism. Its meaning differs considerably from its use in the USA. While in America the term has been equated with highly disputed policies of affirmative action based on ethnicity and race, such programmes have hardly had any relevance in Australia, apart from some positive action schemes for Aborigines. Furthermore, Australian multiculturalism lacks the ideological implication of cultural relativism that has caused much controversy among American academics.

Under the Fraser government the political concept followed primordial notions of ethnicity like those of Clifford Geertz. They were re-interpreted for the Australian context most of all by Jerzy Zubrzycki in his influential reports for the Australian governments on ›Australia as a Multicultural Society‹ (1977), ›Multiculturalism and Its Implications for Immigration Policy‹ (1979) and ›Multiculturalism for All Australians: Our Developing Nationhood‹ (1982). Already the last report stressed that multiculturalism was not to be discussed exclusively in the context of »ethnic affairs« and »something concerned with non-English-speaking minorities«. The ALP governments of the 1980s and early 1990s diminished the socially divisive tendency of an ethnic group approach and put a stronger emphasis on citizenship rights and social justice. Thus they combined conservative elements like the ›recognition of cultural differences‹ with social-democratic demands for ›social justice‹, equity and equal opportunity and added the neo-liberal element of ›economic efficiency‹, later developed under the slogan ›productive diversity‹. However, their understanding of citizenship rights has often been criticised for being rather formal and not substantive in its impact. In 2005, the Geoff Gallop government of Western Australia has reformulated the aim of connecting issues of identity politics and cultural recognition with broader claims for social and political inclusion. It clearly demands for a further developing of Australian multicultural policies along the lines of the Canadian Citizenship Charter. Against the shortcomings of earlier models and policies of multiculturalism, the ›West Australian Charter of Multiculturalism‹ tries to revitalise the spirit of Australian multiculturalism and to confront a widespread backlash against a culturalist multiculturalism criticised for its disuniting implications. The Charter demands a shift from »cultural to democratic pluralism« and argues for an »inclusive multiculturalism« based on four key principles: Civic Ideals, Fairness, Equality, and Participation. It emphasises a need for not only formal but also substantial social equality for indigenous as well as non-indigenous minorities and thus provides for a »meaningful convergence between the indigenous aboriginal and multicultural discourse through an integrative and ›differentiated citizenship‹« (Jayasuriya 2008, 4).

It remains to be seen whether the Rudd government will follow this regional initiative. The regional Charter, however, can be seen as an indication for the flexibility to adjust the meaning of the term ›multiculturalism‹ to changing political and socio-economic contexts and the unusual combination of elements of diverse and otherwise even opposing lines of political thinking that has insured the political and academic success and endurance of the concept of multiculturalism in Australia over nearly 40 years.

3. The strong political emphasis of Australian Labor Party governments on issues of citizenship is widely reflected in Australian research on migration and multiculturalism. Linking questions of multiculturalism to questions of citizenship is by far not a unique Australian invention. Debates on the meaning of ›multicultural citizenship‹ have influenced political theory debates and empirical research projects in many countries. However, only in Australia has multiculturalism been embraced by politicians and researchers alike as an answer to solve unresolved questions of national identity, caused not only by immigration, but also by a fundamental geo-political reorientation of national politics. The introduction of the term in academic and political debate marks the difficult departure from the former colonial settler society of British Australia on its way to form an independent and self-confident new nation of Australians in Asia. While in Western European countries multiculturalism has been mainly discussed as a concept of political and socio-economic inclusion of ›immigrant minorities‹ and in the Eastern European context as a term to conceptualise the co-existence of different culturally defined territorial minorities, in the Australian context it has been developed as a conceptual means to redefine a whole nation. This collective search for a new national identity under the general conceptual frames of multicultural citizenship or a multicultural nation is expressed in numerous books and articles. The success of the concept of multiculturalism as a concept of the new Australian nation can only be explained by referring to some fundamental conceptual problems of Australian nation formation: The Australian settler nation had defined itself up to the 1960s primarily in racial and cultural terms. Australia was mainly seen as a white nation of British heritage. When it opened its borders first to non-British and later non-European immigrants, the old notion of national identity had become inconsistent with the ethnic make-up and cultural identity of significant parts of the population. The government was also challenged to respond to Britain's stronger orientation towards Europe by stressing Australia's independence from its former links to Britain. Old historical links and cultural and racial notions of national identity were questioned. We can even speak of identity crises of the old settler society, as there was no new foundation for national integration apart from the concept of multiculturalism. Australian nationalism was not based on any specific ideology, and it also lacked any specific culture that it could draw on in order to unify its people apart from its British or European heritage. The policy of assimilation, official policy up to the 1960s, was an attempt to deliberately produce or reproduce an Australian national identity. It mainly focussed on the expectations of new settlers to adapt to the so-called ›distinctive Australian way of life‹. The notion of an Australian way of life was, however, a rather vague substance for a postcolonial Australian ›cultural nationalism‹. This cultural nationalism was

un-ideological (compared to US nationalism) and lacked historical myths and narratives. It did not and still does not refer to more than the suburban dream of »the car, family, the garden and a uniformly middle-class lifestyle« (White 1985, 166). Thus the Australian nation state was under-determined by ideology and culture, and it is particularly this under-determination that encouraged and enabled the Australian governments, as Jon Stratton and Ien Ang have argued, to develop multicultural policies in order not only to incorporate migrant communities, but also in order to provide the nation with an ideological foundation for a new mode of self-perception (Stratton and Ang 1998, 153).

Bringing Skin Colour Back In – Discourses on Race and Culture

Many academics have emphatically emphasised the advantages of concepts of ›multicultural citizenship‹ (Stephen Castles), ›civic pluralism‹ (Mary Kalantzis) or ›democratic pluralism‹ (Laksiri Jayasuriya). However, in the 1990s, the concept of multiculturalism was challenged on two different levels: firstly on the political and secondly on the academic level. The rise of the One Nation Party in the mid-1990s and the political shift from ALP governments to the neo-conservative Coalition government under Prime Minister Howard were expressions of a political backlash against high immigration and multicultural policies that was – and still is – supported by a significant part of the Anglo-Saxon population, most of all lower middle-class people especially from the Australian Outback.

The white social and political backlash against multiculturalism has evoked a lot of academic and public resonance. On the one hand, those who like Katherine Betts had already expressed their scepticism of high immigration, and for a long time, multicultural policies saw themselves confirmed by public opinion polls and new shifts of policies. On the other hand, Australian multiculturalism has also been criticised from a cultural critical point of view. Within academia it is particularly the cultural critical discourse on Australia as a ›White Nation‹ (Hage 1998) that has gained much academic and public attention in the last years.

The critical reconstructions of Australian discourses on national unity and multiculturalism are generally inspired by Homi Bhabha's observation that policies of multiculturalism represent »an attempt both to respond to and to control the dynamic process of the articulation of cultural difference, administering a consensus based on a norm that propagates cultural diversity« (Bhabha 1990, 1). From this perspective multiculturalism is seen as ultimately an »exclusionary ideological construct« (Stratton and Ang 1998, 158).

Aborigines, Anglos or Anglo-Celtics, and Asians are identified as the distinctive collective identities that make up the Australian nation. The academic discourse on Australia as a ›White Nation‹ attempts to reconstruct the changing historical formation of these identities as racial or cultural identities. The introduction of multiculturalism in political and academic discourses, it is argued, has only rhetorically replaced race by culture. This change of discourse is thought of as having had little impact on the actual power structure of the Australian society: the power position of the Anglo-Celtic core and the ongoing social exclusion of Aborigines and Asians. While authors like Stephen Castles consider the particular interplay of elements of cultural and social rights as the most important particularity of the Australian mode of dealing with cultural differences caused by immigration, Ghassan Hage, Jon Stratton or Ien Ang argue from a cultural-critical perspective and interpret multiculturalism as a state strategy not only of managing cultural difference but also as a strategy to reproduce the cultural hegemony of the white majority.

Ghassan Hage, influenced by French post-structuralism, focuses his criticism on toleration as one important element of the discourse on multiculturalism. He interprets the discourse of toleration as an expression of unequal distribution of »national capital«. Multiculturalism has been inclusive insofar, he argues, as it has institutionalised the rights of migrants to experience what he calls »homely belonging«, a sense of belonging that allows them to say »this is my nation«. However, it is only the members of the Anglo-Celtic core, the »dominant national culture«, that can also claim a »governmental belonging«, meaning a belonging in terms of »the nation belongs to me«. Thus it is only the powerful, that is the members of the »white nation« who are allowed to tolerate, while »the less powerful endure« toleration. The official multicultural discourse on tolerance, he argues, »is an invitation for the majority to tolerate a cultural minority, it is dependent on an unquestioning belief as to who the majority and the minority are« (Hage 2001, 248). The right-wing populist response to multiculturalism that has gained influence since the mid-1990s only expresses the fear of the mainstream to safely feel to be ›mainstream‹, given the grown and still growing number of NESB migrants.

Jon Stratton and Ien Ang put forward their cultural criticism of Australian multiculturalism from a slightly different angle. Stratton and Ang conclude from the inherent power relation in any act of tolerance that there is an ideological similarity between the homogeneous nation state and multiculturalism: »The ultimate rationale remains national unity; tolerance of diversity is just another means of guaranteeing that unity« (Stratton and Ang 1998, 158). According to their criticism, Australian multiculturalism is based on the hegemony and prior existence of a ›non-ethnicised Australian cultural centre‹. This hegemony, however, they argue, is made invisible in the concept of multiculturalism.

The concept of multiculturalism clearly privileges culture and ethnicity over race. It was built on the assumption that cultural diversity/pluralism was compatible with national unity as long as there was a shared moral order from which this diversity could be negotiated. This common moral order was not negotiated but taken as given and equated in the Australian context with Christian or European moral views. As a concept of social inclusiveness, cultural pluralism failed in the US-context because it was unable to include racial minorities like African-Americans into the common social order. The inclusiveness of cultural pluralism – called multiculturalism in the Australian context – also failed in Australia to include minorities which are perceived as racial minorities, that is Aborigines and Torres Strait Islanders and the growing group of all those summed up under the broad and academically not clearly cut category of Asians.

On Race and Land – The Particular Relevance of Space in Australian Discourses on Migration and Multiculturalism

While in American history whiteness was defined by blackness as its binary opposition, in the Australian context, black was more or less absent. Aborigines were thought of as vanishing from the social map either by extinction or by assimilation. The invisibility of Aborigines in the white Australia policy has been reproduced in the narratives of multiculturalism. Indigenous people are not only socio-economically and politically marginalised, but also often absent in academic literature on multiculturalism. Since the ›black‹ other was more or less absent in Australian historical narratives, the only binary opposition to white was coloured, the latter being most of all identified with the so-called yellow race of Asians. Asians are the only group really challenging the Australian mainstream, the preservation of Christian, European, Anglo-Celtic white morality. There is a growing literature particularly dealing with the so-called Asianisation of the Australian society, its economic and political reasons, its social consequences in terms of ›national fear‹ and racist exclusion by mainstream Australia.

A fear of Asianisation is diagnosed as lying behind the growing criticism of multiculturalism and immigration among the Anglo-Celtic population. These are »deep-seated and deeply ingrained anxieties«, Ien Ang argues, »often articulated as racial anxieties – which have underlain the peculiar structure of feeling of ›white Australia‹« (Ang 1999, 189). Ang stresses that these anxieties not simply resolve around ›race‹, but that they also »have to do with land, with territory – or more precisely, with claims on land and territory«.

It is this particular discourse on the importance of space and geography – their relevance to notions of national identity and their impact on national attitudes to migration – that distinguishes the Australian academic discourse, but generally also the public discourse from discourses in other countries of immigration. The topic of territoriality is important in right-wing discourses of racial anxiety. Discourse analyses have shown that it is also a significant element of discourses on the exclusion of so-called illegal, unauthorised immigrants. It is also the crucial category in the literature challenging the indigenisation of the white presence on the island continent, the colonialist doctrine of Australia as a *terra nullius* and the legal justification of Aboriginal land rights.

According to a reoccurring argument within the academic literature on the issue of Asianisation, the whole migration programme and the hostile public discourse on unauthorised migrants can only be understood by considering the country's particular history and its geographical location. »Geographically, modern Australia was at the other side of the (European) world from which it was born. The contradiction of being ›a far-flung‹ outpost of Europe was deeply ingrained on the white colonist Australian mind: the ›mother country‹ was so far away and yet so emotionally overpowering. This produced a particularly Antipodean sense of place, a special consciousness of self and of the world moulded by the experience of occupying a vast, distant land, which was perceived as nearly empty. The fact that the gravity of settlement was largely in the south-east corner, where Captain Cook first landed, had added to the sense of isolation and separateness« (Ang 1999, 191).

Unlike Canada, Australian landmass was colonised and controlled by only one world power. The colonisation by the British laid the foundation for the creation of the Australian Federation as encompassing the whole landmass of the island continent. Thus settlers had »a singular sense of spatial identity, the integrity of which coincided with that of the whole island-continent« (Ang 1999, 192). However, this idea of an ›island-continent‹ neglects the historic fluidity of the border zone between the north-west coast and the southern islands of Indonesia and Timor, the old links between the Malays and Aborigines in that region, and overemphasises the idea of separateness and distinctiveness and strengthened the sense of wholeness and insularity, but also the feeling of being exposed to external threats. During the nineneenth century, France, Germany and Russia represented the potential other world powers, but since Japan's victory over Russia in 1904/05 the presumed threat of a foreign power was shifted to the non-European demography.

Far from being the »lucky country« that the settler society perceived itself to be in the 1960s the »white nation« has also been an »anxious nation« all through its history (Walker 1999; Burke 2001). The fundamental tension between Australia's white European identity and its Asian, non-European location has been the »cultural logic of that fear«. Racial anxiety has been closely related to spatial anxiety. According to Ien Ang it is particularly this »antagonistic relationship of its history and its geography« that structurally shaped Australian national identity (Ang 1999, 193).

Australia's geographical position as an island-continent renders its approach to immigration an interesting example of migration policy in the absence of shared or disputed borders. The fear of uncontrolled or under-controlled immigration from poorer and more populous Asian neighbours is, as David Walker (1999) has given ample evidence of, deeply grounded in the history of the country. Strict control over immigration was deemed necessary to protect the kind of civilisation that the new settler society imagined itself to develop and to maintain. Its territorial insularity and the seeming naturalness of its borders promoted a »fortress identity« and the idea that in Australia »it was possible to control contact with the rest of the world in a manner not possible for most other nations« (Ang 1999, 194).

For a long time, the fear of an Asianisation of the island-continent has been one of the driving forces of the whole immigration programme. To develop and populate the continent or become an Asian land was the alternative that many Australians saw themselves confronted with. Ironically, this fear of an Asian take-over was even more threatening as it reminded Australians of their own treatment of the Aboriginal inhabitants of the country. A letter published in the *Sydney Morning Herald* in July 1905 made this analogy very clear: »If we cannot people our Commonwealth [...] our race will wane, and eventually be extinguished even as the Aborigines have disappeared before the might and numbers of their white foes« (cit. in Walker 1999, 9).

Discursive reconstructions of the national past are put forward to explain Australia's assimilationist past, but also in order to explain recent political developments: The deep-rooted feeling of territorial vulnerability lies at the heart, so the argument goes, of the public success of the populist One Nation Party and the rigidity of Australian migration policy under the Howard governments. »On the beach, we replay our genocidal past as our apocalyptic future«, Meaghan Morris remarks wryly (Morris 1998, 247).

Summary

If there is a national Australian paradigm to migration studies, it is expressed in the wide-spread consensus to use concepts of multicultural citizenship and post-national nation to describe the particular Australian mode of social and political integration of an ethnically fragmented immigrant society. These concepts have their empirical as well as structural or analytical weaknesses as they overestimate the actual ethnic fragmentation of the Australian society. They also ignore, as the critical discourses on Australia as a white and anxious nation have highlighted, the racial implications of the Australian nation formation and of the conceptualisation and implementation of multicultural citizenship, which is predominantly expressed in the exclusion of Aborigines and Asians and the hardly challenged economic and political power position of the Anglo-Celtic core of the Australian nation.

Many arguments put forward by Australian cultural studies scholars like Hague, Stratton and Ang are convincing. However, there are also inherent problems of their lines of argumentation: By criticising the close connection between race and culture in the Australian discourse and politics of multiculturalism, they often seem to reproduce the very dichotomies they criticise. The dichotomy between Anglos and Asians disregards the ambiguity and flexibility of the meaning of the term ›Asia‹. Who is regarded and classified as ›Asian‹? In popular imagination ›Asia‹ is usually interpreted as meaning East or Southeast Asia and sometimes South Asia. People from what is called ›West Asia‹ (including Turkey, Cyprus, Lebanon and the Middle East) are sometimes included in the broad category of Asians, sometimes not (Ang 2000, 115f.; Hamilton 1990). As debates on the eastern boundaries of Europe show, especially the borders between Europe and Asia have never been clearly defined. Asia is an artificial construct in terms of a geographical as well as a cultural entity. To disregard the heterogeneity of the people subsumed under this category would therefore play into the hands of populist discourses of radicalisation, even if this only occurs unintentionally.

References

A New Agenda for Multicultural Australia. 1999. Canberra: Commonwealth of Australia.

Ang, Ien. 1999. Racial/Spatial Anxiety: ›Asia‹ in the Psycho-Geography of Australian Whiteness. In *The Future of Australian Multiculturalism. Reflections on the Twentieth Anniversary of Jean Martin's The Migrant Presence*, ed. Ghassan Hage and Rowanne Couch, 189–213. Research Institute for Humanities and Social Sciences: University of Sydney.

Ang, Ien. 2000. Asians in Australia: A Contradiction in Terms? In *Race, Colour and Identity in Australia and New Zealand*, ed. John Docker and Gerhard Fischer, 115–30. Sydney: UNSW Press.

Asia Pacific Migration Research Network (APMRN). http://portal.unesco.org/shs/en/ev.php-URL_ID=2879&URL_DO=DO_TOPIC&URL_SECTION=201.html (accessed February 14, 2009).

Betts, Katharine. 1999. *The Great Divide: Immigration Politics in Australia*. Sydney: Duffy & Snellgrove.

Burchell, David. 2001. Multiculturalism and its Discontents: Majorities, Minorities and Toleration. *Ethnicities* 1 (2): 233–49.

Burke, Anthony. 2001. *In Fear of Security. Australia's Invasion Anxiety*. Sydney: Pluto Press.

Castles, Stephen. 1999. Globalisation, Multicultural Citizenship and Transnational Democracy. In *The Future of Australian Multiculturalism. Reflections on the Twentieth Anniversary of Jean Martin's The Migrant Presence*, ed. Ghassan Hage and Rowanne Couch. Research Institute for Humanities and Social Sciences: University of Sydney.

Castles, Stephen. 2000. *Ethnicity and Globalization. From Migrant Worker to Transnational Citizen*. London: Sage.

Dutton, David. 2002. *One Of Us: A Century of Australian Citizenship*. Sydney: UNSW Press.

Galbally, Frank. 1978. *Migrant Services and Programs: Report of the Review of Post-arrival Programs and Services for Migrants* (May). Canberra: AGPS.

Hage, Ghassan. 1998. *White Nation: Fantasies of White Supremacy in a Multicultural Society*. Sydney: Pluto Press.

Hage, Ghassan. 2001. Beyond the Intention of the State: A Response to Burchell. *Ethnicities* 1 (1): 245–49.

Hamilton, Annette. 1990. Fear and Desire: Aborigines, Asians and the National Imaginary. *Australian Cultural History. Special Issue: Australian Perceptions of Asia* 9: 14–35.

Jayasuriya, Laksiri. 2008. Australian Multiculturalism Reframed. *The New Critic* 8 (September). http://www.ias.uwa.edu.au/new-critic/eight/Jayasuriya (accessed February 15, 2009).

Jupp, James. 1996. *Understanding Australian Multiculturalism*. Canberra: Australian Government Publishing Service.

Jupp, James. 1998. Ethnic, Multicultural and Immigration Studies. In *Challenges for the Social Sciences and Australia*, vol. 1, ed. Australian Research Council, 113–18. Prepared by the Academy of Social Sciences in Australia (July).

Jupp, James. 2009. *Social Cohesion in Australia*. Cambridge: Cambridge University Press.

Kalantzis, Mary. 2000. Multicultural Citizenship. In *Rethinking Australian Citizenship*, ed. Wayne Hudson and John Kane, 99–110. Melbourne: Cambridge University Press.

Kymlicka, Will. 2001. Immigrant Integration and Minority Nationalism. In *Minority Nationalism and the Changing International Order*, ed. Michael Keating and John McGarry, 61–83. Oxford: Oxford University Press.

Lyng, Jens. 1935. *Non-British Settlers in Australia*. Melbourne: Melbourne University Press.

Martin, Jean I. 1965. *Refugee Settlers: A Study of Displaced Persons in Australia*. Canberra: Australian National University.

Morris, Meaghan. 1998. White Panic, or Mad Max and the Sublime. In *Trajectories: Inter-Asia Cultural Studies*, ed. Kuan-Hsing Chen, 239–62. London and New York: Routledge.

Office of Multicultural Affairs (OMA). 1989. *National Agenda for Multicultural Australia: Sharing our Future*. Canberra: Australian Government Publishing Service.

Price, Charles A. 1963. *Southern Europeans in Australia*. Melbourne: Oxford University Press and Canberra: Australian National University.

Stratton, Jon, and Ien Ang. 1998. Multicultural Imagined Communities: Cultural Difference and National Identity in the USA and Australia. In *Multicultural States: Rethinking Difference and Identity*, ed. David Bennett, 135–62. London: Routledge.

Walker, David. 1999. *Anxious Nation. Australia and the Rise of Asia 1850–1939*. Brisbane: University of Queensland Press.

White, Richard. 1985. *Inventing Australia*. Sydney: Allen & Unwin.

Zubrzycki, Jerzy. 1964. *Settlers of the Latrobe Valley: A Sociological Study of Immigrants in the Brown Coal Industry in Australia*. Canberra: Australian National University.

Zubrzycki, Jerzy. 1977. *Australia as a Multicultural Society*. Canberra: Australian Government Report.

Zubrzycki, Jerzy. 1979. *Multiculturalism and Its Implications for Immigration Policy*. Canberra: Australian Government Report.

Zubrzycki, Jerzy. 1982. *Multiculturalism for All Australians: Our Developing Nationhood*. Canberra: Government Report.

Part II:
How to Integrate Migration into Old Nation State Narratives

How to Face Reality.
Genres of Discourse within Durch Minorities Research

By Baukje Prins

Abstract

This chapter gives an overview of developments within Dutch minorities studies from the 1980s onward. Starting from a constructivist view of the performativity of language and the situatedness of all knowledge claims, four genres of discourse are discussed, each using its own rhetorical strategies to make readers ›face reality‹, and each appealing to one particular ethical-political value. The genre of denunciation calls for solidarity, the genre of empowerment promotes the value of diversity, while the report is dedicated to the emancipation of minority groups. In the 1990s, due to emerging critical voices in the public debate and the backlash against (Muslim) immigrants since the ›September 11‹ attacks on the US and the murder of Pim Fortuyn in 2002, these three genres gradually lost credibility because of their presumed ›political correctness‹. This led to the dominance of a fourth genre of discourse, that of new realism, which appeals to the value of individual responsibility. Although the four genres seem to be incompatible, this appears to be the case neither in theory nor in practice. Across what look like unsurpassable boundaries, the Dutch discourse has also produced unexpected alliances between these different genres. The chapter concludes with some self-reflexive remarks on the values and political perspective underlying this analysis itself, ending with a plea for exploring an alternative genre, that of heterogeneity, as most suitable to the ethical-political value of a liberal democracy: a responsiveness to otherness and a commitment to justice and fairness for all.

Introduction

Since the early 1980s, the Netherlands have pursued an active policy to further the integration of ethnic minority groups in Dutch society. Subsequent governments put scientific experts to work to investigate the history, socio-economic position and cultural background of different minority groups – investments which testified to a strong belief in social engineering and the ›makeability‹ of Dutch society. In this paper, I will discern four significant *genres* of discourse within Dutch minorities studies that use different rhetorical strategies to make their readers ›face reality‹.[1] Among these are the genre of *denunciation* and the genre of *empowerment*. But the dominant genre within Dutch minorities research has been the genre of the *report*. Until the early 1990s, most reports represented migrants as members of a particular minority group, i.e. as individuals who are socially and/or economically deprived because of their traditional culture. *Emancipation* was assumed to be the only way out, and Dutch government could help minorities achieve that aim. A decade ago, however, a new kind of report has come to the fore, in which cultures of minority groups are not so much perceived from the perspective of deprivation, but from the perspective of deviancy. I will argue that this trend in Dutch minorities research shows a remarkable affinity with a fourth genre of discourse, that of *new realism*. Since the 1980s, against the assumed ›political correctness‹ of the genres of denunciation, empowerment and report, new realism has become ever more dominant in Dutch public and political debates on immigration and ethnic minorities. In the course of my argument it will become clear that the different genres are constituted by different political values and frameworks. Although these differences seem to be of a paradigmatic nature, hence predict the incompatibility of the genres, this appears to be the case neither in theory nor in practice. Across what look like unsurpassable boundaries, unexpected, ›monstrous‹ alliances are made.

The theoretical framework of this research project is constituted by a constructivist view of the performativity of language and the inevitable situatedness of all claims to knowledge. For this reason, I will conclude this paper with an attempt to self-reflexivity: if I think it important to lay bare the constitutive values and political perspectives operative in the Dutch discourse on ethnic minorities, what about the values and political perspective underlying my own analysis?

The Performative Power of Language

According to the constructivist view of language, especially our public speech is neither epistemologically nor politically innocent. I will therefore not only focus on the different standpoints taken within the Dutch minorities research, but also on the different genres of discourse, i.e. the different rhetorical strategies which are used to convince readers of the validity of these standpoints. The reason that I use the term ›genre‹ is because I focus on the performative effects of a particular discourse, i.e. not so much on how it describes reality, as on the ways in which it (co)produces that reality. The way in which terms such as ›discourse‹ and ›genre‹ have come to be used, by Michel Foucault, Jean-François Lyotard, and by many discourse analysts who adopted their views, is actually quite vague. Thus, ›discourse‹ may refer to one particular unit of text, to a corpus of specific texts, or to everything that is said and written during a particular period and in a particular place. For Foucault, dominant discourse is constitutive of the everyday lives and experiences of modern individuals. Power and knowledge are inextricably inter-

---

1   See for a more extensive reading of the Dutch discourse on immigrant integration Prins 2004.

twined, and we become autonomous subjects only as a result of our submission to dominant modes of discipline and normalisation (Foucault 1971; 1979; 1980). Consequently, we are not merely in the sovereign position to make use of our language; our language also makes use of us. Every sentence we utter strikes layers of meaning which may have a serious impact on the social-symbolic world in which we live. According to this constructivist view, language is a form of action with which we construct our selves and our world (Shotter 1993). Lyotard distinguishes between different *genres* of discourse: »a genre of discourse imprints a unique finality onto a multiplicity of heterogeneous phrases by linking that aim to procure the success proper to that genre« (Lyotard 1988, 129). There are stakes tied to the genres of discourse. When these stakes are attained, we talk about success: what we as speakers or as listeners perceive as the intentions of a subject, actually are »tensions exerted by genres upon the addressors and addressees of phrases, upon their referents, upon their senses« (137). Examples of such genres are the genres of seduction, prescription, and persuasion, but Lyotard also talks about the ethical, the tragic, the technical and the erotic genre (136). Sometimes he uses the notion of ›style‹, or the Wittgensteinian concept of ›language games‹ as an equivalent for ›genre‹. And, being the godfather of postmodernism, he puts much emphasis on the heterogeneity or incommensurability of genres of discourse, i.e. on the fact that one genre cannot be reduced to, or translated into another.

The American feminist philosopher Judith Butler has pointed out some striking similarities between such critical (post)structuralist views of language and ›speech act theory‹ as originally elaborated by the British philosopher J.L. Austin (Butler 1997). According to Butler, speech acts such as addressing or naming are paradigmatic for the way in which human individuals are ›subjected‹ through discourse. Like promising, naming and addressing can be seen as acts with so-called illocutionary force: *in* the saying a doing is implied. Thus, *in* expressing a promise, I have made it, and *in* addressing someone, I have assigned her a place in my material-symbolic order. Butler cautions, however, that there is always a difference between *acting* and *acting upon*. The assessment of the actual performative effects of a particular utterance or discourse cannot be made independent of the context in which it takes place. Any speech act can turn out to be infelicitous – because it was not uttered in the appropriate context, or because listeners somehow resisted its appeal. By emphasising this potential gap between saying and doing, between discursive practice and discursive effect, Butler convincingly wards off the frequently voiced accusations against Foucauldian constructivism that it leaves no room for resistance against the ubiquitous power of dominant discourse.

Genres of Discourse

The entire body of Dutch research reports on the socio-economic position and life world of ethnic minority groups, whether scientific or journalistic, can be perceived as practising the *genre of realism*: its aim is to convince readers of the truth of its narratives, i.e. of their faithful representation of the world ›out there‹. However, when one takes a closer look, it appears that within the Dutch minorities discourse, different forms of realism can be distinguished. Most accounts practise a form of what I call *oppositional realism*, i.e. in their exposition of reality, the inscribed authors, the ›narrators‹ of these stories, wish to contradict prejudice, undermine stereotypes and undo the ignorance of their intended audience. But within this oppositional realism, different rhetorical strategies are used to make readers ›face reality‹, differences which appear to be closely connected to the particular standpoint, the ethical-political framework, from which the narrator perceives and constructs that reality.[2]

The Genre of Denunciation

Until the mid-1980s, insofar as there existed a public discourse on racism and discrimination in the Netherlands, it mainly originated from left-wing anti-establishment circles. (Neo)marxist action groups and journalists denounced the exploitation of foreign workers or ›guest workers‹ by big industries, and criticised Dutch government for its complicity. Protests against discrimination and racism were also strongly motivated by memories of the persecution and mass murder of Jewish citizens during the second World War. One very prominent actor in the struggle against contemporary fascism, anti-Semitism and racism, was the Anne Frank Foundation.

Within this genre of *denunciation*, politically conscious ›white‹ Dutch act as the better articulated spokespersons for the victims of exploitation and discrimination who are assumed to be not (yet) able to speak or fight for themselves. Sometimes, the stories have a dramatic impact, enforced by rhetorical questions in an accusative mode, such as: »Is it a wonder they go to the wall?« or »He had learned hard, but had he done his utmost in school only to become an unskilled labourer?« (Soetens 1980, 26, 44). These denunciations are brought to the fore by an impersonal, omniscient narrator, who frequently makes use of free indirect speech, a device by which the narrator cites her[3] protagonists indirectly, using the third personal singular and past tense: »Against her father, the man [Amina] had hardly known during her youth, she felt a dull, helpless hate. She was sold, rendered the property of someone else.« (Soetens 1980, 11). Thus, the author acts as the spokesperson for the person she portrays: by conveying the humiliating and deteriorating conditions under which foreign guest workers live, while at the same time reminding the reader that these are human subjects, capable of feeling, thinking and resisting what is done to them. Free indirect speech, however, is also known as an effective literary device in cases (novels, stories of fiction) where the narrator wants to give words to emotions and insights which the character is

---

2   Note that the analysis presented here focuses exclusively at *qualitative, small-scale* studies. For more extensive analyses of the different genres within the Dutch discourse, see Prins 1997; 2004.
3   For ›she‹ and ›her‹ read also ›he‹ and ›his‹. Still, it is no coincidence, not even (only) a matter of feminist partiality, that I have chosen to use the feminine forms here: a remarkable number of reseachers and authors on ethnic minorities in the Netherlands are female.

assumed not (yet) able to articulate. Hence, although the protagonists (whether a Moroccan girl married off to a much older cousin, or a guest worker who punishes his daughter for not obeying him) is depicted as the *subject* of particular experiences and feelings, they are first and foremost depicted as *subjected* to them. In a sense, the protagonists are put under the ›narrator's guardianship‹ (Meijer 1996, 157).

Another well-tried narrative strategy within the genre of denunciation is the narrator taking her reader to the netherworld of labour brokers, illegal textile shops, kitchens of starred restaurants, and the insides of oil tankers: trials and tribulations of particular individuals are conveyed in a sober tone, full of details such as the names of people, companies and places, wages, working hours, physical problems, secret contracts and slush money. But the narrator abstains from giving comments, expressions of indignation or direct accusations. The denunciation is expected to work best by merely showing the ›naked facts‹ (see for instance Kagie 1987, Braam 1994).[4]

In any case, within the genre of denunciation, the narrator poses as the more articulate, more knowledgeable and literate spokesperson for the people (s)he portrays. Her role is like that of the plaintiff in a court of justice. Just like the prosecutor, who as a ›professional‹ accuser is more skilled in the juridical language game than her clients, the narrator, as a ›professional‹ knower, is more skilled and articulate in the language game of realistic discourse than the guest workers, illegal residents and other members of ethnic minority groups that she represents. She brings her case before a forum of right-minded citizens, supposedly capable of putting themselves into an impartial position and assess the reliability of the narrator's accounts and those of the people on whose behalf she is speaking. She appeals to the ethical-political value of *solidarity* with those who are less well-off. From the denunciatory perspective, the conflict between the Dutch majority and ethnic minorities, is, in the words of Lyotard, a *litigation* [Fr. *litige*]: a conflict in which the plaintiff and the accused use the same ›idiom‹; their different perspectives are commensurable (Lyotard 1988). By making use of the same genre of discourse, they recognise each other as belonging to the same species, they recognise that, in the end, ›we are all human‹. The harm inflicted by one party upon the other involves no less, but also no more than a *damage* [*dommage*], an injustice which, if brought before an impartial court, can be recognised, repaired, and straightened out.

Initially, the number of countervoices against these denunciatory texts was small, and most of them were immediately put in one box with views from the extreme-right. One of the rare exceptions was Herman Vuijsje, a well-known journalist whose social-democratic sympathies were beyond doubt. In his book *Murdered Innocence* (Vuijsje 1986), he argued that Dutch intellectuals and opinion-makers had become overcautious. They had put a ban on any mention of

---

4   In Germany, the work of Günther Wallraff is exemplary for the genre of denunciation (1977; 1985)

ethnic or racial difference, a taboo he traced back to the guilty conscience regarding the Jews which the Dutch developed since the Second World War, and which in the course of time had been applied to all ethnic minority groups. Vuijsje considered this a dangerous tendency, as it forbade ordinary people to express their not always unjustified feelings of fear or anger, a form of repression which could very well lead to frustration and more virulent forms of racism.[5]

The Genre of Empowerment

One of Vuijsje's targets and most outspoken opponents was Dutch-Surinamese anthropologist Philomena Essed. Her assessment of the Dutch situation was exactly the reverse: when it came to interracial relationships, any suggestion that the Dutch people were a racist people was considered taboo. According to Essed, however, the Netherlands was a country pervaded by (overt and covert forms of) racism (Essed 1990; 1991). Some welcomed her work on everyday racism because it finally managed to break the silence concerning a racism which they experienced on a daily basis. Others criticised it for its vague accusations and unsubstantiated claims. Whatever its scientific merits, Essed's studies were among the first in the Netherlands to give public voice to ethnic minority groups themselves. In that sense, they marked the beginning of a gradually emerging genre of discourse, in which allochthone spokespersons entered the public arena to assert the interests of blacks and migrants, i.e. the genre of *empowerment*.

Contrary to the genre of denunciation, in which the inscribed audience consists of the autochthonous Dutch, the genre of empowerment primarily addresses members of ethnic minority groups themselves. These texts attempt to strengthen readers in their struggle to make it in a society which puts many obstacles in their way, such as distrust, prejudice, discrimination and racism. They do so by portraying exemplary individuals, who figure as living proof that, against all odds, you can, with much hard work, perseverance and faith in your own capacities, ›make it if you try‹. Most protagonists are role models, not only because of their individual success, but also because of their belief in political means such as affirmative action and self-organisation. In other words, these are the stories of pioneers, who have successfully integrated in Dutch society, but did so on their own terms. They have not turned into ›bounties‹, but remained loyal to their own group. Within the genre of denunciation, the narrator is the one who ›knows better‹ than her protagonists. Within the genre of empowerment, the roles are reversed: the protagonist here is the real expert, very capable of speaking for herself, whereas the narrator has receded in the background (most frequently in the role of interviewer) as the modest mediator between the protagonist and her readership. Moreover, while within the genre of denunciation, people's privacy is protected by presenting them as anonymous representatives of their group, the genre of empowerment is all about publicity and visibility: protagonists are pre-

---

5   For an English translation of Vuijsje's critique of the ›political correct Netherlands‹, see also Vuijsje 2000.

sented under their own name, and many texts are accompanied by their photographic portraits.

Most significantly, empowerment is not only argued for in terms of group interests and equal rights. The value of *diversity* is considered at least as important. Many protagonists criticise the implicit use of monocultural norms for their exclusive effects. They argue for screening selection procedures in schools and at work on their ethnocentric bias, and for openness to cultural and ethnic differences. Diversity is to be embraced out of respect for the other. On the other hand, diversity is also applauded because it makes for enrichment. It is for instance argued that a diverse body of workers will prove to be profitable for a company because it will heighten its efficiency, flexibility and creativity (see Essed and Helwig 1992).

It may be clear that the genre of empowerment contains many denunciatory elements: the protagonists often strike an accusatory tone against ›white‹ Dutch society, they had to fight »the delusions of superiority and narrow-minded parochialism« (E.A. Latham, cited in: van Lippe-Biesterveld 1986, 9), and »prove themselves twice, perhaps even three times over.« (Goudt 1989, 10). But, contrary to the genre of denunciation, within the genre of empowerment the conflict between majority and minorities is not perceived as a litigation, as an injustice that, if brought before an impartial court, can be resolved. With a neologism by Lyotard, the conflict is perceived rather as a *differend* (Fr. *différend*): it is assumed that, as everyone is a party in the conflict, there is no neutral position from which a judgement can be made. Moreover, as one of these parties (the autochthonous majority) is placed in a position of hegemony towards the others (minorities), impartiality is not to be expected anyway. The injustice done is not a mere damage, but a *wrong*, i.e. »a damage accompanied by the loss of the means to prove the damage« (Lyotard 1988, 5). To translate this to everyday racism: the injustice of racism consists of the structural humiliation, discrimination, distrust and negation of blacks by ›whites‹; consequently, ›whites‹ will not take blacks any more seriously if they would attempt to testify to this injustice. This is precisely the reason why, within this genre, it is only the struggle of minorities themselves, their empowerment, which can undo their structural position of inequality.

The aforementioned studies by Philomena Essed constitute a remarkable mixture of denunciation and empowerment. On the one hand, they clearly belong to the genre of denunciation: Essed's interviews with Dutch-Surinamese women in the Netherlands and Afro-American women in the US are to prove the objective existence of everyday racism in these countries, and how it systematically marks the experiences and lives of even these higher-educated black women. On the other hand, by giving voice to their ›subjugated knowledges‹, Essed's studies likewise portray them as courageous individuals, whose stories of anger and resistance might contribute to the empowerment of their black readers. From the perspective of the ›white‹ reader, however, such a mixture of genres generates a paradoxical message. On the one hand, readers are summoned to take seriously the accusations of the all-pervasive racism in Dutch society. They are assumed to be able to take an impartial position, and judge and consequently repair the injustices done to black people. On the other hand, however, they are told that racism is all-pervasive, hence that all ›whites‹ somehow gain from it, and will show a ›natural‹ reluctance to give up their prejudice and their position as the superior and privileged group. In other words: the conflict between (white) majority and (black) minority is presented by Essed as both a litigation and a differend, as both a conflict to be resolved peacefully because we all belong to the same human ›genre‹ (i.e. share a common language or vocabulary), and as an unresolvable conflict, an unbridgeable gap, between two human ›genres‹, who, due to their radically different positions in society, occupy radically different perspectives (black vs. white, minority vs. majority). A ›white‹ Dutch reader thus receives a paradoxical message, which catches her in a paralysing double bind. Either she accepts the implicit call for solidarity in the genre of denunciation – but then she will be accused of denying her radical partiality as a ›white‹. Or she accepts the implicit call for diversity in the genre of empowerment (the irreducible ›differend‹ between black and white), but then runs the risk of being accused of withholding solidarity, of indifference or denial of responsibility. Consequently, it is by no means clear how the messages of the genres of denunciation and especially that of empowerment should be translated in terms of policy. On the one hand, governmental initiatives to fight racism and discrimination are to be perceived with distrust because of the ›white‹ interests they might protect. Essed for instance denounced Dutch policy measures aimed at preventing ghettoisation and apartheid by forcing ›whites‹ to accept Surinamese or Moroccan neighbours, as a policy of »dispersion [as] a way to undermine resistance to racial oppression« (Essed 1991, 22). On the other hand, a policy of non-interference, which leaves housing to the workings of the free market, was to be approached with just as much distrust, because that would boil down to the encouragement of apartheid and ghettoisation.

Another manifestation of the genre of empowerment could be found in the militant discourse of the Dutch branch of the Arab European League, initiated in 2002 by the Lebanese-Belgian activist Dyab Abou Jahjah who for a short period of time was immensely popular among especially young and well-educated Moroccans. Inspired by the Black Muslim leader Malcolm X, Abou Jahjah combined an angry rhetoric of denunciation concerning racism and discrimination with an equally assertive call for empowerment, in which resistance against cultural assimilation, the preservation of one's religious (i.e. Muslim) identity and the demand for respect were some of the prominent claims (Croonenberg 2002, Gollin and Sommer 2002, Desmet 2003).

The Genre of the Report

For want of a more original term, I have called the next genre – the most dominant genre within the Dutch minorities research – the genre of the report. Most of these studies are carried out at governmental request. They predominantly concentrate on one particular ethnic group (Turks, Moroccans, Hindustani, or Moluccans) or on a particular subgroup, such as Surinamese single mothers, run-away

Turkish youngsters, or Moroccan teenage boys. Some convey a picture of the everyday life and perspectives of one group, while others focus on a specific issue, such as people's position on the labour market, practices of sexuality or practices of birth control. They concentrate on listing the problems these groups face in their integration in society, and conclude with advice for future policy. Inscribed readers are policy-makers, politicians, managers, social workers, teachers – in short: everyone professionally engaged in the integration of minority groups in Dutch society.

In line with the scientific genre, reports are conveyed by an impersonal narrator for whom categorisation is an important means, both to circumscribe the object of research and to structure the ultimate findings. Consequently, in line with the dominant paradigms within sociology and anthropology, the protagonists in these narratives are first and foremost presented as representatives of a particular group. A characteristic which fits in neatly with the long-standing structure of Dutch policy, which until recently basically relied on categorical distinctions between ethnic minorities as target groups of specific policy measures. However, there is a tension within the genre of the report which betrays an internal critique of the performative effects of categorisations. For, apart from the wish to formulate, from a third person impersonal perspective, general and valid conclusions concerning the group studied, there is also a wish to convey a sense of the uniqueness of each individual case, to do justice to the many differences within the group under investigation. This latter wish is often articulated in terms of wishing the objects to ›speak for themselves‹.

Hence, on the one hand, ›reporters‹ merely convey information from a neutral and distanced perspective, on the other hand, they attempt to bring to life particular experiences, personalities and lifeworlds. The genre of the report is thus constituted by an internal tension between a scientific aim on the one hand, and a literary aim on the other. From one perspective, it appeals to the cognitive capacities of the reader, from the other it appeals to capacities such as empathy and imagination. As a consequence, many reports alternate between the impersonal mode of speech, and more personal accounts which are either presented by a first person narrator, or by individual protagonists who thus literally speak ›for themselves‹. Thus, a narrator may tell extensive individual stories, in order to show the heterogeneity within the research population, and remind readers how each case surpasses the boundary of typification: »Reality appears to be too unruly for sound categories of this kind« (De Vries 1987, 16). But that same report may also use individual accounts as examples of certain ›types‹ of individuals, such as the ›modern‹ or the ›traditional‹ Turkish woman. Or, in spite of emphatic statements such as »in reality, pure types do not exist«, individual protagonists are presented as exemplars of a particular type (Brouwer et al. 1992, 269). This alternation of styles betrays the ways in which the genre of the report grapples with the relation between the general and the particular, between smooth categorisations and untidy realities, and how it hesitates between describing the problems of individual protagonists as either generated by social injustices that can be undone, or as the inevitable tragic effects of living ›between two cultures‹.

Despite the purported neutrality of the report vis-à-vis its object of research, and despite the ways in which it gives ample room to the objects of research to ›speak for themselves‹, in the end the author, and inevitably so, is very much present as the authority who, with the help of particular categories and typologies, structures reality. These categories and typologies are not politically innocent. Until quite recently, the ›master‹ dichotomy in most Dutch reports was the dichotomy between traditional and modern cultures or ways of life. Thus, one of the first Dutch studies made a distinction between traditional, transitional and modern Moroccan families (Van den Berg-Eldering 1978), which was adopted in a number of other reports (see for instance Risvanoglu-Bilgin et al. 1986, Mungra 1990). Although the use of the distinction between modern and traditional was quickly criticised for its hierarchical implications, it proved difficult to escape. Thus, a typology of Moroccan families which was meant to replace the dichotomy, relied heavily upon it, insofar as the alternative designations (ambitious, assertive, ambivalent and reluctant) refer to the positive or negative way in which each family related to the values of modern Dutch society (van der Hoek and Kret 1992).

The central value in the genre of the report is emancipation. Reports assume that ethnic minority groups will gradually leave behind their traditional values and ways of life, but that, because of social and economic deprivation, they will not be able to manage that painful process on their own. As a substantial part of fighting the social, economic and cultural deprivation of ethnic minority groups, governmental support is needed to foster their emancipation.

Some reports do manage to abstain from categorisations dependent on the traditional-modern divide. Instead, they focus on the heterogeneity of the group portrayed, whether it consists of Creole lower class youngsters (Sansone 1992), young Moroccan men (Buijs 1993), or ›ethnic‹ schoolboys and -girls (Saharso 1992). They do so by consistently describing reality as experienced by the subjects themselves, i.e. by using their words, their vocabulary. An issue such as successfulness in life is described relative to the criteria that individuals use themselves, or relative to the social status of their own ethnic group, rather than in relation to the standards of modern, middle-class Dutch society. Other studies focus on the way in which not only migrants (›allochthones‹), but also the ›autochthonous‹ Dutch respond to and are affected by the arrival of so many newcomers in society (Hondius 1999, Mak 2000, Meijer and Buikema 2003–2005). As a consequence these reports pay more systematic attention to experiences of racism and discrimination. The focus is not so much on the extent to which a particular group has not yet succeeded in integrating in Dutch society, but on the various ways in which individual migrants fail or succeed in achieving the goals in life they have set for themselves, and on the variety of circumstances that play a part in that. In these studies, the literary aim of evoking the lifeworld of a particular group, of creating a better understanding for the complicated situation they live in and eliciting sympathy for the ways in which they attempt to deal with it, prevails over the (strictly) scientific aim of supplying general conclusions and advice for further policy. One significant characteristic of these reports is their refusal to reduce their accounts to stories of deprivation and the gap between modern and traditional culture.

In the last decade, however, several researchers started challenging this refusal to look at culture. In their view it signified the existence of a taboo. According to anthropologist Frank van Gemert, for instance, many well-meaning Dutch researchers were reluctant to make a causal connection between culture and criminality, merely because they did not want to lapse into the pitfalls of *blaming the victim* or affirming stereotypes (Van Gemert 1998, 10–12). Whereas previous studies on juvenile delinquency therefore mainly ›blamed‹ the (social, economic, etc.) environment, in his own study Van Gemert deliberately describes the criminal behaviour of Moroccan youngsters not in terms of deviancy, but as behaviour that fits in with their normal, everyday ways of interaction (28). However, in spite of his announced intention to focus on the complex *interaction* between culture and environment, his diagnosis does seem to lapse into the kind of culturalist reductionism Van Gemert wanted to avoid. Thus he finds that Moroccans, especially Berbers from the Rif area, are used to mutual relationships based on jealousy and distrust, relations which stimulate secrecy and trying out how far one can go without getting caught. Up to the age of eighteen, according to Van Gemert, Moroccan boys lack internal norms and a sense of responsibility because their community does not expect them to behave well on their own accord. When they are caught, they will be punished, but not morally reproached. It is only when they become adults that Moroccan men are expected to show more respectable and responsible behaviour.

Most outspoken in breaking the taboo on culture in the Dutch research scene has undoubtedly been another young anthropologist, Marion van San. In her report on the delinquent behaviour of that other infamous Dutch problem group, Antillean youngsters, Van San criticised the tendency within minorities studies to evade the question whether aspects of culture might promote criminal behaviour (Van San 1998). She therefore addressed the issue head-on, by investigating whether some forms of delinquent behaviour by boys from Curaçao might be explained by the greater tolerance within the group for particular offences.[6] From interviews with delinquent Curaçao boys and their mothers, Van San reconstructed the ›insider‹ perspective on what she called ›instrumental‹ and ›expressive‹ crimes and concluded that, whereas the boys cannot fall back on their cultural background to legitimise an instrumental crime such as stealing, there does exist a shared subculture which legitimises expressive crimes such as stabbing. The most shocking and controversial element of Van San's findings was the justifying, sometimes even encouraging roles she claims that Curaçao mothers play in toler-

---

6 Van San makes use of the so-called theory of neutralisation, according to which deviant behaviour can be explained away by the person himself or by his significant others with the help of strategies of legitimisation and justification.

ating the criminal behaviour of their sons, especially concerning expressive crimes, where ›honour‹ is at stake. Van San's report met with serious criticisms concerning the negative effects it might have on the public image of Antilleans in Holland. This outburst of political sensitivity, however, must have been peanuts to her compared to the fierce resistance she met when, on request of the Flemish government, she started an investigation into the relationship between ethnicity and criminality in Belgium. When the report was finally published, it was ignored by the intellectual and political establishment, and, to her regret, embraced by the extreme-right party the Flemish Block (De Smedt 2002, Camps 2002).

Rather than perceive the culture of ethnic minority groups in terms of simple, rural traditions that will gradually and self-evidently disappear to be replaced by the more complex, modern ways of life, Van Gemert and Van San assumed that migrants bring with them a deep-seated traditional way of life, a culture of honour and shame which they pass on entirely intact to their children and which is incompatible with the fundamental values of modern Dutch society. In these studies, cultures of minority groups are not so much perceived from the perspective of deprivation, but from the perspective of deviancy. By implication, government is not asked to help members of minority groups with their emancipation, but to press them to take *responsibility*.

New Realism

This latest trend in Dutch minorities research shows affinity with a fourth genre of discourse, which takes us away from the realm of research to the realm of public debate, and from the discourses of oppositional realism to what I will call the genre of *new realism*. Since the 1980s, against the assumed ›political correctness‹ of the genres of denunciation, empowerment and report, new realism has become ever more dominant in Dutch public and political debates on immigration and ethnic minorities. It was radicalised most forcefully by politicians such as the late Pim Fortuyn whose *List Pim Fortuyn* after his murder in May 2002 brought about a political landslide, and the Somali-Dutch Ayaan Hirsi Ali, a member of parliament for the conservative-liberals between 2003 and 2006, who regularly stirred up public controversy by castigating adherents to multiculturalism for their political naïveté, and by her provocative statements about the ›true‹ meaning of Islam. Hirsi Ali achieved worldwide coverage and admiration when her short film *Submission I* in November 2004 led to the murder of its director, Theo van Gogh. The victory of the genre of new realism has had serious consequences for both the position of ethnic minorities in the Netherlands, and for what in the earlier days new realists scornfully referred to as the Dutch ›minorities research industry‹.

The National Minorities Debate

One of the first public expressions of new realism came from the then leader of the conservative liberals (VVD), Frits Bolkestein. In 1991, Bolkestein challenged the dominant Dutch discourse, by stating that from now on the integration of minorities should be handled ›with guts‹ (Bolkestein 1991).

Bolkestein's argument was not so much directed against the goal of emancipation itself, as upon the way in which it could be reached. In its eagerness to help, the attitude of the Dutch government had become too lenient and permissive. Bolkestein's supporters spoke of hugging ›to death‹, ›treading on eggs‹ or a ›culture of pitifulness‹. In their view, this urge to help ethnic minority groups emancipate had made them more rather than less dependent on the welfare state, allowing them to withdraw within their own group rather than stimulate integration into the larger society.

The genre of *new realism* has five distinctive features. First, the author presents himself as someone who dares face the facts, who speaks frankly about ›truths‹ which the dominant discourse has supposedly covered up. Thus Bolkestein spoke firmly about the ›guts‹ and ›creativity‹ needed to solve the problem of integration, and how this would leave no room for ›compromise‹, ›taboos‹ or ›disengagement‹. His supporters accordingly praised him for his show of ›civic courage‹, for the ›mature‹, ›civilised‹ and ›plain‹ way in which he had placed this thorny issue on the political agenda.

Secondly, a new realist sets himself up as the spokesperson of the ›ordinary people‹, i.e. the autochthonous population. Thus, in the television programme *Het Capitool*, broadcasted on March 22, 1992, Bolkestein observed that »below the surface a widespread informal national debate, which was not held in public, was already going on« and in an interview in *NRC Handelsblad* on September 12, 1991, he claimed that »the issue of minorities is a problem incessantly discussed in the pub and in the church«. Why listen to the *vox populi*? On the one hand, ordinary people deserve to be represented because they are realists *par excellence*: they know from their daily experience what is really going on, especially in the poor neighbourhoods of big cities, and they are not blinded by politically correct ideas. On the other hand, one should take the complaints of the ordinary people seriously, in order to keep their emotions under control and channel them in the right direction. As Bolkestein claimed in *de Volkskrant* on September 5, 1992: »[S]omeone who ignores the anxiety, nourishes the resentment he intends to combat.«

A third characteristic of new realism is the suggestion that realism is a characteristic feature of national identity: being Dutch equals being frank, straightforward and realistic. This is particularly manifest in the publications of the aforementioned journalist Herman Vuijsje. In his *Murdered Innocence*, Vuijsje testified to his desire to return to an authentic Dutchness, to the pre-war days when »our country distinguished itself for its pre-eminently matter-of-fact-like treatment of ethnic difference« (Vuijsje 1986, 7).

A fourth feature of new realism is its resistance against the political left. New realists find it is high time to break the power of the progressive elite which for too long has dominated the public realm with its ›politically correct‹ sensibilities regarding fascism, racism and intolerance. This supposedly left-wing censorship of public discourse is also criticised because it is assumed to be accompanied by a relativistic approach to the value of different cultures.

Finally, the discourse of new realism is highly gendered. From the very beginning, when participants in the debate on multiculturalism wanted to prove the practical relevance of the issue at hand, they referred to issues of gender and sexuality, such as the headscarf, arranged or forced marriage, female genital mutilation, honour killing, the cultus of virginity, domestic violence and homophobia. In Bolkestein's initial intervention, for instance, references to the position of women in ›Islamic cultures‹ were quite prominent. When condemning Islam for not living up to the principle of non-discrimination, he stated that the way in which Muslim women were treated ›cast a slur on the reputation of that civilisation‹. And he took issue with cultural relativism, because it would extenuate reprehensible practices such as the custom of *suttee*, female circumcision, and polygamy. For new realists, the equality between men and women is an obvious and uncontested part of Western culture in general and Dutch liberal democracy in particular. But it was only with the rise of the voice Ayaan Hirsi Ali, that the position of Muslim women moved from the margin to the centre of the new realist concern.

A ›Multicultural Drama‹

In January 2000, publicist Paul Scheffer gave an impulse to new realism by castigating his fellow countrymen for closing their eyes to the ›multicultural drama‹ that was developing right under their eyes (Scheffer 2000). Whereas the rates of unemployment, criminality and school drop-out amongst ethnic minorities were extremely high, the Dutch, according to Scheffer, mistakenly held on to their good old strategies of peaceful co-existence through deliberation and compromise. But in doing so, they ignored the fundamental differences between the new situation and the earlier days of pillarised society. Presently, Scheffer argued, there existed fewer sources of solidarity, while Islam, for its refusal to accept the separation between church and state, could not be compared with modernised Christianity; finally, allochthone youngsters were accumulating feelings of frustration and resentment. Teaching Dutch language, culture and history should be taken much more seriously. Only then would allochthone residents acquire a clear view of the basic values of Dutch society.

Scheffer's essay became the intellectual talk of the town. Like Bolkestein's intervention, it was welcomed because of the courageous way in which it challenged the view of the dominant (political as well as academic) elite which, these supporters suggested, had stubbornly refused to face the serious problems of a multicultural society. Scheffer accused politicians of ›looking the other way‹, causing ›a whole nation to lose sight of reality.‹ In this fashion, the rhetorics of Scheffer's article perfectly complied with the genre of new realism. Here, again, was someone who dared to break taboos. Like a decade earlier, several commentators were pleased that it was finally possible to have a ›frank‹ and ›candid‹ conversation without ›politically correct reflexes‹ taking the upper hand. Scheffer, too, claimed that what happened to ordinary people, the stories told ›below the surface‹, remained unseen and unheard, even though his reference was not so much to the autochthonous population as to the feelings of anger and frustration among allochthone youngsters. Yet Scheffer showed a similar ambivalence as to why these feelings should be taken seriously: on the one hand, these youngsters were frustrated for a legitimate reason, i.e. for remaining stuck at the bottom of the social ladder; on the other, government should do more to prevent these frustrations from turning into social upheaval. Like Vuijsje, Scheffer also recommended the affirmation of Dutch identity as a remedy against the problems of multicultural society, although his ideal Dutchman was not the romanticised ›ordinary‹ man or woman in the street, but the decent and politically knowledgeable citizen, finely aware of the good as well as the bad sides of Dutch identity.

Nevertheless, Scheffer shared with his predecessors an impatience with the supposed cultural relativism of the progressive elite, which in his view had deteriorated into an attitude of moral indifference. Resisting the growing leniency and laxity regarding the execution of laws and regulations (the typically Dutch culture of toleration – *gedogen*), Scheffer emphasised that it was high time to draw clear lines on what people were allowed and not allowed to do. But what irritated him was not so much the toleration of anti-western values and practices (although this surely should be tackled too), but the incomprehensible indifference of left-wing intellectuals to the ever-widening gap between a (mostly autochthonous) majority of the well-off, and (mostly allochthone) minorities which remained stuck in a situation of deprivation. Scheffer's version of new realism, in other words, was more ›politically correct‹ than that of his predecessors – his was new realism with a social face.

Pim Fortuyn and the Turn to Hyper-Realism

When, in the global atmosphere of crisis since September 11, Pim Fortuyn suddenly entered the Dutch scene, his rhetorics showed all the characteristics of the genre of new realism. On September 29, 2000, his face appeared on the cover of the weekly magazine *HP/De Tijd*, his mouth tied up with his necktie, accompanied by the caption: »Are you allowed to say everything you think? Dutch taboos.« And, notwithstanding his aristocratic manners and appearance, Fortuyn prided himself on knowing what was going on in the poor neighbourhoods and fully understanding the concerns of the ›ordinary people‹. But, like the new realists before him, Fortuyn's attitude towards his constituency remained ambiguous. On the one hand, the ordinary Dutchman was a new realist like himself. If people living on welfare illegally took on jobs on the black market, their choice was entirely understandable, for »The poor are not at all the pitiful people the left church wants them to be. Most of them are just like us: emancipated, individualised, independent citizens« (Fortuyn 2001, 105). On the other hand, the Dutch people were in need of a true leader, someone who, like himself, could act as their father and mother at the same time: »the father as the one who lays down the law, the mother as the binding element of the herd« (*Het fenomeen Fortuyn* 2002, 40). The third element of new realism, the affirmation of national identity, came to the fore both in Fortuyn's insistence on the preservation of national sovereignty against the ever expanding influence of the EU, and in his warnings against the imminent ›islamisation‹ of Dutch society. Finally, his contempt of the progressive elite pervaded almost every aspect of his writings, resulting in his last book in which he wiped the floor with the purple governments (Fortuyn 2002).

But Fortuyn also further radicalised the new realist discourse. Freedom of opinion, even for an imam who deemed homosexuals like himself lower than pigs, was more important than legal protection against discrimination. According to the notorious interview which cost him his leadership of *Leefbaar Nederland,* Holland was a ›full country‹, Islam ›a backward culture‹, and it would be better to abolish »that weird article of the constitution: thou shall't not discriminate« (cited in *Het fenomeen Fortuyn* 2002, 61; 63). Fortuyn assured people that they could rely on him because he was »a man who says what he thinks and does what he says«. In other words: people were asked to put their trust in him more on account of his new realism than on the basis of his actual political program. And so they did, as was evident in the massive outburst of grief and anger after his murder and at his funeral. Without a doubt, one of the main ingredients of Fortuyn's attractiveness had been his ›frank‹ speech on immigrants. His particular style, this odd mixture of aristocratic appearance and tough talk, turned out to be his strongest political weapon (Pels 2003). In his performance of new realism, which initially was about having the guts to speak freely about problems and how they should be solved, was turned into simply having guts, i.e. giving vent to your gut feelings. Fortuyn thus managed to radicalise the genre of new realism to such an extent that it turned into its very opposite, into a kind of hyper-realism. Frankness was no longer practised for the sake of truth, but for its own sake. References to reality and the facts had become mere indicators of the strong personality of the speaker, proof that a ›real leader‹ had entered the stage who dared migrants to take up their own responsibility rather than wait for help.

Ayaan Hirsi Ali and *Submission Part I*

Not without reason, Ayaan Hirsi Ali has regularly been compared with Pim Fortuyn. Like Fortuyn, she sought confrontation, showed the new realist gut to provoke and thereby imperil her life. Hirsi Ali's apostasy from Islam took place in a remarkably short period of time. In her first publication, November 2001, her rhetorics about Islam had still been inclusive: she had wondered why ›we Muslims‹ cannot look at ourselves, only to answer that question with merciless criticism – but it was phrased as self-criticism: »We Muslims have lost sight of the balance between religion and reason« (Hirsi Ali 2002, 42). But already in her first more outspoken feminist essay, she started to distance herself. She no longer spoke as a Muslim, but as someone »with knowledge of and experience with the Islamic religion« (47). In one of the first television talk-shows she appeared, she referred to herself as a ›secular Muslim‹. Only one evening later, she ›came out‹ as a former Muslim who deemed Islam to be a ›backward culture‹, only to complete her public fall of faith with an interview in the *Trouw* on January 25, 2003, in which she put Mohammed to the pillory as a ›tyrant‹ and a ›perverse man‹. Gender-related issues like female genital mutilation, forced marriages, honour killing and hymen repair, have become part of the Dutch emancipation policies as a direct result of political motions in parliament submitted by Hirsi Ali (see also Hirsi Ali 2004a).

Hirsi Ali's trenchant interventions caused much more commotion than similar statements by Pim Fortuyn had ever done. She was accused of ›fouling her own nest‹, and behaving like ›a bounty‹, and branded as an apostate who washed the dirty linen of an already much stigmatised group in public.

Nothing, however, could make her stop to force both the autochthonous Dutch and Muslim migrants to face the harsh reality of the lives of Muslim women as she perceived it. In the summer of 2004, together with filmmaker Theo van Gogh she made a short movie, *Submission, Part I*. The film, lasting no more than eight minutes and first broadcasted on national Dutch television in August 2004, vehemently denounced the (sexual) violence against Muslim women, suggesting that this violence was legitimised by Islam. Because texts from the Koran were inscribed on the naked skin of the female actresses, the film was extremely blasphemous in the eyes of Muslims. And it soon showed that to some it had indeed exceeded all bounds. On November 2, 2004, Theo van Gogh was brutally slaughtered. His murderer, the 26 year-old Dutch-Moroccan Mohammed Bouyeri, had knived a letter into Van Gogh's body, which made it clear that his deed was actually meant as a warning to Hirsi Ali. She was forced to go underground for a second time in her short career, whereas Dutch government responded with a series of arrests and stricter measures to fight Muslim terrorism. In January 2005, Hirsi Ali returned at the Dutch political scene: deeply touched by the murder of her friend, but unbroken. She took up her work as a member of parliament again, announced that she was working on a new book (in English) entitled *Shortcut to Enlightenment*, and determined to make a sequel to the first film, now with an anonymous director, to be titled: *Submission, Part II*. Meanwhile, the news of the murder of Van Gogh had put her in the spotlight of the international media (see for instance Caldwell 2005). She received numerous awards in different countries, was celebrated by *Time-Magazine* as one of the 100 most influential people of 2005, and her texts were translated in several languages (Hirsi Ali 2004b; 2006).

›Monstrous‹ Alliances

Each of the four genres discussed above fits in with a particular ideological or political framework. As may have become clear, the genres of *denunciation* and *empowerment* are structured by the critical frameworks of Marxism, feminism, anti-racism and the Black consciousness movement. They build on assumptions regarding deep-seated relations of domination and exploitation, to be changed through collective strategies of resistance. The central values here are those of *solidarity* and *diversity*, respectively. The political framework sustaining the genre of the *report*, on the other hand, is that of the social-democratic welfare state, according to which the autonomy of individuals is both the starting point and ultimate aim of democratic government, and the state should create the conditions under which individuals are able to develop their personal capacities. Its central value is *emancipation*. In the Netherlands, this line of thought has been mixed with the heritage of the system of religious pillarisation, which led to the conclusion that the best way for a minority group to achieve collective emancipation was a ›strenghtening of one's own circle‹ first. Within this perspective, emancipation does not imply assimilation. So long as it does not interfere with their socio-economic integration, ethnic minority groups are allowed to hold on to their own culture or religion. All three genres can be perceived as manifestations of *oppositional realism*: accounts of reality made from a particular standpoint. They are partial insofar as they side with the interests of the minority group at hand. But the genres differ in their interpretation of the kind of marginalisation that minority groups suffer. The genre of denunciation presents them as victims of exploitation – *class* being perceived as the main axis of inequality. Within the genre of empowerment the axis of inequality is *race* or *ethnicity*, and minority groups are presented as subjects of resistance. Finally, the genre of the report looks at minorities through the prism of *culture* and consequently speaks of them in terms of deprivation or deviancy.

Emerging at the end of the 1980s, the genre of *new realism* challenged each of these genres of discourse. The political framework underlying new realism is an odd combination of (neo-)liberalism and communitarianism. According to a (neo-) liberal outlook, the state should perform no more than a minimal function in assuring the basic (civic and political) rights of its citizens, granting them maximum freedom to live their lives in their own way. But these rights are to be balanced by civic duties and virtues. *Responsibility* for one's own (individual) welfare and well-being is therefore one of the most important values of a neo-liberal outlook. From a communitarian perspective, responsibility is likewise of crucial importance, be it that here the emphasis is not primarily on one's own individual welfare, but on the welfare of others (i.e. the members of one's community). Moreover, it is not merely individual citizens who should take up responsibility, it is also ethnic, religious and cultural communities that should take responsibility for the state of the larger political community, the nation. No wonder that current integration and immigration policies are almost entirely geared at teaching newcomers, with the help of compulsory integration courses, how to become good Dutch citizens.

If we take these differences in political outlook into consideration, there seems to exist a gap between the genres of denunciation and empowerment on the one hand and the genres of the report and new realism on the other. While authors of the first two genres assume that what is needed to get a more just society is collective struggle, the latter are convinced that what is needed is individual development. An outlook on society as determined by class or other collective struggles seems to be incompatible with the perception of society as the sum of individual activities. One might think that such radically different perspectives consequently lead to different assessments of what is wrong, and to different policy measures to improve the situation. Across such a paradigmatic divide, alliances seem to be unthinkable.

Still, if we take a closer look, we can discern sources for some unexpected, ›monstrous‹ alliances. If we compare the four genres with regard to the question *who* is to do the acting, i.e. who is to struggle or who is to develop, some remarkable agreements come to the fore (see overview on p. 100). Thus, new realists criticise the assumptions in the (scientific) reports that the mechanisms of the welfare state and the model of pillarisation should *help* ethnic groups in their process of emancipation. But in doing so, they tacitly subscribe to one of the main points brought forward by the genre of empowerment, namely that members of minority groups have to help themselves to be successful. Of course, the appeal to ›do it yourself!‹ has a different ring when expressed by a new realist or by an advocate of empowerment: in the first case it is a call in an accusatory mode to finally take responsibility and stop expecting help from others, in the latter it is a critical reminder that dominant society will not help you anyway, and an encouragement to rely on your own (individual and collective) power to show them what you're worth. Thus, although politically spoken the practitioners of the genres of empowerment and new realism are each others' adversaries, they share a strong aversion to an overcaring or paternalistic attitude by the Dutch people or the Dutch state. One example of such an alliance is a publication by new realist Frits Bolkestein, in which he interviews seven key figures from the Dutch Muslim world. Entirely in accordance with the rules of the genre of empowerment, in this book Bolkestein introduces his protagonists as successful migrants who might function as a role model for others. He offers his interlocutors ample space to talk about the way in which they managed to acquire their present position in society. Although they do not agree with Bolkestein's critical view of Muslim culture, they clearly share his dislike of spokespersons and caretakers (*zaakwaarnemers*), as well as his view of integration as not only a matter of rights, but also of responsibilities (Bolkestein 1997).

On the other hand, there is a no less remarkable affinity between the genres of denunciation and report. Although politically far apart, they agree that ethnic minorities are in need of *support* from the Dutch – be it that representatives of the first genre call for support in struggle, while the second genre insists on the importance of support through education. But they find each other in their firm rejection of both the political indifference of new realists, and the too optimistic confidence of the adherents of empowerment that minority groups can manage on their own.

The Genre of Heterogeneity

The findings of the above analysis can be summarised as follows:

Genres within the Dutch minorities discourse

What is to be done?	COLLECTIVE STRUGGLE	INDIVIDUAL DEVELOPMENT
GIVE SUPPORT	genre: **denunciation** value: *solidarity*	genre: **report** value: *emancipation*
DO IT YOURSELF	genre: **empowerment** value: *diversity*	genre: **new realism** value: *responsibility*

This neatly-arranged schedule should not be understood as a (politically) neutral overview of the variety of genres to be found in the Dutch minorities discourse. For one thing, it distinguishes analytically what empirically does not manifest itself along such clear-cut lines at all. This matrix of four genres should rather be perceived as an analytical tool that might be helpful to analyse similar discourses in other countries, as an instrument to be tested for its usefulness in comparative research projects. For another thing, the schedule does not take account of the differences in political impact between the genres. For instance, it does not account for the long-standing dominance of the genre of the report (in terms of numbers of publications and actual influence on policies), nor of the marginality of the genres of denunciation and empowerment (while Abou Jahjah initially attracted a huge following and received much attention by the media, in 2005 his movement has become just another social and political organisation, whose views can be mainly found on its internet-site www.ael.nl). In other words, my critical remarks on these genres notwithstanding, in the above I have practised a form of discursive ›affirmative action‹ regarding the genres of denunciation and empowerment, while downplaying the considerable influence of the genre of the report.

These remarks touch upon the issue of the normative perspective from which the present research project itself has been undertaken. When taking note of its distinction between different genres, which each promote a particular value and political perspective, a perceptive reader might ask which genre of discourse the analysis itself belongs to. To which extent is it part of, or representative of the Dutch discourse it has studied? Does it first and foremost face its readers with reality (i.e. the reality of the Dutch minorities discourse)? Or has it contributed to the empowerment of a particular group, party or genre? Could it be read as a denunciation of the biased nature or lack of self-reflexivity of the discourses it studied? Or should it, in its urge to divide the (discursive) world into separate categories, be seen as a report which surreptitiously supports the actually ›deprived‹ genres of denunciation and empowerment? If it is essential to lay bare the values, political ideologies and rhetorical strategies of the discourses studied, why aren't the values, political standpoints and rhetorical moves on which this (re)construction of (discursive) reality itself rests, made more explicit? Does not this analysis commit the ›sin‹ of pseudo-neutrality or crypto-normativity that it implicitly takes issue with?

These questions are at the heart of this project, insofar as it takes seriously the constructivist claim that power and knowledge are intertwined, that all knowledges are situated, and that descriptions of our (social, discursive) world, however objective, if taken seriously will inevitably affect that very same world (Haraway 1991). If claims to knowledge are never innocent, then neither are the claims defended here.

The position from which the analytical framework elaborated in this paper emerges, i.e. the genre implicitly favoured in and through the above analysis, I will call the genre of heterogeneity.[7] By concentrating on the complexity of (discourses on) interethnic relationships, a focus on heterogeneity implies the attempt to cut across the binary oppositions that play a constitutive role in the four genres I have distinguished so far. Heterogeneity does not support either collective struggle or individual development exclusively. Texts of the genre of heterogeneity (ideally) do not single out victims of oppression, damages to be repaired, arrears to make up, or causes to fight for. Power is rather conceived as a relational and dynamic category, with which individual subjects, members of minorities and majorities, interact in a variety of ways: sometimes they are subdued to forces beyond their reach, sometimes they know how to bend things to their own will, at times they manage to struggle out, at times they exert power over others. Sometimes these accounts even, in an entirely apolitical way, depict human suffering as tragic rather than unjust, associating it with inevitable fate rather than changeable circumstances. Heterogeneous texts distinguish themselves for not being unambiguously on the side of one or other well-defined party, which does not mean that they are not involved with the subject(s) of their investigation. On the contrary, within the genre of heterogeneity, the narrator positions herself constantly, both vis-à-vis her subject-matter and her audience. Only these positions are shifting all the time: the narrator places herself (and henceforth her readers) in a variety of positions, siding then with one, then with another perspective. In doing so, she does not rely upon categorical divisions, such as oppressor versus oppressed, dominant versus marginal, modern versus traditional, or white versus black – let alone good versus bad. Instead, she shows sensitivity to the impurity and inevitable deficiencies of the world as it is. By staging different actors and a multiplicity of voices, she takes account of the complexities and ambiguities of the world described. Her own perspective in these texts is not transparent and univocal either, but split up between different positions. The genre of heterogeneity is a ›non-genre‹, simultaneously situated outside and constitutive of the matrix of discursive genres as elaborated here.

---

7   In the second section, I mentioned some examples of texts that could be perceived as practising the genre of heterogeneity.

To be sure, the performative effects that heterogeneous accounts may produce are not very reassuring. Heterogeneous stories do not offer us certainty in the sense that they confront us with reality as it truly is. They are risky because they are located right in the ›muddle‹ of the complexities and ambiguities which make up the lives of the people portrayed, or, in the case of the current project, the genres depicted. Their authors do not pose as neutral mediators, nor as partisan ventriloquists. They realise themselves to be engaged in non-innocent conversations, without being able to entirely control the effects of their own words, accounts, analyses. But an author who speaks from different perspectives appeals to a variety of understandings within the reader, whose possibly unified views may as a consequence fall apart into an assembly of dispersed positions. The dispersal of the narrator's voice affects her ›authoritative‹ position. It renders it more difficult for a reader to unthinkingly go along with her accounts. S/he might come to realise that clear-cut standpoints cannot be held, that they must make way for more complex and many-sided accounts and for new problems and dilemmas to think through.

The familiar criticism to this approach is that it does not provide readers with a normative standpoint as to how to proceed further and what is to be done. Because it endows each point of view with equal validity, and not offers one last, overall perspective, it leaves its readers empty-handed.

I think such line of criticism is mistaken. It rests on the assumption that normative universalism and a (epistemological or culturally) relativistic outlook are mutually exclusive. I would argue, however, that the genre of heterogeneity fits in precisely with the normative-political framework that lies at the basis of modern Western societies and that is the framework of liberal democracy.[8] Within the political regime of liberal democracy it is of the utmost importance to have an open eye for, as Seyla Benhabib has phrased it, »the many subtle epistemic and moral negotiations that take place across cultures, within cultures, among individuals, and even within individuals themselves in dealing with discrepancy, ambiguity, discordancy, and conflict« (Benhabib 2002, 31). In that sense, the liberal democratic framework differs from (the stronger forms of) cultural relativism, insofar as the latter starts from assumptions concerning the incommensurability of different cultures, and aims to preserve their (presumed) purity. Within a liberal democracy, on the other hand, it is acknowledged and accepted that the political inclusion of new groups will lead to the hybridisation of the cultural heritage of the groups concerned as well as of the society that includes them. Benhabib emphasises the importance of openness in public deliberations to what she calls »the standpoint of the concrete other«, i.e. to other people's specific needs and interests, to the ways in which ›they‹ truly differ from ›us‹, in order to enlarge »the standpoint of the general other«, i.e. the standpoint from which we

---

8 Elsewehere, I have given an extensive account of the normative political position underlying my constructivist analysis of the Dutch minorities discourse and my defense of the genre of heterogeneity (Prins 2004, especially chapters 6 and 7).

perceive others as equal bearers of rights and duties (Benhabib 1992, 148–177). The ultimate aim of this responsiveness to otherness is to ensure that our institutions and laws live up to their claims of justice and fairness for all, to their liberal claims of universality. In my opinion, the performative effects of texts of the genre of heterogeneity as envisioned above, would be extremely beneficial in fostering democratic forms of life and in enlarging our normative-political standpoint such that it indeed becomes more inclusive and may justifiably lay claim to universal validity.

Epilogue

The above text stems from the beginning of 2006. How did things in the Netherlands proceed since then?

While her international reputation rose, Hirsi Ali's popularity at home was gradually waning. Her final fall from grace was no less dramatic than her rise to fame had been. She had always wholeheartedly supported the tough policy line of her fellow party member and Minister of Alien Affairs and Integration, Rita Verdonk. She agreed that asylum seekers should not be handled with too much pity – especially Somali refugees, she once emphasised, were prone to fraudulent practices. But Hirsi Ali herself had also committed fraud when applying for asylum back in 1992 – something she always had been quite open about. Nevertheless, when on May 11, 2006, a television documentary by the VARA, entitled *Saint Ayaan*, supposedly ›revealed‹ those facts, Verdonk was quick to declare that, formally speaking, Hirsi Ali had never acquired Dutch citizenship. Although the Minister was soon forced to retrace her steps, in May 2006 Hirsi Ali left the Netherlands to take up a position at the American Enterprise Institute, a conservative Washington D.C. think-tank with close ties to the Bush administration (see also Hirsi Ali 2007).

The national elections of November 2006 resulted in the installation of the Balkenende IV Cabinet, a coalition of Labour Party, Christian Democrats, and Christian Union. This government has replaced the individualistic, neoliberal approach of its predecessor with a more communitarian outlook emphasising the importance of social cohesion, civic duties and family values. It launched a *Deltaplan inburgering* (›Deltaplan civic integration‹) focussing on the emancipation of immigrants with the help of better education and equal job opportunities, while conceiving of integration in terms of ›active citizenship‹: the acceptance of the core values of the constitutional state, knowledge of each other's backgrounds, willingness to fight discrimination and participation in communal activities (*Integratienota 2007–2011*, 2007, 7).

Consequently, Dutch policy-makers remain highly interested in studies focusing on the integration and emancipation of immigrants, hence in studies that fall within the genre of the report. Research projects such as those by Van Gemert and Van San, in which culture figures as the main explanatory factor for deviant immigrant behaviour, are far outnumbered by reports focusing on emancipation, which mostly show that rapid (cultural) changes are taking place within immigrant communities. Thus, a study like *Emancipation of the Second Generation* (Pels and De Gruijter 2006), written at the request of the Ministry of Justice, concludes that young mothers of Moroccan and Turkish descent are actively trying to lead a more autonomous life than their mothers. The authors give several suggestions on how to support these women in their desire to find a balance between care for their family and community on the one hand, and their desire for individual independence on the other.

Some research reports attracted a lot of attention, because they reported about what especially the media present as the most problematic group, that of second-generation Dutch Moroccans. One of these, also commissioned by the Ministry of Justice, *Homegrown Warriors* (Buijs et al. 2006) addresses the issue of Islamic radicalism. The authors point out that the causes of religious radicalisation are multifarious. Feelings of estrangement from their own community, combined with a strong focus on Dutch society make especially Moroccan youngsters sensitive to social-economic deprivation and discrimination and prone to look for a clear alternative in orthodox Islam. In *Kapot Moeilijk* (De Jong 2007), anthropologist Jan Dirk de Jong draws an unembellished image of the hostile attitude and behaviour of delinquent Dutch-Moroccan boys towards representatives of the dominant society. Going against the popular image that their deviant behaviour is due to their cultural (i.e. Moroccan) or religious (i.e. Islamic) background, De Jong argues that the group-dynamical processes among the boys should be understood as a typical case of ›street culture‹, similar to that of other gangs. Hence, in these studies, no one is ›looking the other way‹ and denying the problematic sides of immigrant integration, as the rhetoric of new realism has it.

Within the realm of minority studies and local policy-making the new realist rhetoric has not really taken root. But among the elite of opinion makers (journalists, politicians, columnists) its core ideas have become mainstream.[9] Thus many welcomed Paul Scheffer's book *The Country of Arrival* (2007) as the long awaited impartial, knowledgeable and hopeful account of the thorny issues of immigration and integration. Scheffer gives a lengthy argumentation for an unprejudiced perspective on the conflicts and frictions caused by recent immigration. His treatment of the perspectives of immigrants and natives, however, is remarkably asymmetrical. On the one hand, immigrants are required to become knowledgeable about the language, culture and history of their new home country, Muslims should learn to deal with criticism and acknowledge that freedom of religion implies the freedom of others, too, and the Dutch political elite should take the large following of populists like Fortuyn as a reason for some serious soul-searching. The Dutch ›ordinary people‹, however, although admittedly inclined to conformity and informal pressure to assimilate, are not urged to change their outlook. Scheffer's ›we‹ thus remains the exclusive ›we‹ of the ›autochthonous‹

---

9 For this discrepancy between local policies and public discourse, see also Prins and Saharso 2008.

Dutch. The leadership of the Labour Party felt much inspired by Scheffer's work, as showed in a first draft of a party memorandum on integration, which demanded that »newcomers, their children and grandchildren make an unconditional choice for the Netherlands«, and claimed that if they wanted to emancipate, they needed to »abandon« where they came from (Partij van de Arbeid 2008).

Also among the larger Dutch public, new realism has gained a firm foothold. This for instance showed from the indignant reactions in September 2007 to a speech held by crown princess Maxima on the occasion of the presentation of a report of the Scientific Council for Government Policy (the WRR) on the issue of (national) identity (WRR 2007). In this speech, published by *NRC Handelsblad* on September 25, 2007, the princess (herself from Argentinian background) related how in her search for Dutch identity she had discovered that »the Netherlands is too many-sided to capture it in one cliché. ›The‹ Dutchman does not exist.« This remark, obviously meant as a compliment, and entirely in the spirit of the WRR report, was taken by many as an insult and as an unacceptable relativisation of Dutch norms and values. And although the elections of 2006 resulted in a progressive majority in parliament and a centre-left government, the winners of the popular vote were the extreme-right Freedom Party (PVV) and the leftist Socialist Party (SP). In line with new realism, both parties know how to tap into fears regarding the undermining Dutch sovereignty and identity. Especially Geert Wilders, the autocratic leader of the Freedom Party, has proven to be an excellent manipulator of xenophobic feelings. When his anti-Islam movie *Fitna* came out in March 2008, it did not induce the radical response from Dutch Muslims that the government feared and Wilders probably hoped for. But it did bring him awards and applause (at home and abroad) by adherents of radical freedom of speech – and ever higher scores for the Freedom Party (up to 20 per cent of the votes) in opinion polls.

Which is all to show that a significant part of the Dutch public still has problems with facing the complexities, multi-layeredness and heterogeneity that according to scientific studies constitutes the reality of Dutch multicultural society today.

References

Benhabib, Seyla. 1992. *Situating the Self. Gender, Community and Postmodernism in Contemporary Ethics*. Cambridge: Polity Press.

Benhabib, Seyla. 2002. *The Claims of Culture. Equality and Diversity in the Global Era*. Princeton: Princeton University Press.

Berg-Eldering, Lotty van den. 1978. *Marokkaanse gezinnen in Nederland*. Alphen a/d Rijn: Samson.

Bolkestein, Frits. 1991. Integratie van minderheden moet met lef worden aangepakt. *De Volkskrant*, September 12.

Bolkestein, Frits. 1997. *Moslim in de polder. Frits Bolkestein in gesprek met Nederlandse moslims.* Amsterdam and Antwerpen: Contact.

Braam, Stella. 1994. *De blinde vlek van Nederland. Reportages over de onderkant van de arbeidsmarkt.* Amsterdam: Van Gennep.

Brouwer, Lenie, Bea Lalmahomed, and H. Josias. 1992. *Andere tijden, andere meiden. Een onderzoek naar het weglopen van Marokkaanse, Turkse, Hindoestaanse en Creoolse meisjes.* Utrecht: Jan van Arkel.

Buijs, Frank. 1993. *Leven in een nieuw land. Marokkaanse jongemannen in Nederland.* Utrecht: Jan van Arkel.

Buijs, Frank, Froukje Demant, and Atef Hamdy. 2006. *Strijders van eigen bodem. Radicale en democratische moslims in Nederland.* Amsterdam: Amsterdam University Press.

Butler, Judith. 1997. *Excitable Speech. A Politics of the Performative.* New York: Routledge.

Caldwell, Christopher. 2005. Daughter of the Enlightenment. *New York Times Sunday Magazine*, April 3.

Camps, Hugo. 2002. Ik werd als tweede Filip de Winter neergezet. Marion van San, getergd criminoloog. *Elsevier*, June 6.

Croonenberg, Ed. 2002. ›Wij zijn niet te gast, wij zijn thuis.‹ *HP/De Tijd*, November 29.

Desmet, Yves. 2003. Malcolm X van de lage landen? *Het Parool*, March 8.

Essed, Philomena. 1990. *Everyday Racism. Reports of Women from Two Cultures.* Claremont, CA: Hunter House.

Essed, Philomena. 1991. *Understanding Everyday Racism. An Interdisciplinary Theory.* Newbury Park, CA: Sage.

Essed, Philomena, and Lydia Helwig. 1992. *Bij voorbeeld. Multicultureel beleid in de praktijk.* Amsterdam: FNV.

Fortuyn, Pim. 2001. *Droomkabinet. Hoe Nederland geregeerd moet worden.* Amsterdam: Van Gennep.

Fortuyn, Pim. 2002. *De puinhopen van acht jaar paars.* Rotterdam: Karakter/Speakers Academy.

Foucault, Michel. 1971. *L'ordre du discours.* Paris: Gallimard.

Foucault, Michel. 1979. *Discipline and Punish. The Birth of the Prison.* Middlesex: Penguin Books.

Foucault, Michel. 1980. *Power/Knowledge. Selected Interviews & Other Writings 1972–1977.* Ed. Colin Gordon. New York: Pantheon Books.

Gemert, Frank van. 1998. *Ieder voor zich. Kansen, cultuur en criminaliteit van Marokkaanse jongens.* Amsterdam: Aksant.

Gollin, Rob and Martin Sommer. 2002. Held en demon. *De Volkskrant*, December 7.

Goudt, Mieke. 1989. *In de gemeenteraad! Gesprekken met de eerste zwarte en migranten raadsvrouwen in Nederland.* Leiden: Stichting Burgerschapskunde.

Haraway, Donna Jeanne. 1991. Situated Knowledges: The Science Question in Feminism and the Privilege of Partial Perspective, in: *Simians, Cyborgs, and Women: The Reinvention of Nature,* ed. idem, 183–201. London: Free Association Press.

Het Fenomeen Fortuyn. 2002. Amsterdam: De Volkskrant/Meulenhoff.

Hirsi Ali, Ayaan. 2002. *De zoontjesfabriek.* Amsterdam and Antwerpen: Augustus.

Hirsi Ali, Ayaan. 2004a. *De maagdenkooi.* Amsterdam and Antwerpen: Augustus.

Hirsi Ali, Ayaan. 2004b. *Ich klage an. Plädoyer für die Befreiung der muslimischen Frauen.* Munich: Piper.

Hirsi Ali, Ayaan. 2006. *The Caged Virgin. An Emancipation Proclamation for Women and Islam.* New York: Free Press.

Hirsi Ali, Ayaan. 2007. *Infidel.* New York: Free Press.

Hoek, Jannet van der, and Martine Kret. 1992. *Marokkaanse tienermeisjes, gezinsinvloeden op keuzen en kansen.* Utrecht: Jan van Arkel.

Hondius, Dienke. 1999. *Gemengde huwelijken, gemengde gevoelens.* Den Haag: Sdu.

Integratienota 2007–2011 Zorg dat je erbij hoort! 2007. Den Haag: Ministerie VROM/WWI.

Jong, Jan Dirk de. 2007. *Kapot moeilijk. Een etnografisch onderzoek naar opvallend delinquent groepsgedrag van ›Marokkaanse‹ jongens.* Amsterdam: Aksant.

Kagie, Rudie. 1987. *Berichten uit een Hollands gastenboek. Over de werkomstandigheden van buitenlandse arbeiders.* Amsterdam: Van Gennep.

Lippe-Biesterveld, Irene van. 1986. *Van daar. Portretten van buitenlandse vrouwen in Nederland.* Amsterdam: Sara/Van Gennep.

Lyotard, Jean-François. 1988. *The Differend. Phrases in Dispute.* Manchester: Manchester University Press.

Mak, Geertje. 2000. *Sporen van verplaatsing.* Kampen: IJsselacademie.

Meijer, Maaike. 1996. *In tekst gevat. Inleiding tot een kritiek van representatie.* Amsterdam: Amsterdam University Press.

Meijer, Maaike, and Rosemarie Buikema, ed. 2003–2005. *Cultuur en migratie in Nederland* (in five parts). Den Haag: Sdu.

Mungra, G. 1990. *Hindoestaanse gezinnen in Nederland.* Leiden: Centrum voor Maatschappelijke Tegenstellingen.

Partij van de Arbeid. 2008. *Verdeeld verleden, gedeelde toekomst,* PB-resolutie Integratie. www.pvda.nl/download.do/id/320250112/cd/true/ (accessed 10 February 2009).

Pels, Dick. 2003. *De geest van Pim. Het gedachtegoed van een politieke dandy.* Amsterdam: AMBO/Anthos.

Pels, Trees, and Marjan de Gruiter, ed. 2006. *Emancipatie van de tweede generatie. Kiezen en kansen in de levensloop van jonge moeders van Marokkaanse en Turkse afkomst.* Assen: Van Gorcum.

Prins, Baukje. 1997. *The Standpoint in Question. Situated Knowledges and the Dutch Minorities Discourse.* Ph.D. diss., Utrecht University.

Prins, Baukje. 2004. *Voorbij de onschuld. Het debat over de multiculturele samenleving.* 2nd rev. ed., Amsterdam: Van Gennep.

Prins, Baukje, and Sawitri Saharso. 2008. In the Spotlight. A Blessing and a Curse for Immigrant Women in the Netherlands. *Ethnicities* 8 (3): 365–84.

Risvanoglu-Bilgin, Silbin, Lenie Brouwer, and Marijke Priester. 1986. *Verschillend als de vingers van een hand. Een onderzoek naar het integratieproces van Turkse gezinnen in Nederland.* Leiden: COMT.

Saharso, Sawitri. 1992. *Jan en alleman. Etnische jeugd over etnische identiteit, discriminatie en vriendschap.* Utrecht: Jan van Arkel.

San, Marion van. 1998. *Stelen & steken. Delinquent gedrag van Curaçaose jongeren in Nederland.* Amsterdam: Het Spinhuis.

Sansone, Livio. 1992. *Schitteren in de schaduw. Overlevingsstrategieën, subcultuur en etniciteit van Creoolse jongeren uit de lagere klasse in Amsterdam 1981–1990.* Amsterdam: Het Spinhuis.

Scheffer, Paul. 2000. Het multiculturele drama. *NRC Handelsblad*, January 29.

Scheffer, Paul. 2007. *Het land van aankomst.* Amsterdam: De Bezige Bij.

Shotter, John. 1993. *Conversational Realities. Constructing Life Through Language.* London: Sage.

Smedt, Dirk de. 2002. Van San spreekt. *Vlaams Blok Magazine* 26 (7/8).

Soetens, Nelly. 1980. *Kinderen van gastarbeiders.* Rotterdam: Futile.

Vuijsje, Herman. 1986. *Vermoorde onschuld. Etnisch verschil als Hollands taboe.* Amsterdam: Bert Bakker.

Vuijsje, Herman. 2000. *The Politically Correct Netherlands.* Westport, CN: Greenwood Press.

Vries, Marlene de. 1987. *Ogen in je rug. Turkse meisjes en jonge vrouwen in Nederland.* Alphen a/de Rijn: Samson.

Wallraff, Günther. 1977. *Der Aufmacher.* Cologne: Kiepenheuer & Witsch.

Wallraff, Günther. 1985. *Ganz unten.* Cologne: Kiepenheuer & Witsch.

WRR. 2007. *Identificatie met Nederland.* Amsterdam: Amsterdam University Press.

Beyond the Race Relations Model: Old Patterns and New Trends in Britain

By Karen Schönwälder

Abstract

In Britain, research into ethnic relations, migration and racism is a well-established field. For a long time, the race paradigm was dominant. The relationship with US-American research and politics remains close while links to other European research traditions developed late. Many scholars are now favouring a replacement of a black-white dualism with more complex concepts – and the trend is pointing in this direction. A non-political approach, however, has no future in Britain, a political commitment to anti-racism remains a moving force at British universities. New demands of the government have encouraged policy-oriented research efforts and a greater interest in the integration of immigrants and refugees.

British ›Race Relations‹ Research: Model or Disaster?

The work of British academics on issues of immigration and what is usually called ›race relations‹ has, among European academics, in the past few decades been particularly influential. In the 1980s and 1990s, British research was often seen as more advanced than the work of colleagues in other countries – if not as a model. This status came under attack around the year 2000, when a group of younger scholars in Britain demanded that »dispassionate analysis« should replace »ideological denunciation« (Hansen 1999, 437) and that higher quality research and more comparative work were needed (Favell 2000; 2001).[1] Were such harsh attacks justified or mainly self-marketing strategies? What are the main features of the research field, what is typically British about them, and how can we explain – rather than praise or condemn – such features? The following text was written in 2002 and reviews the development and characteristics of British research on migrant integration and ethnic relations up to that point.

---

1   Adrian Favell, in particular, has issued harsh attacks on colleagues in the field. He criticizes a »hegemony of British ›black‹ cultural studies«, a tradition he regards as »sociologically and comparatively incompetent« and as incompatible with a »serious sociology of race and ethnicity« (Favell 2000, 360, 362f.).

The Disciplinary Structure of British Research

Dominant perspectives are to some extent an expression of the disciplinary structure of the field: In Britain one obvious feature is the long-term dominance of sociology and social anthropology, which relatively early began to study questions related to immigration.[2] There are a number of geographers in the field (e.g. Vaughan Robinson, Eleonore Kofman, Susan Smith, Russell King), while demography remains marginal. The latter is not particular to migration research but an expression of the overall limited British interest in demography and population policy.[3] Furthermore, although there is an enormous body of work on the educational system, the influence of pedagogy and social work in academic and wider public debates has been weaker than e.g. in Germany with its paternalistic welfare state. In comparison with Germany, the most striking features are the almost total absence of economists and the relatively minor role of legal scholars in the field (of course there are exceptions like Anthony Lester, Andrew Nicol, Sebastian Poulter). To a considerable extent, this situation reflects the political framework. Unlike Germans, the British do not tend to discuss political questions as legal ones, thus jurists are less prominent in political debates. The limited development of economic research into migration is an expression of the fact that, for a long time, government policy was marked by an absence of economic considerations. As immigration was seen through the race-relations lens, its economic implications seemed of lesser importance (see Schönwälder 2001, 414–26; Hatton and Wheatley Price 1999). And as dark-skinned immigrants had been qualified as a problem, their contribution to the country's economy was often neglected.

Political science – as everywhere? – entered the field late. However, already in 1992 Zig Layton-Henry (1992, xv) stated that »The neglect of ›race‹ issues by political scientists is much less significant now than it was even five years ago«.[4] Studies of elections and the political participation of people with a Caribbean or Asian background are now well established (e.g. Anwar 2001, 533–49; Saggar 1997; for an early example see Deakin 1965). The effects of the race-relations legislation have regularly been investigated (although systematic evaluations are rare), and there are a number of studies of the development of migration policy since 1945 (Solomos and Jenkins 1987; Blackstone, Parekh and Sanders 1998; Dean 1992; Hansen 2000; Spencer 1997; Lunn 1989), while the political process, actor constellations, and interest groups in the last twenty years seem underinvestigated. A political-theory perspective is weakly developed. Bhikhu Parekh has made important contributions (see for instance Parekh 1998), but altogether

---

2 Already in 1969 the British Sociological Association devoted its conference to the ›Sociology of Race and Racialism‹.
3 David Coleman's and John Salt's »The British Population« (1992, 519) contains a subheading »No population policy please, we're British«, and the authors argue that »There is no overall population policy« (528).
4 In 1986, John Solomos had noted that »the political analysis of racism is relatively backward« (1986a, 313).

British scholars were latecomers in the recent theoretical debates about minority rights, multiculturalism and social cohesion. There is also no parallel to the US-American international-political-economy approach as represented e.g. by James Hollifield. The predominance of sociology and social anthropology has encouraged an emphasis on social relations and – more recently – on questions of identity.

If we trust a rather optimistic assessment of John Solomos and Les Back (1996a, xii, 1), »the study of race and racism [is] no longer a highly specialised field but has attracted interest in all branches of the social sciences and humanities«; it »has become an established field of study in a number of social science disciplines«. At the same time, a strong trend is noticeable towards the establishment of ›race‹ or ›ethnic relations‹ as a separate discipline, a development which not only expresses a strength but could turn out to be a danger as it could further an isolation of this field from the disciplinary mainstream. Generally, the field is more established than in other European countries.

The Race Paradigm:
Brief Remarks on the Development of a Tradition

The terms academics choose to describe the subject of their inquiries usually reflect their view of its main features: Where others do research on migration and integration, British research is concerned with race and racism. Sometimes, the different terminology refers to the same things. But more often, the choice of the terms ›race‹ and ›racism‹ (or ›race relations‹) reflects a focus on social relations structured by a belief in the significance of phenotypical differences, on discrimination and on hostility against migrants and minorities. On the other hand, perspectives that centre on the willingness and ability of the immigrants to adjust to conditions in the host society and to adopt the majority culture are less common. There is, for instance, no British parallel to the US-American and German debates about assimilation as represented by scholars like Richard Alba or Hartmut Esser.

Historically, there are two main reasons for the development of this particular perspective: Firstly, post-war immigration occurred in the context of decolonisation and of difficult negotiations about the co-existence of privileged European settlers and dark-skinned Africans in the former colonies. It was inviting to perceive the migration of dark-skinned people to Britain as a transfer of the same black-white conflict to Europe, and research perspectives initially related to inter-ethnic relations in e.g. Africa seemed applicable to social relations in British cities.[5] Early studies by Kenneth Little or Michael Banton were strongly influenced by the American sociology of group relations and prejudice. However, in the 1950s and 1960s some publications appeared that were not shaped by a race-

---

5   On perceptions of immigration in the 1950s and 1960s see Schönwälder 2001.

relations perspective, like studies of Polish, Italian, or other European immigrants (see e.g. Tannahill 1958; Deakin 1972).[6]

The crucial shift occurred in the 1960s under the influence of the US-American civil rights movement. The violent riots e.g. in 1967 in Denver and in 1968, following the murder of Martin Luther King, together with broader movements towards civil rights for African-Americans, made a deep impression on the British public and its political elites. Now, in addition to a political leadership obsessed with the threats of an emerging ›race‹ question, the political Left (in the widest sense) began to focus on the centrality of a black-white relationship. *Colour and Citizenship*, a major study intended to disclose a Myrdal-style »British dilemma«, insisted »that we must break away from the focus of an immigrant-host relationship and turn instead to a study of the relationships between groups within a society in which one of the groups was distinguished by the factor of colour.« And as the study further emphasised, »this discrimination against coloured citizens is not to be equated with discrimination against foreigners who are white« (Rose et al. 1969, 6, 677). Academics who still dared to compare the situation of, say, Italian and Caribbean immigrants to Britain, came under fire.[7] Comparisons of the British and e.g. the German migratory experience seemed senseless if, on the one hand, a race-relations situation and, on the other, an immigrant-host relation existed. To the present day, British research is overwhelmingly shaped by the interaction with US-American discussions. As Tariq Modood (1996a, 93) puts it, British researchers have traditionally »looked to the race relations scene in America as an explanatory and normative guide«.

This close relationship partly rests on strong links between the British and the US-American academic worlds. Books based on American doctoral theses have been influential contributions to the British debate (Freeman 1979; Katznelson 1973; Studlar 1985; Messina 1989), and academics frequently move between the two countries, in particular from Britain to the richer American universities. The more or less common language makes comparative studies relatively easy. And increasingly books and articles are being written for a joint British-American audience, a fact that encourages authors to adopt a common language – and this of course means concepts as well as words – and to refer to (seemingly) familiar experiences.

Additionally, the personal background of the people who shaped the field of British race/ethnic relations studies has to be taken into account. British research traditions reflect the heritage of the British Empire. People like John Rex, Stuart Hall, Bhikhu Parekh, Paul Gilroy, Tariq Modood or John Solomos, to name just a few, were themselves born or have a family background in South Africa, the Caribbean, India or other countries that were once part of the British Empire. While perspectives are not exactly insular (as claimed by Favell), there is a bias

---

6 The influential magazine *New Society* also published articles about Polish and Italian immigration: Britain's community of Poles, no. 42, 18 July 1963: 13f.; Napoli, Bedfordshire, no. 57, 31 October 1963: 6–8.
7 This was the case with Sheila Patterson's work, see e.g. Patterson 1969.

towards the old world of British influence. Furthermore, to a greater extent than in other countries, academic perspectives are shaped by intellectuals who themselves belong to minorities and, to a certain degree, represent their political demands. More strongly than research in other countries, British research is associated with the political movements of some minorities and with the political Left.

Already in the early 1970s, scholars like Stephen Castles and Annie Phizacklea criticised a trend to see the British situation as unique or as comparable mainly to the US. Instead they suggested a Europeanisation of perspectives and a stronger focus on the common »features of all advanced capitalist countries« (Castles, Booth and Wallace 1984; Castles and Kosack 1973)[8]. Its Marxist credentials, the limits of a fairly narrow economic approach, and (probably) the hostility of the British Left towards ›Europe‹ ensured that this call for a reorientation remained largely unheeded. Robert Miles' work (Miles and Phizacklea 1979; Miles 1989) which combined the political economy approach with a critique of the process of racialisation, i.e. cultural processes, became however extremely influential. The fact that he (like e.g. historian Colin Holmes) constantly emphasised parallels between the discrimination against Caribbeans, Asians, Jews, the Irish, etc. illustrates that a black-white dualism was and is not universally adopted.

Western Marxism with its main basis, the Centre for Contemporary Cultural Studies (with Stuart Hall, John Solomos, Paul Gilroy) paved the way for cultural studies. Academics at the CCCS were »unified through a common concern with developing an analysis of racism which fully accepts its relative autonomy from class-based social relations«. They shared a critical attitude towards the class-oriented Left and a belief in the »centrality of racism in relations of power and domination in post-war Britain« (Solomos 1986b, 89, 91). Without reference to the political context, i.e. the advent of Thatcherism and a ›New World‹ of modern capitalism, this tradition would remain incomprehensible. As the group around Stuart Hall believed, racism occupied a central place in the political strategy of the Conservatives who were implementing a »shift from a ›consensual‹ to a more ›coercive‹ management of the class struggle by the capitalist state« (Hall et al. 1978, 218). Politically and academically the group was committed to understanding, and thus helping to counter, the new right. But it is also characteristic for this approach to demand that the societal context of scholarly work be reflected and disclosed.

Thus ten years after the publication of *Colour and Citizenship,* race and racism were re-emphasised as the key concepts. Again this occurred in response to the political environment – now of Thatcherism and, for a short period of time, a radicalising Left and more self-conscious and combative minorities. In the 1980s, anti-racism was probably the key concept academics as well as activists subscribed to while, at least among more radical activists, the study of ethnicity and culture was discredited. As for instance Bourne and Sivanandan demanded, rather than the minorities, white racism should be the object of research – rather than culture,

---

8   For a more general comment see Phizacklea 1984.

power, class, and racism should be at the centre of attention (Bourne 1980). This latter approach has now disappeared, as, on the one hand, its political basis more or less vanished and, on the other, cultural forms and ethnic or hybrid identities became new research foci.

Current Trends

Increasing Criticism of the Race Relations Model

Considering the situation at the beginning of the 21st century, it is hardly disputable that ›race‹, ›racism‹ and ›race relations‹ are still predominant concepts in British research. There may be »little agreement about what it is that researchers in this field [which Solomos and Back call the analysis of race and racism] are actually investigating« (Solomos and Back 1996b, 213), but the terminology is widely used. Sometimes the term ›ethnic relations‹ is preferred, while other researchers distinguish between racial and ethnic relations. Often this distinction implies that phenotypical differences (or the belief in their social relevance) indeed constitute social relations different from those marked by cultural identities and cultural differences, but in terms like ›culture racism‹ or when a ›race-relations‹ concept is transferred to relations between immigrants of, say, Turkish descent and a German majority, distinctions get blurred.[9] Generally, the term ›race‹ is far more widely and loosely used than for instance in Germany.

As pointed out above, research into ›race relations‹ was, in the last few decades, far from uniform. And yet, there is currently a widely-held perception that the race relations paradigm has encouraged a black-white dualism which – among other things – has led to a concentration of research interests on resident minorities, while migratory movements and newcomers were neglected. A report for the Home Office concludes that »overall there is relatively little research on recent immigrants in the UK, and almost nothing on certain groups and aspects of integration. This seems to be due to two circumstances: first the UK is not generally perceived as a country of immigration and there is no immigration policy as such [...] second the race relations model has been dominant in research and has concentrated attention on longer established ethnic minorities.« As the authors further argue, »this model may be appropriate for longer established ethnic minorities, but its relevance for newer immigrant and refugee groups needs to be investigated. Clinging to this model may be a barrier to adaptive policy-making in the current situation« (Castles et al. 2001, 21).

Indeed, migratory movements and asylum are relatively new topics in British research. When, in the early 1990s, asylum became a politically contentious issue, there was hardly any research on refugees and asylum (see Joly 1988), a situation

---

9 For a discussion of the merit in distinguishing the two concepts, see Jenkins 1996. David Mason argues that »race remains a pivotal concept in sociology because it denotes a social relationship in which symbolic representations which emphasise the social and cultural relevance of biologically rooted characteristics play a central role« (Mason 1996, 198).

that reflected the minor importance of the asylum issue in the political field. It was also typical for the British debate that, when refugee policy became an issue, one predominant question was whether a more restrictive policy would have racially discriminatory effects, i.e. whether darker-skinned people would be negatively affected. Albanians or Kurds attracted less solidarity.[10] Furthermore, it now seems that a belief in the restrictive character of British migration policy prevented academics from realising that in fact migratory movements were taking place. Thus a study for the British Home Office suggests that »although there has, in the past, been a perception that the UK has restrictive migration policies, these policies have, during the period under study, allowed in an increasing number of short and medium term migrants to meet labour market needs« (Dobson et al. 2001, 274). Studies of these movements as well as of the migrants involved are, however, rare.

Even for longer-established ethnic minorities the race-relations model has its problems. Thus Tariq Modood, the most prominent academic voice of Asian-Muslim minorities, insists that ethnic minorities should not solely be seen as objects of racism but that they need to be studied as real collectivities, and »have a reality of their own« (Modood 1996a, 98). As he points out, there is not only a colour-racism but also a racism directed against Muslims which, in a unifying Europe, could become the more important dividing line towards the Islamic world. Altogether, he argues that it is pluralism that marks what he still calls »race relations« – not dualism (see Modood 1996b).

It is now widely accepted that, in contemporary Britain, the living conditions of ethnic minority groups are marked by a considerable diversity (Modood et al. 1997). However, the state of research is extremely uneven as attention has, for a considerable time, focussed on those of Caribbean and ›Asian‹ descent. As Steve Fenton pointed out, the emphasis on racism has also led to a neglect of the empirical study of social mobility (Fenton 1996, 160). And Roger Penn, with reference to a major empirical survey, noted »the invisibility of relationships *between* ethnic minority groups« and the silence of researchers on an issue which seems to be taboo (Penn et al. 2000, 358).

In sum, many scholars have, since the 1990s, criticised perspectives which assume a black-white ›dualism‹.[11] In fact, some of the deficits noted above have been addressed. Thus quite a lot is currently being written about asylum and refugees, and more research is being undertaken on non-Black immigrants, such as the Irish. Nevertheless, the dualistic approach still seems to exercise considerable influence – maybe more so among the ›activists‹ rather than among academic scholars.

---

10 On the beginning asylum-debate see Schönwälder 1997.
11 See also the contributions of Michael Banton and Phil Cohen in Modood 1996b, 13–15, 15–21.

De-politicisation – Re-politicisation?

Above it was argued that British research was marked by a particularly strong link with ethnic-minority (and left-wing) politics but that, with the decline of the Left, the influence of left-wing politics on ›race relations‹ studies has become weaker. Generally, the relationship between research/researchers and minority politics, i.e. the demands and interests of the people they investigate, is a subject of controversies. Thus John Solomos and Les Back (1995, 5, 10) distance themselves from allegedly »disengaged scholarship« as well as from a position of »advocacy«. As they contend, »researchers in this field are almost inevitably forced to confront questions about politics«; a separation from political action »is in some ways impossible and even undesirable« (Solomos and Back 2000, 23). Claire Alexander and Brian Alleyne (2002, 544) have adopted a more radical stance and voiced their regret about what they perceive as the disconnection of the academy from, and its irrelevance to, activist work. At the same time, a new and rather different politicisation is taking place. It is linked to shifts in migration policy implemented by the Labour government and to its demand for a knowledge-based policy. Given the new political interest in questions of migration and integration, research activities are flourishing, and there is a new trend towards applicable, policy-oriented research.[12] Three issues are central to the new migration policy and the related demand for research evidence: Firstly, the government has announced its plan to introduce an effective managed migration programme and a migration policy based on economic interests. So far, there is very little research on the economic effects and implications of labour migration, i.e. research that could guide such a policy.[13] Secondly, the immigration of refugees has become a burning political issue. While up to 1989 less than 10,000 people per year applied for asylum, the United Kingdom more recently received about 100,000 annual applications (including dependents). This has motivated an urgent interest in understanding the background to this development as well as raising new requirements as regards the integration of refugees. And, finally, the integration of immigrants and longer-term ethnic minorities is altogether perceived as unsatisfactory, and the government responded with a novel »national approach to integration«.[14] While the existing knowledge about forms and levels of discrimination and racism as well as about identities of people with a migratory background provides a basis,

---

12 As Sarah Spencer of the influential think-tank IPPR points out: »Accompanying the shift towards management of migration to meet the UK's economic and social objectives has been a recognition by government of the importance of research, not least on migrants' motivation, on the skills that they bring and factors influencing successful settlement. It published its first study, ›Migration: An economic and social analysis‹, in 2001 and has since initiated a wider research programme.« (Spencer 2002, 2). As one example of government-sponsored work, see the report ›Integration: Mapping the field‹ which is meant to be a contribution to »new and modified policies based on solid evidence and sound vision« (Castles et al. 2001, 1).
13 Hatton and Wheatley Price (1999, 41) state that: »Although migration has been a controversial issue, its effects on the economy have been the subject of surprisingly little research«. A study for the Home Office tried to provide some answers: Glover et al. 2001.
14 See the government's White Paper (Home Office UK 2002, 74).

there is a demand for additional research on e.g. the ability of the state to encourage integration, social cohesion and identification with the national community.[15] The new political interest in research on migration together with the newly available financial resources has encouraged some academics to enter the field and others to respond to political demands. Thus we may see the development of a new relationship between academia and politics and a trend towards politically applicable research. If the latter came true, this new trend could balance or even overcome the often disapproved of theoretical overload of British ›race relations‹ research.

Too Much Culture, Too Much Theory?

As Ralph Grillo (2002) noted in a review of a compendium on *The Sociology of Race and Ethnicity*, a preference for theoretical over empirical work is clearly visible. Indeed, scholars like John Rex, Stuart Hall and Robert Miles represent a tradition of research that aimed to place issues of ›race‹ and ›race relations‹ in broader theoretical frameworks of, once, mainly Weberian or Marxist thinking. Since the 1990s, a shift towards an emphasis on culture and identity has been the predominant trend. This was often linked with a preference for post-structuralism and postmodernism. The emphasis on culture and identity reflects an international development, which was possibly more pronounced in Britain and the US than in other European countries. Indeed Homi Bhabha and Paul Gilroy, two of the most influential representatives of the study of identities, now teach in the US. There has been a proliferation of studies on the media, literature, identity and youth cultures. Increased attention has been given to colonialism and post-colonialism or rather to colonial and post-colonial discourses. Gender studies have also profited from the shift towards culture and difference. In this field, »more recent work has been heavily influenced by cultural analysis, with a focus on representations of migrants and on the meanings that they attach to their lived experiences« (Erel and Kofman 2003, 73).[16]

On the other hand, the relatively minor importance of gender perspectives in mainstream research may also be taken as an indicator for an »acceptance of diversity« within the academic field which nevertheless leaves some new perspectives on the margins. Thus we may have seen a »proliferation of feminist writings« (Solomos and Back 2000, 16) while, on the whole, »gender has rarely been considered a significant analytical category within the European literature on migration, which has remained gender blind« (Erel and Kofman 2003, 74).

Multiculturalism – for many years not really an issue in British debates – is now being discussed. For many years, Roy Jenkins' famous 1966-dictum about integration not as a »flattening process of assimilation but as equal opportunity, accom-

---

15   See for instance the special issue of Parliamentary Affairs 55 (2002), no. 3, on citizenship education.
16   Erel and Kofman continue: »resulting in a relative neglect of new forms of migration and the changing structural factors and immigration legislation which has shaped migratory flows« (ibid., 73).

panied by cultural diversity, in an atmosphere of mutual tolerance« seemed to have settled the question. Critics of an »ethnicisation« of individuals were almost non-existent.[17] Ethnic monitoring and the reference to ethnic communities (rather than individuals) were and are rarely questioned. But the situation has changed in two respects: Increasingly, anti-racism and the fight against discrimination are perceived as insufficient, and there is a search for an attractive political project to complement the struggle against exclusion. As for instance Tariq Modood argues, the struggle for equality and racial justice has to be complemented by a greater public recognition of difference. Recognition is contrasted with mere toleration, and – like assimilation – a »culture-free liberal individualism« (Commission on the Future of Multi-Ethnic Britain 2000, 37)[18] is rejected. The Commission on the Future of Multi-Ethnic Britain and its chair Bhikhu Parekh call for a »purposeful process of change«, a deliberate effort at creating a new identity of Britain as both a community of citizens and of communities (ibid., 11).[19] Multiculturalism appeared to be a vision that could be offered to dark- and light-skinned Britons alike.

But as a response to the riots of 2001 in Bradford, Burnley and Oldham, there is also a new concern with the negative consequences of a policy that accepts or even promotes separation. Thus a committee investigating the Bradford riots (headed by Herman Ouseley, a former chairman of the Commission for Racial Equality) criticised the fact that economic and social programmes had been allowed »to develop along self-styled cultural and faith-dominant tracks that have fuelled the drift towards segregation« (Ouseley 2001, 18). And Home Secretary David Blunkett (2003) has rejected »forced assimilation into a monoculture, [as well as] an unbridled multiculturalism which privileges difference over community cohesion«. In the British debate, these are new voices, and they may soon be reflected in parallel research questions.

As regards the shift towards the study of culture, identities, and difference, there are different views. It is alternatively seen as a yet uncompleted »process of reclaiming ›culture‹ in critical debate« (Solomos and Back 1996b, 224), as an »obsession« with difference which tends to render invisible the true situation of the mass, the »harsh, unfashionable and curiously static political economy of inequality and neglect« (Alexander and Alleyne 2002, 545), or, as Favell contends, an annoying, academically unsatisfactory cul-de-sac. Indeed, while not sharing the dislike of cultural studies, John Solomos and Les Back agree that »not much of the mainstream research in this field is theoretically informed in any substantial way« (Solomos and Back 1996b, 229). And John Solomos (1998, 48) bemoans that »much of the academic debate [...] has remained unsatisfactorily abstract«.

---

17 For an influential German example of this critique see Dittrich and Radtke 1990.
18 The Commission was appointed by the influential Runnymede Trust. The report provoked a controversial debate.
19 See also Parekh 1999. For the new interest in multiculturalism see the special issue of Patterns of Prejudice 35 (2001), no. 1, entitled ›New perspectives on multiculturalism and citizenship‹; Solomos 1998; Modood and Werbner 1997.

However, it should not be overlooked that, apart from the more theoretical writing that sometimes seems to attract more attention, scholars working in Britain have also produced a range of sound, down-to-earth studies on questions like the development of migration policy (Spencer 1997; Layton-Henry and Rich 1986; Hansen 2000), the socio-economic situation of ethnic minorities (Coleman and Salt 1996; Peach 1996), etc. And, of course, many studies of identities and cultural developments represent sound, empirically-based scholarship (Baumann 1996; Jacobson 1997).

Internationalisation

Anyone criticising the unsatisfactory development of international and comparative perspectives in the social sciences and the humanities is nowadays likely to meet with widespread approval. This whole volume is devoted to the difficulties such endeavours still face, such as problems of language, concepts, and knowledge of different national frameworks. But is British research particularly insular and self-centred?

If there exists a certain temptation for scholars to place themselves mainly within a big and lively British research community, there have, in the past decade, also been a number of efforts towards an internationalisation and Europeanisation of perspectives. Volumes by Russell King (1993), John Solomos and John Wrench (1993), Malcolm Cross (1992), David Cesarani and Mary Fulbrook (1996) document this trend (see also Bloch and Levy 1999; Kofman et al. 2000). Furthermore, the European Union itself has become a subject of academic inquiries.[20]

As in other countries, the development of transnational communities has recently attracted enormous attention and focussed interests on developments extending the borders of the nation state.[21]

Journals previously dominated by articles on British affairs have redesigned their profile in order to incorporate additional perspectives. Thus *New Community* in 1998 became the *Journal of Ethnic and Migration Studies*. *Ethnic and Racial Studies* has also published many articles on developments in continental Europe.

British universities, with their relatively international community of scholars, provide opportunities for post-graduate students and academics of Greek, Italian etc. descent to use their cultural capital in order to investigate issues of migration and inter-ethnic relations in other countries and/or involving ›their‹ ethnic group.

However, the greater internationalisation and Europeanisation has its limits. International exchange and cooperation are based on the English language. This encourages a hegemony of the native speakers and of concepts predominant in Britain and the US. Only if they write in English and, to some extent, within an Anglo-American framework, will scholars from other countries be noticed. The

---

20 See the special issue of the Journal of Ethnic and Migration Studies 24 (1998), no. 4; Favell and Geddes 2000.
21 See in particular research done in the context of the transnational communities network coordinated by a team at Oxford University: www.transcomm.ox.ac.uk.; Vertovec 2001.

major journals in the field, which happen to be published in English, still hardly ever review books written in other languages.

Furthermore, internationalisation may involve a reaffirmation of the strong links with the US, partly because of increasingly connected academic communities, partly because of the requirements of a book market in which authors increasingly write for a British and American readership. Additionally, some scholars insist on a special relationship with the US because of the influence on the ›Black‹ community in Britain of events and discussions there (David Gillborn as quoted by Gabriel 1998, 40f.).

Conclusions

British research on migration, racism, on people with a migration background and on social relations shaped by a belief in the significance of ethnic bonds and physical differences, is certainly not uniform and, given the current debates, its future shape and directions are not easy to predict. There is a strong demand for an internationalisation of perspectives, while at the same time the relationship with US-American research and politics remains close. Many scholars are now favouring a replacement of a black-white dualism with more complex concepts – and the trend is pointing in this direction. A non-political approach, however, has no future in Britain. A political commitment to anti-racism remains a moving force at British universities, and new demands of the government are encouraging policy-oriented research efforts.

Anyone cooperating with British academics is likely to encounter confident colleagues who look back on a developed tradition of empirical and theoretical work. In all probability, the encounter would take place in their native language. They would be sensitive to moral and ethical questions. The usage of terms like ›race‹ or ›integration‹ would be a subject of debates, while the use of terms like ›assimilation‹ would not be permitted. And yet, to a considerable extent, the cooperating European scholars would know the same literature and ask similar questions. As shown above, this literature and the research questions are to a considerable extent shaped by the national political framework. Comparative endeavours need to be aware of these different contexts in which research evidence and theories originated, and it is necessary to reflect carefully the possibilities and problems of transferring concepts and results to other contexts.

References

Alexander, Claire, and Brian Alleyne. 2002. Introduction: Framing Difference: Racial and Ethnic Studies in Twenty-first-century Britain. *Ethnic and Racial Studies* 25: 541–51.

Anwar, Muhammad. 2001. The Participation of Ethnic Minorities in British Politics. *Journal of Ethnic and Migration Studies* 27: 533–49.

Baumann, Gerd. 1996. *Contesting Culture. Discourses of Identity in Multi-ethnic London.* Cambridge: Cambridge University Press.

Blackstone, Tessa, Bhikhu Parekh, and Peter Sanders. 1998. *Race Relations in Britain: A Developing Agenda.* London: Routledge.

Bloch, Alice, and Carl Levy. 1999. *Refugees, Citizenship and Social Policy in Europe.* London: Macmillan.

Blunkett, David. 2003. Integration with Diversity: Globalisation and the Renewal of Democracy and Civil Society. In *Rethinking Britishness*, ed. Phoebe Griffith and Mark Leonard. London: Foreign Policy Centre, as printed in *The Observer*, September 15, 2002.

Bourne, Jenny, with the assistance of A. Sivanandan. 1980. Cheerleaders and Ombudsmen: The Sociology of Race Relations in Britain. *Race and Class* 11: 331–52.

Castles, Stephen, and Godula Kosack. 1973. *Immigrant Workers and Class Structure in Western Europe.* London: Oxford University Press.

Castles, Stephen, Heather Booth, and Tina Wallace. 1984. *Here for good: Western Europe's New Ethnic Minorities.* London: Pluto Press.

Castles, Stephen, Maja Korac, Ellie Vasta, and Steven Vertovec. 2001. *Integration: Mapping the Field.* Synopsis of a report by the Centre for Migration and Policy Research (CMPR) and Refugee Studies Centre (RSC), University of Oxford under contract to the Home Office Immigration Research and Statistics Service (IRSS), presented to an IPPR Seminar, London, July 2001.

Cesarani, David, and Mary Fulbrook. 1996. *Citizenship, Nationality and Migration in Europe.* London: Routledge.

Coleman, David, and John Salt. 1992. *The British Population: Patterns, Trends and Processes.* Oxford: Oxford University Press.

Coleman, David, and John Salt. 1996. *Ethnicity in the 1991 Census. Vol. 1: Demographic Characteristics of the Ethnic Minority Populations.* London: Office of Population Censuses and Surveys.

Commission on the Future of Multi-Ethnic Britain. 2000. *The Future of Multi-ethnic Britain.* Report of the Commission on the Future of Multi-Ethnic Britain. London: Profile Books.

Cross, Malcolm. 1992. *Ethnic Minorities and Industrial Change in Europe and North America.* Cambridge: Cambridge University Press.

Deakin, Nicholas. 1965. *Colour and the British Electorate 1964: Six Case Studies.* London: Institute of Race Relations.

Deakin, Nicholas. 1972. *Immigrants in Europe.* London: Fabian Society.

Dean, D.W. 1992. Conservative Governments and the Restriction of Commonwealth Immigration in the 1950s: The Problems of Constraint. *Historical Journal* 35: 171–94.

Dittrich, Eckhard J., and Frank-Olaf Radtke. 1990. *Ethnizität. Wissenschaft und Minderheiten*. Opladen: Westdeutscher Verlag.

Dobson, Janet, Khalid Koser, Gail McLaughlan, and John Salt. 2001. International Migration and the United Kingdom: Recent Patterns and Trends. RDS Occasional Paper 75. London: Home Office.

Erel, Umut, and Eleonore Kofman. 2003. Female Immigration in Post-war Europe: Counteracting a Historical Amnesia. In *European Encounters: Migrants, Migration and European Societies since 1945*, ed. Rainer Ohliger, Karen Schönwälder and Triadafilos Triadafilopoulos, 71–95. Aldershot: Ashgate.

Favell, Adrian. 2001. Multi-ethnic Britain: An Exception in Europe? *Patterns of Prejudice* 35: 35–57.

Favell, Adrian, and Andrew Geddes. 2000. Immigration and European Integration: New Opportunities for Transnational Political Mobilization? In *Challenging Immigration and Ethnic Relations Politics: Comparative European Perspectives*, ed. Ruud Koopmans and Paul Statham, 407–28. Oxford: Oxford University Press.

Fenton, Steve. 1996. The Subject is Ethnicity. In *The Racism Problematic: Contemporary Sociological Debates on Race and Ethnicity*, ed. Rohit Barot, 139–65. Lewiston: Mellen.

Freeman, Gary P. 1979. *Immigrant Labour and Racial Conflict in Industrial Societies*. Princeton: Princeton University Press.

Gabriel, John. 1998. New Contours of Anti-racist Politics. *Patterns of Prejudice* 32: 35–44.

Glover, Stephen, Ceri Gott, Anais Loizillon, Jonathan Portes, Richard Price, Sarah Spencer, Vasanthi Srinivasan, and Carole Willis. 2001. *Migration: An Economic and Social Analysis*. RDS Occasional Paper 67. London: Home Office.

Grillo, Ralph. 2002. Review of *The Sociology of Race and Ethnicity*. Ed. Malcolm Cross. *Journal of Ethnic and Migration Studies* 28 (1): 181–7.

Hall, Stuart, Chas Critcher, Tony Jefferson, John Clarke, and Brian Roberts. 1978. *Policing the Crisis: Mugging, the State, and Law and Order*. London: Macmillan.

Hansen, Randall. 1999. Migration, Citizenship, and Race in Europe: Between Incorporation and Exclusion. *European Journal of Political Research* 35: 415–44.

Hansen, Randall. 2000. *Citizenship and Immigration in Post-war Britain: The Institutional Origins of a Multicultural Nation*. Oxford: Oxford University Press.

Hatton, Timothy J., and Stephen Wheatley Price. 1999. *Migration, Migrants and Policy in the United Kingdom*. iza Discussion Paper 81. Bonn: IZA.

Home Office UK. 2002. *Secure Borders, Safe Haven: Integration with Diversity in Modern Britain*. White Paper. London: Home Office.

Jacobson, Jessica. 1997. Religion and Ethnicity: Dual and Alternative Sources of Identity among Young British Pakistanis. *Ethnic and Racial Studies* 20: 238–56.

Jenkins, Richard. 1996 ›Us‹ and ›Them‹: Ethnicity, Racism and Ideology. In *The Racism Problematic: Contemporary Sociological Debates on Race and Ethnicity*, ed. Rohit Barot, 69–88. Lewiston: Mellen.

Joly, Daniele. 1988. *Refugees in Britain: An Annotated Bibliography*. Warwick: CRER.

Katznelson, Ira. 1973. *Black Men, White Cities: Race, Politics, and Migration in the United States, 1900–30, and Britain, 1948–68*. London and New York: Oxford University Press.

King, Russell. 1993. *Mass Migrations in Europe: The Legacy and the Future*. London: Wiley.

Kofman, Eleonore, Annie Phizacklea, Parvati Raghuram, and Rosemary Sales. 2000. *Gender and International Migration in Europe*. London: Routledge.

Layton-Henry, Zig. 1992. *The Politics of Immigration: Immigration, ›Race‹ and ›Race‹ Relations in Post-war Britain*. Oxford: Blackwell.

Layton-Henry, Zig, and Paul Rich. 1986. *Race, Government and Politics in Britain*. London: Macmillan.

Lunn, Kenneth. 1989. The British State and Immigration, 1945–51: New Light on the Empire Windrush. *Immigrants and Minorities* 8: 161–74.

Mason, David. 1996. Some Reflections on the Sociology of Race and Racism. In *The Racism Problematic: Contemporary Sociological Debates on Race and Ethnicity*, ed. Rohit Barot, 193–211. Lewiston: Mellen.

Messina, Anthony M. 1989. *Race and Party Competition in Britain*. Oxford: Oxford University Press.

Miles, Robert. 1989. *Racism*. London: Routledge.

Miles, Robert, and Annie Phizacklea. 1979. *Racism and Political Action in Britain*. London: Routledge and Kegan Paul.

Modood, Tariq. 1996a. If Races Don't Exist, Then What Does? Racial Categorisation and Ethnic Realities. In *The Racism Problematic: Contemporary Sociological Debates on Race and Ethnicity*, ed. Rohit Barot, 89–105. Lewiston: Mellen.

Modood, Tariq. 1996b. The Changing Context of ›Race‹ in Britain: A Symposium. *Patterns of Prejudice* 30: 3–13.

Modood, Tariq, Richard Berthoud, Jane Lakey, James Nazroo, Patten Smith, Satnam Virdee, and Sharon Beishon. 1997. *Ethnic Minorities in Britain: Diversity and Disadvantage: The Fourth National Survey of Ethnic Minorities*. London: PSI.

Modood, Tariq, and Pnina Werbner. 1997. *The Politics of Multiculturalism in the New Europe: Racism, Identity and Community*. London: Zed Books.

Ouseley, Herman. 2001. *Community Pride not Prejudice: Making Diversity Work in Bradford: Bradford Race Review Report*. Bradford: Bradford Vision.

Parekh, Bhikhu. 1998. Integrating Minorities in a Multicultural Society. In *European Citizenship, Multiculturalism, and the State*, ed. Ulrich K. Preuss and Ferran Requejo, 67–86. Baden-Baden: Nomos.

Parekh, Bhikhu. 1999. National Identity in a Multicultural Society. In *From Legislation to Integration? Race Relations in Britain*, ed. Muhammad Anwar, Patrick Roach, and Ranjit Sondhi, 196–211. Basingstoke: Palgrave Macmillan.

Patterson, Sheila. 1969. *Immigration and Race Relations in Britain, 1960–1967*. London: Oxford University Press.

Peach, Ceri. 1996. *Ethnicity in the 1991 Census. Vol. 2: The Ethnic Minority Population in Great Britain*. Office of Population Censuses and Surveys. London: HMSO.

Penn, Roger, Adrian Favell, and Malcolm Cross. 2000. Review Symposium: Ethnic Minorities in British Social Science: Three Views. *Journal of Ethnic and Migration Studies* 26: 357–67.

Phizacklea, Annie. 1984. A Sociology of Migration or ›Race Relations‹? A View from Britain. *Current Sociology* 32: 199–218.

Rose, Eliot J.B. and Associates. 1969. *Colour and Citizenship: A Report on British Race Relations*. London: Oxford University Press.

Saggar, Shamit. 1997. *Race and British Electoral Politics*. London: Routledge.

Schönwälder, Karen. 1997. Einwanderungspanik und »multirassische Gesellschaft«: Großbritannien Anfang der neunziger Jahre. In *Die Sprache des Migrationsdiskurses: Das Reden über »Ausländer« in Medien, Politik und Alltag*, ed. Karin Böke, Matthias Jung, and Martin Wengeler, 349–61. Opladen: Westdeutscher Verlag.

Schönwälder, Karen. 2001. *Einwanderung und ethnische Pluralität: Politische Entscheidungen und öffentliche Debatten in Großbritannien und der Bundesrepublik von den 1950er bis zu den 1970er Jahren*. Essen: Klartext.

Solomos, John. 1986a. Trends in the Political Analysis of Racism. *Political Studies* 34: 313–24.

Solomos, John. 1986b. Varieties of Marxist Conceptions of ›Race‹, Class and the State. In *Theories of Race and Ethnic Relations*, ed. John Rex and David Mason, 84–109. Cambridge: Cambridge University Press.

Solomos, John. 1998. Beyond Racism and Multiculturalism. *Patterns of Prejudice* 32: 45–62.

Solomos, John, and Les Back. 1995. *Race, Politics and Social Change*. London: Routledge.

Solomos, John, and Les Back. 1996a. *Racism and Society*. Basingstoke: Macmillan.

Solomos, John, and Les Back. 1996b. Race and Racism in Social Theory. In *The Racism Problematic: Contemporary Sociological Debates on Race and Ethnicity*, ed. Rohit Barot, 212–30. Lewiston: Mellen.

Solomos, John, and Les Back. 2000. Introduction: Theorising Race and Racism. In *Theories of Race and Racism: A Reader*, ed. idem, 1–28. London: Routledge.

Solomos, John, and Richard Jenkins. 1987. *Racism and Equal Opportunity Policies in the 1980s*. Cambridge: Cambridge University Press.

Spencer, Ian R.G. 1997. *British Immigration Policy Since 1939: The Making of Multi-racial Britain*. London: Routledge.

Spencer, Sarah. 2002. *Recent Changes and Future Prospects in UK Migration Policy*. Paper presented at the Ladenburger Discourse on Migration, February 14–15.

Studlar, Donley T. 1985. »Waiting for the Catastrophe«: Race and the Political Agenda in Britain. *Patterns of Prejudice* 19: 3–15.

Tannahill, J.A. 1958. *European Volunteer Workers in Britain*. Manchester: Manchester University Press.

Vertovec, Steven. 2001. *Transnational Challenges to the ›New‹ Multiculturalism*. Paper presented to the ASA Conference, University of Sussex, 2001, available on: www.transcomm.ox.ac.uk.

Wrench, John, and John Solomos. 1993. *Racism and Migration in Western Europe*. Oxford: Berg.

Migration Research in Germany: The Emergence of a Generalised Research Field in a Reluctant Immigration Country

By Michael Bommes

Migration in Germany at present circumscribes a differentiated and increasingly specialised field of research which includes various disciplines of the social sciences such as sociology, geography, history, linguistics, education, political science, economics, law, psychology and social anthropology. But this type of generalised migration research dealing with all kinds of migration and the social structures emerging from them has developed only during the 1980s and 1990s as a merger of those research traditions which dealt in discrete fashion with the different migration strands in Germany after the Second World War. In this sense migration research in Germany has been initially to a large extent part of the so-called applied sciences reacting to problems as they were perceived in various social contexts like the political system, the economy, law, education, housing, the health system or social work.

Migration has neither been a major topic in the core of the various disciplines of the social sciences in Germany nor has it been addressed by major social theorists as a central challenge for theory-building – a clear difference from the history of thinking in the social sciences of the US where the intellectual formation of early sociology was strongly inspired by the challenge to understand the socio-structural development of emerging urban cities like Chicago as a result of immigration processes (Lindner 1990; Thomas and Znaniecki 1958).

The focus of our interest are here, on the one hand, the mutual relations between immigration processes and the resulting social and political changes in Germany, and the social sciences dealing with international migration and social integration on the other hand. We assume that research in this field does not just describe and explain these processes but is itself an internal part of the social and political dynamics of migration, settlement and integration processes in this field. We are interested in the ways in which the socio-historical context of immigration in Germany resonates in the concepts, theories and methodological approaches of German migration research.[1]

---

1 This is a shortened and revised version of Bommes, Michael (2006): Migration and Migration Research in Germany, in: Ellie Vasta/Vasoodeven Vuddalamay (ed.), International Migration and the Social Sciences: Confronting National Experiences in Australia, France and Germany, pp. 143–221, Basingstoke et al.: Palgrave Macmillan.

This endeavour, however, seems to imply a methodological trap since we, the observers of the relation between migration research and the social context of its production, cannot claim to be placed somewhere outside the social world at a neutral vantage point of observation. There is no way out of this circularity but the only option is to identify this vantage point as the social system of science itself. This system, like any other system, can provide a version of itself, of other social systems like politics, the economy, law, education etc. and the relation between these different systems and science. In other words, like any sociology of knowledge the following section is a case of the self-appliance of science which treats science as an internal part of the social reality – without being placed itself outside of this reality.

We divide the following text into three parts. In the first part we look at migration research in Germany dealing with refugees, expellees and ethnic Germans entering since 1945 the territory of what became in 1949 the Federal Republic of Germany (FRG). As we will see this research tradition ended in the late 1950s and remained unlinked with migration research since the early 1970s dealing with the immigration of the guest-workers and their families. This research started as so-called *Ausländerforschung* (›foreigner research‹) and developed from there to a generalised migration research. This will be discussed in the second part. The *Ausländerforschung* provided the grounds for a settled, more differentiated and internationalised migration research in Germany since the end of the 1980s when international migration was reconceptualised as an internal structural element of modern society since its emergence.[2] This will be discussed in the third part.

Migration Research on Expellees, Refugees and Ethnic Germans: A Means to Cope with Irreversible Outcomes of the National Catastrophe

The social sciences in Germany dealing with the immigration and settlement of refugees, expellees and ethnic Germans after the war have been closely oriented to policy and to practical applicability. Research on expellees and refugees of the late 1940s and 1950s was motivated and subsidised for reasons of political fear that ›political radicalisation‹ might spread among these immigrant groups under the severe social conditions of the immediate post-war period, i.e. a lack of housing, employment and insecure supply of food and clothes. This was expected to cause serious competition and social conflict in labour markets, to overstrain the social infrastructure heavily damaged by the war and to dissolve the »social institutions of German life«[3] through the import of ›alien‹ cultural behaviour by these immigrant groups (Müller 1956). The social effect and political duty resulting from the

---

2 On this conceptualisation of migration see, from a historical point of view, Page Moch 1992 and Bade 2000; from a sociological point of view, Bommes 1999 and Castles and Miller 2003.
3 The influential sociologist Schelsky developed some of his ideas on »the change of the contemporary German family« (1953) first by studying refugee families (1950).

immigration of the expellees and refugees was defined as a necessary recomposition of »a new German people from the internal Germans and the eastern expellees« (Lemberg 1950a; also Lemberg 1952). Various initial forms of political mobilisation and the formation of political unions and parties among these immigrants were perceived as indicators of a potential failure of this recomposition.

In order to prevent any such ethnic or class mobilisation among the expellees and refugees, political programmes of social integration had already been issued by the American and British occupying administrations (Schraut 1996; Jordan 1996) in the western zones of divided Germany, and they were further elaborated by the newly formed FRG after 1949. The aim was to ease social tensions especially by means of employment and housing policies. This integration policy was legitimised with reference to the »national community of fate« which had to share »the burden« and to divide the shortages in a just manner among all Germans based on »national solidarity« (Rogge 1959, 178).

Research on refugees and expellees was essentially designed corresponding to this political approach and dealt primarily with problems of ›incorporation‹ or ›integration‹. This is particularly well documented in a comprehensive collection of studies in a three-volume edition on the expellees in Western Germany (Lemberg and Edding 1959) financially and politically subsidised by the Federal Ministry for Expellees, Refugees and Claimants of the War (FME).[4] The aim of this collection was »to provide a complete and reliable picture of the state of incorporation and the problems related to it« (Ackermann 1990, 16). A number of wide-ranging studies were presented dealing with the economic and occupational incorporation of the expellees and refugees, their regional distribution and patterns of internal migration, legal problems of integration, the structure and effects of the burden-sharing programmes, the provisions of charity organisations, political integration, housing problems, religious change and integration, cultural and linguistic change and integration, and the social organisation of the expellees and refugees. These studies were the outcome of the collaboration of a ›research group on incorporation‹ initiated in 1954 by the FME which comprised thirty social scientists from various disciplines such as law, sociology, geography, economy, linguistics and cultural studies. The aim of this group was to provide a comprehensive study of high practical value and applicability for future decisions in politics, administration and jurisdiction concerning all aspects of incorporation of the expellee and refugee population. The main result of these studies was, however, to show that the integration of this population had been much less problematic than expected and proved to be quite advanced after the relatively short time period since the war.

This research, driven by the idea to articulate the extent and state of incorporation was not, however, characterised by any coherent conceptual or theoretical framework. The terms ›integration‹ and ›incorporation‹ had very different meanings. Usage and meaning of these terms varied according to the political context of

---

4   Bundesministerium für Vertriebene, Flüchtlinge und Kriegsgeschädigte.

their employment which predefined the relevant problems and the frame of reference. Faced with an urgent need for applied science no autonomous interest in developing an original theory of social integration or incorporation emerged. Embedded in contemporary discourse the terms ›integration‹ and ›incorporation‹ employed in research preserved strong political connotations and were embedded in a semantic field of terms like ›partnership‹, ›participation‹, ›gaining ground‹, ›to arrange in a whole‹, ›adaptation‹, ›assimilation‹, ›to settle in‹, ›organic insertion‹, ›to accustom‹, ›to ingrain‹, ›constitution of a new people‹ (cf. Pfeil 1952, 65). Only in 1959 did the FME propose to develop a new ›theory of integration and incorporation‹. A three-step model was proposed: in the first step the provision of labour and housing was seen as essential, to be followed by the second step of increasing access to social security, both assumed to prepare the ground for the third step, namely cultural integration and identificatory incorporation (Ackermann 1990, 22).

The national embeddedness of contemporary research on expellees, refugees and ethnic Germans resonates with these usages and meanings of the terms ›integration‹ and ›incorporation‹. A closer look, however, allows us to distinguish two underlying but closely related approaches: a more ›structural approach‹ and a ›national community approach‹. Related to the central political fear of social conflicts and the aim to prevent these, social integration was interpreted as participation »in the national economy, in the distribution of property and in cultural life« (Nahm 1959, 151).[5]

In structural terms economic incorporation proved to be relatively successful by the end of the 1950s. Contrary to fears of major social conflicts the ›economic miracle‹, the full inclusion of the refugees and expellees into citizenship and the compensation programmes provided by the state under the heading of ›compensation for burden‹, had provided the conditions for the integration of the immigrant population in a constantly expanding labour market allowing them to regain social status.

The legitimising political frame of reference for these structural forms of integration was the ›nation‹ reconstituted after the war as the ›national community of fate‹ (*nationale Schicksalsgemeinschaft*). This national community conceptualised in ethno-cultural terms was also the underlying frame of reference of the ›national community approach‹ in research linked with the structural approach by means of defining the economy, social rights and welfare in national terms, i.e. the economy, social rights and welfare of the German people. The main challenge of the presence of refugees, expellees and the ethnic Germans was perceived as the reconstitution of a common German people. And the ›common fate of the national community‹ was seen as the historical and cultural basis for the possibility of facing this challenge (Boehm 1959; Karasek-Langer 1959).

---

5   In German political semantics the reference to ›cultural life‹ (*Kulturleben*) connotes the nation as the frame of reference of the homogeneous culture of the people.

Research focusing on the structural conditions of social integration has been essentially embedded in this frame with its final centre of reference being the nation. Integration in the last instance referred to a process of national community-building, equal rights of the members of this community and the absence of social conflicts being at the same time a precondition and a result of this same process. In case of its success ›ethnic melting‹ was seen as possible and »the emergence of a new people from domestic and expelled Germans from the east« (Lemberg 1950a) should be its expected result. Social participation of the expellees and its success was conceptualised as mediated by the category of national belonging seen as a precondition for individual integration: the essential moderator of the relation between society and the individual was the nation state. The way contemporary research on expellees, refugees and ethnic Germans investigated the conditions and options for successful enlargement of economic, political, legal, social and cultural participation of these immigrants presupposed the nation state and the indispensable conjunction of these options with national belonging. Membership in the national community was seen as a central condition for the restriction and solution of social tensions and conflicts linked with expulsion and escape and the resulting social frictions.

Research on expellees, refugees and ethnic Germans during the 1940s and 1950s involved various social sciences. The different disciplinary approaches and research questions, however, found a common and comprehensive basis by employing ›the nation‹ and ›the people‹ as the centre of reference for their analysis which was committed to the objective of reconstituting and maintaining the people and the nation, in the end the defining criterion of successful integration and incorporation. Seen from a current perspective the categories of ›the people‹ and ›the national community‹ provided the nearly unreflected ground for analysis and the assumptions about the meaning and the options of social integration. This does not imply that contemporary research was naïve concerning the structure of nation states and the violent history of state-building processes in Europe.[6] It indicates, however, the deep structural embeddedness of the social sciences in the historical development of the nation state which affects their conceptual design up to their most general understanding of society or rather societies identified as national societies.

In recent debates on transnationalism the critique of ›methodological nationalism‹ has become almost fashionable. But the deep implicit correspondence between the conceptual design of the social sciences and the rise of the modern nation state articulated especially in the concept of society has been identified much earlier in general sociology (Tenbruck 1989, 1992). This is not the place to go into details of

---

6   This holds especially true for Lemberg who had published already in 1950 a book on the history of the nation state in Europe, an effort to identify the structural context for the emergence of the horrifying post-war constellation of escape, expulsion and forced mass immigration (Lemberg 1950b). Lemberg's book is an illusive description of the conflict-driven European state-building processes in the nineteenth and twentieth centuries (see also Lemberg et al. 1959 and Rhode 1959).

the conceptual status of the nation in sociological theory.[7] For our purposes it is important to differentiate between subsequent migration research which was based implicitly on the concept of a national society, but in the modernised version provided by the Parsonian tradition, and modernisation theories, on the one hand, and the contemporary research approaches on expellees, refugees and ethnic Germans during the 1940s and 1950s, on the other hand. This research had been carried out before the German social sciences went through a process of ›re-education‹ and conceptual redesign as a consequence of scientific exchange programmes and the (re-)import of Anglo-Saxon sociological approaches and research techniques. This can easily be grasped not only from the conceptual language of this earlier research but also from the explicit modes of reference to ›the nation‹ and ›the people‹. This was certainly due to the lack of a strictly scientific, i.e. abstract and consistent, conceptual language. But primarily it indicates the deep entanglement of the early migration research in post-war Germany with the project of the nation. This nearly identificatory relation to the nation was grounded in the effort to cope with the catastrophe which clearly was a national one and which had to be faced – by the nation. The affirmative and unreflective relation to the concepts of ›the nation‹ and ›the people‹ as a centre of reference in the early German migration research was based in the negative evidence of the national catastrophe urgently in need of solution.[8] Research subscribed to the duty to contribute to the search for such solutions.

When many of the studies during the 1950s had demonstrated that the integration of the refugees and expellees made good progress, the political funding of this research was more or less completely stopped. The three-volume edition of Lemberg and Edding (1959) proved to be the high peak and the end point of research on expellees and refugees after the war. Opinion polls showed that the attitudes of the indigenous population towards the expellees and refugees were characterised

---

7   With Marx, Weber and Durkheim the concept of the nation still stood at right angles to their theoretical interpretations of modern society. The nation-state concept found no systematic place either in Marx's theory of capitalism, nor in Weber's theory of rationalisation and legitimacy of the modern bureaucratic state. Neither did it find a systematic place in Durkheim's theory of the ›conscience collective‹. Only Parsons, following Durkheim's claim that integration is the central problem of modern societies, assigns the ›nation‹ a systematic place in his modernisation theory: ›the societal community‹ allows for the integration of modern society and according to Parsons the ›nation‹ is a universalistic form of inclusion in the ›societal community‹. According to Parsons this form has been successively disentangled from criteria of ethnic belonging in the modern, functionally differentiated society. This disentanglement was to be expected at each place where differentiation was making progress. Parsons' theory conceptualises societies as nationally and territorially delineated units. The troubling potential of the nation as a politically mobilising form of community as it was irritating the older tradition, is tamed by Parsons' theory of modern society. Parsons' interpretation that modern societies are integrated by nation states has been the unquestioned ground for sociological theorising until the end of the 1980s.

8   Another aspect of this is that quite a few of these researchers started their careers during the time of National Socialism and had been partially or deeply entangled with the politics of the NSDAP; see Gerhardt 2000.

by social indifference. During the 1960s only very few studies were published (for an overview, see Bade 1987, 145, passim).

Only when the numbers of ethnic Germans in the early 1970s were rising slightly were a few studies requested by the government investigating the economic and social integration of ethnic Germans and the long-term impact of this immigration on the national economy. During the 1980s, especially, historians published a number of studies revisiting the immigration of expellees and refugees in the disciplinary analytical frame of ›sociohistorical migration research‹. The aim of these studies was to situate the immigration of expellees systematically in the history of Germany running through a process of change from a country of emigration to a country of immigration (in particular Bade 1987; 1990; 1992).[9] In this context a new interest in the historical positioning and definition of expellee and ethnic German immigration since 1945 emerged and a variety of detailed and regionally oriented historical case studies was published.[10]

The situation changed completely when since 1987 a new process of mass immigration of ethnic Germans from Eastern Europe started as a consequence of the collapse of the socialist states. This caused a new interest in these immigrants from the general social sciences. But this new research started in a context where Germany had already had nearly thirty years of labour immigration and settlement. Part of this process was the emergence of another strand of migration research which started as *Ausländerforschung* (›research on foreigners‹).

Migration Research on Labour Migration: The Emergence of Social Integration as the Main Research Paradigm in the German *Sozialstaat*

The early research on refugees, expellees and ethnic Germans came to an end in the late 1950s. The connection between this and subsequent migration research on the guest-workers' immigration and settlement since the late 1960s has not yet been explored. There are two main reasons for this. Firstly the frame of reference of this early research was defined negatively: by the national catastrophe. Any positive reference to the nation in political and scientific semantics was more or less blocked. The emergent and more and more successful FRG described itself positively in relation not to the nation, but to the implementation of the *soziale*

---

9   It is striking that until the end of the 1980s the immigration of expellees, refugees and ethnic Germans, i.e. immigration structured by the history of nation-state building, was mainly treated by the historical sciences and remained outside the focus of other social sciences. It seems that the orientation of migration research of the 1970s and 1980s to modern social sciences provided the background for this blind spot.

10 Grieser 1980; Schier 1981; Bauer 1982; Bethlehem 1982; Steinert 1986. An extensive volume on ›Refugees and Expellees in Western German Postwar History‹ (Schulze, von der Brelie-Lewien and Grebing 1987) and the book ›New Home in the West‹ (Bade 1990) can be regarded as conclusive volumes of this research strand. But see also the overviews on the early research concerning expellees and refugees of Brelie-Lewien 1987, Sywottek 1989 and more recently Rautenberg 1997 and Hoffmann et al. 2000.

Marktwirtschaft (›social market economy‹) and the *Sozialstaat* (welfare state). The mantra of *Modell Deutschland* (›Model Germany‹) employed by Chancellor Helmut Schmidt during the election campaign of 1976 sums up this success story of the *Sozialstaat* and the newly gained and rather denationalised political identity. This mantra precisely did not refer to any national mode of community-building. The political semantics of the nation which were still strongly present in the texts of the early research on the expellees and refugees became devalued as a result of the growth of the welfare state and related processes of individualisation (Beck 1986; Lepsius 1990; Bommes 1995). Secondly, research on labour migration started slowly in the early 1970s reaching its high peak at the end of the 1970s and early 1980s. It has mainly been carried out by another and younger generation of researchers trained in the universities of the FRG.[11] This research started in a social context which was characterised by the high peak of welfare state expansion, the recruitment of high numbers of labour migrants and the political and cultural context of post-1968. One central element was the expansion of the education system including the growth of universities combined with the institutionalisation of the social sciences and especially sociology during the 1960s and the early 1970s. The research techniques, terminology and types of theories employed were mainly taken from the ›re-educated‹ and modernised social sciences. We should not conclude, however, that the terms in which problems were conceptualised were completely different. As will be seen, a different frame of reference was chosen, i.e. the problem of integration in a specific model of the modern welfare state. In other words: the state remained the relevant frame for the definition of the relevant types of problems to be dealt with in research.

Migration research on labour migration started as *Gastarbeiterforschung* (›guest-worker research‹), named soon afterwards *Ausländerforschung* (›foreigner research‹) and only during the 1980s was it slowly reconceptualised as general migration research. The design of German migration research up to the present is still strongly influenced by the theoretical and methodological conceptualisations of migration developed in the early phases of research during the 1970s and 1980s. This was the formative context for the emergence of migration research as a more and more differentiated subdiscipline of sociology and other disciplines of the social sciences like education, political science and social anthropology. In 1985 a working group – ›Migration and Ethnic Minorities‹ – of the German Sociological Association was founded which, after some reluctance, became institutionalised as a formal research section in 1990. Other centres established included: the Centre for Studies on Turkey at the University of Essen in 1995, the Institute for Migration Research and Intercultural Studies (IMIS) at the University of Osnabrück in 1991, the European Forum for Migration Studies (EFMS) at the University of Bamberg in 1993, and the Institute for Interdisciplinary Research on

---

11 Influential sociologists like Pfeil and Schelsky who had been involved in research on the refugees and expellees after the war and during the 1950s retired in the late 1960s and 1970s. The most influential German sociologists in labour migration research published their results in 1973 (Hoffmann-Nowotny), 1980 (Esser) and 1981 (Heckmann).

Conflicts and Violence at the University of Bielefeld in 1997. The 1990s saw the emergence of further research centres dealing with migration especially at the Universities of Mannheim, Berlin (Humboldt University) and the Wissenschaftszentrum Berlin. The main protagonists of research on labour migration in the 1970s and 1980s – such as Klaus J. Bade, Hartmut Esser, Friedrich Heckmann, Hans-Joachim Hoffmann-Nowotny and Ursula Mehrländer were involved in these institutionalisation processes of migration research.

Research on labour migration during the 1960s and 1970s was, however, initially primarily designed as applied science reacting to ›social problems‹ which were publicly perceived as most urgent. It had become clear that the labour migrants started to settle by leaving the accommodation centres where many of them had been living in during the 1960s and reuniting as families in Germany. Problems of housing, health, political participation and especially education in schools and occupational training of the second generation became major topics of concern and much of the research was taking these up as main issues.

In a study on the *Westdeutsche Ausländerforschung* (West German foreigner research), Treibel (1988) has argued that much of the research of the 1970s and early 1980s was characterised by a strong political and normative involvement and a corresponding lack of scientific detachment.[12] Treibel differentiates four phases of research between 1955 and 1986: a pre-phase between 1955 and 1970, an early phase between 1970 and 1973, a phase of consolidation between 1974 and 1978 and a phase of expansion between 1979 and 1983. The years after 1983 she saw characterised by multiple efforts to take stock and to reflect the empirical, methodological and theoretical limits of the *Ausländerforschung* (for similar classifications see Auernheimer 1984; Wilpert 1984).

In the mid-1980s a number of reflexive publications on migration research register that the field had expanded enormously and that it has become impossible for a single researcher to encompass the field as a whole. During the 1970s and 1980s there was a tremendous output of formal and informal, so-called grey publications (IAB 1982, 1982–9; Vink 1977–82; Weidacher 1981/2; Weidacher and Lopez-Blasco 1982). After excluding the so-called grey publications Treibel counts more than 400 publications between 1970 and 1985 taking into account only sociological approaches (Treibel 1988, 27). In discussing this literature in terms of Elias' distinction of involvement and detachment she identifies a gap between research before 1974 which she classifies as more detached and research afterwards during the consolidation and booming phases which she classifies as being to a large extent involved.

A closer look at the research of the early phase shows that the authors of those studies which Treibel classifies as detached situated their research less in a special-

---

12   She employs the distinction of Norbert Elias (1956) who argued that any social science has to face the challenge of balancing the tension between involvement and detachment. Involvement refers to an attitude which takes the urgent problems of a presence and its frame of reference for granted. Detachment refers to an attitude which tries to grasp the various modes of problem perceptions themselves as an important aspect of the object of study.

135

ised subfield of migration research – which was then non-existent in Germany – but in general theoretical fields like group sociology (Kurz 1965) or various system theoretical approaches (Hoffmann-Nowotny 1970; 1973; Albrecht 1972). Many of these authors published little or nothing on migration in their subsequent careers. In other words these authors built their scientific careers not primarily on migration as a subject but entered the field of migration by starting from intrinsic general scientific problems of their (sub-) disciplines. This is an indication of the fact that migration was not at that time a central field for research in the German-speaking social sciences and therefore offered only very limited career opportunities. Consequently, those who entered the field afterwards found little to build upon.

Most of the *Ausländerforschung* of the 1970s, i.e. during the phases of consolidation and expansion, did not start from intrinsic scientific problems but presented itself primarily as applied sciences trying to tackle ›the social problems‹ resulting from labour migration which were largely described as *Ausländerproblem*. Research took the problem definitions articulated in the various societal fields of politics, employment, education, housing, family and health as starting grounds.

Most of the research projects on labour migrants and their families have been carried out at universities.[13] Additionally, public research institutes like the Institute for Employment Research (Institut für Arbeitsmarkt- und Berufsforschung), the German Youth Institute (Deutsches Jugendinstitut), the German Institute for Urban Studies (Deutsches Institut für Urbanistik), the Federal Institute for Occupational Training (Bundesinstitut für Berufsbildung), the German Institute for Economic Research (Deutsches Institut für Wirtschaftsforschung), statistical offices and the research institutes of the political foundations Friedrich-Ebert-Stiftung and Konrad-Adenauer-Stiftung and some private research companies have been involved during the 1970s and 1980s to differing degrees. The main funding bodies were the German Research Council, the Volkswagen Foundation, the Federal Ministry of Education and Research, and the Bund-Länder Commission for Educational Planning and Research Promotion (Bund-Länder Kommission für Bildungsplanung und Forschungsförderung).

During the 1970s problem orientation of research was expected by the funding bodies. In 1974 the Volkswagen Foundation implemented a research programme called ›Migration Movements of Workers in Europe‹ in order to fund research projects which were supposed to address the following objectives among others: empirical research on the state of affairs which had emerged from migration; analysis of the structural problems resulting from migration by means of economics, sociology, demography and economics of education; analysis of forthcoming problems and consequences of migration and provision of solutions; and contributions to theories of migration (Korte and Schmidt 1983, 105). The Foundation intended to fund primarily those projects which were dealing with the most urgent and relevant problems in a limited time frame (104). The research programme

---

13 According to Angenendt (1992, 179) about two-thirds.

originally planned from 1974 until 1978 was expanded until 1981. After the first period it was stressed that there exists especially a need for action and solution-oriented research dealing with barriers and chances of social integration of foreign workers and their families, on the one hand, and fundamental research on the other. The research programme was slightly redesigned and announced under the title ›Guestworker Research – Migration and its Social Consequences‹. The funding activities of the Foundation were co-ordinated with the funding activities of the Federal Ministry of Research and Technology and the research priorities of the Institute for Employment Research.

The Volkswagen Foundation funded 62 research projects between 1974 and 1982 covering the following areas (Korte and Schmidt 1983): economic development and the employment of foreign workers; education and socialisation; occupational training; language acquisition; housing and segregation; remigration and integration; political participation; medical condition and health care; and fundamental research. One-third of the funded projects dealt with return migration, largely conceptualising and exploring it as an alternative to social integration in Germany. Another third treated various aspects of social integration in different social realms with a special emphasis on the second generation, families and women. According to the evaluation of Korte and Schmidt (1983) the area of ›fundamental research‹ was covered by two projects: one by Hartmut Esser developed a general model of assimilation and social integration and statistical methods of analysis (Hill 1984) using data sets produced by a research project funded by the Federal Ministry of Research and Technology (see below); another by Hermann Bausinger[14] explored the cultural patterns of orientation by means of social anthropological and cultural studies approaches.

From 1975 until 1979 the Federal Ministry of Research and Technology funded an interdisciplinary research network, ›Problems of Foreigner Employment‹, which included three subprojects on ›Social and Cultural Determinants of Behaviour of Foreign Employees in the Federal Republic of Germany‹, ›Integration of Foreign Employees in Companies‹, and ›The Interdependency between Decisions of Companies on Investment and Location and the Availability of Foreign Employees‹ (Didzolat 1979; Korte 1980). This research network claimed to employ a common theoretical framework based on ›methodological individualism‹ (Esser et al. 1979). In this context Hartmut Esser developed his approach to migration sociology based on rational choice assumptions (Esser 1980) which has remained up to the present one of the most influential research paradigms in German migration sociology (see below). Based on this research project he published numerous articles on the social determinants of assimilation and social integration of labour migrants and their families during the 1980s (e.g. Esser 1981; 1982; 1985a; 1985b; Esser and Friedrichs 1990). The study on the integration of foreign em-

---

14 Director of the Ludwig-Uhland Institute for Empirical Cultural Studies at the University of Tübingen.

ployees in companies (Gaugler et al. 1978; 1985) did not have the same impact.[15] It is, however, interesting that the integration of foreign employees has always been seen as a key to overall integration. And recent studies have argued that one reason for the relative stability of employment of foreigners has been their inclusion in the social insurance systems, the labour legislation and the labour relations at the workplace based on the statutory framework for the rights of employees (Böcker and Thränhardt 2003).

In parallel a first big ›Representative Study on the Situation of Foreign Employees and their Family Members in the Federal Republic of Germany‹ was financed by the Federal Ministry of Labour and Social Order and carried out by the Research Institute of the Friedrich-Ebert-Foundation directed by Ursula Mehrländer (Mehrländer and Hoffmann 1981). This study was replicated twice (König et al. 1986; Mehrländer et al. 1996). Additionally, statistical material and other relevant information were published regularly by the Commissioner for Foreigners of the Federal Government institutionalised in 1979, now the Commissioner for Migration, Refugees and Integration.

A large number of so-called ›model projects‹ in the area of education were financed by the Bund-Länder Commission for Educational Planning and Research Promotion (Bund-Länder Kommission 1980; Esser and Steindl 1987). These projects were largely based on varying types of action research involving a practical component, testing new models of education or social work and an accompanying research element, evaluating these models and their effects.

The outcome of this variety of funding activities was the emergence of a large body of publications in the field of migration research. We try to identify some of the main conceptual and theoretical research strands which were influential in the course of the 1970s and 1980s. We start from some of the literature which Treibel has categorised as belonging to the self-reflexive phase beginning, in her view, in the early 1980s. We finish this section with an outline of those general theoretical approaches of migration research which were developed during the 1970s and 1980s and which have remained influential up to the present.

Wilpert (1984) has characterised much of the research during the 1970s as being driven by a ›social problem approach‹, arguing that most of the research adopted the problem definitions articulated in the fields of politics, employment, education, law, housing, family or health (see also Griese 1984; Hamburger et al. 1983; Thränhardt 1984). The social consequences of labour immigration and settlement during the 1960s and 1970s were called the *Ausländerproblem*. Much research started from the more or less unquestioned assumption that labour migrants and their families cause problems and are confronted with a number of social problems due in large part to their inadequate capacity to integrate. In other words, the immigration and settlement process of labour migrants and their families were not conceptualised as an internal and foreseeable permanent socio-

---

15 Two reviews (Genosko 1981; Heckmann 1986) characterised both collections as incoherent presentations of empirical data without any deeper theoretical insights.

structural element of society but rather as an unintended external element affecting ›German society‹ which needed to be adapted to the existing structures.

The preparedness of the emergent research during the 1970s to tackle the *Ausländerproblem* and to fulfil the expectations of problem and solution orientation needs to be understood against two backgrounds. On the one hand, migration research was not at all embedded in the social sciences as a generalised subdiscipline. This is indicated by its specific name *Ausländerforschung*. On the other hand, the expansion of the welfare state during this period was also a time of institutionalisation and expansion of the social sciences in the universities. One reason for this was the strong post-war belief that welfare policies and their implementation based on the insights of modern social sciences would finally allow society to run free from economic crisis, unemployment and poverty (Lutz 1984). This general trust in the steering capacities provided by modern social sciences was already shrinking and the expansion of the social sciences had come to an end by the mid-1970s. In this context the detection of the emergent *Ausländerproblem* as a consequence of the settlement process of the labour migrants provided a new field which obviously seemed to be in urgent need of research and advice by the social sciences.

During the 1980s much of the research of the 1970s and early 1980s was criticised for three core deficiencies: the absence of general theories of migration and integration, the failure to develop these and the reliance instead on ad hoc theories (Genosko 1981; Boos-Nünning 1983; Esser 1980; 1984); the inadequacy of research methods and methodologies employed (Sievering 1985; Hoffmeyer-Zlotnik 1986); and a parallel lack of historical awareness and embeddedness of the *Ausländerpolitik* and *Ausländerforschung* (Bade 1992).

Additionally, a number of conceptual failures and implicit or explicit biases were criticised. Most striking was the strong integration orientation of migration research during the 1970s and 1980s. The subject of this research were indeed the *Ausländer* and the core problem was social integration. This frame organised to a large extent most conceptual approaches independent of all other differences between them. This may be demonstrated by the way in which the concepts of culture and ethnicity/ethnic minorities were employed in research.

A salient publication in the 1970s was a book by Schrader et al. (1976) on ›The Second Generation. The Socialisation and Acculturation of Foreign Children in the Federal Republic‹. Based on an evolutionary model of cultural socialisation they argue that immigrant children entering the destination country before schooling age will be easily acculturated to the norms and values of the host society and therefore will be able to assimilate and to cope with the challenges of social integration. Immigrant youth entering the country older than 14 and more or less after the end of their school education will be completely socialised to the norms and values of the society of origin. They may well be able to cope with the immigration situation but will never be fully integrated into the host society due to their inability to acculturate and assimilate. The most problematic case, however, in this view are those immigrant children who enter the country during their schooling age, because they will be torn between the two cultures and the differing norms and values of both societies. This model became very popular in the German *Ausländerpädagogik* (›foreigner pedagogy‹) providing schools and the education system with a frame that allowed them to treat the presence of immigrant children as an exceptional situation challenging the integrative capacities of schools and the education system to the extreme (Czock and Radtke 1984; Czock 1990). At the same time, it gained relevance in a political debate of the early 1980s as to whether it would be appropriate to restrict the right of family reunification by allowing only children up to the age of 6 to join their families. The main argument, i.e. the claim that only this could secure a successful social integration of migrant families and their children, was backed up by migration researchers explicitly supporting this claim (e.g. Esser 1982). Immigrant youth entering the country were labelled as a potentially ticking social bomb by the first Commissioner for Foreigners of the Federal Government if no adequate measures of social integration were installed (Kühn 1979).

In the same context, Turkish immigrants in particular were seen as living torn between two cultures and their conflicting expectations. This provided the organising principle for a famous exhibition touring in Germany called ›Germany in the Morning, Turkey in the Evening‹ (Kunstamt Kreuzberg 1981). In the same manner, socio-linguistic approaches identified a »bisected linguistic ability in two languages« (*doppelseitige Halbsprachigkeit*; Stölting 1980) among immigrant children, an analytical model which was largely adopted for the analysis of integration problems of second-generation immigrant youth (Stüwe 1982; Kalpaka 1986; Bielefeld et al. 1982; for a critique see Bommes 1993). This same approach was supported by social anthropological studies on Turkish immigrant youth arguing that serious cultural misunderstandings and conflicts arose from problems of appropriate symbolic decoding of everyday behaviour by these youth based on their socialisation experiences in Turkish peasant society (Schiffauer 1983). It was also dominant in a number of studies on Turkish immigrant women and girls, explaining their preparedness to accept patriarchal domination in terms of their traditional peasant socialisation.[16]

At first glance there seems to be a striking similarity in the usage of the concept of culture in sociological approaches using the assimilation model of Hartmut Esser (Esser 1980; Esser and Friedrichs 1990). The assumption here is that the

---

16 See e.g. Baumgartner-Karabak and Landesberger 1978; Karasan-Dirks 1980; Petersen 1985; Straube 1988; for a critique see Bennholdt-Thomsen 1987; Hebenstreit 1984, 1986; Elke Esser 1982; Otyakmaz 1995; Gümen 1996; Schöttes and Treibel 1997, arguing that migrant women were presented as a kind of counter-image to the ideal-type modernised and emancipated German or West European woman. What was striking was the general preparedness of migration research to believe in the myth that Turkish immigrants were socialised in a traditional society, i.e. Turkey. Based on very limited knowledge and a peculiar reading of the existing literature this myth became a topos; see Bommes 1993, 77; for an exception see Kleff 1984. In current debates on fundamentalism and the oppression of Turkish women by male immigrants the same myth is revived and an amazingly naïve study by a second-generation immigrant woman – trained as a sociologist in Germany – is used as a major reference for reasons of authenticity; see Kelek 2005 and the discussion of Beck-Gernsheim 2005.

social integration of immigrants is dependent on the success of cultural, structural and social assimilation processes. And two variables are seen as responsible: the equipment of the immigrants themselves and the responsiveness of social structures to the assimilation efforts of individual migrants. Esser has argued recurrently up to the present (Esser 2004) that it is mainly the lack of adequate cultural capital and tendencies of ethnic segregation that account for much of the relative failure of the (especially) Turkish immigrant population. The difference, however, is that for methodological reasons cultural capital is operationalised in a very formal manner using language and education as the main indicators. The concept is designed for empirical test procedures and keeps away from any substantialist concepts interpreting culture as an insurmountable worldview and code of action once adopted in socialisation processes.

The limits of these concepts and their account of immigrant cultures as inherently deficient were soon criticised by so-called inter- or multicultural approaches which gained political, scientific and practical prominence. In the fields of education and social work it was claimed that the deficit perspective needed to be replaced by a perspective of difference: cultures are different but of equal value. This approach criticised the former perspective for its one-sidedness ignoring the fact that the structures of society itself, especially of the education system, proved to be ill-equipped to deal with the challenge of immigration and its multicultural impact on society and its predominantly monocultural national education system (prominent in the early 1980s was Hohmann 1982). Interculturalism then refers to the practical methods required for the ability to cope with this new situation allowing for both the exchange of culturally different views and expectations and learning the social competence of mutual cultural tolerance (Auernheimer 1990).

In parallel a politically ambivalent debate on the emergence of a ›multicultural society‹ came to be promoted by left liberals as well as by rather conservative and even right-wing-oriented politicians and intellectuals (Miksch 1983; Leggewie 1990; Cohn-Bendit and Schmidt 1992; Ulbrich 1991). Authors like Leggewie and Cohn-Bendit and Schmidt interpret multiculturalism as a challenge to the nation state and its implicit model of a culturally homogeneous society. In their view multiculturalism implied the necessity to come to terms with cultural plurality resulting from migration and the gains and conflicts linked with it. From the conservative side multiculturalism was rather taken as a proof of the insurmountable distinctiveness of national and ethnic cultures.

Both perspectives, the former stressing the deficits of immigrant cultures to cope with conflicting expectations and the latter stressing their difference, were soon criticised for their primary focus on culture as the decisive variable for explaining the socio-structural position and life chances of immigrants (Radtke 1990; Bade 1996a). There were early warnings against relying on social anthropological and culturalist approaches for the analysis of labour immigration and its structural impacts from a Marxist point of view (Meillasoux 1980). In particular, migration research on migrant families and the second generation – involving not only educational sciences and social work but also sociology, linguistics and social anthropology – with its strong emphasis on problems of education and social work was criticised for creating the societal construction of immigrants as a social problem, i.e. the *Ausländerproblem*, with scientific means, and largely ignoring the main underlying socio-structural conditions for the emergence of the immigration situation since the 1980s. This critique was elaborated at a conference in 1987 on ›The Contribution of the Social Sciences to the Construction of Minorities‹ (Dittrich and Radtke 1990).

The critique of the contribution of the social sciences to the construction of minorities was illuminating but it is striking, however, that it seemed not quite appropriate in the German context. Minority approaches like those in the Netherlands, Britain or Australia never really gained ground in German migration politics and research. In her review of the *Ausländerforschung* Czarina Wilpert (1984) identifies this as one of the desiderata of research. And Stephen Castles (1984) argued that politics and research will have to cope with the emergence of ethnic minorities. It was Friedrich Heckmann (1981) who made a serious effort to introduce such approaches when he argued that during the 1970s Germany had become an immigration country and that the labour migrants had entered social positions which could best be analysed by resorting to the minority approaches of the Chicago School tradition and by combining them with aspects of socio-structural analyses. In his view the long-term effect of immigration was the emergence of minority colonies of varying immigrant groups. Based on this model Heckmann (1992) described the life and options of most Turkish immigrants as indeed socially placed in the infrastructural context of ethnic colonies. There has also been a debate between Elwert (1982) and Esser (1986) as to whether these colonies were to be interpreted either as a kind of sluice for newly arriving immigrants, allowing them to find their ways into the destination society by providing them with the necessary support, or rather as barriers to successful social integration, effecting in the long run the isolation of the immigrant population from the core institutions of society. Similarly, social anthropologists like Schiffauer (e.g. 1984) discussed the development of Islam and changes of religious orientation primarily with a focus on the integrative capacity of religious identification.

But minority approaches never gained real prominence in German migration research.[17] One reason for this becomes obvious from the type of debate between Elwert and Esser: the emergence and existence of minorities and the related social infrastructure were analysed in a functional perspective evaluating minorities in terms of their contribution to social integration. They were not interpreted as a regular structural outcome of immigration processes as had been suggested by Wilpert and Castles.

---

17 This holds true even if the research section of the German Sociological Association initiated by Heckmann was named ›Migration and Ethnic Minorities‹. A look at the conferences and debates of this organisation support this claim. The publication of an ›Encyclopedia of Ethnic Minorities in Germany‹ (Schmalz-Jacobsen and Hansen 1995) also did not change this situation.

Another important reason was that immigrants in Germany never really articulated themselves as ethnic minorities. This was certainly an effect of both: (a) the German migration policy which was primarily *Ausländerpolitik* and never based on ethnic minority approaches; (b) the recruitment of low qualified labour migrants. Although immigrant groups were addressed in national terms concerning, for example, the organisation of ›foreigner counselling‹ (*Ausländerberatung*) by charities or the subsidising of immigrants' self-organisations and clubs (Puskeppeleit and Thränhardt 1990) this did not effect the emergence of strong ethnic minorities and leadership. Rather, the different national groups and their self-organisations remained dependent client groups of the charities and local governments. One main reason for the reproduction of this clientelistic position of the immigrants was the lack of intellectuals among them who could have built a career on ethnic mobilisation and community formation. This lack was due to the mode of migrant recruitment in the 1960s and 1970s.

In other words: the sociological minority approach failed not only because it was rarely acknowledged among migration researchers but also because the immigrants themselves did not strongly articulate as minorities. This defines a constitutive part of the social existence of ethnic minorities: the identification and description of social groups as minorities by themselves and by others in such a way that this distinction becomes relevant for the modes of social inclusion and exclusion, of political articulation and the distribution of resources in various realms of society.

This also throws some light on the specific meaning of a certain line of criticism which addressed the ethnicisation and culturalisation of migration and its consequences (Bukow and Llayora 1988; Auernheimer 1988; Radtke 1990; Bommes and Radtke 1993; Bommes and Scherr 1992a): Its target was not a minority policy, which never gained ground in Germany, but the usage of ethnic and cultural distinctions made by organisations of the education system, social work, local administrations or labour offices. They tended to rely on these distinctions in an opportunistic manner dependent on their capacity to cope with organisational everyday problems: refusal of duties, claims of organisational resources like money or staff, legitimation of organisational decisions etc. Even here the overall framework remained the social integration approach.

To sum up: despite all differences the common frame of German migration research dealing with the labour immigrants was the strong orientation to problems of social integration. Seen from a general sociological background this is not surprising since the integration paradigm had been dominant in sociology and the social sciences for a long time. But the definitions and meanings of integration in much of the literature followed closely the perspective of the German welfare state which in a peculiar and rather ironic way defined the immigration problem in a non-ethnic manner as the *Ausländerproblem* as far as social integration in education, housing or labour markets was concerned. Ethnic and cultural belonging referred to hindrances to integration which needed to be dealt with. The key expectation was not assimilation in national terms in order to make the immigrants Germans but acculturation or assimilation in order to master the barriers of inclusion. And even multiculturalists argued by underlining the advantages of multicultural approaches for the prospects of social integration. In this sense there was a striking homology between the perspective of the social sciences and the *Sozialstaat*.

How does this fit with the international reputation of the German state that it excluded the labour migrants and their families from any political citizenship rights until the end of the 1980s – and the striking absence of a citizenship perspective in research? Referring to the ethnic foundations of the German citizenship law from 1913, reinstalled in 1949, there was no political willingness to grant those rights – but at the same time national citizenship was never a big public issue. The national substance of German citizenship was practically eroded in two ways. In the German *Sozialstaat* national modes of politics were largely devalued for historical reasons and political identity was based on the successful welfare state model. Additionally, the enduring presence of immigrants in various social contexts further devalued social presuppositions of national homogeneity (Bommes 1995; Bade and Bommes 2000). In the political forefront there was the enduring denial of immigration and the refusal to allow for citizenship rights of immigrants. In the background the main policy was driven by the German model of *Sozialstaat* and its paradigm of integration concerning labour, education, housing and the family. Many of the German migration researchers opted politically for an expansion of immigrant rights. But their research was primarily concerned with the conditions of social integration in those realms mentioned before, i.e. practical migration research subscribed to the model of social integration of the German *Sozialstaat*.

As a consequence of this subscription international migration and its consequences were never really regarded as a process that affected the core structures of society itself. The main question was not how migrations change the economic, legal, political, educational, religious or residential structures of society but rather how migrants could be included in and adapted to these structures. This is not to say that there was not much criticism of the lack of societal preparedness to change in order to allow for the social integration of migrants and their families. But the implicit or explicit perspective remained the option of social integration and the main indicator for integration was the degree of social inequality of migrants compared to the indigenous population. By the end of the 1980s it was even assumed that labour immigration and the consequent settlement processes were coming to an end. Discussing the migration theories of Hoffmann-Nowotny and Esser, Bernhard Nauck argued that this comparison »may be historically legitimated by the fact that there are some indicators that the theoretical discussion (and the empirical research) in the field of the German migration sociology can be regarded for the time being as concluded« (1988, 18). This obviously proved to be wrong and perspectives changed completely after 1989.

Nevertheless migration research in Germany in its present form is strongly impregnated by those research traditions which emerged during the 1970s and

1980s. One outcome of this period has been a number of general theories of migration and research approaches that proved to be sustainable. With an overview of these approaches we finish this subsection.

The first explicitly theoretical approach which remained one of the major frames of reference for research was developed by Hans-Joachim Hoffmann-Nowotny (1970; 1973). His *structural functionalist approach* focuses on prevailing prestige power relations as fundamental structural conditions of ›societal subsystems‹. On the basis of a power-theoretical modification of structural functional class theories Hoffmann-Nowotny distinguishes different levels of such systems from national subsystems of different sizes up to the international system and the system of world society (1970, 16; 1998). Prestige legitimises power and a disequilibrium of the distribution of power and prestige leads to structural tensions in these systems. Migration is conceptualised as a mechanism of compensation and transfer of structural tensions in and between social systems, resulting from status inconsistencies in the relations of power and prestige endowments. The thesis that became most prominent (and still is) was his claim that the effect of labour migrations was the emergence of new classes at the bottom of pre-existing class systems. Hoffmann-Nowotny has applied his theoretical approach in empirical research on labour migration in Switzerland (1973) and in a joint comparative research project with Karl-Otto Hondrich on Germany and Switzerland funded by the Volkswagen Foundation in the late 1970s (Hoffmann-Nowotny and Hondrich 1982). The approach of Hoffmann-Nowotny has influenced many scholars for more than thirty years and he was influential in a number of scientific and political committees during that period.

In 1980 the book ›Aspects of Migration Sociology‹ by Hartmut Esser was published. His approach has been by far the most influential in Germany. There are two reasons for this. The book introduced a vigorous theoretical approach based on ›methodological individualism‹ and rational choice assumptions. It blamed most of international migration research for a lack of theoretical rigour and claimed that any theoretically serious claim employed implicitly or explicitly assumptions that could be and needed to be reconstructed in terms of methodological individualism and a theoretical model of the rational actor. Esser elaborated this ›strong programme‹ of the unity of science during the 1980s and 1990s when he drew back from migration research and produced an impressive series of books, one on ›general sociology‹ (Esser 1993) and six on ›specific sociologies‹ covering the main fields. During the 1980s few researchers in the field of migration followed Esser's approach in terms of its methodological rigour (Hill 1984; Nauck 1985; Esser and Friedrichs 1990). This has changed since the 1990s when a number of his younger scholars and those of Bernhard Nauck entered the field working on various topics of migration and social integration (for example, Kalter, Granato, Diehl, Haug, Kristen, Diefenbach and Steinbach). The advantages of the model of social integration proposed by Esser are obvious. Migrants are not conceptualised as cultural dopes but rational actors trying to realise aims and ends in order to maximise their subjective benefits. It entailed a precise definition of

minority transition model

assimilative actions of migrants and it distinguishes clearly between the cultural and social equipment of migrants, on the one hand, and social barriers in various realms of society on the other. The interaction between both is seen as decisive for the success or failure of the assimilative efforts of migrants and their social integration.

The model has been subscribed to by many researchers for reasons of its simplicity and operational clarity.[18] Another reason was that it conceptualises social integration in terms of social inequality – thereby confirming the adequacy of the main focus of migration research. The prominence of the approach in Germany, however, was not confirmed in international or at least European discussions. The rigour of the rational choice approach of Esser[19] is not really appreciated and regarded rather sceptically. Some of the scepticism is also politically grounded in a reluctance to accept the assimilation model. Assimilation is seen as deeply linked with the worst parts of the history of European nation-state building. Political constellations, however, have been changing and with »the return of assimilation« (Brubaker 2001) a new debate on the relevance of assimilation has started in Europe and in the US (Bade and Bommes 2004c).

A third important approach in migration research have been Marxist theories of the labour market. Part of the expansion of the social sciences during the 1960s and early 1970s and the students' revolt of 1968 has been a revival of Marxist theories in the universities. Labour migration in this period provided an occasion for new research efforts on international class relations. Migration was interpreted as an expression of internationalised exploitation and inequality relations and provided new evidence that modern society was still a capitalist class society.[20] One of the most detailed and informative studies was published in 1981 by Knut Dohse which provided a theory of the ›bourgeois state‹ and described migration policy in Germany in the nineteenth and twentieth centuries as a conflictual interplay between a capitalist market economy and the state interested in reproducing its power basis. But in the mid-1980s Hartwig Berger (1987; 1990) complained that a class approach had never seriously applied to the German situation. After 1989 Marxism lost much of its ground. But this should not be taken as the end of its relevance. It has been incorporated in approaches which adopt parts of Piore's (1979) theory of segmented labour markets, of the world system approach of Wallerstein and some of the work of Sassen (Potts 1990; Parnreiter 2000; 2001). It also resonates in numerous texts which employ Bourdieu's prominent distinction between different modes of capital (economic, social and cultural).

---

18 See e.g. the textbook of Treibel 1990 and later editions and also Han 2000. It has also been adopted by Heckmann during the 1990s when he gave up his minority approach.
19 Esser is usually counted as a rational choice theorist. There are, however, many differences between his model of the rational actor and other rational choice theories. We ignore this here.
20 Castles and Kosack 1973; Nikolinakos 1972; Harbach 1976; Berger et al. 1978; Heckmann 1981; Augustin and Berger 1984; Castles 1984 (German translation: 1987); Kleff 1984; Castles and Kosack 1973 was published in English but it was a main reference text in German discussions.

During the 1980s and the early 1990s ethnic minority approaches were prominently introduced (Heckmann 1981; Castles 1984; 1987). There was also a debate in German sociology on the failure of different theories of modern society to account for ethnicity (Esser 1988; Kreckel 1989; Nassehi 1990). In the 1990s the relation between migration and ethnic conflict was a recurrent topic of research but ethnic minority approaches lost ground for the reasons explained above.

If we compare these approaches the reason for their sustainability is grounded in the capacity of each to provide a relatively consistent theoretical frame which allows important aspects of the social complexities linked with migration to be accounted for and the underlying structural relations to be analysed. Despite all the differences between these approaches some similarities are striking: Marxist efforts and the work of Hoffmann-Nowotny and Esser share the assumption that the generating mechanisms of social inequality – exploitation (Marxism), power/prestige differences (Hoffmann-Nowotny) or conflicts over resources between utility maximising actors (Esser) – are the foundation of the core structures of society in which the emergence and reproduction of class, strata or underprivileged groups are anchored. The three approaches also share the assumption of a close relationship between social inequality and social integration. This fits well with the overall tradition of migration research in which the problems of ›inequality‹ and ›integration‹ are conceptualised in a way that they interpret and underpin each other: identifiable inequalities in the distribution of labour, income, education, housing etc. are interpreted as indicators of problems of integration; potential integration problems of migrants are proved vice versa by referring to social inequalities. The development of the relations of inequality are interpreted as a seismograph of the conflictual potential of migration.

This corresponds to a long tradition of general sociology. There are, however, problematic consequences linked with this: (1) The stress on social inequality and integration implies a tendency to limit migration research to the analysis of the relations of distribution and inequality. This causes a tendency to perceive social changes effected by international migration only in so far as they affect these relations. The limited concept of social structure and differentiation basically referring to relations of capital and power distribution is one of the main reasons why migration research notoriously fails to focus on the consequences of international migration for the social structures of society in its various differentiated realms as a whole. Somehow migration remains conceptionally external to the structural development of society. (2) The subscription to the concept of integration is theoretically problematic. Despite all terminological differences – assimilation, incorporation, inclusion, integration, cohesion – there remains a notorious indeterminacy in the meaning of either the integration of individuals in society or the integration (or more recently: social cohesion) of society. Migration research, however, was and is well able to come to terms with this indeterminacy because this allows for an operationalisation of social integration explicitly or implicitly closely linked with the political conceptualisations and semantics of integration provided by the welfare state.

Michael Bommes

It was the socio-historical approach in migration research which programmatically and substantially defined its subject as less restricted to the paradigm of social integration and social inequality. Klaus J. Bade (1987) argued in one of his programmatic articles on socio-historical migration research that any research on migration and settlement processes needs to be embedded in the demographic, economic, social and cultural history of both the region of origin and destination. The best examples of this approach do not read like highly specialised historical studies on certain migration strands but give an impressive account of the structural impacts of migration processes on the societal contexts in which they occurred (e.g. Bade 1979; 2000; 2004; Herbert 1986; 2001; Oltmer 2005; Bade, Emmer, Lucassen, and Oltmer 2007; for an excellent overview see Oltmer 2010). This may well have to do with the internal disciplinary challenges: historical migration researchers aim to underline the overall meaning of migration processes for the development of history, its continuities and discontinuities. They strive for the meaning of their subject in the discipline as a whole and thereby may be less in danger of falling into the traps of subdisciplinary differentiation and specification (see Lucassen and Lucassen 1997). Historical studies on migration and the socio-historical approach gained a major influence on migration research in various disciplines. Social historians were among the founders of the main migration research institutes in Germany and became members and chairs of evaluation committees for research funding and advisory boards of the government.

Migration Research after 1989: The Institutionalisation of General Migration Research in Germany

1989 turned out to be a decisive year for Germany and the wider world – and also for migration research. Nothing remained as it was. Harbingers of change had been apparent before: for example, the dramatically rising numbers of ethnic Germans entering the country since 1988. Migration research which had previously struggled for conceptual generalisations, to leave behind the peculiarities of the *Ausländerforschung* after 1989 went through a process of empirical differentiation and generalisation. Next to the ethnic Germans the numbers of asylumseekers and refugees of civil wars were rising dramatically, new forms of labour migration like seasonal and contract workers gained increasing relevance and the progressing European integration process induced new forms of labour migration based on the legal freedom of services. It became clear that migration had lost its comparatively simple layout as *Ausländerproblem* and that migration research would have to deal with all of these different forms of immigration. Empirical differentiation became another impulse for generalisation.

Not only the sheer numbers but also the structural embedding of these migration processes caused change. The reunification of Germany suddenly confronted the eastern part of the population with the implications of the freedom of movement: a shrinking population in many areas from where young East Germans moved towards the western parts of the country after the decay of the economic infrastructure, on the one hand, and the arrival of asylum-seekers, refugees and ethnic Germans in East Germany, on the other. In this context, there were attacks against asylum-seekers in Eastern as well as Western cities. They were presented by the media worldwide as a moral catastrophe for the newly united Germany. In several cities in West Germany conflicts between old and new immigrant youth, especially Turks and ethnic Germans gained public attention. The arrival of ethnic Germans turned out to be just another immigration wave linked with many implications known already from the guest-worker immigration affecting especially the labour market and the education system. In the construction sector the employment of contract workers and subcontracting to firms from Portugal, Britain and Ireland based on the European freedom of services caused serious conflict.

Migration and the perceived social tensions linked with it became again a major political topic and this provided the context for the firm institutionalisation of migration research at several universities and research institutes. During the 1990s this was accompanied by extensive funding activities. The main relevant institutions were, among others, the German Research Council, the Volkswagen Foundation and the Federal Ministry of Education and Research.

At the beginning of the 1990s the German Research Council set up a main research area called ›The Consequences of (Labour-)Migration for Education‹ (FABER). This research area was funded from 1991 until 1997 allowing for 21 research projects involving education, linguistics, psychology, psychiatrics, sociology and law (Gogolin and Nauck 2000, 9). A graduate school on ›Migration in Modern Europe‹ at the Institute for Migration Research and Intercultural Studies (IMIS) of the University of Osnabrück was financed from 1995 until 2004. Additionally, a substantial number of research projects was funded via the normal application procedure.

The Volkswagen Foundation set up a research area first called ›The Alien and the Intimate‹ and later renamed ›The Construction of one's own and the Alien‹ (Gunsenheimer 2007). The establishment of this research area was an immediate reaction to the conflictual situation after 1989. In this framework more than 180 research projects between 1991 and 2005 were funded[21] but not all or even most of them dealt with migration. The focus was put on constellations in which potentially conflictual relations between ›the alien and the intimate‹ are made socially relevant. Additionally, in 2003 a call for applications of international research networks in the field of ›Migration and Integration‹ was published and in autumn 2004 seven networks were approved. A second call was published in late 2005 and a third one in 2007. Additionally, a chair in ›Sociology/Methodology of Interdisciplinary and Intercultural Migration Research‹ was established in 2003 at the IMIS funded by the Foundation.

---

21 See press announcements of the Volkswagen Foundation from 14 April 2003 and the announcement of funded projects in this research area between 2000 and 2005 at (www.VolkswagenStiftung.de).

Apart from single research projects the Federal Ministry of Education and Research financed between 2002 and 2005 a major research network named ›Processes of Disintegration – Strengthening Potentials of Integration of Modern Society‹. This network included seventeen single research projects placed at different universities all over Germany and quite a number of these projects dealt with ethnic conflicts, problems of social integration in cities, right-wing extremism and problems of religious integration and recognition. Additionally a ›Programme on Intercultural Conflict and Societal Integration‹ (*Arbeitsstelle für interkulturelle Konflikte und gesellschaftliche Integration*) based at the Science Centre in Berlin was funded for three years from 2003. The main aim was to promote communication between academics, policy-makers and the wider public.

It is of course impossible to provide a complete overview of the subjects of this internally highly differentiated research. Instead we shall identify some of the main topics which have been dealt with in this period and at the end of this section we discuss if there have been any new theoretical or methodological developments in the field and if there were any major shifts concerning the overall embedding of research orientations.

The main topics of research were: (1) immigration and social integration of ethnic Germans; (2) social integration of the first and second generations of the former guest-workers; (3) migration and education; (4) migration, citizenship and the welfare state; (5) migration and ethnic conflicts; (6) migration and religion/Islam; (7) migration, the labour market and the fiscal effects of migration; and (8) illegal migration.

(1) The most striking development in the field of ethnic German immigration has been the approximation of their status during the 1990s to the status of other immigrant groups and the restriction of former privileges. In a parallel manner ethnic Germans became just one subject group in migration research among others. The German libraries network catalogue offers more then 300 titles between 1990 and 2005 including all relevant scientific disciplines in migration research. Among those who have published in this field it is easy to find a number of authors that are usually counted as general migration researchers. Research in this field has become quite consolidated, applying the main instruments of migration research to the various aspects of settlement and integration of the ethnic Germans. A vast number of studies on social integration in the labour market, the education system, the housing market and the health system are available. Additionally much attention has been paid specifically to families and the second generation.[22] The outcomes of this research demonstrate that the restriction of former privileges combined with a change of resource equipment concerning especially linguistic abilities and cultural capital on the side of the immigrant

---

22 For an overview see the contributions in Bade and Oltmer 2003; also Herwartz-Emden 2003; on the second generation see Dietz 1998 and on the labour market Zimmermann 1999. On the political assimilation of the status of the ethnic Germans to other immigrant groups see Heinelt and Lohmann 1992 and Bommes 1996.

population cause all kinds of problems of social integration well known from other immigration processes. It should be noted, however, that the inclusion of the ethnic Germans in the main paradigm of migration research, i.e. social integration and the focus on their cultural and social equipment as main conditions for successful integration, has been experienced by ethnic Germans as a loss of social status. Migration research has contributed to lowering the social status of ethnic Germans by ascribing them a migrant status while they were stressing their national belonging as the foundation for the legitimate claim of recognition and equality with all Germans.[23]

(2) The 1990s and the early years of the twenty-first century saw also a continuation of research on the social integration of the first and second generations of the former guest-workers. This research has been important for a number of reasons. It succeeded in showing that the integration of the labour migrants of the first generation and their families up to the 1990s was much more successful than many former alarming scientific and political announcements had expected (Thränhardt et al. 1994; Thränhardt 1998; Seifert 1995; 2000). This result has been undermined by two other developments: unemployment in Germany has been constantly rising and was very high during the 1990s and early 2000s. This affects labour migrants in at least two ways: they are more strongly hit by unemployment than the indigenous population, and the second generation especially seems to be losing ground because many of them are less competitive in the education system compared to their indigenous peers and have fewer chances to enter employment (Baumert 2001; 2003; Kalter and Granato 2004; Kristen and Granato 2004). These findings have become relevant in a European perspective since many countries see themselves confronted with the challenging question as to whether they may have to pay at present and in the future the price of a migration policy which failed to take into account the long-term perspective of an immigrant population that had been recruited under highly specific conditions and with no intention of long-term immigration (Bade and Bommes 2004c).

(3) Another main field of research was closely linked with this: the issue of education. Research on migration and education has been an intensively researched topic funded in numerous ways. In the FABER research network many aspects have been addressed: among others the role of families and their capital equipment; cultural conflicts and their impact on teachers; social evaluation processes of language competencies among Turkish and German youth in urban neighbourhoods; the impregnation of the education system by a national linguistic habitus; the role of national school policy traditions for the handling of migration; and the organisational conditions of discrimination of migrant children in schools.[24] In

---

23 The legitimacy of this claim was continually challenged by migration researchers (e.g. Otto 1990).
24 An overview of some of the results is provided by the journals *Unterrichtswissenschaft* (no. 2, 1993), and *Zeitschrift für Pädagogik* (no. 1, 1994; no. 5, 1998) and by Gogolin and Nauck 2000.

this context two points may be stressed: (a) though the research area was headed ›Consequences of Migration for Education‹ most research projects did not concentrate on the structural implications of migration for the field of education but instead focused again mainly on migrants and their social and cultural equipment[25]; (b) research on migrant families done in this context succeeded in making some headway insofar as it started to focus not just on the failures but the potential of migrant families to support their members when confronted with the challenges of migration and social integration.[26]

The publication of *PISA* (Baumert 2001; 2003) had some irritating effects. It seemed that research on education had accumulated a large body of differentiated knowledge but that it was incapable of providing a convincing answer to the question as to why the German education system proved was a central factor in the reproduction of the unequal distribution of chances. This affected especially the children of immigrants. There is no valid theory at hand which is convincingly able to account for the reproduction of this positioning of migrant children. Therefore a new debate on migration and education and the conditions for success and failure of migrants has started and is still going on (Bade and Bommes 2004a; Steinbach and Nauck 2004).

(4) Research on the social integration of immigrants was the continuation of the former research practices. But parallel international changes, the rising numbers of immigrants and the new relevance of ethnic immigration at the beginning of the 1990s, the reinstitutionalisation of the sovereign German nation state, new political debates on the social costs of immigration and its effects on the welfare state, and new forms of welfare chauvinism all put the role of the national welfare state on the agenda of migration research. Up to the end of the 1980s the state had been criticised by many migration researchers and political actors for its hesitant migration policy, the lack of legal security and citizenship rights for immigrants and the inadequacy of its integration policy. But with the exemption of Dohse (1981) the state was the addressee of normative claims and not an object of study. The national welfare state had been an agenda setter but it had not been analysed itself as an internal socio-structural condition of the forms and size of international migration. During the 1990s a number of books and articles were published[27] and international conferences and related research projects were started.[28] The main

---

25 An exception was Gomolla and Radtke 2002, a study of the organisational discrimination of migrant children in schools.
26 This perspective was already present in the early work of Nauck (1985), but see now Herwartz-Emden 2003; Nauck 2001; 2002; Steinbach and Nauck 2004 and Steinbach 2004a. This perspective was also taken in the Sixth Family Report of the Federal Government (Deutscher Bundestag 2000).
27 Heinelt and Lohmann 1992; Bommes and Halfmann 1994; Bommes 1995; 1996; 1999; Faist 1995; Kleger 1997; Mackert 1999; Mackert and Müller 2000.
28 Bommes and Halfmann 1998 which presents the results of a conference on ›Migration and National Welfare States in International Comparison‹ held in 1996 at the University of Osnabrück, funded by the Volkswagen Foundation, and Bommes and Geddes 2000 which presents the results of a conference held at the European University Institute in Florence in 1998, funded by the EU.

problems tackled in this field were, among others: the interrelation between welfare and migration policies; international migration and the loss or restructuration of state sovereignty; forms of citizenship and forms of migration; political inclusion/ citizenship and inclusion or exclusion of migrants; and the relation between organisational traditions of states and the design of migration policies. This research succeeded in demonstrating that states in their different shapes need to be understood much more as important internal elements of the structural dynamics linked with international migration and its various social consequences for society and less as a kind of external leader steering and controlling this process. This myth and its unintended consequences are part of the game. However, the constant promotion of international migration to a high level of political importance in many nation states and in the EU during the last decade, was associated with a substantial extension of funding of a kind that insists increasingly on policy relevance. There is an implicit tendency to instrumentalise research linked with the danger that researchers and research institutes involved in competition for fund-raising restrict analytic perspectives and subscribe (again) to some of the unavoidable self-mystifications of the political system.

(5) A further important research field was reacting to rising fears that ethnic conflicts may gain increasing relevance. Empirical evidence for this was provided not least by the attacks on asylum-seekers in the early 1990s and conflicts between right-wing youth and immigrant youth but also between ethnic German and Turkish youth. A number of edited volumes on the relation between migration, ethnicity and social conflict were published (e.g. Bade 1996b; Eckert 1998; Heitmeyer and Dollase 1996). These volumes collected the existing knowledge, made use of existing general models of social conflict and tried to determine the specificity of ethnic conflicts. It is, however, striking that many of the relevant empirical studies focus on youth. This holds true for large-scale studies (e.g. Heitmeyer et al. 1992; Heitmeyer et al. 1997) and for qualitative research (e.g. Tertilt 1996; Eckert et al. 2000; Dannenbeck et al. 1999; Weißköppel 2001). There remain, however, a number of open questions. Do research results indicate a dangerous potential for violent conflicts based on growing radical orientations linked with ethnic and religious fundamentalism? This interpretation is forcefully proposed by the Bielefeld school around Heitmeyer.[29] Others argue that ethnicity has become just one form among others for youth to engage in everyday conflicts (Eckert et al. 2000; Dannenbeck et al. 1999; Weißköppel 2001). After all, ethnic conflicts have not gained the continuous and public relevance in Germany which many authors saw coming during the 1990s (Bommes 2004a). The flipside of this are less public forms of social distance and demarcation between immigrants and the indigenous population (Steinbach 2004b).

---

29 He has, however, been criticised on methodological and theoretical grounds for his studies on right-wing youth and on growing fundamentalism among Turkish youth; e.g. Bommes and Scherr 1992b; Santel 1998; Proske and Radtke 1999.

(6) The mode, however, in which religious practices of Turkish migrants have become the subject of research is indicative of the guiding orientation of migration research in Germany – not least when it deals with religion: Islam and its forms of organisation as well as the religious orientations of migrants are primarily observed guided by the question as to whether they contribute or hinder the social integration of migrants.[30] A number of studies focus on Islamic organisations and some authors interpret them as a fundamentalist threat to Europe (e.g. Binswanger 1990a; 1990b; 1990c) whereas others expect that the embedding of Islam in the legal institutional setting of Germany will cause internal change towards a ›Euro-Islam‹ adopting much more church-like organisational forms and becoming more individualised (Leggewie 1993a; 1993b). Some authors focus on the religious practices and orientations of Turkish Muslims. Schiffauer, in particular, followed the religious orientations and organisational development of Turkish immigrant groups for more than twenty years (1983; 1984; 1991; 2000; 2004). He analyses the micro-structural changes of the religious life of Turkish migrants and interprets them as active and constructive forms of handling the challenges of social integration. A quite opposite position involves studies like Tertilt (1996) and Heitmeyer et al. (1997) who interpret the Islamic orientations of Turkish youth as strong barriers to social integration. They are presented as traditionalist cultural forms binding these youth to their cultures of origin, containing a fundamentalist or extremist potential and keeping youth away from the values of ›enlightenment‹.[31] In recent years this has become a dominant perspective putting quite naïve but strongly ›anti-fundamentalist‹ studies like Kelek (2005) at the centre of debate. Irrespective of agreement or disagreement with the one or the other interpretation both share as the focal point of analysis the question of social integration. The emergence of Islam in Europe as the most important religion next to Christianity has not really been grasped as a major structural change of society in Europe and in Germany. It remained to be pointed out by US scholars that the institutionalisation of Islam in Europe brings the history of social differentiation between religion(s), law and politics back on the agenda. The relations between religion(s) and states in Europe are based in historical compromises and the arrival of Islam is challenging these compromises (Fetzer and Soper 2005; Klausen 2005). The highly generalised suspicions of fundamentalism seem to a large extent to articulate this challenge. Committed to its guiding orientation of social integration migration research has paid only very little attention to these structural effects of migration on society, the role of religion and its meaning for ongoing migration and settlement processes. Islam – like many other effects of migration – has for a long time been perceived as an external element of society which will lose its structural relevance if only migrants manage to integrate in society.

---

30 The title of Jonker 1997 is paradigmatic.
31 Tietze (2001) points out that ›enlightenment‹ has the same discursive position in the German debate on Islam as *laïcité* in the French debate.

(7) Labour market and fiscal effects of migration again became an important topic of research during the 1990s. It had been dealt with during the 1970s from two angles: (a) the guest-worker recruitment of the 1960s and 1970s had been analysed by questions like the costs and benefits of migration, the impact of migration on economic growth cycles and the functioning of the labour market, and the future demand of labour migrants (e.g. Kaiser 1977; Körner 1976; Pöhlmann 1974). These approaches lost relevance in between and had been replaced by the foreigner research with its focus on social integration. During the 1990s the topic returned for two reasons. New forms of labour migration emerged as an effect of (a) the restructuration of Eastern European countries and the opening of the German labour market for immigrants from Eastern Europe on the basis of contract and seasonal labour; (b) the liberalisation of the EU labour market based on the rule of freedom of services; and (c) the slight opening of the German labour market for highly qualified migrants. Quite a number of studies concentrated on contract and seasonal labour migration[32] which proved to have a major impact especially on the construction sector with the effect of its Europeanisation, the change of sectoral labour relations and occupational structures in Germany and high unemployment for construction workers with a permanent resident status. The opening of the German labour market for highly qualified migrants and its symbolic staging for the ›Green Card‹ found much public attention. It became a political symbol for a change of perspective on immigration (Ette 2003). Empirical research on the outcomes of this policy shows that Germany had indeed adapted its labour market policy to the needs of the highly internationalised ICT sector (Kolb 2004).

In a more abstract manner economists have analysed the impact of migration on labour markets (e.g. Pischke and Velling 1997; Bauer 1998; Bauer and Zimmermann 2002; Trabold and Trübswetter 2003). These studies are telling if we compare them to other approaches in migration research: a common outcome of these studies is that migration seems to have only minor effects on wage levels as well as on the employment conditions for indigenous workers. This outcome is often referred to by defenders of more open migration policies in political debates about the effects of migration on labour markets and social welfare. Economists themselves, however, generally do not engage directly in those debates or in debates on social integration. Economists are primarily interested in the structural effects of migration on markets and what this means for the disciplinary established economic models. They may opt for open labour markets and/ or the reduction of social welfare (e.g. Straubhaar 1996), but the reasons for this are scientifically established model assumptions. Economists have a disciplinary capacity to avoid political expressions and to preserve their autonomy by means of a scientific frame of reference. Economists' models are criticised, however, by sociologists and other disciplines for the normativism implied in their basic assumptions concerning

---

32 See Faist et al. 1999; Hunger 2000a; 2000b; Hunger and Santel 2003; Bommes et al. 2004; Worthmann 2001; on legal implications see Hanau 1996; Junker and Wichmann 1996.

utility maximising behaviour, market equilibria and efficiency. Economists favour efficiency and assume that the market is the institution that can best guarantee this (Lazear 2000). To be sure, economists often intervene politically but these interventions are guided by disciplinary biases in favour of open and competitive markets. This provides an internal basis for keeping distant from political or alternative normative expectations.

This marks a clear difference from debates on fiscal effects of migration which have recently gained prominence in many European countries. The taken-for-granted starting point of these debates is the politically institutionalised fact that migrants are seen as a part of the population on state territories that may possibly be excluded from the consumption of public goods if they turn out to consume more of these goods than they contribute to their production. European welfare states have been much more inclusive of migrants since 1945 than has been expected by many scholars. The capacity to exclude them shrinks the longer migrants manage to stay on a state's territory (Hollifield 1992; Soysal 1994). This, however, has not wholly destroyed the assumption that migrants – different from the indigenous population – somehow constitute a disposable part of the population whose stay may depend on whether they prove to be a relief to or a burden on public spending. The debate itself is dominated by controversial positions, the one strongly favouring restrictions by arguing that immigrants have negative impacts on public budgets unless they stay longer than 25 years in a country like Germany (Birg 2002), the other stressing that on the whole the indigenous population benefits strongly from immigration (Loeffelholz and Heilemann 1998; Bonin 2001; 2002; Loeffelholz et al. 2004). But even those who argue that immigration is necessary for demographic reasons and pays off in terms of public budgets in the long term subscribe to the underlying state perspective that migration remains an external element of society to be managed and guided by political priorities.

(8) In a similar manner illegal migration has gained increasing public attention since the end of the 1990s when the presence of illegal migrants in many social areas like construction, farming, restaurants and catering, private households and health care became evident. But recent studies conclude that not very much reliable knowledge is available and that more systematic research is needed. A number of studies, however, have appeared which look at sectors where illegal migrants are primarily employed like construction and private households (e.g. Cyrus and Vogel 2002; Hochstadt 2003; Worthmann and Zühlke-Robinet 2003; Gather and Meißner 2002; Hess 2002; Lutz 2002). Other studies describe illegal migrants as entrepreneurs (Elwert 2002), compare the life conditions of illegal migrants in different countries (Jordan et al. 1997; Cyrus et al. 2004), analyse the situation of illegal migrants in cities (Alt 1999; 2003; Anderson 2003; Bommes and Wilmes 2007) or examine the structures of illegal migration and employment for migrants from different countries of origin (Morokvasic 1994; Irek 1998; Schäfter and Schultz 1999). A further strand deals with the mutual relation between informal economies and illegal migration (Schneider and Enste 2000). Additionally, the

legal and political implications of illegality for migrants and for states are discussed in a number of texts (Alt and Bommes 2006; Eichenhofer 1999; Fodor 2001; Hailbronner 2000; Hailbronner et al. 1998; Hofherr 1999). However, the extent of illegal migration and the numbers of illegal migrants remained fairly unclear.[33]

Despite the insecurities of knowledge much of the research on illegal migration is embedded in a political debate which is largely structured in a bipolar manner. Illegal migrations and their social consequences are analysed, on the one hand, from a ›humanitarian‹ viewpoint, stressing the exploitation of illegal migrants by trafficking, human smuggling and in black economies as well as their severe life conditions resulting from their restricted access to security, housing, health and education. On the other hand, illegal migration is analysed as a challenge for migration policies concerning the control of access, the enforcement of legal regulations and appropriate forms of handling illegal migrants torn between efforts of detention and the preservation of humanitarian standards. In this field again the political and normative challenges of illegal migration tend to push migration research and many researchers to adopt positions and to place themselves within normative and/or political frameworks. Few studies attempt to grasp illegal migrations as an internal element of society and more specifically as the structural backdrop to the migration policies of the individual European welfare states and the EU as a whole (but see Cyrus 2004).

German migration research has gone through a process of differentiation as an effect of the differentiation of migration and its social effects. This involved a process of growing internationalisation of research, the involvement of researchers in international cooperation, conferences and publications. But has this also implied the emergence of new research approaches and theories in addition to those established during the 1970s and 1980s? Without any doubt the paradigm of social integration remained the guiding perspective for most of migration research in Germany after 1989/90 even when the topics of research were broadened. Two efforts, however, have been made to challenge this paradigm: (a) transnationalism started mainly from *empirical* grounds and recent international discussions (e.g. Glick-Schiller et al. 1995; Vertovec and Cohen 1999; Portes 2001), in order to argue for new concepts and theories of migration and integration; (b) the introduction of recent sociological system theory into the field of migration research started from *theoretical* grounds arguing that this approach allows a more solid understanding of migration as an internal element of the structural development of modern society.

(a) Transnationalists[34] have argued that migration research needs to redesign its more or less outdated basis in methodological nationalism. They argue that trans-

---

33 For an overview on methods, the difficulties of assessment and the insecurity of existing knowledge see Vogel 2003; AKI 2004, and the website of the Hamburgisches Welt-WirtschaftsInstitut: www.hwwi.org
34 In Germany the main protagonists are Thomas Faist 2000a; 2000b and Ludger Pries 1997; 1998; 2001a; 2008.

national structures render visible the constraints of the concept of national society which is criticised as a ›container concept‹. In the eyes of transnationalists, assimilation research is therefore characterised by a limited frame of analysis since it still conceptualises migration and its social consequences as a problem of migrants' assimilation and integration to the host society. But transnational migrants no longer orientate their modes of life towards this type of container society but rather to the structural contexts provided by emergent transnational spaces. These emergent structures cannot be grasped adequately by a nation-state concept of society. Instead we need a new concept of transnational social relations or spaces.

At the centre of this argument is the claim that more and more migrants are becoming so-called ›transmigrants‹. The life courses of migrants are more and more marked by their participation in transnational social relations. They are leading not just one- or bi-directional, but multi-directional lives. The result is the emergence of pluri-local modes of life for these migrants. According to transnationalists many migrations are becoming continuous in time and space. Transmigration and the new pluri-local social spaces are not just seen as the extension of the migrants' origin communities but as an independent social structure. According to transnationalists, as a result we can observe the emergence of combined ›bounded-nomadic‹ modes of life. Under the conditions of globalisation and the diffusion of new technologies of communication and transport these new types of transmigrants are becoming more and more relevant. Transnationalists argue that the developments identified as transnational social structures or spaces can best be grasped by research approaches which have become prominent as network analyses, theories of cumulative causation, migration systems theories and globalisation theories.

These rather straightforward positions have been confronted with a whole array of objections in the international and also the German debate. Scholars like Alba, Nee, Brubaker and Esser claim that a theoretically reflected concept of assimilation still provides the best frame for the analyses of even the most recent immigration processes in Europe or the US. They stress empirical evidence for the relevance of ongoing assimilation processes even among the most recent migrants and argue against an overestimation of ethnic economies and their transnational character. Their conclusion is: Assimilation still matters.

Without doubt transnationalist approaches (not only) in Germany have succeeded in challenging established research frameworks and reveal that globalisation and the resulting importance of international migration call for new approaches that leave behind the restrictions of the social integration paradigm, the implied ›methodological nationalism‹ (Wimmer and Glick-Schiller 2001) of the social sciences, and that account adequately for emergent transnational social structures. But at the same time the conceptual and theoretical devices have remained vague so far and concepts like ›transnational social spaces‹ and ›networks‹ need further theoretical elaboration (Bommes 2003b).

(b) The introduction of recent developments of system theoretical approaches in migration research was motivated less by empirical changes in international migration and more by the claim that the self-restriction of migration to the paradigms of social integration and social inequality had limited strongly its capacity to take fully into account the impacts of migration on the differentiated social structures of society (Bommes 1999; 2001).[35] The stress of migration research on integration and inequality always implied a silent decision in favour of the first of the two most important theoretical strands in sociology dealing with structural differentiation (Schimank 1998; Schwinn 1998). The one tradition which started from Marx and Weber later differentiated into various approaches and research schools focusing on relations of social inequality. Societal structures are interpreted in this perspective as the outcome of the unequal distribution of social resources and the resulting social dynamics and conflicts. The other tradition, linked to Marx and Weber, but also to Durkheim, Simmel and Parsons, has focused on the effects of the functional differentiation of modern society. The most vigorous theory of modern society as functionally differentiated has been elaborated in the system theory of Luhmann (1984; 1997).

The argument in favour of the latter approach can be summarised as follows. The main advantage is that the theory develops a differentiated model of modern society conceptualised as a world society. This provides a ground for observing the differentiated effects of migration on society in its various realms and avoids the restriction of analyses to the relations of social distribution and integration. It allows migration to be conceptualised as a form of social mobility institutionalised in modern society and based on its functional differentiation structure. This can be made visible by comparing it with other differentiation structures of society. It also allows us to account for the specificity of international migration by analysing the peculiarities of the political system in the modern world society differentiated in nation states. This society may be conceptualised as differentiated in various functional realms, i.e. mainly politics, the economy, law, science, education, health, religion, sports and the family, and it is argued that there are several levels of social systems, i.e. function systems, organisations, interactions and networks. It is claimed that this approach also allows us to analyse societal relations of distribution and social inequality (Bommes 2004b).[36] A central claim is that the approach may lead to an opening of the field of research in such a way that (a) the differentiated contexts in which migration occurs and has a structural impact, i.e. the various functional realms, the different types of organisations, the modes of interaction and emerging networks, can be taken fully into account – at the centre of interest is the evolution of social structures as an effect of migration; (b) migra-

---

35   What follows is heavily biased since it refers to the approach of the author and it may downplay criticisms which may deserve more attention and may overestimate the importance of the perspective.
36   This, as well as the adequacy and introduction of the approach in the field of migration research, is contended by Schwinn 1998 and Esser 2001. See also the special issue of *Geographische Revue* with contributions from Esser 2003, Pries 2003 and Bommes 2003c.

tion is ›deconstructed‹ as a kind of single and compact event – it means very different things depending on the system-specific context in which it becomes relevant and is perceived and constructed as such; (c) the notion of integration in ›the society‹ gets abandoned because no individual – not only a migrant – is integrated in *the* society because there is no such holistic unit which anyone can get integrated into. The modes of inclusion of individuals in social systems are unstable, time-limited and dependent on the differentiated forms of interdependencies between social systems.

As in the case of transnationalism the impact of this approach is unsure and open. It was echoed by scholars who had already come from a system theoretical background (e.g. Stichweh 1998; 2001; Halfmann 1998; 2005; Groh and Weinbach 2005). The approach has also been applied recently in the field of migration and education (Gomolla and Radtke 2002) and in the field of sociology of knowledge (Boswell 2009). The background rationale for the setting up of the research networks on ›migration and integration‹ of the Volkswagen Foundation has been the idea to open the field of research, i.e. to explore the effects of migration on the differentiated structures of society and to identify its structural barriers and potentials for the integration of migrants. If we distinguish between the peculiar system-theoretical approach of Luhmann and the conceptualisation of society as functionally differentiated then we see that only a limited number of scholars are willing to subscribe to system theory and its radical assumptions, whereas there is a greater willingness to accept the argument that the analytic potential of differentiation theory has been underused in migration research.

Conclusion

The expansion and differentiation of migration research in Germany mirrors the history of migration and the modes of its political handling in this country. Until the end of the 1980s migration research in Germany did not refer to a differentiated and generalised field of research firmly institutionalised in universities and other research institutes. Immediately after the war migration research was research on refugees, expellees and ethnic Germans who came to Germany as a consequence of escape and expulsion during and after the war. This type of research came to an end in the late 1950s. It was followed by the guest-worker and foreigner research during the 1970s and 1980s. Only after 1989 did migration become a differentiated and generalised research field as an internal effect of former scientific developments and as an external effect of the diversification of immigration and its impact on society.

The review of migration research during the three distinct phases shows that much of German research and its approaches are – implicitly or explicitly – embedded in the model of the German national welfare state. This model provides the framework for the dominant integration paradigm even after – or better, especially after – the decline of the nation as the defining semantic distinction and framework for integration. The nation had been the explicit framework for the integration of expellees, refugees and ethnic Germans after the war and research was clearly committed to support the political effort to promote the integration process of these migrants by means of analysing the conditions for success. This explicit and close link between research and integration policies had its foundation in the evident social catastrophe of the German nation which had to be reconstructed from the devastation of the war which affected all aspects of social life. The main difference between research during this era and subsequent migration research is the explicit and specific mode of reference to the nation, i.e. the duty to face the catastrophe and to shoulder its burdens and challenges. Subsequently, the nation more or less disappeared as an explicit frame of reference.

This was due, on the one hand, to the different careers of social researchers that engaged in the guest-worker and foreigner research of the 1970s and 1980s. They had been trained in modernised social sciences and were also largely academically socialised in the social and cultural context of 1968, at a time when the West German state based its political self-presentation on the success of the *Sozialstaat* model and its capacity for social integration. The semantics of the nation had been undergoing a process of social devaluation as a result of the National Socialist disaster and for the socio-structural reason of accelerated individualisation processes during the 1960s and 1970s. The models of analysis employed in German migration research were to a large extent embedded in the political model of society articulated by the *Sozialstaat*: individuals are expected to strive for success in the fields of education and the labour market, to maintain the family and to care for their health. Success is defined as the capacity to reproduce the achieved social status. The welfare state supports these efforts of individuals and deals with the provision of conditions that increase the likeliness of success.[37] During the 1970s this also provided the frame for the conceptualisation of the labour migrants and their families as a potential problem once it became evident that an irreversible settlement process had started. Failure of integration was conceptualised as primarily due to the social and cultural equipment of migrant families. And the absence of the nation as a frame of reference of integration provided the context for the specific meaning of cultural and ethnic differences in the political and scientific perspective on integration. The key expectation was not assimilation in national terms in order to make the immigrants Germans but acculturation or assimilation in order to master the barriers of integration in the education system, the labour and the housing market. Failure of integration referred to a problem defined by the *Sozialstaat* and not by the nation. Cultural and ethnic differences, therefore, were either perceived as hindrances to social integration which required an effort of modernisation to be carried out especially by the migrant families themselves and the *Sozialstaat*, especially the education system and social work. Or they were interpreted as a challenge, i.e. the emergence of a multicultural society requires a change in social and political habits towards more cultural

---

37 Esping-Andersen (1990) classifies this appropriately as the conservative character of the German (and more generally, continental) type of welfare state.

tolerance as a necessary precondition for the social integration of migrants. Despite all the differences described in the previous sections the common frame of German migration research dealing with labour migration in the 1960s and 1970s and its social consequences was a strong orientation to problems of social integration as defined by the *Sozialstaat*.

There was a striking homology between the perspectives of the social sciences and the *Sozialstaat*. This is underlined, on the one hand, by the weak impact of minority approaches and, on the other hand, by the fact that the important theoretical approaches in German migration research, i.e. Marxism, rational choice, system theory and the minority approach, focus on problems of social integration and social inequality. Despite all the differences between these approaches they share a notorious indeterminacy of the precise meaning of the applied concepts of social integration in society. But migration research proved to be competent to come to terms with this indeterminacy precisely because this allowed for a pragmatic operationalisation of social integration explicitly or implicitly closely linked with the political conceptualisations and semantics of integration provided by the welfare state, i.e. the German *Sozialstaat* model.

This did not imply a relation of determination between migration research and the political system in Germany. Most of the research was indeed carried out by independent research organisations and funding was provided to a large extent by independent funding institutions like the German Research Council or the Volkswagen Foundation. It was rather a relation of correspondence and mutual support between science and politics: the orientation of research to the public and political definitions of migration and integration and the effective message that migration and integration constitute important issues of the present and future, succeeded in creating political resonance and a corresponding willingness to provide the means required for research.

The emphasis on topics of social integration and social inequality was certainly firmly based in a long tradition of general sociology and its ›methodological nationalism‹. But the external orientation of research to the political framing of the problems of migration and integration allowed at the same time the distancing of irritations resulting from internal debates of general sociology and the social sciences concerning the methodological problems of the concepts of society, integration and social inequality which could have had some impact. In this way there emerged no real pressure to review the variety of theories and concepts employed and to search for new approaches. There was largely a lack of vigour to conceptualise problems in internal scientific terms. The dominant orientation to the political salience of migration diverted the attention of migration research from some of the important scientific debates. The primacy of problems was defined rather in politically than scientifically embedded frames. As a result, migration research failed to broaden its perspective. One major effect of this was that the impact of migration on the whole range of social structures of society was not fully and systematically taken into account. With a slight exaggeration we may say that migration remained a social phenomenon that affected society from the outside and needed to be adapted to the institutionalised social structures by means of social integration.

Linked with the changes since 1989, German migration research has gone through a process of differentiation as an effect of the differentiation of migration processes themselves and of their social consequences. By now, it is a firmly established field of research attracting quite a number of young academics trying to build a career. This has involved also a process of growing internationalisation of research and the involvement of researchers in international cooperation, conferences and publications. But on the whole the paradigm of social integration has remained the guiding perspective for most of migration research in Germany after 1989/90 even if the topics of research were broadened. We have referred to some new approaches in the fields of education and family and we discussed the ways in which research on migration in national welfare states since the 1990s has shown that the political system needs to be understood more as an important internal element of the structural developments linked with international migration and its social consequences for society, and less as a privileged observer and leader steering and controlling this process.

The internationalisation and especially Europeanisation of migration research during the last decade, however, seems to have had the surprising effect that it has strengthened the paradigm of integration. This is due to the fact that European countries underwent a process of mutual adaptation based on reconstruction processes affecting the relation between states and their populations. Due to severe budget problems under conditions of globalisation welfare states change the conditions of provision by redefining the relation between themselves and their population as a relation of ›rights and duties‹: social rights have been strongly linked to expectations to accept duties, i.e. to engage actively in education, to search for employment, to accept low-paid jobs etc. This ›new deal‹ includes the long-term resident migrant population as well as new immigrants (Bommes 2003a). Despite former and actual large differences between national migration policies since the late 1990s a European-wide search for models and ›best practices‹ of social integration has been established and research networks have been set up comparing national models of social integration (Heckmann and Schnapper 2003; Michalowski et al. 2008). On the European level a Network of Excellence has started dealing with ›Immigration, Integration and Social Cohesion in Europe‹. A number of research calls published in recent years underline the expectation of policy-oriented research. The result is a double-layered context for the revival and strengthening of the integration paradigm or ›the return of assimilation‹ (Brubaker 2001). Firstly, a number of individual states fear repeating what they perceive as the failures of the labour migration policies of the 1960s and 1970s. They redesign their migration policies and set up different versions of social integration programmes. In this context the demand for the social sciences, i.e. migration research, is based in the expectation to back up these programmes in two dimensions: in terms of effectiveness and of political legitimacy. Secondly, on the European level the paradigm of social integration has gained new relevance by defining it as a challenge that affects all European member states and therefore creates a demand for common European solutions. In other words the conceptualisation of the social integration of migrants as a European problem has become part of the dynamics of the self-invention of the EU and the forced expansion of its responsibilities (Boswell 2009).

It is indeed a quite surprising and ironic effect. The ›return of assimilation‹ seems now to encourage the integration and assimilation approaches which have been dominant in German migration research since the 1970s and which were formerly criticised for their parochialism and ignorance concerning especially the emergence of ethnic minority formation, the dimensions of ethnic conflict and discrimination and their political implications. There may be good reasons for this revival (Bade and Bommes 2004a; 2004b). But the implied danger of a general willingness to accept the expectation of policy orientation on an internationalised level is a scientific self-restriction of migration research. Forced to compete for research money this may lead to a repetition of former restrictions. The most important among those are: (a) the continuation of a conceptualisation of international migration which fails to conceive it as an internal form of social mobility of modern society which affects the differentiated social structures of all societal realms; this carries forward time and again a notion of migration as something that comes from outside; (b) the tendency to omit the analysis of the political system as just one part of the structural evolution of social reality which needs to be analysed like any other object of the social sciences. The requested policy orientation of research tends to subscribe to some of the myths of the political system – not least that processes of migration and integration can be steered and controlled. Social scientists are tempted to participate in the reproduction of political myth since this affirms also the relevance of the social sciences and provides social occasions which allow scientists to imagine that they take part in the shaping of society. The history of migration research in Germany should teach us that the activities of social researchers and their scientific products have indeed a number of effects on society. Research is part of the game which it analyses. This is neither wrong nor could it be changed and it can even become the subject of analyses itself. The point is: the social sciences are like any science part of society. But it makes a difference if they claim the relevance of their contributions primarily with reference to the urgency of externally, e.g. politically, economically or educationally articulated problems or to the urgency of internal, i.e. theoretical, methodological and empirical problems of the relevant scientific disciplines. Migration research defines an interdisciplinary field of research which is particularly confronted with the challenge to find the appropriate balance between external and internal perspectives of relevance. The history of migration research in Germany is a case in point that demonstrates that the constitutive political embeddedness of research certainly does not facilitate the effort to find the right balance.

References

Ackermann, Volker. 1990. Integration: Begriff, Leitbilder, Probleme. In *Neue Heimat im Westen: Vertriebene, Flüchtlinge, Aussiedler*, ed. Klaus J. Bade, 14–36. Münster: Westfälischer Heimatbund.

AKI (Arbeitsstelle interkulturelle Konflikte und gesellschaftliche Integration). 2004. *Migration und Illegalität in Deutschland, AKI-Forschungsbilanz 1.* Berlin: Wissenschaftszentrum Berlin.

Albrecht, Günter 1972. *Soziologie der geographischen Mobilität.* Stuttgart: Enke.

Alt, Jörg. 1999. *Illegal in Deutschland. Forschungsprojekt zur Lebenssituation ›illegaler‹ Migranten in Leipzig.* Karlsruhe: Von-Loeper-Literaturverlag.

Alt, Jörg. 2003. *Leben in der Schattenwelt. Problemkomplex illegale Migration.* Karlsruhe: Von-Loeper-Literaturverlag.

Alt, Jörg, and Michael Bommes, ed. 2006. *Illegalität: Grenzen und Möglichkeiten der Migrationspolitik.* Wiesbaden: VS Verlag für Sozialwissenschaften.

Anderson, Philip 2003. *›Dass Sie uns nicht vergessen...‹ Menschen in der Illegalität in München. Eine empirische Studie im Auftrag der Landeshauptstadt München.* Munich: Sozialreferat.

Angenendt, Steffen. 1992. *Ausländerforschung in Frankreich und der Bundesrepublik Deutschland. Gesellschaftliche Rahmenbedingungen und inhaltliche Entwicklungen eines aktuellen Forschungsbereiches.* Frankfurt am Main and New York: Campus.

Auernheimer, Georg. 1984. Ausländerforschung (Migrationsforschung). In *Handwörterbuch Ausländerarbeit*, ed. idem, 58–62. Weinheim and Basel: Beltz.

Auernheimer, Georg. 1988. *Der sogenannte Kulturkonflikt. Orientierungsprobleme ausländischer Jugendlicher.* Frankfurt am Main and New York: Campus.

Auernheimer, Georg. 1990. *Einführung in die interkulturelle Erziehung.* Darmstadt: Wissenschaftliche Buchgesellschaft.

Augustin, Viktor, and Hartwig Berger. 1984. *Einwanderung und Alltagskultur.* Berlin: Publica.

Bade, Klaus J. 1979. *Transnationale Migration und Arbeitsmarkt 1879–1929. Studien zur deutschen Sozialgeschichte zwischen großer Deflation und Weltwirtschaftskrise*, Bd. 1: 1879–1914 (postdoctoral thesis Erlangen 1979); internet version 2005: *Land oder Arbeit? Transnationale und interne Migration im deutschen Nordosten vor dem Ersten Weltkrieg.* www.imis.uni-osnabrueck.de/BadeHabil.pdf

Bade, Klaus J. 1987. Sozialhistorische Migrationsforschung und ›Flüchtlingsintegration‹. In *Flüchtlinge und Vertriebene in der westdeutschen Nachkriegsgeschichte*, ed. Schulze, von der Brelie-Lewien and Grebing, 126–62.

Bade, Klaus J., ed. 1990. *Neue Heimat im Westen: Vertriebene, Flüchtlinge, Aussiedler.* Münster: Westfälischer Heimatverbund.

Bade, Klaus J. 1992. *Deutsche im Ausland – Fremde in Deutschland. Migration in Geschichte und Gegenwart*. Munich: C.H. Beck.

Bade, Klaus J., ed. 1996a. *Die multikulturelle Herausforderung: Menschen über Grenzen – Grenzen über Menschen*. Munich: C.H. Beck.

Bade, Klaus J., ed. 1996b. *Migration – Ethnizität – Konflikt. Systemfragen und Fallstudien*. Osnabrück: Universitätsverlag Rasch.

Bade, Klaus J. 2000. *Europa in Bewegung. Migration vom späten 18. Jahrhundert bis zur Gegenwart*. Munich: C.H. Beck.

Bade, Klaus J. 2004. *Sozialhistorische Migrationsforschung* (Studien zur Historischen Migrationsforschung, vol. 13), ed. Michael Bommes and Jochen Oltmer. Göttingen: V&R unipress.

Bade, Klaus J., and Michael Bommes. 2000. Politische Kultur im ›Nicht-Einwanderungsland‹: Appellative Verweigerung und pragmatische Integration. In *Migrationsreport 2000: Fakten – Analysen – Perspektiven*, ed. Klaus J. Bade and Rainer Münz, 163–204. Frankfurt am Main and New York: Campus.

Bade, Klaus J., Michael Bommes, and Rainer Münz, ed. 2004. *Migrationsreport 2004. Fakten – Analysen – Perspektiven*. Frankfurt am Main and New York: Campus.

Bade, Klaus J., and Michael Bommes, ed. 2004a. *Migration – Integration – Bildung. Grundfragen und Problembereiche* (IMIS-Beiträge 23), Osnabrück: IMIS.

Bade, Klaus J., and Michael Bommes. 2004b. Einleitung. In *Migration – Integration – Bildung*, ed. idem, 7–20.

Bade, Klaus J., and Michael Bommes. 2004c. Einleitung: Integrationspotentiale in modernen europäischen Wohlfahrtsstaaten. In *Migrationsreport 2004*. ed. idem and Rainer Münz, 11–42.

Bade, Klaus J., and Jochen Oltmer, ed. 2003. *Aussiedler: Deutsche Einwanderer aus Osteuropa*. 2nd ed. Göttingen: V&R unipress.

Bade, Klaus J., Pieter C. Emmer, Leo Lucassen, and Jochen Oltmer, ed. 2007. *Enzyklopädie Migration in Europa*. 2nd ed. Paderborn: Schöningh.

Bauer, Franz J. 1982. *Flüchtlinge und Flüchtlingspolitik in Bayern 1945–1950*. Stuttgart: Klett-Cotta.

Bauer, Thomas. 1998. *Arbeitsmarkteffekte der Migration und Einwanderungspolitik: Eine Analyse für die Bundesrepublik Deutschland*. New York and Heidelberg: Physica.

Bauer, Thomas, and Klaus F. Zimmermann. 2002. *The Economics of Migration. International Library of Critical Writings in Economics* 151. Cheltenham: Edward Elgar.

Baumert, Jürgen. 2001. *PISA 2000 – Basiskompetenzen von Schülerinnen und Schülern im internationalen Vergleich*. Opladen: Leske & Budrich.

Baumert, Jürgen. 2003. *PISA 2000 – ein differenzierter Blick auf die Länder der Bundesrepublik Deutschland*. Opladen: Leske & Budrich.

Baumgartner-Karabak, Andrea, and Gisela Landesberger. 1978. *Die verkauften Bräute. Türkische Frauen zwischen Kreuzberg und Anatolien.* Reinbek bei Hamburg: Rowohlt.

Beck, Ulrich. 1986. *Risikogesellschaft.* Frankfurt am Main: Suhrkamp.

Beck-Gernsheim, Elisabeth. 2005. Türkische Bräute. Ein Blick auf die Migrationsdebatte in Deutschland. Unpublished manuscript. University of Erlangen-Nürnberg.

Bennholdt-Thomsen, Veronika. 1987. *Frauen aus der Türkei kommen in die Bundesrepublik. Zum Problem der Hausfrauisierung.* Bremen: Edition Con.

Berger, Hartwig. 1987. Arbeitswanderung im Wandel der Klassengesellschaft – Für einen Perspektivenwechsel in der Migrationsforschung. *Migration* 1: 7–20.

Berger, Hartwig. 1990. Vom Klassenkampf zum Kulturkonflikt – Wandlungen und Wendungen der westdeutschen Migrationsforschung. In *Ethnizität, Wissenschaft und Minderheiten*, ed. Eckhard J. Dittrich and Frank-Olaf Radtke, 119–38. Opladen: Westdeutscher Verlag.

Berger, Hartwig, Manfred Heßler, and Barbara Kavemann. 1978. *Brot für heute, Hunger für morgen.* Frankfurt am Main: Suhrkamp.

Bethlehem, Siegfried. 1982. *Heimatvertreibung, DDR-Flucht, Gastarbeiterzuwanderung. Wanderungsströme und Wanderungspolitik in der Bundesrepublik Deutschland.* Stuttgart: Klett-Cotta.

Bielefeld, Ulrich, Reinhard Kreissl, and Thomas Münster. 1982. *Junge Ausländer im Konflikt. Lebenssituationen und Überlebensformen.* Munich: Deutsches Jugendinstitut.

Binswanger, Karl. 1990a. Islamischer Fundamentalismus in der Bundesrepublik. Entwicklungen – Bestandsaufnahme – Ausblick. In *Im Namen Allahs. Islamische Gruppen und der Fundamentalismus in der Bundesrepublik Deutschland*, ed. Bahman Nirumand, 38–54. Cologne: Dreisam.

Binswanger, Karl. 1990b. Ökonomische Basis der Fundamentalisten. In *Im Namen Allahs. Islamische Gruppen und der Fundamentalismus in der Bundesrepublik Deutschland*, ed. Bahman Nirumand, 81–93. Cologne: Dreisam.

Binswanger, Karl. 1990c. Fundamentalisten-Filz – getrennt marschieren, vereint schlagen. In *Im Namen Allahs. Islamische Gruppen und der Fundamentalismus in der Bundesrepublik Deutschland*, ed. Bahman Nirumand, 129–48. Cologne: Dreisam.

Birg, Herwig. 2002. *Auswirkungen und Kosten der Zuwanderung nach Deutschland. Gutachten für das Bayerische Staatsministerium des Innern (Materialien des Instituts für Bevölkerungsforschung und Sozialpolitik 29).* Universität Bielefeld.

Böcker, Anita, and Dietrich Thränhardt. 2003. Erfolge und Misserfolge der Integration – Deutschland und die Niederlande im Vergleich. *Aus Politik und Zeitgeschichte* 26: 3–11.

Boehm, Max Hildebert. 1959. Gruppenbildung und Organisationswesen. In *Die Vertriebenen in Westdeutschland. Ihre Eingliederung und ihr Einfluß auf Gesellschaft, Wirtschaft, Politik und Geistesleben*, ed. Eugen Lemberg and Friedrich Edding, 521–605. Kiel: Hirt.

Bommes, Michael. 1993. *Migration und Sprachverhalten. Eine ethnographisch-sprachwissenschaftliche Fallstudie*. Wiesbaden: Deutscher Universitätsverlag.

Bommes, Michael. 1995. Migration and Ethnicity in the National Welfare State. In *Migration, Citizenship and Ethno-National Identities in the European Union*, ed. Marco Martiniello, 120–43. Aldershot: Avebury.

Bommes, Michael. 1996. Migration, Nationalstaat und Wohlfahrtsstaat – kommunale Probleme in föderalen Systemen. In *Migration – Ethnizität – Konflikt*, ed. Bade, 213–48.

Bommes, Michael. 1999. *Migration und nationaler Wohlfahrtsstaat. Ein differenzierungstheoretischer Entwurf*. Wiesbaden: Westdeutscher Verlag.

Bommes, Michael. 2001. Migration in der funktional differenzierten Gesellschaft. *Schweizerische Zeitschrift für Politikwissenschaft* 7 (2): 108–16.

Bommes, Michael. 2003a. The Shrinking Inclusive Capacity of the National Welfare State: International Migration and the Deregulation of Identity Formation. In *The Multicultural Challenge (Comparative Social Research 22)*, ed. Grete Brochmann, 43–67. Oxford: Elsevier.

Bommes, Michael. 2003b. Der Mythos des transnationalen Raumes. Oder: Worin besteht die Herausforderung des Transnationalismus für die Migrationsforschung? In *Migration im Spannungsfeld von Globalisierung und Nationalstaat (Leviathan Sonderheft 22)*, ed. Dietrich Thränhardt and Uwe Hunger, 90–116. Wiesbaden: Westdeutscher Verlag.

Bommes, Michael. 2003c. Migration in der modernen Gesellschaft. *Geographische Revue* 5 (2): 41–58.

Bommes, Michael. 2004a. Über die Aussichtslosigkeit ethnischer Konflikte in Deutschland. In *Friedens-und Konfliktforschung in Deutschland – Eine Bestandsaufnahme*, ed. Ulrich Eckern, Leonie Herwartz-Emden and Rainer-Olaf Schultze, 155–84. Wiesbaden.

Bommes, Michael. 2004b. Zur Bildung von Verteilungsordnungen in der funktional differenzierten Gesellschaft. Erläutert am Beispiel ›ethnischer Ungleichheit‹ von Arbeitsmigranten. In *Differenzierung und soziale Ungleichheit. Die zwei Soziologien und ihre Verknüpfung*, ed. Thomas Schwinn, 399–428. Frankfurt am Main: Humanities Online.

Bommes, Michael, and Andrew Geddes, ed. 2000. *Welfare and Immigration: Challenging the Borders of the Welfare State*. London: Routledge.

Bommes, Michael, and Jost Halfmann. 1994. Migration und Inklusion. Spannungen zwischen Nationalstaat und Wohlfahrtsstaat. *Kölner Zeitschrift für Soziologie und Sozialpsychologie* 46: 406–24.

Bommes, Michael, and Jost Halfmann, ed. 1998. *Migration in nationalen Wohlfahrtsstaaten. Theoretische und vergleichende Untersuchungen*. Osnabrück: Universitätsverlag Rasch.

Bommes, Michael, Kirsten Hoesch, Holger Kolb, and Uwe Hunger, ed. 2004. *Organisational Recruitment and Patterns of Migration. Interdependencies in an Integrating Europe (IMIS-Beiträge 25)*. Osnabrück: IMIS.

Bommes, Michael, and Frank-Olaf Radtke. 1993. Institutionalisierte Diskriminierung von Migrantenkindern. Die Herstellung ethnischer Differenz in der Schule. *Zeitschrift für Pädagogik* 39: 483–97.

Bommes, Michael, and Albert Scherr. 1992a. Multikulturalismus: Ein Ansatz für die Praxis der Jugendarbeit? *Deutsche Jugend* 5: 199–208.

Bommes, Michael, and Albert Scherr. 1992b. Rechtsextremismus: Ein Angebot für ganz gewöhnliche Jugendliche. In *Reaktionen Jugendlicher auf gesellschaftliche Bedrohung*, ed. Jürgen Mansel, 210–27. Weinheim: Juventa.

Bommes, Michael, and Maren Wilmes. 2007. *Menschen ohne Papiere in Köln: eine Studie zur Lebenssituation irregulärer Migranten (im Auftrag des Rates der Stadt Köln)*. Osnabrück: IMIS.

Bonin, Holger. 2001. Fiskalische Effekte der Zuwanderung nach Deutschland: eine Generationenbilanz. *Migration in Europa. Beihefte der Konjunkturpolitik* 52: 127–56.

Bonin, Holger. 2002. Eine fiskalische Gesamtbilanz der Zuwanderung nach Deutschland. *Vierteljahreshefte zur Wirtschaftsforschung* 71: 215–29.

Boos-Nünning, Ursula 1983. Die Zukunft der ausländischen Arbeitnehmer und ihrer Familien. *Soziologische Revue* 6: 129–39.

Boswell, Christina. 2009. *The Political Uses of Expert Knowledge: Immigration Policy and Social Research*. Cambridge: Cambridge University Press.

Brelie-Lewien, Doris von der. 1987. Zur Rolle der Flüchtlinge und Vertriebenen in der westdeutschen Nachkriegsgeschichte. Ein Forschungsbericht. In *Flüchtlinge und Vertriebene in der westdeutschen Nachkriegsgeschichte*, ed. Schulze, von der Brelie-Lewien and Grebing, 24–45.

Brubaker, Rogers. 2001. The Return of Assimilation? Changing Perspectives on Immigration and its Sequels in France, Germany, and the United States. *Ethnic and Racial Studies* 24 (4): 531–48.

Bukow, Wolf-Dietrich, and Roberto Llayora. 1988. *Mitbürger aus der Fremde. Soziogenese ethnischer Minoritäten*. Opladen: Westdeutscher Verlag.

Bund-Länder Kommission für Bildungsplanung und Bildungsforschung. 1980. *Förderung ausländischer Kinder und Jugendlicher. BLK-Materialien zur Bildungsplanung 2*. Bonn.

Castles, Stephen. 1984. *Here for Good. Western Europe's New Ethnic Minorities*. London: Pluto Press.

Castles, Stephen. 1987. *Migration und Rassismus in Westeuropa*. Berlin: Express-Edition.

Castles, Stephen, and Godula Kosack. 1973. *Immigrant Workers and Class Structure in Western Europe*. Oxford: Oxford University Press.

Castles, Stephen, and Mark J. Miller. 2003. *The Age of Migration: International Population Movements in the Modern World*, 3rd ed. London: Macmillan.

Cohn-Bendit, Daniel, and Thomas Schmidt. 1992. *Heimat Babylon. Das Wagnis der multikulturellen Demokratie*. Hamburg: Hoffmann und Campe.

Cyrus, Norbert. 2004. *Aufenthaltsrechtliche Illegalität in Deutschland: Sozialstrukturbildung – Wechselwirkungen – Politische Optionen. Bericht für den Sachverständigenrat für Zuwanderung und Integration*, Berlin. http://www.bamf.de/template/ zuwanderungsrat/expertisen/expertise_cyrus.pdf

Cyrus, Norbert, Franck Düvell, and Dita Vogel. 2004. Illegale Zuwanderung in Großbritannien und Deutschland: ein Vergleich. In *Migration and the Regulation of Social Integration (IMIS-Beiträge 24)*, ed. Anita Böcker, Betty de Hart and Ines Michaloskwi, 45–74. Osnabrück: IMIS.

Cyrus, Norbert, and Dita Vogel. 2002. Ausländerdiskriminierung durch Außenkontrollen im Arbeitsmarkt? Fallstudienbefunde – Herausforderungen – Gestaltungsoptionen. *Mitteilungen aus der Arbeitsmarkt- und Berufsforschung* 35: 254–70.

Czock, Heidrun. 1990. *Der Fall Ausländerpädagogik. Erziehungswissenschaftliche und bildungspolitische Codierungen der Arbeitsmigration*. Frankfurt am Main: Cooperative Verlag.

Czock, Heidrun, and Frank-Olaf Radtke. 1984. Sprache – Kultur – Identität. Die Obsessionen der Migrationspädagogen. In *Lebenszusammenhänge von Ausländern und pädagogische Problematik. Zur Kritik traditioneller Lernorte und Beispiele aktivierender Sozialarbeit*, ed. Gerd Stüwe, 37–79. Bielefeld: AJZ.

Dannenbeck, Clemens, Felicitas Eßler, and Hans Lösch. 1999. *Herkunft (er)zählt. Befunde über Zugehörigkeiten Jugendlicher*, Münster: Waxmann.

Deutscher Bundestag. 2000. *Familien ausländischer Herkunft in Deutschland. Leistungen – Belastungen – Herausforderungen. Sechster Familienbericht der Bundesregierung*, Drucksache 14/4357. Berlin.

Didzolat, Beate. 1979. *Gastarbeiter in der Bundesrepublik Deutschland. Ergebnisse des Forschungsverbundes ›Probleme der Ausländerbeschäftigung‹. Kurzfassung des Forschungsberichts*, ed. Bundesminister für Forschung und Technologie, Bonn.

Dietz, Barbara. 1998. *Jugendliche Aussiedler – Portrait einer Zuwanderergeneration*. Frankfurt am Main and New York: Campus.

Dittrich, Eckhard J., and Frank-Olaf Radtke, ed. 1990. *Ethnizität, Wissenschaft und Minderheiten*. Opladen: Westdeutscher Verlag.

Dohse, Knut. 1981. *Ausländische Arbeiter und bürgerlicher Staat. Genese und Funktion von staatlicher Ausländerpolitik und Ausländerrecht. Vom Kaiserreich bis zur Bundesrepublik Deutschland*. Königstein im Taunus: Athenaeum.

Eckert, Roland, ed. 1998. *Wiederkehr des ›Volksgeistes‹? Ethnizität, Konflikt und politische Bewältigung*. Opladen: Leske & Budrich.

Eckert, Roland, Christa Reis, and Thomas A. Wetzstein. 2000. *›Ich will halt anders sein wie die anderen!‹ Abgrenzungen, Gewalt und Kreativität bei Gruppen Jugendlicher*. Opladen: Leske & Budrich.

Eichenhofer, Eberhard, ed. 1999. *Migration und Illegalität (IMIS-Schriften, vol. 7)*, Osnabrück: Universitätsverlag Rasch.

Elias, Norbert. 1956. Problems of Involvement and Detachment. *British Journal of Sociology* 7: 226–52.

Elwert, Georg. 1982. Probleme der Ausländerintegration: Gesellschaftliche Integration durch Binnenintegration? *Kölner Zeitschrift für Soziologie und Sozialpsychologie* 34: 717–31.

Elwert, Georg. 2002. Unternehmerische Illegale. Ziele und Organisationen eines unterschätzten Typs illegaler Einwanderer. *IMIS-Beiträge* 19: 7–20.

Esping-Andersen, Gøsta. 1990. *The Three Worlds of Welfare Capitalism*. Cambridge: Polity Press.

Esser, Elke. 1982. *Ausländerinnen in der Bundesrepublik Deutschland. Eine soziologische Analyse des Eingliederungsverhaltens ausländischer Frauen*. Frankfurt am Main: Fischer.

Esser, Hartmut. 1980. *Aspekte der Wanderungssoziologie. Assimilation und Integration von Wanderern, ethnischen Gruppen und Minderheiten*. Darmstadt and Neuwied: Luchterhand.

Esser, Hartmut. 1981. Aufenthaltsdauer und die Eingliederung von Wanderern: Zur theoretischen Interpretation von soziologischen ›Variablen‹. *Zeitschrift für Soziologie* 10: 76–97.

Esser, Hartmut. 1982. Sozialräumliche Bedingungen der sprachlichen Assimilation von Arbeitsmigranten. *Zeitschrift für Soziologie* 11: 279–306.

Esser, Hartmut. 1984. Ein neues Forschungsgebiet und alte Fehler? Arbeitsmigration und ethnische Minderheiten. *Soziologische Revue* 7 (1), special issue: 151–60.

Esser, Hartmut. 1985a. Soziale Differenzierung als ungeplante Folge absichtsvollen Handelns: Der Fall der ethnischen Segmentation. *Zeitschrift für Soziologie* 14: 435–49.

Esser, Hartmut. 1985b. Zur Validität subjektiver Sprachkompetenzmessungen bei Arbeitsmigranten. In *Arbeitsmigrantenforschung in der Bundesrepublik Deutschland*, ed. Ulrich O. Sievering, 192–225. Frankfurt am Main: Haag und Herchen.

Esser, Hartmut. 1986. Ethnische Kolonien: ›Binnenintegration‹ oder gesellschaftliche Isolation? In *Segregation und Integration*, ed. Hoffmeyer-Zlotnik, 106–17.

Esser, Hartmut. 1988. Ethnische Differenzierung und moderne Gesellschaft. *Zeitschrift für Soziologie* 17: 235–48.

Esser, Hartmut. 1993. *Soziologie. Allgemeine Grundlagen.* Frankfurt am Main and New York: Campus.

Esser, Hartmut. 2001. Kulturelle Pluralisierung und strukturelle Assimilation: das Problem der ethnischen Schichtung. *Schweizerische Zeitschrift für Politikwissenschaft* 7 (2): 97–108.

Esser, Hartmut. 2004. Welche Alternativen zur ›Assimilation‹ gibt es eigentlich? In *Migration – Integration – Bildung*, ed. Bade and Bommes, 41–59.

Esser, Hartmut, and Jürgen Friedrichs, ed. 1990. *Generation und Identität: Theoretische und empirische Beiträge zur Migrationssoziologie.* Opladen: Westdeutscher Verlag.

Esser, Hartmut, Eduard Gaugler, and Karl-Heinz Neumann. 1979. *Arbeitsmigration und Integration. Sozialwissenschaftliche Grundlagen. Materialien zur Arbeitsmigration und Ausländerbeschäftigung, vol. 4.* Königstein im Taunus: Peter Hanstein.

Esser, Hartmut, and Michael Steindl. 1987. *Modellversuche zur Förderung und Eingliederung ausländischer Kinder und Jugendlicher in das Bildungssystem. Bericht über eine Auswertung.* Bonn: Köllen.

Ette, Andreas. 2003. Politische Ideen und Policy-Wandel: die ›Green Card‹ und ihre Bedeutung für die deutsche Einwanderungspolitik. In *Die deutsche ›Green Card‹: Migration von Hochqualifizierten in theoretischer und empirischer Perspektive (IMIS-Beiträge 22)*, ed. Uwe Hunger and Holger Kolb, 39–50. Osnabrück: IMIS.

Faist, Thomas. 1995. *Social Citizenship for Whom? Young Turks in Germany and Mexican Americans in the United States.* Aldershot: Avebury.

Faist, Thomas. 2000a. *The Volume and Dynamics of International Migration and Transnational Social Spaces.* Oxford: Oxford University Press.

Faist, Thomas, ed. 2000b. *Transstaatliche Räume. Politik, Wirtschaft und Kultur in und zwischen Deutschland und der Türkei.* Bielefeld: Transcript.

Faist, Thomas, Klaus Sieveking, Uwe Reim, and Stefan Sandbrink. 1999. *Ausland im Inland. Die Beschäftigung von Werkvertragsarbeitnehmern in der Bundesrepublik Deutschland.* Baden-Baden: Nomos.

Fetzer, Joel S., and J. Christopher Soper. 2005. *Muslims and the State in Britain, France and Germany.* Cambridge, MA: Cambridge University Press.

Fodor, Ralf. 2001. Rechtsgutachten zum Problemkomplex des Aufenthalts von ausländischen Staatsangehörigen ohne Aufenthaltsrecht und ohne Duldung in Deutschland. In *Rechtlos? Menschen ohne Papiere*, ed. Jörg Alt and Ralf Fodor, 125–223. Karlsruhe: Von-Loeper-Literaturverlag.

Gather, Claudia, Birgit Geissler, and Maria S. Rerrich, ed. 2002. *Weltmarkt Privathaushalt. Bezahlte Haushaltsarbeit im globalen Wandel.* Münster: Westfälisches Dampfboot.

Gather, Claudia and Hanna Meißner. 2002. Informelle Erwerbsarbeit in privaten Haushalten. Ein blinder Fleck in der Arbeitssoziologie? In *Weltmarkt Privathaushalt,* ed. Gather, Geissler and Rerrich, 120–39.

Gaugler, Eduard, and Wolfang Weber et al. 1978. *Ausländer in deutschen Industriebetrieben. Ergebnisse einer empirischen Untersuchung. Materialien zur Arbeitsmigration und Ausländerbeschäftigung,* vol. 1. Königstein im Tausnus: Peter Hanstein.

Gaugler, Eduard et. al. 1985. *Ausländerintegration in deutschen Industriebetrieben. Materialien zur Arbeitsmigration und Ausländerbeschäftigung,* vol. 6. Königstein im Taunus: Peter Hanstein.

Genosko, Joachim. 1981. Migration. *Soziologische Revue* 4: 355–66.

Gerhardt, Uta. 2000. Bilanz der soziologischen Literatur zur Integration der Vertriebenen und Flüchtlinge nach 1945. In *Vertriebene in Deutschland. Interdisziplinäre Ergebnisse und Forschungsperspektiven,* ed. Dierk Hoffmann, Marita Krauss and Michael Schwartz, 41–63. Munich: Oldenbourg.

Glick Schiller, Nina, Linda Basch, and Cristina Szanton Blanc. 1995. From Immigrant to Transmigrant: Theorizing Transnational Migration. *Anthropological Quarterly* 68: 48–63.

Gogolin, Ingrid, and Bernhard Nauck. 2000. *Migration, gesellschaftliche Differenzierung und Bildung. Resultate des Forschungsschwerpunktprogramms FABER.* Opladen: Leske & Budrich.

Gomolla, Mechthild, and Frank-Olaf Radtke. 2002. *Institutionelle Diskriminierung – Die Herstellung ethnischer Differenz in der Schule.* Opladen: Leske & Budrich.

Griese, Hartmut, ed. 1984. *Der gläserne Fremde. Bilanz und Kritik der Ausländerforschung und Ausländerpädagogik.* Opladen: Leske & Budrich.

Grieser, Helmut. 1980. *Die ausgebliebene Radikalisierung. Zur Sozialgeschichte der Kieler Flüchtlingslager im Spannungsfeld von sozialdemokratischer Landespolitik und Stadtverwaltung 1945–1950.* Wiesbaden: Steiner.

Groh, Kathrin, and Christine Weinbach. 2005. *Zur Genealogie des politischen Raums. Politische Strukturen im Wandel.* Wiesbaden: VS Verlag für Sozialwissenschaften.

Gümen, Sedef. 1996. Die sozialpolitische Konstruktion ›kultureller‹ Differenzen in der bundesdeutschen Frauen- und Migrationsforschung. *Beiträge zur feministischen Theorie und Praxis* 19 (42): 77–89.

Gunsenheimer, Antje, ed. 2007. *Grenzen. Differenzen. Übergänge: Spannungsfelder inter- und transkultureller Kommunikation.* Bielefeld: transcript.

Hailbronner, Kai. 2000. The Regularisation of Illegal Immigrants in Germany. In *Les Régularisations des Étrangers Illégaux dans l'Union Européenne* [Regularisations of Illegal Immigrants in the European Union], ed. Philippe de Bruycker, 251–71. Bruylant and Brussels: Université Libre de Bruxelles.

Hailbronner, Kai, David Martin, and Hiroshi Motomura. 1998. Immigration Admissions and Immigration Controls. In *Immigration Controls: the Search for Workable Policies in Germany and the United States*, ed. idem, 203–24. Oxford: Berghahn Books.

Halfmann, Jost. 1998. Politischer Inklusionsuniversalismus und migratorisches Exklusionsrisiko. *Berliner Journal für Soziologie* 4: 119–30.

Halfmann, Jost. 2005. World Society and Migrations: Challenges to Theoretical Concepts of Political Sociology. In *International Migration Research. Constructions, Omissions and the Promises of Interdisciplinarity*, ed. Michael Bommes and Ewa Morawska, 129–51. Aldershot: Ashgate.

Hamburger, Franz et al. 1983. *Sozialarbeit und Ausländerpolitik (Neue Praxis, Sonderheft 7)*. Neuwied: Luchterhand

Han, Petrus. 2000. *Soziologie der Migration*. Stuttgart: Lucius & Lucius.

Hanau, Peter. 1996. Das Arbeitnehmerentsendegesetz. *Neue Juristische Wochenschrift* 49: 1369–74.

Harbach, Heinz. 1976. *Internationale Schichtung und Arbeitsmigration*. Reinbek bei Hamburg: Rowohlt.

Hebenstreit, Sabine. 1984. Rückständig, isoliert, hilfsbedürftig – das Bild ausländischer Frauen in der Literatur. *Frauenforschung. Informationsdienst des Forschungsinstituts Frau und Gesellschaft* 2 (4): 24–38.

Hebenstreit, Sabine. 1986. *Frauenräume und weibliche Identität. Ein Beitrag zu einem ökologisch orientierten Perspektivenwechsel der sozialpädagogischen Arbeit mit Migrantinnen*. Berlin: Express Edition.

Heckmann, Friedrich. 1981. *Die Bundesrepublik: Ein Einwanderungsland? Zur Soziologie der Gastarbeiterbevölkerung als Einwandererminorität*. Stuttgart: Klett-Cotta.

Heckmann, Friedrich. 1986. Rezension zu Gaugler et al., Ausländerintegration in deutschen Industriebetrieben. *Kölner Zeitschrift für Soziologie und Sozialpsychologie*: 623–7.

Heckmann, Friedrich. 1992. *Ethnische Minderheiten, Volk und Nation. Soziologie inter-ethnischer Beziehungen*. Stuttgart: Enke.

Heckmann, Friedrich, and Dominique Schnapper, ed. 2003. *The Integration of Immigrants in European Societies. National Differences and Trends of Convergence*. Stuttgart: Lucius & Lucius.

Heinelt, Hubert, and Anne Lohmann. 1992. *Immigranten im Wohlfahrtsstaat am Beispiel der Rechtspositionen und Lebensverhältnisse von Aussiedlern*. Opladen: Leske & Budrich.

Heitmeyer, Wilhelm et al. 1992. *Die Bielefelder Rechtsextremismus-Studie*. Weinheim and Munich: Juventa.

Heitmeyer, Wilhelm, and Rainer Dollase, ed. 1996. *Die bedrängte Toleranz: Ethnisch-kulturelle Konflikte, religiöse Differenzen und die Gefahren politisierter Gewalt*. Frankfurt am Main: Suhrkamp.

Heitmeyer, Wilhelm, Joachim Müller, and Helmut Schröder. 1997. *Verlockender Fundamentalismus: Türkische Jugendliche in Deutschland*. Frankfurt am Main: Suhrkamp.

Herbert, Ulrich. 1986. *Geschichte der Ausländerbeschäftigung in Deutschland 1880–1980. Saisonarbeiter, Zwangsarbeiter, Gastarbeiter*. Bonn: Dietz.

Herbert, Ulrich. 2001. *Geschichte der Ausländerpolitik in Deutschland. Saisonarbeiter, Zwangsarbeiter, Gastarbeiter, Flüchtlinge*. Munich: C.H. Beck.

Herwartz-Emden, Leonie, ed. 2003. *Einwandererfamilien: Geschlechterverhältnisse, Erziehung und Akkulturation*, 2nd ed. Göttingen: V&R unipress.

Hess, Sabine. 2002. Au Pairs als informalisierte Hausarbeiterinnen. Flexibilisierung und Ethnisierung der Versorgungsarbeiten. In *Weltmarkt Privathaushalt*, ed. Gather, Geissler and Rerrich, 103–19.

Hill, Paul Bernhard. 1984. *Determinanten der Eingliederung von Arbeitsmigranten*. Königstein im Taunus: Peter Hanstein.

Hochstadt, Steven. 2003. Die Bedeutung der neuen Arbeitsmigration für die Institutionen und die Arbeitskräftepolitik in der Bauwirtschaft. In *Migration im Wettbewerbsstaat*, ed. Uwe Hunger and Bernhard Santel, 119–52. Opladen: Leske & Budrich.

Hoffmann-Nowotny, Hans-Joachim. 1970. *Migration. Ein Beitrag zu einer soziologischen Erklärung*. Stuttgart: Enke.

Hoffmann-Nowotny, Hans-Joachim. 1973. *Soziologie des Fremdarbeiterproblems. Eine theoretische und empirische Analyse am Beispiel der Schweiz*. Stuttgart: Enke.

Hoffmann-Nowotny, Hans-Joachim. 1998. Weltgesellschaft, internationale Migration und Wohlfahrtssysteme. In *Migration in nationalen Wohlfahrtsstaaten*, ed. Bommes and Halfmann, 297–302.

Hoffmann-Nowotny, Hans-Joachim, and Karl-Otto Hondrich, ed. 1982. *Ausländer in der Bundesrepublik Deutschland und in der Schweiz*. Frankfurt am Main and New York: Campus.

Hoffmann, Dierk, Martina Krauss, and Michael Schwartz, ed. 2000. *Vertriebene in Deutschland. Interdisziplinäre Ergebnisse und Forschungsperspektiven*. Sondernummer der Schriftenreihe der Vierteljahreshefte für Zeitgeschichte. Munich: Oldenbourg.

Hoffmeyer-Zlotnik, Jürgen, ed. 1986. *Qualitative Methoden der Datenerhebung in der Arbeitsmigrantenforschung*. Mannheim: Forschung, Raum und Gesellschaft.

Hofherr, Karin. 1999. *Die illegale Beschäftigung ausländischer Arbeitnehmer und ihre arbeitsvertragsrechtlichen Folgen.* Frankfurt am Main: Peter Lang.

Hohmann, Manfred. 1982. *Unterricht mit ausländischen Kindern.* Munich: Oldenbourg.

Hollifield, James F. 1992. *Immigrants, Markets and States: The Political Economy of Postwar Europe.* Cambridge, MA: Harvard University Press.

Hunger, Uwe. 2000a. Temporary Transnational Labour Migration in an Integrating Europe: the Challenge to the German Welfare State. In *Welfare and Immigration*, ed. Bommes and Geddes, 189–208.

Hunger, Uwe. 2000b. *Der ›rheinische Kapitalismus‹ in der Defensive. Eine komparative Policy-Analyse zum Paradigmenwechsel in den Arbeitsmarktbeziehungen am Beispiel der Bauwirtschaft.* Baden-Baden: Nomos.

Hunger, Uwe, and Bernhard Santel, ed. 2003. *Migration im Wettbewerbsstaat.* Opladen: Leske & Budrich.

IAB, ed. 1982. *Materialien zur Ausländerbeschäftigung.* Beiträge zur Arbeitsmarkt- und Berufsforschung. Nürnberg: Institut für Arbeitsmarkt- und Berufsforschung (IAB).

IAB, ed. 1982–9. *Ausländische Arbeitnehmer. Literaturdokumentation zur Arbeitsmarkt- und Berufsforschung.* Beiträge zur Arbeitsmarkt- und Berufsforschung, Nürnberg: Institut für Arbeitsmarkt- und Berufsforschung (IAB).

Irek, Malgorzata. 1998. *Der Schmugglerzug: Warschau – Berlin – Warschau. Materialien einer Feldforschung.* Berlin: Das Arabische Buch.

Jonker, Gerdien. 1997. Die islamischen Gemeinden in Berlin zwischen Integration und Segregation. In *Zuwanderung und Stadtentwicklung (Leviathan-Sonderband 17)*, ed. Harald Häußermann and Ingrid Oswald, 347–64. Opladen and Wiesbaden: Westdeutscher Verlag.

Jordan, Ulrike. 1996. Operation Stork: Kinder im Kontext der Britischen Flüchtlingspolitik. In *Die Flüchtlingsfrage in der deutschen Nachkriegsgesellschaft*, ed. Sylvia Schraut and Thomas Grosser, 141–60. Mannheim: Palatium.

Jordan, Bill, Dita Vogel, and Estrella Kylza. 1997. Leben und Arbeiten ohne regulären Aufenthaltsstatus. Ein Vergleich von London und Berlin am Beispiel brasilianischer Migranten und Migrantinnen. In *Zuwanderung und Stadtentwicklung (Leviathan-Sonderband 17)*, ed. Harald Häußermann and Ingrid Oswald, 215–31. Opladen and Wiesbaden: Westdeutscher Verlag.

Junker, Abbo, and Julia Wichmann. 1996. Das Arbeitnehmer-Entsendegesetz – doch ein Verstoß gegen europäisches Recht. *Neue Zeitschrift für Arbeitsrecht* 13: 502–12.

Kaiser, Hanna Maria. 1977. *Die Auswirkungen der sektoralen Produktions- und Produktivitätsentwicklung auf den Bedarf an ausländischen Arbeitskräften.* Bonn: Eichholz Verlag.

Kalpaka, Anita. 1986. *Handlungsfähigkeit statt Integration. Schulische und außerschulische Lebensbedingungen und Entwicklungsmöglichkeiten griechischer Jugendlicher*. Munich: Deutsches Jugendinstitut.

Kalter, Frank, and Nadia Granato. 2004. Sozialer Wandel und strukturelle Assimilation in der Bundesrepublik. Empirische Befunde und Mikrodaten der amtlichen Statistik. In *Migration – Integration – Bildung*, ed. Bade and Bommes, 61–81.

Karasan-Dirks, Sabine. 1980. *Die türkische Familie zwischen gestern und morgen (Mitteilungen des Deutschen Orient-Instituts 13)*. Hamburg.

Karasek-Langer, Alfred. 1959. Volkstum in der Wandlung. In *Die Vertriebenen in Westdeutschland*, ed. Lemberg and Edding, 606–94.

Kelek, Necla. 2005. *Die fremde Braut*. Cologne: Kiepenheuer & Witsch.

Klausen, Jytte. 2005. Muslim Elites in Europe. Manuscript American Academy of Sciences. Berlin and Brandeis University, Waltham, MA.

Kleff, Hans-Günther. 1984. *Vom Bauern zum Industriearbeiter: Zur kollektiven Lebensgeschichte der Arbeitsmigranten aus der Türkei*. Ingelheim: Manthano.

Kleger, Heinz, ed. 1997. *Transnationale Staatsbürgerschaft*. Frankfurt am Main and New York: Campus.

Kolb, Holger. 2004. *Einwanderung zwischen wohlverstandenem Eigeninteresse und symbolischer Politik. Das Beispiel der deutschen ›Green Card‹*. Münster: Lit.

König, Peter, Günther Schultze, and Rita Wessel. 1986. *Situation der ausländischen Arbeitnehmer und ihrer Familienangehörigen in der Bundesrepublik Deutschland – Repräsentativuntersuchung '85'. Forschungsbericht 133*. Bonn: Bundesminister für Arbeit und Sozialordnung.

Körner, Hellmut. 1976. *Der Zustrom von Arbeitskräften in die Bundesrepublik Deutschland 1950–1972. Auswirkungen auf die Funktionsweise des Arbeitsmarktes*. Frankfurt am Main and Munich: Peter Lang.

Korte, Herrmann. 1980. Forschungsverbund ›Probleme der Ausländerbeschäftigung‹, gefördert vom Bundesminister für Forschung und Technologie. Erfahrungsbericht des Leitinstituts. Manuscript. Rheda-Wiedenbrück.

Korte, Herrmann, and Alfred Schmidt. 1983. *Migration und ihre sozialen Folgen. Förderung der Gastarbeiterforschung durch die Stiftung Volkswagenwerk 1974–1981*. Göttingen: Vandenhoeck & Ruprecht.

Kreckel, Reinhart. 1989. Ethnische Differenzierung und moderne Gesellschaft. Kritische Anmerkungen zu Hartmut Essers Aufsatz. *Zeitschrift für Soziologie* 18: 162–67.

Kristen, Cornelia, and Nadia Granato. 2004. Bildungsinvestitionen in Migrantenfamilien. In *Migration – Integration – Bildung*, ed. Bade and Bommes, 123–41.

Kühn, Heinz. 1979. *Stand und Weiterentwicklung der Integration der ausländischen Arbeitnehmer und ihrer Familien in der Bundesrepublik Deutschland. Memorandum des Beauftragten der Bundesregierung*. Bonn.

Kunstamt Kreuzberg. 1981. *Morgens Deutschland – Abends Türkei*. Berlin: Kunstamt Kreuzberg.

Kurz, Ursula. 1965. Partielle Anpassung und Kulturkonflikt. Gruppenstruktur und Anpassungsdispositionen in einem italienischen Gastarbeiter-Lager. *Kölner Zeitschrift für Soziologie und Sozialpsychologie* 17: 814–32.

Lazear, Edard P. 2000. Economic Imperialism. *Quarterly Journal of Economics* 115: 99–146.

Leggewie, Claus. 1990. *Multi Kulti – Spielregeln für die Vielvölkerrepublik*. Berlin: Rotbuch.

Leggewie, Claus. 1993a. Der Islam im Westen. Zwischen Neo-Fundamentalismus und Euro-Islam. *Kölner Zeitschrift für Soziologie und Sozialpsychologie, special issue* 33: 271–91.

Leggewie, Claus. 1993b. *Alhambra. Der Islam im Westen*. Reinbek bei Hamburg: Rowohlt.

Lemberg, Eugen, ed. 1950a. *Die Entstehung eines neuen Volkes aus Binnendeutschen und Ostvertriebenen. Untersuchungen zum Strukturwandel von Land und Leuten unter dem Einfluß des Vertriebenen-Zustromes*. Marburg: Elwert.

Lemberg, Eugen. 1950b. *Geschichte des Nationalismus in Europa*. Stuttgart: Curt E. Schwab.

Lemberg, Eugen. 1952. *Volk in der Wanderung. Einheimische und Vertriebene in der werdenden Volksordnung*. Dortmund: Ardey.

Lemberg, Eugen, and Friedrich Edding, ed. 1959. *Die Vertriebenen in Westdeutschland. Ihre Eingliederung und ihr Einfluß auf Gesellschaft, Wirtschaft, Politik und Geistesleben*, 3 vols. Kiel: Hirt.

Lemberg, Eugen, Gotthold Rhode, and Herbert Schlenger. 1959. Voraussetzungen und Zusammenhänge des deutschen Vertriebenenproblems. In *Die Vertriebenen in Westdeutschland*, ed. Lemberg and Edding, 8–37.

Lepsius, M. Reiner. 1990. *Interessen, Ideen, Institutionen*. Opladen: Westdeutscher Verlag.

Lindner, Rolf. 1990. *Die Entdeckung der Stadtkultur: Soziologie aus der Erfahrung der Reportage*. Frankfurt am Main: Suhrkamp.

Loeffelholz, Hans Dietrich von, and Ulrich Heilemann. 1998. *Ökonomische und fiskalische Implikationen der Zuwanderung nach Deutschland*. RWI-Papiere 52. Essen.

Loeffelholz, Hans Dietrich von, Thomas Bauer, John Haisken-DeNew, and Christoph Schmidt. 2004. Fiskalische Kosten der Zuwanderer. Gutachten für den Sachverständigenrat für Zuwanderung und Integration. http://www.bamf.de/template/zuwanderungsrat/ expertisen/expertise_loeffelholz.pdf.

Lucassen, Jan, and Leo Lucassen, ed. 1997. *Migration, Migration History, History. Old Paradigms and New Perspectives*. Bern: Peter Lang.

Luhmann, Niklas. 1984. *Soziale Systeme*. Frankfurt am Main: Suhrkamp.

Luhmann, Niklas. 1997. *Die Gesellschaft der Gesellschaft*. Frankfurt am Main: Suhrkamp.

Lutz, Burkhart. 1984. *Der kurze Traum immerwährender Prosperität*. Frankfurt am Main and New York: Campus.

Lutz, Helma. 2002. Transnationalität im Haushalt. In *Weltmarkt Privathaushalt*, ed. Gather, Geissler and Rerrich, 86–102.

Mackert, Jürgen. 1999. *Kampf um Zugehörigkeit: Nationale Staatsbürgerschaft als Modus sozialer Schließung*. Wiesbaden: Westdeutscher Verlag.

Mackert, Jürgen, and Hans Peter Müller, ed. 2000. *Citizenship – Soziologie der Staatsbürgerschaft*. Wiesbaden: Westdeutscher Verlag.

Mehrländer, Ursula, Carsten Ascheberg, and Jörg Ueltzhöffer. 1996. *Situation ausländischer Arbeitnehmer und ihrer Familienangehörigen in der Bundesrepublik Deutschland – Repräsentativuntersuchung '95'. Forschungsbericht 263*. Bonn: Bundesminister für Arbeit und Sozialordnung.

Mehrländer, Ursula, and R. Hoffmann. 1981. *Situation der ausländischen Arbeitnehmer und ihrer Familienangehörigen in der Bundesrepublik Deutschland – Repräsentativuntersuchung '80'. Forschungsbericht 50*. Bonn: Bundesminister für Arbeit und Sozialordnung.

Meillassoux, Claude. 1980. Gegen eine Ethnologie der Arbeitsmigration in Westeuropa. In ›*Dritte Welt*‹ *in Europa. Probleme der Arbeitsimmigration*, ed. Jochen Blaschke, 53–59. Frankfurt am Main: Syndikat.

Michalowski, Ines, Uwe Hunger, Can M. Aybek and Andreas Ette, ed. 2008. *Migrations- und Integrationsprozesse in Europa. Vergemeinschaftung oder nationalstaatliche Lösungswege?* Wiesbaden: VS Verlag für Sozialwissenschaften.

Miksch, Jürgen, ed. 1983. *Multikulturelles Zusammenleben. Theologische Erfahrungen*. Frankfurt am Main: Lehmbeck.

Morokvasic, Mirjana. 1994. Pendeln statt auswandern. Das Beispiel der Polen. In *Wanderungsraum Europa, Menschen und Grenzen in Bewegung*, ed. idem and Hedwig Rudolph, 166–87. Berlin: Edition Sigma.

Müller, Karl Valentin. 1956. *Heimatvertriebene Jugend. Eine soziologische Studie zum Problem der Soziltüchtigkeit des Nachwuchses der heimatvertriebenen Jugend*. Würzburg: Holzner-Verlag.

Nahm, Peter Paul. 1959. Der Wille zur Eingliederung und seine Förderung. In *Die Vertriebenen in Westdeutschland*, ed. Lemberg and Edding, 145–55.

Nassehi, Armin. 1990. Zum Funktionswandel von Ethnizität im Prozess gesellschaftlicher Modernisierung. Ein Beitrag zur Theorie funktionaler Differenzierung. *Soziale Welt* 41: 261–82.

Nauck, Bernhard. 1985. *Arbeitsmigration und Familienstruktur. Eine Analyse der mikrosozialen Folgen von Migrationsprozessen*. Frankfurt am Main and New York: Campus.

Nauck, Bernhard. 1988. Sozialstrukturelle und individualistische Migrationstheorien. *Kölner Zeitschrift für Soziologie und Sozialpsychologie* 40: 15–39.

Nauck, Bernhard, ed. 2001. *Immigrant and Ethnic Minority Families (Journal of Comparative Family Studies*, special issue).

Nauck, Bernhard. 2002. *Solidarpotentiale von Migrantenfamilien.* Expertise. Bonn: Friedrich-Ebert-Stiftung.

Nikolinakos, Marios. 1972. *Politische Ökonomie der Gastarbeiterfrage. Migration und Kapitalismus.* Reinbek bei Hamburg: Rowohlt.

Oltmer, Jochen. 2005. *Migration und Politik in der Weimarer Republik.* Göttingen: Vandenhoeck & Ruprecht.

Oltmer, Jochen. 2010. *Migration im 19. und 20. Jahrhundert (Enzyklopädie deutscher Geschichte, vol. 86).* Munich: Oldenbourg Wissenschaftsverlag.

Otto, Karl A. 1990. Aussiedler und Aussiedlerpolitik im Spannungsfeld von Menschenrechten und Kaltem Krieg. Historische, politisch-moralische und rechtliche Aspekte der Aussiedlerpolitik. In *Westwärts-Heimwärts. Aussiedlerpolitik zwischen ›Deutschtümelei‹ und Verfassungsauftrag*, ed. idem, 11–68. Bielefeld: AJZ.

Otyakmaz, Berrin Özlem. 1995. *Auf allen Stühlen. Das Selbstverständnis junger türkischer Migrantinnen in Deutschland.* Cologne: ISP.

Page Moch, Leslie. 1992. *Moving Europeans. Migration in Western Europe since 1650.* Bloomington, IN: Indiana University Press.

Parnreiter, Christof. 2000. Theorien und Forschungsansätze zu Migration. In *Internationale Migration: Die globale Herausforderung des 21. Jahrhunderts?* ed. Karl Husa, Christof Parnreiter and Ingrid Stacher, 25–52. Frankfurt am Main: Brandes und Apsel.

Parnreiter, Christof. 2001. Die Mär von den Lohndifferentialen. Migrationstheoretische Überlegungen am Beispiel Mexikos. *IMIS-Beiträge* 17: 55–89.

Petersen, Andrea. 1985. *Ehre und Scham. Das Verhältnis der Geschlechter in der Türkei.* Berlin: Express Edition.

Pfeil, Elisabeth. 1952. Soziologische und psychologische Aspekte der Vertreibung. In *Europa und die deutschen Flüchtlinge*, ed. Institut zur Förderung öffentlicher Angelegenheiten, 40–71. Frankfurt am Main: Institut zur Förderung öffentlicher Angelegenheiten.

Piore, Michael J. 1979. *Birds of Passage. Migrant Labour and Industrial Societies.* Cambridge: Cambridge University Press.

Pischke, Jörn-Steffen, and Johannes Velling. 1997. Employment Effects of Immigration to Germany: An Analysis Based on Local Labour Markets. *Review of Economics and Statistics* 79: 594–604.

Pöhlmann, Hartmut. 1974. *Wachstumseffekte und wachstumspolitische Beurteilung der Gastarbeiterbeschäftigung in der Bundesrepublik Deutschland.* Würzburg: Schmitt & Meyer.

Portes, Alejandro. 2001. *Transnational Entrepreneurs: the Emergence and Determinants of an Alternative Form of Immigrant Economic Adaptation.* ESRC Transnational Communites Research Programme Working Paper WPTC-01-05, University of Oxford.

Potts, Lydia. 1990. *The World Labour Market. A History of Migration.* London: Zed Books.

Pries, Ludger. 1997. Neue Migration im transnationalen Raum. In *Transnationale Migration (Soziale Welt, Sonderband 12)*, ed. idem, 15–44. Baden-Baden: Nomos.

Pries, Ludger. 1998. Transnationale soziale Räume. In *Perspektiven der Weltgesellschaft*, ed. Ulrich Beck, 55–86. Frankfurt am Main: Suhrkamp.

Pries, Ludger. 2001a. The Disruption of Social and Geographic Space. Mexican-US Migration and the Emergence of Transnational Social Spaces. *International Sociology* 16: 55–74.

Pries, Ludger. 2003. Transnationalismus, Migration und Inkorporation. Herausforderungen an Raum- und Sozialwissenschaften. *Geographische Revue* 5 (2): 23–40.

Pries, Ludger, ed. 2008. *Rethinking Transnationalism: the Meso-Link of Organisations.* London and New York: Routledge.

Proske, Matthias, and Frank-Olaf Radtke. 1999. Islamischer Fundamentalismus und jugendliche Gewaltbereitschaft. *Neue Sammlung* 39 (1): 47–61.

Puskeppeleit, Jürgen, and Dietrich Thränhardt. 1990. *Vom betreuten Ausländer zum gleichberechtigten Bürger.* Freiburg im Breisgau: Lambertus.

Radtke, Frank-Olaf 1990. Multikulti: Das Gesellschaftsdesign der 90er Jahre? *Informationsdienst zur Ausländerarbeit* 4: 27–34.

Rautenberg, Hans-Werner. 1997. Die Wahrnehmung von Flucht und Vertreibung in der deutschen Nachkriegsgeschichte bis heute. *Aus Politik und Zeitgeschichte* 53: 34–46.

Rhode, Gotthold. 1959. Phasen und Formen der Massenzwangswanderung in Europa. In *Die Vertriebenen in Westdeutschland*, ed. Lemberg and Edding, 17–36.

Rogge, Heinrich. 1959. Vertreibung und Eingliederung im Spiegel des Rechts. In *Die Vertriebenen in Westdeutschland*, ed. Lemberg and Edding, 174–245.

Santel, Bernhard. 1998. Töten für den Islam? Eine holzschnittartige Studie über junge Türken in Deutschland. *Frankfurter Allgemeine Zeitung*, 13 July: 14.

Schäfter, Elke, and Susanne Schultz. 1999. Putzen, was sonst? Latinas in Berlin: Bezahlte Hausarbeit als Arbeitsmarkt für Migrantinnen. In *Migrationen. Lateinamerika Analysen und Berichte*, no. 23, ed. Karin Gabbert, 97–110. Bad Honnef: Horlemann.

Schelsky, Helmut. 1950. Die Flüchtlingsfamilie. *Kölner Zeitschrift für Soziologie und Sozialpsychologie* 3: 159–78.

Schelsky, Helmut. 1953. *Wandlungen der deutschen Familie in der Gegenwart*. Dortmund: Ardey.

Schier, Siegfried. 1981. *Die Aufnahme und Eingliederung von Flüchtlingen und Vertriebenen in der Hansestadt*. Lübeck and Kiel: Schmidt-Römhild.

Schiffauer, Werner. 1983. *Die Gewalt der Ehre*. Frankfurt am Main: Suhrkamp.

Schiffauer, Werner. 1984. Religion und Identität. Eine Fallstudie zum Problem der Reislamisierung bei Arbeitsmigranten. *Schweizerische Zeitschrift für Soziologie* 10: 485–516.

Schiffauer, Werner. 1991. *Die Migranten aus Subay. Türken in Deutschland: Eine Ethnographie*. Stuttgart: Klett-Cotta.

Schiffauer, Werner. 2000. *Die Gottesmänner. Türkische Islamisten in Deutschland*. Frankfurt am Main: Suhrkamp.

Schiffauer, Werner. 2004. Die Islamische Gemeinschaft Milli Görüş – ein Lehrstück zum verwickelten Zusammenhang von Migration, Religion und sozialer Integration. In *Migrationsreport 2004*, ed. Bade, Bommes and Münz, 67–96.

Schimank, Uwe. 1998. Funktinale Differenzierung und soziale Ungleichheit: die zwei Gesellschaftstheorien und ihre konflikttheoretische Verknüpfung. In *Konflikt in modernen Gesellschaften*, ed. Hans-Joachim Giegel, 61–88. Frankfurt am Main: Suhrkamp.

Schmalz-Jacobsen, Cornelia, and Georg Hansen, ed. 1995. *Ethnische Minderheiten in der Bundesrepublik Deutschland. Ein Lexikon*. Munich: C.H. Beck.

Schneider, Friedrich, and Dominik Enste. 2000. *Schattenwirtschaft und Schwarzarbeit. Umfang, Ursachen, Wirkungen und wirtschaftspolitische Empfehlungen*. Munich and Vienna: Oldenbourg.

Schöttes, Martina, and Annette Treibel. 1997. Frauen – Flucht – Migration. In *Transnationale Migration (Soziale Welt, Sonderband 12)*, ed. Ludger Pries, 85–117. Baden-Baden: Nomos.

Schrader, Achim, Bruno Nikles, and Hartmut Griese. 1976. *Die zweite Generation: Sozialisation und Akkulturation ausländischer Kinder in der Bundesrepublik*. Kronberg: Athenäum.

Schraut, Sylvia. 1996. »Make the Germans do it« – Die Flüchtlingsaufnahme in der amerikanischen Besatzungszone. In *Die Flüchtlingsfrage in der deutschen Nachkriegsgesellschaft*, ed. idem and Thomas Grosser, 119–40. Mannheim: Palatium.

Schulze, Rainer, Doris von der Brelie-Lewien, and Helga Grebing. ed. 1987. *Flüchtlinge und Vertriebene in der westdeutschen Nachkriegsgeschichte. Bilanzierung der Forschung und Perspektiven künftiger Forschungsarbeit*, Hildesheim: Lax.

Schwinn, Thomas. 1998. Soziale Ungleichheit und funktionale Differenzierung. Wiederaufnahme einer Diskussion. *Zeitschrift für Soziologie* 27: 3–17.

Seifert, Wolfgang. 1995. *Die Mobilität der Migranten. Die berufliche, ökonomische und soziale Stellung ausländischer Arbeitnehmer in der Bundesrepublik.* Berlin: Express Edition.

Seifert, Wolfgang. 2000. *Geschlossene Grenzen – offene Gesellschaften? Migrations- und Integrationsprozesse in westlichen Industrienationen.* Frankfurt am Main and New York: Campus.

Sievering, Ulrich O., ed. 1985. *Arbeitsmigrantenforschung in der Bundesrepublik Deutschland.* Frankfurt am Main: Haag und Herchen.

Soysal, Yasemin. 1994. *Limits of Citizenship. Migrants and Postnational Membership in Europe.* Chicago: University of Chicago Press.

Steinbach, Anja. 2004a. Solidarpotentiale in Migrantenfamilien. In *Familie in der Einwanderungsgesellschaft (Beiträge der Akademie für Migration und Integration, vol. 8)*, ed. Marianne Krüger-Potratz, 39–48. Göttingen: Vandenhoeck & Ruprecht.

Steinbach, Anja. 2004b. *Soziale Distanz. Ethnische Grenzziehung und die Eingliederung von Zuwanderern in Deutschland.* Wiesbaden: VS Verlag für Sozialwissenschaften.

Steinbach, Anja, and Bernhard Nauck. 2004. Intergenerationale Transmission von kulturellem Kapital in Migrantenfamilien. Zur Erklärung von ethnischen Unterschieden im deutschen Bildungssystem. *Zeitschrift für Erziehungswissenschaft* 7: 20–32.

Steinert, Johannes-Dieter. 1986. *Flüchtlinge, Vertriebene und Aussiedler in Niedersachsen: Eine annotierte Bibliographie.* Osnabrück: Kommisionsverlag H.Th. Wenner.

Stichweh, Rudolph. 1998. Migration, nationale Wohlfahrtsstaaten und die Entstehung der Weltgesellschaft. In *Migration in nationalen Wohlfahrtsstaaten*, ed. Bommes and Halfmann, 49–61.

Stichweh, Rudolph. 2001. Systemtheorie der Exklusion. Zum Konflikt von Wohlfahrtsstaatlichkeit und Globalisierung der Funktionssysteme. In *Die Weltgesellschaft. Soziologische Analysen*, idem, 85–102. Frankfurt am Main: Suhrkamp.

Stölting, Wilfried. 1980. *Die Zweisprachigkeit jugoslawischer Schüler in der Bundesrepublik Deutschland.* Wiesbaden: Harrassowitz.

Straube, Hanna. 1988. *Türkisches Leben in der Bundesrepublik.* Frankfurt am Main and New York: Campus.

Straubhaar, Thomas. 1996. Schutzzoll auf Arbeit: das neue Gesicht des Protektionismus. *List Forum für Wirtschafts- und Finanzpolitik* 22 (3): 209–21.

Stüwe, Ger. 1982. *Türkische Jugendliche: Eine Untersuchung in Berlin-Kreuzberg.* Bensheim: päd. extra buchverlag.

Sywottek, Arnold. 1989. Flüchtlingseingliederung in Westdeutschland. Stand und Probleme der Forschung. *Aus Politik und Zeitgeschichte* 51: 38–46.

Tenbruck, Friedrich H. 1989. *Die kulturellen Grundlagen der Gesellschaft. Der Fall der Moderne*. Opladen: Westdeutscher Verlag.

Tenbruck, Friedrich H. 1992. Was war der Kulturvergleich, ehe es den Kulturvergleich gab? In *Zwischen den Kulturen? (Soziale Welt Sonderband 8)*, ed. Joachim Matthes, 13–35. Göttingen: Schwartz.

Tertilt, Herrmann. 1996. *Turkish Power Boys. Ethnographie einer Jugendbande*. Frankfurt am Main: Suhrkamp.

Thomas, William I., and Florian Znaniecki. 1958. *The Polish Peasant in Europe and America* (1st ed. 1918), New York: Knopf.

Thränhardt, Dietrich. 1984. Ausländer als Objekt deutscher Interessen und Ideologien. In *Der gläserne Fremde*, ed. Griese, 115–32.

Thränhardt, Dietrich. 1998. *Regionale Ansätze und Schwerpunktaufgaben der Integration von Migrantinnen und Migranten in Nordrhein-Westfalen*. Studie im Auftrag des Ministeriums für Umwelt, Raumordnung und Landwirtschaft des Landes Nordrhein-Westfalen. Münster: Institut für Politikwissenschaft der Universität Münster.

Thränhardt, Dietrich, Renate Dieregsweiler, and Bernhard Santel. 1994. *Ausländerinnen und Ausländer in Nordrhein-Westfalen. Die Lebenslage der Menschen aus den ehemaligen Anwerbeländern und die Handlungsmöglichkeiten der Politik*. Landessozialbericht vol. 6, ed. Ministerium für Arbeit, Gesundheit und Soziales des Landes Nordrhein-Westfalen.

Tietze, Nikola. 2001. *Islamische Identitäten. Formen muslimischer Religiösität junger Männer in Deutschland und Frankreich*. Hamburg: Hamburger Edition.

Trabold, Harald, and Parvati Trübswetter. 2003. Beschäftigungs- und Lohneffekte der Migration. In *Migration. Potential und Effekte für den deutschen Arbeitsmarkt*, ed. Herbert Brücker, Harald Trabold, Parvati Trübswetter and Christian Weise, 101–51. Baden-Baden: Nomos.

Treibel, Annette. 1988. *Engagement und Distanzierung in der westdeutschen Ausländerforschung. Eine Untersuchung ihrer soziologischen Beiträge*. Stuttgart: Enke.

Treibel, Annette. 1990. *Migration in modernen Gesellschaften*. Weinheim and Munich: Juventa.

Ulbrich, Stefan, ed. 1991. *Multikultopia. Gedanken zur multikulturellen Gesellschaft*. Vilsbiburg: Arun-Verlag.

Vertovec, Steven, and Robin Cohen, ed. 1999. *Migration, Diasporas and Transnationalism*. Cheltenham and Northampton, MA: Elgar.

Vink, Jan. 1977–82. *Ausländische Arbeiter und ihre Familien*. Frankfurt am Main: Institut für Sozialarbeit und Sozialpädagogik.

Vogel, Dita. 2003. Illegaler Aufenthalt. Konzepte, Forschungszugänge, Realitäten, Optionen. In *Migration im Spannungsfeld von Globalisierung und National-*

staat *(Leviathan Sonderheft 22),* ed. Dietrich Thränhardt and Uwe Hunger, 161–79. Wiesbaden: Westdeutscher Verlag.

Weidacher, Alois. 1981/2. *Ausländische Arbeiterfamilien, Kinder und Jugendliche. Situatuionsanalysen und Maßnahmen,* 2 vols. Munich: Deutsches Jugendinstitut.

Weidacher, Alois, and Andres Lopez-Blasco. 1982. *Ausländerpolitik und Integrationsforschung in der Bundesrepublik Deutschland. Eine Darstellung wichtigster Ergebnisse mit Auswahlbibliographie.* Munich: Deutsches Jugendinstitut.

Weißköppel, Cordula. 2001. *Ausländer und Kartoffeldeutsche. Identitätsperformanz im Alltag einer gemischten Realschulklasse.* Weinheim: Juventa.

Wilpert, Czarina. 1984. International Migration and Ethnic Minorities. New Fields for Post-War Sociology in the Federal Republic of Germany. *Current Sociology* 22: 305–52.

Wimmer, Andreas, and Nina Glick-Schiller. 2001. Methodological Nationalism and Beyond. Nation-State Building, Migration and the Social Sciences. Paper presented at the workshop on ›Transnational Migration: Comparative Perspectives‹, June, Princeton University.

Worthmann, Georg. 2001. Industrielle Beziehungen und politische Steuerung in der deutschen Bauwirtschaft: eine empirische Untersuchung zur Normgenese der deutschen Entsenderegulierung. Diss. Universität Duisburg.

Worthmann, Georg, and Klaus Zühlke-Robinet. 2003. Neue Arbeitsmigration im Baugewerbe und ihre Regulierung – Das Arbeitnehmer-Entsendegesetz als Instrument zur Re-Regulierung des Bauarbeitsmarktes. In *Migration im Wettbewerbsstaat,* ed. Hunger and Santel, 91–118.

Zimmermann, Klaus F. 1999. *Ethnic German Migration since 1989: Results and Perspectives.* Forschungsinstitut zur Zukunft der Arbeit. Discussion Paper Series. Bonn: IZA.

Migration Studies in Austria – Research at the Margins?

By Bernhard Perchinig

Abstract

The article analyses the interconnections between migration policy and migration research in Austria. Despite its multicultural past, Austria has followed a ›guest worker‹ policy, drawing sharp distinctions between ›foreigners‹ (›Ausländer‹) and ›citizens‹ since the 1960s, which only was mitigated due to Austria's accession to the EU and the development of an EU integration acquis. The strong legal divide between foreigners and nationals was reflected in the research, which focused on citizenship policies, and, due to the rising influence of the xenophobic Freedom Party (FPÖ), on issues of discrimination and racism. Interestingly, the positive attitude towards cultural diversity with regard to Austria's ›autochthonous‹ minorities was never reflected in migration policy, where cultural diversity was perceived as a threat. The article argues that this perception is linked to the cultural gap between the Social Democratic and the Conservative ›camp‹ after World War II and the lack of public debate on the history of Antisemitism and the extermination of the Jewish community during Nazism. After World War II, cultural diversity was associated with the deep societal and political division and pillarisation of the Austrian society. Nation-building and the production of cultural homogeneity characterised most of the 1970s and 1980s, and several consecutive governments declined to accept immigration as a reality. The state of migration research reflects the long history of supersession, as only research uncritical towards government policies is supported and critical researchers often have to leave Austrian research institutions and universities.

Introduction

The editors of the volume have asked the authors to concentrate on the following questions:

- Are there national paradigms of migration research? One or many? And are they contested or widely shared?
- Is migration reflected as a part of the changes in social-structural development?
- What is the role of the organisational and funding structure?
- Is there a mutual influence of research and politics?

Before dwelling on these questions, I would like to add some considerations on the idea and meaning of ›paradigm‹. The traditional concept of ›paradigm‹ has been shaped by Thomas Kuhn's analysis of scientific developments, where a paradigm is seen as a shared set of concrete solutions to central problems in a specific scientific field guiding the work of the scientific community, which is committed to the paradigm because of training and institutional rules. According to Kuhn, intellectual progress is not shaped by scientific logic and advancement, but by intellectually violent revolutions leading to a paradigm shift, a new world-view on existing problems, often brought forward by academic outsiders or scientists critical to the established rules in academia (cf. Kuhn 1962).

For this understanding of paradigm, the existence of an institutionalised academic discipline with a well-formulated subject, specific methods and clear demarcation lines to the outside world is a precondition. Nowhere in academia migration research has established itself as such a kind of discipline, at best the issue of migration is accepted as an important area of research for different disciplines. On the contrary, migration research often is defined as an »interdisciplinary« endeavour, which, like many interdisciplinary activities, often leads to scepticism within the academic communities of the established disciplines.

Due to these considerations, I would prefer to analyse the situation of migration research in terms of competing narratives than of paradigms, where the concept of a narrative is characterised by an intermingling of discourses in different social fields, e.g. academia and politics. Thus we might not find one single ›grand narrative‹, but a layer of different (hi)stories reflecting the interaction of the academic and political development of the field. At least this is the case in Austria.

One Paradigm or Many?

Given the importance of immigration to Vienna, Lower Austria and Vorarlberg in the nineteenth and early twentieth century, on the one hand, and the history of emigration on the other, one could imagine that migration research would have a long academic tradition in Austria. The opposite is the case. Neither the thick history of emigration nor the more recent waves of immigration since the end of the Second World War received a lot of attention in the academic world. Only some ten years after Austria had started to recruit labour migrants under a guestworker scheme in the late 1960s and early 1970s, the first studies on migration were contracted.

The political background of immigration policy at this time was mainly characterised by two aspects: The overwhelming influence of the social partners in the field of migration policy on the one hand and the idea of organising labour migration according to a principle of rotation on the other.

Until the end of the twentieth century, the elaborate system of social partnership has been a main arena of policy making in Austria. In the areas of labour market and social policy neither the political parties in parliament nor the government, but the social partners – mainly the Chamber of Labour and the Trade Unions on the one hand and the Chamber of Commerce and the Association of Industrialists on the other – were the decisive actors. Based on personal, formal and informal linkages to the government, the parliament and the two larger parties, the social partners were able to transform their politics into parliamentary decisions. The trade unions secured their influence within the workforce by pursuing an insider policy focusing on male workers with Austrian citizenship in stable employment, downplaying the interest of women and immigrants (cf. Talos 1993).

For the government the inclusion of the social partners secured the broad acceptance of decisions in the field of economic and social policy, moderate unions and a virtually strike-free economy. In this framework, the trade unions acted as a part of the government system and not of the opposition, as in many other European countries.

Ironically, a conflict about immigration of foreign labour stood at the beginning of social partnership in the early 1960s, when the Austrian economy was struck by severe labour shortage (cf. Wollner 1996). While the Chamber of Commerce pressed for recruitment of labour from abroad, the Trade Union Federation and the Chamber of Labour strongly opposed it. Due to hardened front lines no agreement could be reached in the first instance. In this situation, the Chamber of Labour and the Unions used their bargaining power to increase their influence in the central negotiation arena within the social partnership, the ›wages and prices commission‹ in exchange for the acceptance of a first temporary immigration agreement for 47,000 ›guest workers‹ for the year 1961. The unions pressed for a system of rotation privileging Austrian citizens. ›Guest workers‹, as they were called, should have the right to equal pay, but should only get an employment contract for one year, and each year a new contingent for immigration should be negotiated between the social partners. In the case of job-losses non-Austrian workers should be dismissed before their Austrian colleagues. In the following years, the Chamber of Labour and the trade unions used the yearly negotiations of the contingent of foreign workers as lever to increase their influence within the social-partnership regime (Böse et al. 2001, 3). The initial social partnership-agreement of 1961 remained the determining framework for further regulations of the labour market access by immigrants until the 1980s. In the 1970s, Austria developed a system of restricted labour market access for immigrants, transforming them into an easily dismissible labour market reserve. The main tool of labour-market control was an elaborated system of work permits, which made immigrants more vulnerable than other groups on the labour market, as they needed at least five years of employment to receive an unrestricted labour-permit, which could be lost again in case of prolonged unemployment (cf. Bauböck and Wimmer 1988).

The guest-worker system with its idea of ›rotation‹ in reality never worked. Employers did not want to recruit inexperienced personnel, as long they could rely on trained staff, and most immigrants, who themselves often also planned a short period of stay, could not earn enough to start the desired business in their home country. Thus most immigrants decided to stay longer and brought their family members to Austria. Since the beginning of the 1970s, family immigration surpassed new labour immigration, and Austria became a de-facto immigration country, although the authorities still denied this fact (Böse et al. 2001, 2).

Despite these developments, a labour market approach dominated migration policy until the end of the 1980s. Thus the social partners stayed the main actors and the Ministry for Social Affairs was the only responsible authority. The unions, which by inclusion into the system of social-partnership had become a part of the system of government, did not open their structures for immigrants, but instead focused their activities on workers and employees holding Austrian citizenship. They did not bother about the exclusion of non-Austrian citizens from passive voting rights at the shop floor level, so immigrants did not enter their ranks and files. Instead of opening their own political structure, the unions and the chamber concentrated on funding migrants' sports and cultural associations (cf. Gächter 1995, 47). One of the most pertinent effects of Austria's ›guest-worker‹ policy was the development of an ethnically segmented labour market with immigrants occupying the lower positions of the occupational hierarchy even in the second and third generation and the development of an immigrant underclass.

In this political context, the first studies published in the early 1980s signified two opposing trends of thought still influential in this research area. Whereas Elisabeth Lichtenberger's monograph on *Guest Workers – Living in two Societies* (1984) positively echoed the guiding political principle of migration policy and focused on the socio-economic position and the assimilation of immigrants, the first study on *Foreign Labour in Austria* (Wimmer 1986), which had been commissioned in 1982 to the Austrian Institute for Economic Research and the Institute for Advanced Studies by the Ministry of Social Affairs and the Ministry of Science and Research, questioned the concept of rotation.

The study explained the development and implementation of Austria's guest-worker policy by the overwhelming influence of the social partners in that field of policy, and criticised that both social partners jointly had decided to make use of immigrants as a buffer on the labour market to reduce unemployment of the native workforce. Confronted with the results of the study, the funding ministries – headed by Social Democratic ministers – raised serious concerns about the »lack of objectivity« and even threatened to withdraw funding.

This study did not only mark the beginning of migration research in Austria, but also stands for the beginning of a tradition of highly politicised research challenging governmental migration policies. Most of the researchers contributing to these studies came from the academic left; some of them had privately been involved in action groups in favour of immigrants. Until today, there is a split in the research landscape between a more economically or demographically oriented research which tries to avoid political connotations, and research referring critically to the state of migration policy in Austria. Although the latter had got some hold at the universities and the Austrian Academy of Sciences in the late 1990s, most critical researchers left or were forced to leave these state-funded research institutions and either left Austria for good or left the research field in that decennium. State-sponsored research institutions are now dominated by empirical research abstaining from political criticism.

Are Paradigms Contested or Widely Shared?

Also this question has to be answered with regard to migration policy and migration research history. Two areas of discourse, the growing influence of demographic and of normative arguments in the 1980s and early 1990s, have to be mentioned here. Both of them cannot be understood without a short reference to major changes in the institutional setting of immigration policy in the late 1980s and early 1990s.

As already mentioned, until the end of the 1980s immigration policy was a part of labour market policy with the social partners and the Ministry for Social Affairs as the main actors. Following the epochal changes in the political setting of Europe in the beginning of the 1990s and the huge influx of refugees from Bosnia-Herzegovina, the Ministry of the Interior approached the scene and became a proactive player, defining immigration as a problem of internal security (Sohler 1999). This view was fostered by the largest influx of immigrants Austria had experienced ever since: Between 1987 and 1994 the resident immigrant population more than doubled, from 326,000 to 713,000 (Böse et al. 2001, 5). The prevailing system of migration control by way of labour market regulation was unable to cope with this new situation.

Even more important than the shift of actors were the dramatic changes the established ›two and a half‹-party system with its strong linkage to the system of social-partnership was undergoing. Two parties never had been a part of the informal elite-cooperation in the system of social partnership: The Freedom Party (FPÖ), in the early 1980s a far right-wing, German nationalistic party with an electorate of around 6 per cent on the one hand, and the newly formed Green party, which in its early years comprised activists from the ecological movement, human rights activists and disappointed former left-wing Social Democrats and activists from the radical academic leftist groups.

When in 1986 the late Jörg Haider was elected head of the FPÖ, he started to transform the former elitist party to a right-wing populist party with a mainly male working class electorate of up to 30 per cent. The former all-German tendency of the FPÖ, which presented Austria as a part of the larger German nation and was strongly opposing minority rights for the ethnic groups traditionally settling in Austria, was replaced by an Austrian nationalism and a strict anti-immigrant position. On the other hand, the Green party sharpened its profile in human rights, particularly with regard to immigrant integration. Thus migration issues, which formerly were regulated in the closed political framework of elite cooperation of the social partners, entered the parliamentary arena from the fringes: The transformed FPÖ and the newly founded Greens gained political profile by focusing on an issue neglected by the two large mass parties dominating the parliament, the conservative ÖVP and the Social Democrats, and transformed migration policies to a central parliamentary issue in the 1980s.

Both parties had never been a part of the social-partnership elite-consensus and did not feel bound by the traditional interests shaping migration policy. So they were free to use the issue to sharpen their political profile. Migration policy, which had been decided behind the closed doors of the social partners before, was transferred into the parliamentary arena and became a major public issue in the 1990s.

The shift of migration policy into the parliamentary arena led to a short phase of open scientific and political discussion on the future of Austria's migration policy. Between 1989 and 1992, the Ministry of the Interior together with the Chancellery initiated several dialogue groups including civil servants, migration researchers and intellectuals. One outcome of the dialogue was a draft of an »immigration law« suggesting a system of immigration control instead of the existing labour-market regime and an equalisation of the legal status of immigrants and natives after a few years. The break-up of Yugoslavia and the huge influx of refugees from Bosnia stopped this short phase of rational discourse. Now the risk of mass immigration from Eastern Europe became a central issue, and the Freedom Party gained considerable support for its anti-immigration policies. Trade unions as well as all parliamentary parties except for the Greens defined control of immigration, and not integration, as their major goal.

At the end of the 1980s a new subject entered the arena: The ageing of society. A study commissioned by the City of Vienna, which at that time was envisaging a continuous decline of population, was the first to use demographic arguments in favour of controlled immigration (Anatalovsky 1990). Known demographers like Heinz Fassmann and Rainer Münz argued to accept the reality and try to develop a quota-system for immigration aimed at compensating the foreseeable loss of population with its dramatic consequences on the pension and the health system (Fassmann and Münz 1995, 10). The idea of migration as a means of demographic planning found acceptance among the government, which had realised that the existing mode of migration management via control of the labour market was inefficient. The discussion led to the implementation of a new immigration control regime based on annual immigration quotas, but without improvements of the legal status of immigrants.

Already in 1987 the existing labour market regime was amended introducing a percentage quota to control access to the labour market. The maximum percentage of employment of foreign citizens was set at 10 per cent (later lowered to 8 per cent), with a complicated procedure for overdrawing the quota. Between 1991 and 1993 a comprehensive reform of the existing legal migration regime entered into force. The idea behind the reforms was to prevent the use of the asylum procedure as a door to immigration and to regulate new immigration not via the labour market, but via a quota regime, which should be adapted yearly. Contrary to immigration countries employing quota regimes, the right of residence was not connected with the right of access to the labour market, and the existing labour-market quota system only underwent minimal reforms. Thus many legally resident immigrants – especially young people, women and self-employed – were not allowed to work. Beyond that, the new law stipulated new income and housing thresholds as preconditions for residence. In contrast to official declarations, the new acts also applied to legal residents in the country without giving any credit to that fact. Bad housing, long-term unemployment or the omission to apply for the prolongation of an existing residence permit in time often lead to the loss of one's residence rights and the need to apply for a residence permit anew and from the country of origin (Bauböck 1997, 686).

The drastic consequences of the new laws did not only raise protest among human rights organisations, but also lead to a new interest in the field of migration and integration in research. It might not be by chance that in the beginning of the 1990s, legal scholars and political scientists started to compare the Austrian legislation with international norms and developments in other European countries and connected themselves with centres of legal research in the Netherlands and in Germany. On the other hand, the strong legal division between natives and foreigners in Austria also aroused growing interest in the then developing discussion about theories of citizenship. In the early 1990s the Department of Political Science at the Institute of Advanced Studies in Vienna became a focal point of citizenship studies in Austria. Rainer Bauböck's *Transnational Citizenship* (1994) was the first in a series of publications in the area of comparative citizenship-studies financed by the Ministry of Science and directed by Rainer Bauböck, which involved former scholars of the department and actively reached out to the international scientific community by organising conferences – and by publishing in English. Two theoretical strands received growing attention: citizenship studies in the tradition of Thomas H. Marshall (1965) and Tomas Hammar (1990), and theories of racism in the tradition of British cultural studies. During the early 1990s, also a reorientation of the reception of theory took place: Whereas German research had been the main reference point in the books and papers written in the 1970s and 1980s, the Anglo-Saxon discussion became much more influential now. This was partly a result of the fact that several researchers had got grants for British universities and partly due to a re-import of British cultural studies through the German publishing house *Argument Verlag*.

Moreover, the normative focus on theories of citizenship shifted the discussion about the integration of immigrants from the older labour-market paradigm to a more political paradigm, questioning the adequacy of nation-state citizenship as a solution to integration and served as a new framework for the academic discourse. ›Citizenship‹ may be the only uncontested research paradigm among migration researchers, and there might even be a normative consensus about the need to enlarge citizenship rights to immigrants within the research community.

Citizenship studies also formed a major part of the research programme on ›Xenophobia‹ of the Ministry of Science from 1996 to 2001. As this programme also included regular lectures of renowned British scholars, like Robert Miles and Stuart Hall, the orientation on research in the German-speaking world further was complemented by a growing interest in the British and American tradition of theory-building. A second large research programme of the Ministry of Science on ›Cultural Studies‹ with a strong focus on British and American theory-building reinforced this reorientation.

The high degree of involvement of researchers into human rights' NGOs and the significant growth of right-wing extremism and xenophobia in Austria in the 1990s as well as the development of new forms of self-organisation of immigrants from Africa and Asia were reflected by the reception of the international debate about the concept of ›racism‹, especially among younger scholars and students (cf. Görg and Pühretmeyer 2000, Van Dijk and Wodak 2000). Whereas the term ›racism‹ in social science had only been used in the context of the National Socialist regime in the 1970s and 1980s, in the mid-1990s the concept of ›cultural racism‹ entered the discussion.

Further to the research programmes of the Ministry of Science, the focus of the European Union on anti-discrimination policies and the funding of anti-racist networks and research were a highly influential factor in developing a ›migration research community‹ in Austria. In this area, mostly young researchers at extra-university institutes, which are often also activists of the European Network against Racism or other policy-oriented NGOs developed a new area of discourse strongly linked with the reception of cultural theory and postcolonial approaches (cf. Görg and Pühretmeyer 2000).

Are There Blind Spots in Migration Research?

Autochthonous minorities in Austria face a completely different legal and social framework with regard to their cultural rights than immigrant minorities. The legal term used for autochthonous ethnic groups is *Volksgruppe*. Whereas the 1976 Ethnic Groups Act (Volksgruppengesetz BGBl. [Bundesgesetzblatt, Federal Law Gazette] 396/1976) and other legal provisions guarantee a set of cultural rights to the autochthonous minorities, there are no such rights for immigrant ethnic groups. On the contrary, the legal provisions governing naturalisation and the right of residence directly and indirectly demand assimilation to the ›Austrian way of life‹. The Ethnic Groups Act does not apply to immigrant minorities (cf. Baumgartner and Perchinig 1995).

The Ethnic Groups Act guarantees the preservation of the ethnic groups (*Volksgruppen*) and stipulates that their language and national characteristics (*Volkstum*) should be respected. An ethnic group is defined as those groups of Austrian citizens traditionally residing (›*wohnhaft und beheimatet*‹) in parts of the Austrian state territory who speak a non-German mother tongue and have own national characteristics. The federal state recognises its obligation to subsidise measures that safeguard the existence of the ethnic groups and their national characteristics. Members of these minority groups have the right to use their mother tongue before the authorities in the areas where they live, and education in their mother tongue – bilingual schooling – is granted in certain areas.

Special advisory bodies comprising representatives of the different ethnic minorities, the *Volksgruppenbeiräte,* were set up at the Chancellor's office to advise the federal government on minority policies and the distribution of subsidies for the organisations of the representative ethnic minorities (*Volksgruppenförderung).* This body is intended to safeguard the cultural, social and economic interests of the ethnic groups and is composed of representatives of the minorities, political parties and the religious groups. The implementation of these rights often is prevented by reluctance of politicians and/or, as in the case of the Carinthian Slovenes, a strong nationalist climate with organisations like the *Kärntner Heimatdienst*, acting as vociferous and influential anti-minority pressure groups. Nevertheless, the importance of group-rights for the autochthonous minorities is an accepted fact, at least at the level of the federal government (cf. Baumgartner et al. 2001).

There are no similar legal provisions safeguarding the cultural rights of immigrant ethnic groups. On the contrary, the naturalisation law and Austrian residence law implicitly favour assimilation. According to the 1988 Naturalisation Act (BGBl. 124/1998), the »integration of the applicant« was the most important criterion for the granting of naturalisation. According to the internal regulations of the provincial government of Vienna, »complete integration« was understood as fluent knowledge of German, a sound professional education and proven activities for the coexistence of the indigenous and immigrant population in Vienna (Wiener Integrationsfonds 1999, 43). Until 1998, the naturalisation law demanded »assimilation to the Austrian way of life« as a precondition for naturalisation. Only in 2006 the reform of the nationality act replaced these demands by a naturalisation test. How can this different treatment of diversity and pluralism be explained?

Here a look at the ›grand narratives‹ of Austrian nation-building might be helpful. The first narrative concerns the destruction of the First Austrian Republic by civil war in 1933, leading to the Austro-fascist regime and the ›consenting occupation‹ by Nazi Germany in 1938. Here the narrative tells a story of society sharply divided by class, region and religion, where both the Social Democratic and the Conservative ›camp‹ were unable to solve conflicts of interest in the parliamentary arena and instead resorted to violence leading to civil war. This incapability to forge a consensus on the future of Austria, so the narrative goes, was the base for the high level of support for the NSDAP in Austria and later allowed Nazi Germany to consentingly occupy the country.

This division, so the foundation narrative continues, was overcome in the national-socialist concentration camps, where Conservatives as well as Social Democrats were jailed and decided to build a new state after liberation based on cooperation and peaceful conflict-resolution overcoming the old cleavages – cleavages which, after all, had not only been defined in political, but also in cultural terms by both ›camps‹. The Social Democratic Party of the First Republic (1918–1938) had always understood itself as a political as well as cultural movement shaping a new way of life ranging from housing styles to clothing and greeting modes confronting the dominant Catholic culture, whereas the Conservatives had a strong leaning towards political Catholicism fostering a Catholic and rural lifestyle associated with folk customs and traditions and a patriarchal family. In the 1920s and 1930s, nearly all areas of life were pillarised according to these two camps, and until the 1980s a ›learned Austrian‹ could tell from the name of the insurance company of a car which political camp the owner was aligned to. And even today, greeting with the traditionally conservative »Grüß Gott«[1] in the (Social Democratic) Viennese City Hall and the traditionally liberal or Social Democrat »Guten Tag«[2] in the (Conservative) Chamber of Commerce may lead to a penetrating glance.

The reduction of the differences between the two camps was one of the major political successes of the late chancellor Bruno Kreisky, who together with the then archbishop Franz König forged a new understanding between the Catholic Church and the Social Democratic Party, the narrative continues. Thus in the 1970s and 1980s, integration mainly meant overcoming the political and lifestyle difference between the two former camps by opening up access to education, raising mass incomes and mass consumption. The institution of ›social partnership‹ was seen as a major tool to accomplish this appeasement. Homogeneity in everyday culture should help to overcome the traditional conflicts between the two competing camps and lifestyles. Cultural pluralism was associated with the traditional pillarisation of the society and assessed as a threat rather than as an asset.

But this story carries a hidden subtext: In the 1920s, the Conservatives as well as the developing German-nationalist camp were united by anti-Semitism, which both used to campaign against the Social Democratic government in Vienna, denouncing »red Vienna« as being dominated by Jewish influence. After the liberation from Nazism in 1945, the consecutive Conservative-Social Democratic coalition governments jointly decided to block restitution as far as possible and soon began to compete for the support of former Nazis, whereas no move was made to invite the survivors of the Holocaust back to Austria. Instead, the definition of Austria as the first victim of Nazi Germany became the second ›grand narrative‹ of Austrian nation building after 1945. In this context, a reference to ›cultural pluralism‹ was a hidden reference to the destroyed Jewish tradition of Vienna, and the agreement to overcome the traditional cleavages by fostering (class)cultural homogeneity also included a hidden agreement not to touch on Austria's involvement in the Holocaust. So the founding myth of the reconciliation of the two camps of the interwar period merged with the myth of Austria as the first victim of Nazi Germany and effectively silenced further public discussion on this topic.

In this context, conflicts involving the autochthonous minorities were mainly seen as destabilising the newly reached societal consensus. Within the academic left which, although critical, nevertheless supported Kreisky's government, the

---

1 There is no literal English translation for this formula. »Greetings and God Bless You« might come closest.
2 »Good day, How are you?«

leading discourse was not a discourse on cultural pluralism, but, following the reception of Gramsci, on cultural predominance. ›Cultural pluralism‹ and ›multiculturalism‹ as political concepts entered the arena of discourse only in the early 1980s, at a time when most politicians still had been socialised in a tradition emphasising the risks of cultural pluralism.

In the 1960s and 1970s, however, the narrative of a new Austria did not go uncontested by the former predominant narrative of Austria as a part of the ›German nation‹, which was strongly associated with NS-ideology. The right-wing Freedom Party, the incorporated student leagues at the universities and right-wing newspapers depicted Austria as a part of the ›German cultural nation‹ (›*deutsche Kulturnation*‹) and were united in their opposition against granting cultural group rights to the Carinthian Slovenes and the Croats in the Burgenland as guaranteed in the Austrian State Treaty of 1955. The passing of the Ethnic Groups Act in 1976 can be seen as the culmination point of the fight between these two competing narratives, leading to the inclusion of the autochthonous ethnic groups into the prevailing narrative of a new Austrian nation.

Linguistic rights for both the Carinthian Slovenes and the Croats of the Burgenland had been guaranteed in Article 7 of the Austrian State Treaty of 1955, which constituted an independent Austrian State. Their implementation into the State Treaty had been a result of the strong involvement of Carinthian Slovene fighters in the Yugoslav Partisan resistance against Nazi Germany, whereas a majority of the German-speaking Carinthian population did not oppose the Nazi regime, and many supported it. In the negotiations of the State Treaty Yugoslavia, supported by the then Soviet Union, demanded to grant linguistic rights to the Carinthian and Styrian Slovenes and the Croats in the Burgenland (Stourzh 1975, 76ff.). After the end of the war, Yugoslavia demanded parts of the province of Carinthia as its territory, and withdrew these demands only after an agreement of linguistic rights for ethnic minorities in Austria was reached.

The implementation of these rights had been neglected by the government until the mid-1970s, when the then chancellor Bruno Kreisky ordered to implement the provision for bilingual street signs in Southern Carinthia in 1972. These signs were demounted in a mass turmoil organised by the *Kärntner Heimatdienst*, a right-wing German-nationalist anti-minority pressure group with strong historical connections to the NSDAP (cf. Perchinig 1989, 131ff). Violent blast and arson attacks against memorials and offices of both sides characterised the following years. To appease the conflict, chancellor Kreisky installed an expert commission, which called for a »special census« defining the number of minority members and drafted the Ethnic Groups Act, granting group rights to autochthonous ethnic minorities in Austria, which was passed by all parliamentary parties, including the Freedom Party (FPÖ).

But the conflict could not be held in the parliamentary arena any more. Socialised in the late 1960s, younger activists began to forge a coalition of Catholic, Protestant and left-wing youth and students' organisations and the left wing of the Social Democrats. Their arguments focused on the strong links between the organisations opposed to minorities with the far-right wing and the roots of their thinking in National Socialism. Commitment for minority rights became a decisive political issue not only for the left, but also for Catholic organisations, who met in the ›solidarity committees‹ for the Slovene minority and formed a new kind of social movement. One of the reasons for the success of this emerging new social movement was the strong link of the conflict with history. On the one hand, the *Kärntner Heimatdienst* and other organisations campaigning against minority rights had strong links to a Nazi past and to right-wing extremism, whereas many Carinthian Slovenes had actively fought in the Yugoslav Partisan Army and were politically supported by Yugoslavia, at that time well respected among the academic left as an interesting model of Socialism.

At the same time the influence of the students' revolution lead to a growing interest in the role of Austrians in the Nazi regime, and many students questioned their parents about their past. As many Slovenes had been involved into the fight against the Nazis, their narrative could serve as a model for identification with a ›better part‹ of Austria – and for many also as a model for a ›better father‹ than one's own, who had not opposed to or who had even supported the Nazi regime.

This new coalition organised a boycott of the planned special census leading to the result that more Slovenes would live in Vienna than in Carinthia. This symbolic victory laid the foundation for a gradual shift in the public understanding of the role of ethnic groups: Whereas in the 1960s and 1970s the majority of Austrians stressed the ›German‹ character of Austria, a positive esteem of the existence of traditional, autochthonous minorities began to characterise the discourse on Austrian ›national identity‹ in the 1980s and 1990s. A positive view of the traditional minorities went well together with the growing interest in the multinational Habsburg Empire, as depicted in the books of Claudio Magris, which were bestsellers in Austria. So Austrian national identity was reconnected with its Habsburg past, and this discourse also helped to downgrade Austria's involvement into National Socialism. Now the narrative of the ›*Deutsche Kulturnation*‹ was not convenient for Austria's image anymore, an image which now relied on the more fashionable notion of a long lasting tradition of cultural diversity.

Even within the Freedom Party, references to the ›Austrian nation‹ gradually began to replace the traditional ›German‹ orientation. Under the heading »*Österreich zuerst*« (priority for Austria), this ›Austrian nationalism‹ was made instrumental in a major anti-immigrant campaign of the FPÖ arguing in favour of a reduction of rights for immigrants, whereas at the same time the FPÖ tried to improve its relations to the autochthonous minorities. As Carinthian governor, the late Jörg Haider was the first provincial governor to install an Ethnic Minorities Office within the provincial administration and to found a Carinthian Institute for Ethnic Studies, which should present Carinthia as a model for ethnic relations in Central Europe, but was closed down in the late 1990s.

This switch of narratives was also reflected in scientific research. During the 1980s, a huge variety of critical studies on the situation of the autochthonous ethnic groups was published. In this context, Peter Gstettner and Dietmar Larcher of the Institute of Pedagogics at the University of Klagenfurt, the capital of Carinthia, developed a research focus on bilingual education and intercultural pedagogics, but without reference to immigration. Intercultural pedagogies also had become a focus of research at the Pedagogical Institute of the City of Vienna, where teachers and teacher-trainers were discussing alternatives to the existing framework of ›*Ausländerpädagogik*‹ (›foreigners' pedagogy‹). Seizing a window of opportunity, they succeeded in influencing the Ministry of Education to introduce intercultural education as an educational principle and to install team-teaching in many Viennese schools.

Although these two institutions were working in a comparable field, they had little contact until the beginning of the 1990s. Only then some researchers working on the autochthonous minorities became aware of the issue of immigration and started to question their theoretical concepts, which often were based on the tradition of ›*völkisch*‹ thinking around the late Theodor Veiter, who held a professorship of international law in Innsbruck. Until today, there is only a weak link between the research community working on autochthonous groups and migration researchers, and often the concepts of ethnicity applied are quite different, with a focus on sociological concepts in the field of migration research and a dominance of legal research and primordial concepts of ethnicity in the research on autochthonous minorities.

The Institutional Framework

As already mentioned, the development of migration research in Austria strongly depended on a few researchers, most of them political scientists and sociologists, who started to work in the field in the early 1980s. Until now, migration research is not well established in the Austrian academic world. There exists one institute devoted to migration policy (International Centre for Migration Policy Development, ICMPD) which is organised as an intergovernmental organisation and concentrates on consultancy to governments and international bodies, but also hosts a small research unit. In the academic area, neither an institute nor a specific journal for migration research exists. The Austrian Academy of Science has established a Commission on Migration and Integration Research with the aim to coordinate academic research in the field of migration and integration at the institutes of the Academy, but is not engaged in research itself. The only activities of the Commission were to organise public lectures on migration issues and to act as an organisational platform for the edition of the *Second Austrian Migration and Integration Report 2007* (Fassmann 2007).

Basic and applied research on migration and integration is more or less regularly pursued at three or four extra-university institutes. Their research efforts depend on project funding by the ministries and research programmes. In total, there might be at most some 10–15 persons earning their living solely from migration research, with some 30–40 more doing research on migration issues from time to time. As a matter of fact, there is a high amount of fluctuation out of academia or to universities and research centres abroad.

At the end of the 1990s, the relationship between the academic world and policy makers has been described as characterised by mutual distrust (ICMPD 1998). The study reported that many researchers feared that their work would be misused by the government, while governmental officials often suspected researchers to be keen on attacking migration policy decisions. This precarious relationship has somehow improved since. With the growing importance and accessibility of EU funding, the research world has developed into a bifurcated structure: Most research funded by Austrian authorities is devoted to a governmental research perspective (e.g. immigration control, labour market integration, housing and social questions) and focuses on applied research. As freedom of access to information is not regulated by law in Austria, the funding authorities often prevent the publication of undesired results or put pressure on the scientists to reformulate their reports. This is not the case with research programmes funded by the Ministry of Science and Research and the Funds for the Advancement of Scientific Research, the main Austrian research funding agency, and with EU funding, which is largely independent from political interference, but funding possibilities from these sources are scarce.

This divide between academic and applied research is further exacerbated by the move of the Ministry of the Interior to develop in-house research facilities at its Police Academy, with a dominant focus on security issues. Together with the Austrian Fund of Integration, a foundation dependent on the Ministry of the Interior, an internal research and documentation infrastructure is recently in the making. This development has raised fears within the research community that access to data will be further restricted and governmental funding for research will be redirected to state-controlled bodies.

Nevertheless, migration researchers have gained growing public recognition in the last few years. This development does not only reflect the growing importance of the field in politics, but is also an effect of continuous research and publication activities and international academic networking. In 2003 the first Austrian report on migration and integration, involving all relevant researchers, was published by the ICMPD (Fassmann and Stacher 2003), followed by a second report published by the Austrian Academy of Sciences in 2007 (Fassmann 2007). Both reports were well received by the public and serve as a source of information for researchers, students, administrators and NGOs. As a result of the research programme on xenophobia administered by the Ministry of Science and Research between 1997 and 2001, a series of seven books presenting all research results was published by *Drava* between 1998 and 2002 (see the titles in the references), which also helped to establish the field in the academic world. In the early 2000s, several networks at the European level came into existence involving Austrian researchers, like e.g. the European Migration Dialogue with its regular reports on migration politics (König and Perchinig 2003; 2005) or the EU-funded European Migration Network which regularly published comparative reports on migration issues (e.g. IOM 2004).

Austria's migration research community has also been able to link rather well with the European research infrastructure in this field. Austrian researchers are involved in the EU-funded Network of Excellence IMISCOE (Immigration and Social Cohesion in Europe, www.imiscoe.org) and have secured several research projects under the diverse EU-funding schemes and published widely in the IMISCOE publication series (Bauböck 2006; Bauböck et al. 2006; 2007; Fassmann et al. 2008; Jandl 2007; Jandl et al. 2008). EU funding has also helped to liberate academic researchers from the political pressures of applied research described above and to develop to a critical mass of competence. As two recent evaluations have shown (FAS 2008; Kozeluh 2008), migration research is one of the fields of proven competence of social sciences in Austria and has produced a high output, particularly due to involvement in European projects. Both evaluations point at the negative consequences of fragmentation and the disastrous effects of the lack of stable funding.

This positive development is not adequately reflected by funding or within the traditional academic institutions. When the programmes of the Ministry of Sciences expired in the early 2000s, only a few researchers could secure their involvement in this field through more action-oriented programmes like the EU-funded EQUAL initiative, and only a few got some temporarily funded positions at state-funded institutions. In the last few years a number of researchers either left the research area or left Austria; and with cutting research budgets also the few temporarily funded positions in state institutions are being closed down. In particular researchers publicly critical towards Austria's migration and integration policies have been forced out of state funded academic institutions in the last few years. Critical debates on migration issues are now virtually reduced to private circles or academic initiatives, which nowadays find their home more often at the Universities of the Arts than at the social science institutes of the big universities, which have largely lost their critical impetus (not only) in this field.

References

Antalovsky, Eugen. 1990. Wien 2010. Stadtentwicklung bei Bevölkerungswachstum und offenen Grenzen; Ergebnisse der Arbeitstagung vom 20. April 1990 im Wiener Rathaus. Vienna: Institut für Wirtschafts- und Sozialforschung.

Bauböck, Rainer. 1994. Transnational Citizenship. Membership and Rights in International Migration. Aldershot: Elgar.

Bauböck, Rainer. 1997. Migrationspolitik. In *Handbuch des politischen Systems Österreichs. Die zweite Republik*, ed. Herbert Dachs et al., 678–90. Vienna: Manz.

Bauböck, Rainer. 2006. Migration and Citizenship. Legal Status, Rights and Political Participation. Amsterdam: Amsterdam University Press.

Bauböck, Rainer, and Hannes Wimmer. 1988. Social Partnership and »Foreigners Policy«. *European Journal of Political Research* 16: 659–81.

Bauböck, Rainer, Eva Ersboll, Kees Groenendijk, and Harald Waldrauch, ed. 2006. *Acquisition and Loss of Nationality. Policies and Trends in 15 European Countries*, 2 vols. Amsterdam: Amsterdam University Press.

Bauböck, Rainer, Bernhard Perchinig, and Wiebke Sievers, ed. 2007. *Citizenship Policies in the New Europe*. Amsterdam: Amsterdam University Press.

Baumgartner, Gerhard, and Bernhard Perchinig. 1995. Minderheitenpolitik. In *Handbuch des politischen Systems Österreichs. Die zweite Republik*, ed. Herbert Dachs et al., 628–41. Vienna: Manz.

Baumgartner, Gerhard, Andrea Ellmeier, and Bernhard Perchinig. 2001. *Transversal Study: Cultural Policy and Cultural Diversity. Country Report: Austria*. Strasbourg: Council of Europe.

Böse, Martina, Regina Haberfellner, and Ayhan Koldas. 2001. *Mapping Minorities and their Media: The National Context – Austria*. http://www.lse.ac.uk/collections/EMTEL/Minorities/papers/austriareport.doc

FAS. 2008. *Netzwerke der Wissensproduktion*. Vienna: FAS-Research. http://fasshop.at/catalog/download/Netzwerke_der_Wissensproduktion.pdf (accessed June 12, 2008).

Fassmann, Heinz, ed. 2007. *2. Österreichischer Migrations- und Integratonsbericht 2001–2006*. Klagenfurt/Celovec: Drava.

Fassmann, Heinz, and Rainer Münz. 1995. *Einwanderungsland Österreich? Historische Migrationsmuster, aktuelle Trends und politische Maßnahmen*. Vienna: Braumüller.

Fassmann, Heinz, and Irene Stacher, ed. 2003. *Österreichischer Migrations- und Integrationsbericht*. Klagenfurt/Celovec: Drava.

Fassmann, Heinz, Ulrike Reegers, and Wiebke Sievers, ed. 2008. *Statistics and Reality: Concepts and Measurements of Migration in Europe*. Amsterdam: Amsterdam University Press.

Gächter, August. 1995. Integration und Migration. *SWS-Rundschau* 35 (4): 435–8.

Görg, Andreas, and Hans Pühretmeyer. 2000. Antirassistische Initiativen in Österreich. Zur Diskussion ihrer Positionen und ihrer strategischen Potentiale. In *Trennlinien. Imagination des Fremden und Konstruktion des Eigenen*, ed. Josef Berghold, Elisabeth Menasse, and Klaus Ottomeyer, 237–58. Klagenfurt/Celovec: Drava.

Hammar, Tomas. 1990. *Democracy and the Nation-State. Aliens, Denizens and Citizens in a World of International Migration*, Aldershot: Avebury.

ICMPD (International Centre for Migration Policy Development). 1998. *Feasibilitystudie zur Errichtung eines Österreichischen Forums für Migrationsforschung*. Vienna: ICMPD.

IOM. 2004. *The Impact of Immigration on Austria's Society*. Vienna: IOM.

Kozeluh, Ulrike. 2008. *Struktur der Geistes-, Sozial- und Kulturwissenschaften in Österreich. Bericht im Auftrag des RFTE-Rates für Forschung und Technolo-*

gieentwicklung. Vienna: RFTE. http://www.ratfte.at/UserFiles/File/080331_GSK inOesterreich_Kozeluh_final.pdf (accessed June 2, 2008).

Jandl, Michael, ed. 2007. *Innovative Concepts for Alternative Migration Policies: Ten Innovative Approaches to the Challenges of Migration in the 21st Century*. Amsterdam: Amsterdam University Press.

Jandl, Michael, et al. ed. 2008. *Migration and Irregular Work in Austria*. Amsterdam: Amsterdam University Press.

König, Karin, and Bernhard Perchinig. 2003. Austria. In *EU and US Approaches to the Management of Immigration. Comparative Perspectives*, ed. Jan Niessen, Yongmi Schibel, and Raphaële Magoni, 13–47. Brussels: Migration Policy Group.

König, Karin, and Bernhard Perchinig. 2005. Austria. In *Current Immigration Debates in Europe: A Publication of the European Migration Dialogue*, ed. Jan Niessen, Yongmi Schibel, and Cressida Thompson, 11–56. Brussels: MPG.

Kuhn, Thomas S. 1962. *The Structure of Scientific Revolutions*. Chicago: University of Chicago Press.

Lichtenberger, Elisabeth (with Heinz Fassmann). 1984. *Gastarbeiter. Leben in zwei Gesellschaften*. Vienna: Böhlau.

Marshall, Thomas H. 1965. Citizenship and Social Class. In *Class, Citizenship, and Social Development. Essays*, ed. idem, 71–134. New York: Anchor Books.

Perchinig, Bernhard. 1989. *»Wir sind Kärntner und damit hat's sich.« Deutschnationalismus und politische Kultur in Kärnten*. Klagenfurt/Celovec: Drava.

Sohler, Karin. 1999. Zur Neuformulierung der Politik der inneren Sicherheit im Kontext der Immigrationskontrolle in Österreich 1989–1999. Diploma thesis, Vienna University.

Stourzh, Gerald. 1975. *Kleine Geschichte des Österreichischen Staatsvertrages*. Graz: Styria.

Talos, Emmerich, ed. 1993. *Sozialpartnerschaft – Kontinuität und Wandel eines Modells*. Vienna: Verlag für Gesellschaftskritik.

Volf, Patrik, and Rainer Bauböck. 2001. *Wege zur Integration. Was man gegen Diskriminierung und Fremdenfeindlichkeit tun kann*. Klagenfurt/Celovec: Drava.

Wiener Integrationsfonds, ed. 1999. *MigrantInnen in Wien. Daten & Fakten & Recht. Report 98, part II*. Vienna.

Wimmer, Hannes, ed. 1986. *Ausländische Arbeitskräfte in Österreich*. Frankfurt am Main: Campus.

Wodak, Ruth, and Teun A. van Dijk, ed. 2000. *Racism at the Top. Parliamentary Discourses on Ethnic Issues in Six European States*. Klagenfurt/Celovec: Drava.

Wollner, Eveline. 1996. Auf dem Weg zur sozialpartnerschaftlich regulierten Ausländerbeschäftigung in Österreich. Die Reform der Ausländerbeschäftigung und der Anwerbung bis Ende der 1960er Jahre. Diploma thesis, Vienna University.

Books published as a result of the research programme on xenophobia mentioned above:

Bauer, Ingrid, Josef Ehmer, and Sylvia Hahn, ed. 2002. *Walz – Migration – Besatzung. Historische Szenarien des Eigenen und des Fremden.* Klagenfurt/Celovec: Drava.

Berghold Josef, Elisabeth Menasse, and Klaus Ottomeyer, ed. 2000. *Trennlinien. Imagination des Fremden und Konstruktion des Eigenen.* Klagenfurt/Celovec: Drava.

Fassmann, Heinz, Helga Matuschek, and Elisabeth Menasse-Wiesbauer, ed. 1999. *Abgrenzen – Ausgrenzen – Aufnehmen. Empirische Befunde zu Fremdenfeindlichkeit und Integration.* Klagenfurt/Celovec: Drava.

Fassmann, Heinz, Josef Kohlbacher, and Ursula Reeger, ed. 2002. *Zuwanderung und Segregation. Europäische Metropolen im Vergleich.* Klagenfurt/Celovec: Drava.

Liebhart, Karin, Elisabeth Menasse, and Heinz Steinert, ed. 2002. Fremdbilder – Feindbilder – Zerrbilder. Zur Wahrnehmung und diskursiven Konstruktion des Fremden. Klagenfurt/Celovec: Drava.

Van Dijk, Teun A., and Ruth Wodak, ed. 2000. Racism at the Top. Parliamentary Discourses on Ethnic Issues in Six European States. Klagenfurt/Celovec: Drava.

Volf, Patrik, and Rainer Bauböck. 2001. Wege zur Integration. Was man gegen Diskriminierung und Fremdenfeindlichkeit tun kann. Klagenfurt/Celovec: Drava.

Part III:
Emerging Research
in New Migration Countries

Italy – Migration Research Coming of Age

By Tiziana Caponio

Abstract

The developing of migration studies in Italy can be depicted as marked by the shift from one prevailing macro-structural paradigm to the emerging of a new, more agent-oriented perspective looking at immigration and at immigrants' integration as the result of a multitude of individual and/or networks' strategies and decisions, both on the part of immigrants and of the receiving society. Two factors contributed to such a shift: the greater awareness of immigration as a structural phenomenon and its increasing relevance in the political agenda; the emerging of a new, more internationally oriented generation of migration scholars, influenced by the main theoretical concepts elaborated throughout the 1990s in the European and, most of all, US literature, such as the notion of transnationalism and the policy-making perspective in the study of migration policy.

The article reconstructs such a process of paradigm shift and investigates the main theoretical assumptions, methodological approaches and research streams underlying ›old‹ and ›new‹ migration studies in this latecomer immigration country. If it goes without saying that Italian migration research is today far more developed and promising than two decades ago, still a number of gaps can be pointed out. A major issue is represented by the scarce institutionalisation of migration studies in the academic structure, which accounts for the unevenness in terms of interest and level of research on migration in Italian social sciences.[1]

Introduction

Using the concept of paradigm in social sciences does not only bring problems of definition and clarity, but this is even more the case with an interdisciplinary area like migration, and in a country like Italy, where the overlapping between academic/scientific and NGO/policy-oriented research is still a characterising feature of the field. As a consequence, the notion of paradigm cannot be intended here but in soft manner, to indicate a prevailing approach to the study of migration composed of theoretically driven narratives on its causes and dynamics, of a set of research questions and scientifically relevant issues, and – last but not least – a

---

1 I would like to thank Giuseppe Sciortino for his helpful suggestions and comments. Thanks also to Camille Schmoll and Ferruccio Pastore for their reading of previous versions.

repertory of methods and research techniques. In the social sciences, hardly one such soft paradigm has ever gained unconditional consensus: the coexistence of different paradigms is a far more frequent situation. Immigration research in Italy is no exception.

Actually, as argued below, the development of migration studies in this latecomer immigration country can be depicted as a shift from the dominating macro-structuralist paradigm, looking at immigration to Italy as an exceptional phenomenon produced by a number of push and – later also – pull factors, to the emerging of a more agent-oriented perspective. In this context, immigration and, more and more, immigrants' integration started to be regarded as the result of a multitude of individual and/or networks' strategies and decisions, both on the part of immigrants and of the receiving society.

Such a (quasi)paradigm shift was favoured by two factors: the increasing awareness in the public debate of immigration as a structural phenomenon and the parallel increasing relevance of the issue in the political agenda, as pointed out by the passing of the first framework law in 1998, reformed just four years later in 2002; and the emergence of a new, more internationally oriented generation of migration scholars. This facilitated the penetration in Italian research of the main theoretical concepts elaborated throughout the 1990s in the European and, most of all, US literature, thus contributing to a great extent to the internationalisation of Italian research and to the enhancing of its scientific profile.

This includes the network approach and the notion of transnationalism, that inform a great deal of contemporary research on immigrants' integration, as well as, in the study of migration policy, of the policy-making approach that has contributed to address the limits of macro-institutional analysis based on citizenship models.

The chapter is structured as follows: The following paragraph illustrates the macro-structural paradigm guiding the first Italian studies on immigration, and its main theoretical assumptions, research questions and methods. The second paragraph turns to the public discourse and political agenda on immigration in Italy from the late 1980s until today, to point out their intertwining, throughout the 1990s, with the experts' research priorities and agendas. In the third paragraph, developments in the paradigms and theoretical approaches informing the most recent scientific research on migration public policy and social integration will be analysed. It goes without saying that these topics do not exhaust the debate on immigration in the Italian scholarly literature, yet they can be considered as crucial concerns raised largely by the late 1990s political agenda. The final paragraph gives some conclusive remarks on the state of affairs of Italian migration studies today as compared to the ›old‹ European immigration countries.

Making Sense of Italian Exception.
The Prevailing Macro-Structuralist Paradigm

The start of immigration flows towards Italy is conventionally identified with the mid-1970s, when for the first time in Italian modern history the migratory balance scored a positive sign, i.e. inflows overcame outflows (Bonifazi 2007). Yet, as pointed out by historians (Corti and Sanfilippo 2009) as well as by other social sciences scholars adopting a *longue durée* perspective (see for instance: Colombo and Sciortino 2004), even during the transoceanic migration era, i.e. in the decades between 1880 and 1920, internal migratory movements as well as transfrontalier ones especially in the Alps area did never completely stop. The arrival in the 1920s of first Chinese traders from France can probably be regarded in such a context of continuous exchanges and movements across Italian borders.

Nevertheless, this migratory legacy does not seem to have been considered by the first studies on immigration flows and immigrants in Italy, that, at the beginning of the 1980s, appear to be essentially concerned with making sense of the dramatic U-turn from an emigration to an immigration country (Caponio 2008). In a context of economic stagnation in Italy at that time, immigration does not seem to have been perceived as a structural phenomenon, but rather as an anomaly: the priority in the research agenda was to explain the exceptional Italian case, a new receiving country which was still being perceived as a major sending one. This is clearly pointed out by Rella and Vadalà's (1984) account on ›Sociological Literature on Migration in Italy‹, published in a monographic issue of *Current Sociology* on immigration research in Europe edited by Morokvašić (1984). Not only was Italy listed among the sending countries along with Yugoslavia, Spain, and Portugal, but just two pages were dedicated to immigration research. The article closed up with this final remark: »The immigration of foreigners [...] does not imply that Italy will become a country of large-scale immigration« (Rella and Vadalà 1984, 151).

The literature review carried out by Rella and Vadalà is also revealing under another respect. Two trends were distinguished in the study of Italian emigration, which actually can be regarded as two alternative theoretical perspectives of the prevailing macro-structuralist paradigm. The first one can be identified with a functionalist and assimilationist approach, which considered (e)migration as a positive factor for the country of origin, i.e. as »a safety valve capable of preventing an outburst of social tensions« (144), and focused essentially upon migrants' living conditions and assimilation in the host countries. Such an approach was influenced, according to the authors, by North American sociology, on the one hand, and by humanitarian Catholic thinking on the other.

The second theoretical approach, which is suggested to be more advanced as it »originated in secular progressive thinking« (143), started to get ground in the late 1960s and can be identified with a Marxist perspective explaining emigration in terms of theories of imperialism. Particular attention was now paid to the role played by immigrants in the labour market of receiving societies as well as to the negative consequences of the Italian unplanned and widely spread exodus. On the other hand, an increasing number of researchers were also concerned with the denunciation of – Italian – immigrants' subalternity and marginalisation both in the economy and in the receiving societies at large (1984, 145).

Actually, both theoretical perspectives influenced the early studies on foreign immigration to Italy. In particular, four research streams can be identified in the 1980s and early 1990s: 1) studies analysing the causes of immigration flows towards Italy; 2) descriptive research aimed at providing basic data and information on the main characteristics of the immigrants present in the country; 3) qualitative analyses improperly labelled »community studies« (Zanfrini 1998, 14) because of the focus on national groups and the emphasis on immigrants' different cultures; 4) policy-oriented social problems research.

As for the first research stream, Marxist theorising clearly exerted a strong influence. First accounts, especially by demographers, emphasised the role of world population imbalances, determining movements of people from overpopulated, underdeveloped third-world countries towards wealthier European ones, while analyses carried out by sociologists underlined the crucial relevance of push factors such as unemployment, social and economic inequalities, political turmoil and dictatorship. The supposed specificity of the Italian case, according to these accounts, consisted in the lack of pull factors in terms of attractive opportunities in the economy and the labour market. Italy was regarded as an immigration country *malgré-soi*, i.e. as a product of world disparities in the distribution of wealth, population growth rates and political stability. According to first politological explanations (see for instance: Melotti 1993), such disparities would have been enhanced by the introduction of entry restrictions on the part of northern and central European immigration countries after the 1973 oil crisis. Migration flows started to redirect to southern Europe as a second choice, this part of the continent not – yet – closed to immigration and enjoying wealthier conditions than most of the areas of origin.

However, some sociologists and economists objected to such a primacy of push factors by pointing out the attractiveness of the Italian segmented labour market, and thus of a number of pull factors structurally interrelated with the Italian model of economic development (i.e., small and medium-sized manufactories, care services etc.). Yet, this did not change the terms of reference in the debate: immigrants continued to be regarded as passively reacting to more elaborated *push and pull* factors constellations and a ›reserve army of labour‹. Curiously enough, such an approach overlooked some of the concepts elaborated by research studies on Italian emigration abroad such as that of ›migratory chain‹, introduced by Reyneri (1979) to account for continuous new flows of immigrants and for their choice of destinations.

The second research stream obviously answered to the practical need of providing adequate information and knowledge about the migrant population arriving in Italy. It was far less theoretically driven. In 1979, the Centro Studi Investimenti Sociali (Censis) for the first time collected quantitative data about immigrants' numbers, origins, economic sectors and geographic areas of settlement. Estimates were also provided, since it was acknowledged that the phenomenon escaped the control of Italian authorities to a large extent, and in-depth investigations were carried out into four local areas: i.e., the city of Milan and three regions, Veneto, Emilia Romagna and Sicily. The case studies drew attention to the structural dynamics of local labour markets: foreigners answered a persistent need for low-skilled workers in unattractive sectors for the national workforce, such as fishing, agriculture and other demanding jobs in the small and medium-sized firms of the north-eastern region.

At the beginning of the 1980s, local surveys were promoted in the context of the first inter-university project on foreign workers in Italy, encompassing different regions, e.g. Piedmont, Tuscany, Umbria, Marche, Abruzzo, Campania, Apulia, and cities like Rome and Milan (see for instance contributions in Cocchi 1990). Experts in different disciplines were involved, even though the majority were demographers, as reflected by the critical analysis of official statistics and a preference for quantitative methods.

Two other research streams developed throughout the end of the 1980s and early 1990s, rising issues of immigrant settlement and patterns of integration. As for the community studies, these somehow recall British and French critical studies of the 1970s in their refusal of straight-line assimilation theory (Caponio 2008, 447f.). Nevertheless, most of these studies lacked systematicity and theoretical solidity, often conveying over-simplified and stereotypical knowledge about the different groups present in Italy. Actually, and in line with the local-level studies of the late 1980s, this research stream was primarily concerned with the need to provide general information on immigrant communities and cultures rather than advancing any critical approach to issues of ethnicity, difference and social integration.[2]

As for the policy-oriented social problems research, together with a continuity with critical, Marxist-oriented studies denouncing the living conditions of Italian emigrants abroad, a strong influence of what Rella and Vadalà (1984) considered ›old style‹, functionalist Catholic social thinking can also be pointed out. On the eve of and right after the approval of the second immigration law in 1990[3], a number of national conferences were held (see Cocchi 1990; Censis 1991; Delle Donne, Melotti and Petilli 1993), aimed at gathering together experts in different immigration policy subfields (children's education, labour market, health care, housing etc.), some of them – but not all – being affiliated with Catholic NGOs such as Caritas. Political scientists and lawyers also entered the field, often with the explicit purpose of supporting policy-oriented research and influencing poli-

---

2   See, for instance, the contributions on the Tunisian, Pakistani, Chinese, Egyptian, Cape Verdean, Eritrean, Filipino, Moroccan, Senegalese, Ghanaian, Sri Lankan, Tamil and Somali communities collected in Mottura 1992.
3   The first immigration law approved in 1986 was quite vague in its content and lacked instruments and resources for implementation. As a consequence, four years later, a reform was already needed. On this point see: Zincone 2006.

cymakers in their search for solutions. To some of these conferences, European scholars were also invited, in order to frame the analysis of the Italian case in a broader perspective.

Thus, at the beginning of the 1990s, immigration was becoming a key issue in the political agenda. In this favourable climate, the infrastructuring of migration research in Italy started to take place, essentially developing in close relation with those Catholic NGOs originally involved in supporting emigrant communities abroad. This is the case of the Centro Studi Emigrazione (CSER) founded in 1963 by the Scalabrinian Missionaries that in the late 1980s turned more and more of its attention to immigration, as indicated by the growing number of contributions on this subject published by the journal *Studi Emigrazione* (Caponio 2008, 459); and of Caritas that in 1991 published its first annual report on immigration (*Dossier Immigrazione*), which is still published today. In that same year the Istituto per lo Studio della Multietnicità (ISMU) was founded in Milan. It can be considered the first Italian independent research centre specialising on immigration. Chaired by Vincenzo Cesareo, of the Catholic University of Milan, ISMU actually showed since the very beginning a research approach oriented towards social problems. This is still evident in its main research areas today, dealing with education and training, health, employment, family and children.[4]

Despite this gradual institutionalisation of the migration research field and the opening to comparison with other European countries, the idea of Italy as an exceptional case was still prevailing. The macro-structural paradigm based on the assumption of the primacy of structural factors acting well above the heads of individual immigrants was actually pervading most Italian research in the 1990s, even though with a theoretical shift from Marxism to functionalism, which was more consistent with the Catholic background of the first Italian research institutions on immigration mentioned above, and with the perspective of most academic experts who in this period started to take part in policy-making processes.

From Emergency to Integration, to Security. The Framing of Immigration in the Italian Changing Political Agenda

Analysing processes of political framing of immigration in Italy throughout the 1990s and 2000s is revealing with respect to the development of Italian migration studies. Especially in the first decade, a strong research-policy nexus can be pointed out, as underscored by a number of *ad-hoc* commissions of experts on immigration appointed at ministerial level. Yet, from the 2000s onwards such a nexus weakened, giving way to an increasing distance between the two spheres, as will be pointed out below. But let us see in more detail the phases of such a framing process and its impact on academic research on migration.

If the first Italian immigration law, approved in February 1986, did not raise any public debate and was essentially aimed at complying with international

---

4 See: www.ismu.org

obligations (Colombo and Sciortino 2004, 53), this was not the case with the second law approved only four years later in January 1990. Some events underpinned such a dramatic change in the visibility of migration in the public sphere, as the squatting of deserted buildings in Milan and Rome and racist attacks against immigrants working irregularly in the tomato harvesting in the south of the country, with the murder of a South African asylum seeker.[5] The 1990 law reacted to these pressures by providing only buffer solutions: funds were assigned to regional authorities to establish first accommodation facilities for regular immigrants, while a regularisation was enacted to legalise irregular workers. Yet, in the lack of any consistent integration framework, squatting continued to represent a hot issue throughout the mid-1990s, leading to a situation of continuous emergency, further exacerbated by the unexpected mass arrivals from Albania in 1992 and of refugees from Kosovo in 1993. Last but not least, the tightening of entry controls envisioned by the 1990 law actually produced increased irregularity in the following years (Colombo and Sciortino 2004, 57), leading to a new legalisation in 1995.

In the early 1990s, immigration was featured in the Italian public debate as a series of dramatic and emergency events requiring urgent and immediate buffer solutions. Yet, among some quarters of the political class, especially Catholic and left-wing politicians, there was already some awareness of the structural character of migratory flows towards the country. In 1993, the appointment by the then Minister of Social Affairs of a commission of top-level civil servants and academic experts charged with the task of elaborating a consolidated bill on immigration and immigrant rights, set for the first time the entering of the integration issue in the political agenda. Yet, it took five more years to come to the approbation of the third immigration law.[6] A new commission was appointed, composed of more or less the same team of experts and civil servants (Zincone 2008, 23).

Law n. 40/1998, also known as Turco-Napolitano after the names of the then Ministers of Social Affairs and Home Affairs of the centre-left first Prodi government, for the first time dealt extensively with immigrant integration. The concept of »reasonable integration« was set in the law preamble, implying both nationals' and immigrants' physical and psychological well-being, on the one hand, and positive interaction between different groups, on the other (see also Zincone 2000). On the basis of these two principles, a number of policy measures aimed at fostering individual equality and at promoting intercultural relations were devised in all the crucial spheres of immigrant incorporation, i.e. employment, health, education and professional training, housing and civic participation. Last but not least, the law established also a National Fund for Immigrant Policy, to be distributed to the regions on the basis of the annual and pluriannual integration pro-

---

5 See also Zincone 2008, 20.
6 Actually, according to Zincone 2008, part of the proposals of the 1994 Contri draft were already included in a Decree Law on immigration (n. 489/1995) which was enacted in 1995.

grammes that the regions had to agree upon with the municipalities.[7] Moreover, a Commission for the Integration of Immigrants was appointed to monitor the implementation of the law as well as the progress in the social integration of immigrants.

The Commission, chaired by Giovanna Zincone, a political scientist and expert on migration that had already taken part in the two previous commissions, gave a considerable boost to research on immigrants' integration and related policies. Two reports were published in 2000 and 2001 (Zincone 2000; 2001), gathering contributions from academics and experts in the spheres of immigrants' incorporation identified by the law and mentioned above. Moreover, the second report launched, for the first time in Italy, a discussion among academics on the measurement of immigrants' integration in the Italian society (Zincone 2001, 17; Golini, Strozza and Amato 2001). This represents a relevant research stream still nowadays, as will be pointed out below. Last but not least, the Commission organised three international conferences on crucial topics in the Italian public debate, i.e.: the reform of the 1992 citizenship law (February 1999); immigrants' political participation and representation (June 1999); and the integration of Roma and Sinti minorities (June 2000).

The Commission for the Integration of Immigrants is a clear example of the research-policy nexus that characterised the centre-left policy style on migration throughout the 1990s (i.e., since the 1993 Commission). The Commission was composed of eight top-level officials, nine experts (seven of which from the Academia, one from the National Council for Research and one from an NGO working on interculture), and two representatives of the entrepreneurial world one of which of Somali origin. As is clear, a certain representation of pro-immigrant instances was envisaged, as emphasised also by the background of some of the Academic experts.[8] The Commission clearly reflected the overlapping between scientific research and pro-immigrant activism mentioned above in relation to the emerging of the Italian research infrastructure on migration.

This participation of (partly pro-immigrant) experts to national decision-making was interrupted in 2001 by the return into power of Berlusconi[9], after a hot electoral campaign where the centre-right coalition succeeded in putting the issue of illegal migration on the top of the political agenda (Colombo and Sciortino 2004, 66). The centre-right coalition did not appoint the Commission for the Integration of Immigrants anymore, even though it was not formally abolished by the new immigration law approved in 2002. Actually, Law n. 189/2002, named

---

7 In order to get funding, regional programmes had to be approved by the national government and to secure 20 per cent co-funding.
8 Udo Clement Enwereuzor, appointed as expert on interculture, was actually an active member of a NGO working on international cooperation and anti-racism, Cospe (Cooperation for the Development of Emergent Countries); Giuseppe Pittau, from the Pontifical Academy of Sciences, is also the coordinator of the Caritas Statistical yearly book on immigration.
9 The first Berlusconi government entered into power after the 1994 April elections and lasted until January 1995. After the elections of May 2001, Berlusconi was elected again as Prime Minister and formed his second cabinet.

Bossi-Fini after the names of the two centre-right political leaders that undertook the initiative, was essentially concerned with the tightening of entry and residence requirements, and did not substantially intervene in the area of integration (Zincone 2008, 33).

However, more striking is the fact that the second centre-left Prodi government elected in May 2006 did not re-establish the Commission. A new bill on immigration was presented, which dealt essentially with the reform of the extremely strict regulations of entry and residence permits of the Bossi-Fini[10], while as far as integration is concerned the only relevant novelty was the introduction of immigrants' active and passive franchise at local elections. Moreover, another important bill presented by the then Home Office Minister Giovanni Amato was the reform of the 1992 citizenship law, aimed essentially at reducing the residence time required to apply for naturalisation from ten to five years, while introducing at the same time an integration test (knowledge of the language and of the Italian Constitution). Yet both bills remained unapproved.

Beginning in 2001, immigrants' integration lost centrality in the political agenda. This was probably the main consequence of the centre-right second Berlusconi government capacity to impose issues of illegality and security to the fore, which was not effectively countered by the following – extremely weak – centre-left majority. Yet, one has also to consider the (quasi-)federal reform approved in October 2001 that assigned to the regions the entire responsibility for welfare policies, immigrant ones included.[11] As a consequence, immigrant integration started to be perceived less and less as a national issue, but rather as a regional and local one.

In April 2008, the electoral victory of the centre-right coalition and the constitution of a new Berlusconi government definitively ruled out any discourse on integration and/or citizenship. Security and illegality became key issues again, as pointed out by the recent approbation (July 2009) of the so-called Security Law, putting together various norms on security many of which targeting illegal immigrants, and depicting them as potential criminals. Yet, as will be pointed out below, integration still represents a crucial concern in Italian migration studies today. This seems to signal a greater autonomy of the research agenda from the political one, what could be regarded, from an academic and scientific point of view, as a positive result. However, an opposite view blaming the risk of research marginality and abstract thinking is also shared by a non negligible number of Italian migration scholars, especially by those with a militant NGO's background, who represent an important share of the migration research community to this day.

---

10 For details see Zincone 2008, 38.
11 Starting from the 2003 Budgetary Law, the regions are the only authorities held responsible for the setting of social policy priorities. The National Fund for Immigrant Policy was abolished and merged into the more general National Social Fund, divided among the regions on the basis of a number of socio-economic indicators: the number of legally resident immigrants is one of such indicators, yet this does not imply that the regions have an obligation to devise specific measures for their integration.

Bringing Actors Back In? Competing Paradigms in Contemporary Migration Research

The overcoming of the exceptionality thesis and of the macro-structural paradigm described above did not come overnight, and in a way, as pointed out, it was the product of the centre-left majorities' attempts throughout the 1990s to put the issue of immigrants' integration at the top of the political agenda. Another factor that favoured such a process was indeed the emergence of a new, more internationally oriented generation of migration scholars. This facilitated the penetration in Italian research of the main theoretical concepts elaborated throughout the 1990s in the European and, most of all, US literature.

However, it is difficult to identify a unique, coherent paradigm that would have replaced the ›old‹ macro-structuralist one. Speaking, once again, in very general terms, a more agent-oriented perspective can be pointed out, looking at immigration and, more and more, at immigrants' integration, as the result of a multitude of individual and/or networks' strategies and decisions, either on the part of immigrants themselves or of the receiving society. We shall attempt to reconstruct the emergence of such a (quasi)paradigm, as well as of the main theories and research approaches stemming from it, by looking at two of the main research topics characterising migration literature throughout the 1990s to this day, i.e. migration policy and immigrants' social integration.

Beyond Citizenship Models. Italian-style Migration Policy Studies

As mentioned above, the first studies on migration policy adopted either a strictly juridical or a more socially oriented perspective and were essentially of a descriptive kind. However, already at the beginning of the 1990s, a few comparative studies started to propose a more theoretically grounded perspective, analysing the Italian case in the context of the European literature on immigrants' incorporation regimes. The neo-institutionalist citizenship model approach was adopted by Melotti (1993) and Zincone (1994) to stress once more the exceptional Italian situation: according to these authors, immigrant policies in this country could neither be framed in terms of an assimilationist nor of a multicultural model. Italy lacked, in its political culture, a tradition of colonial rule and/or immigrant recruitment and accommodation, as was the case in other central and northern European countries (Melotti 1993). As a matter of fact, immigration was suffered rather than planned. According to Zincone (1994), in such a context, immigrants' opportunities of access to citizenship rights were extremely differentiated across the country, according to the varying levels of administrative efficiency and resources, as well as to differences in the local policy networks mobilised on the issue. A dramatic gap was pointed out between northern and southern cities (Lostia and Tomaino 1994): Whereas throughout the 1990s, the former had developed specific projects in the area of immigration, the latter lacked first assistance and information services. However, these first observations on local-level immigrant policy were essentially of a descriptive kind.

Yet, at the end of the decade a greater concern for theoretical explanation was emerging: The myth of Italy as a ›case apart‹ started to lose acceptance in the context of new streams in European research emphasising more and more the need for comparison and drawing greater attention to the local[12] and regional[13] dimension of immigrant policy. A great deal of the comparative edited books of the end of the 1990s, either on immigrant policy or on immigration control, started to pay attention to the Italian case, often regarded as somehow representative of the later southern European migratory system.[14] More recent analyses have also looked at Italian immigration and immigrant policies in the context of theories on southern European familistic welfare states (Sciortino 2004): The entry of foreign women to be employed irregularly in the domestic sector has been explained as a product of welfare policies that privilege monetary transfers to the families rather than the provision of care services, as well as of cultural values assigning the burden of care to women.

If these comparative studies essentially focused on the macro institutional factors accounting for cross-country differences in immigrant and immigration policy contents, in these same years a different, more processual and actors' centred policy-making perspective also started to gain ground in Italian migration policy studies following the American policy approach. Such a perspective actually provided a number of consistent theoretical frameworks and concepts, which could represent an alternative to the prevailing macro-structural, national models paradigm. Three research streams can be listed under this rubric in Italy, i.e.: national-level policy-making studies; local-level implementation and policy-making analyses; research on the outcomes of specific pieces of legislation. Along with the prevailing policy-making approach, the influence of the collective action and social movements scholarship has to be mentioned, which appears to be particularly relevant in a number of young scholars' recent studies.

As for the first research stream, right after the approbation of the 1998 immigration law, a number of studies focused on top-level decision-making institutions, i.e. the Italian parliament, government and central bureaucracy (Fedele 1999; Zucchini 1999; Colombo and Sciortino 2003), to find out, on the basis of the analysis of official documents (like parliamentary proceedings, drafts of the law etc.), the main political parties' positions and strategies, the key actors in mediating between the different views etc. A different approach can be found in the analyses carried out by Zincone (2008) and Zincone and Di Gregorio (2002),

---

12   See a number of comparative projects promoted by international organisations, such as the Council of Europe (1995), that focused on the specific issue of immigrants' housing segregation and urban renewal policy; the UNESCO programme ›Multicultural Policies and Modes of Citizenship in European Cities (MPMC)‹, promoted in 1996; and the OECD report ›Immigrants, Integration and Cities. Exploring the Links‹ (OECD 1998), which also included cities in Australia, the United States, and Canada.

13   See Thränhardt 1992 for an analysis of German *Länder* and Blommaert and Martiniello 1996 on regional policies in Belgium.

14   See for instance Zincone 1998 on Italian integration and citizenship policy; Sciortino 1999 and Pastore 2000 on migration controls.

these latter being more concerned with relations between levels of government and different – public, private, civil society – actors in policy-making (governance approach).[15]

In the second stream, i.e. local-level policy-making studies, two research pathways can be singled out: classical implementation studies, focusing on administrative discretion and bureaucratic practices in regularisation procedures (Zucchini 1998), permits' renewal (Triandafyllidou 2003), and in the issuing of the permanent residence permit (*carta di soggiorno*) introduced by Law n. 40/1998 (Fasano and Zucchini 2001); and studies that analyse local policy-making as a process starting from below, i.e. from local policy networks and/or organisations in civil society that are mobilised on specific issues. Most of these studies are of a comparative kind and consider city policies at large[16], while others rather focused on specific issues such as housing and first reception policies (Ponzo 2008) or mosques' building as a highly politicised policy-making process (see Saint-Blanc and Schmidt di Friedberg 2005).

Compared with the first studies on local policy, this second generation of research is clearly more influenced by international debates and theorising not only in migration studies, but also in other research traditions such as implementation and policy-making, on the one hand, and local welfare mix, on the other. As a consequence, their contribution is not limited to merely showing the pitfalls of the national models approach in the ›exceptional‹ Italian context. Local immigrant policy in Italy is actually regarded as a case study for exploring more general hypotheses and – middle-range – theories on bureaucratic behaviour, multilevel governance and/or welfare state restructuring.

The third research stream identified above is concerned with policy outcomes, i.e. with the intended and unintended, expected and unexpected consequences of specific legislative measures, and in particular of amnesties for irregular immigrants on the one hand, and Italian citizenship and nationality laws on the other. As for the first topic, the incredible success of the amnesty approved right after the 2002 Bossi-Fini law stimulated a great number of studies overtly questioning the efficacy of such policies in tackling with issues of entry control and labour market regulation (Barbagli, Colombo and Sciortino 2004; Strozza and Zucchetti 2006). On the other hand, research on the unexpected consequences and side-effects of the Italian nationality laws have acquired a particular relevance in the recent years and following the centre-left Amato bill mentioned above. These studies have highlighted the irrational and somehow paradoxical consequences of those norms that favour the descendants of emigrants in South America, most of whom apply for Italian passports to get easier access to the US or to Spain (Zincone 2006; Tintori 2009). Furthermore, recent studies on the second-generation immigrants in Italy have pointed out how the difficulties of becoming Italian citizens despite

---

15 See Zincone and Caponio 2006.
16 See for instance CeSPI 2000 on the cases of Milan and Rome; Caponio 2006 on Milan, Bologna, and Naples; Campomori 2008 and Barberis 2007 on medium-sized cities.

being born in the country undermines the sense of national identity of these youngsters (Bosisio et al. 2005).

If the three research streams described so far have focused on policy and policy-making, a fourth emerging research path is that on political mobilisation on immigration related issues. Most of these studies have investigated immigrant associations using the theoretical lens of collective action and social mobilisation theory, looking in particular at *political opportunity structures* (Danese 2001; Caponio 2005) and at networks and societal organisational resources (Eggert and Pilati 2007). Resource mobilisation theory lies also behind Ruzza's (2008) analysis of the Italian antiracist movement. Other studies on immigrants' mobilisation have adopted either a social capital perspective (Caselli 2006) or a more micro-sociological one, focusing on practices of social recognition and identity formation taking place within immigrants and/or mixed voluntary associations (Mantovan 2007; Camozzi 2008).

Research on Immigrants' Social Integration. Competing Perspectives

Along with public policy and mobilisation on immigration, another issue that received increasing attention by scholarly research on migration in Italy throughout the 1990s to this day is that of immigrants' integration. Such an interest can be traced back to the demographic enquiries on the immigrant population of the beginning of the decade (see above) that already attempted to collect data on the living conditions of immigrants, with a particular attention to employment and housing (Blangiardo, Strozza and Terzera 2006, 153). On the other hand, the first – above mentioned – naïve ›communities studies‹, too, were actually concerned with investigating how the different immigrant cultures were adapting to the Italian receiving society.

However, it is only in the late 1990s that a quality leap in such a debate actually occurred, with the emergence of two different, even though almost not communicant, research pathways: the quantitative path aimed at measuring social integration, developed in particular by demographers and, to a lesser extent, by sociologists; and the qualitative one, prevailing among sociologists and anthropologists, and more concerned with patterns of immigrants' incorporation and/or relations with the countries of origin. Let us analyse both research paths in-depth here, by looking in particular at the implications in terms of research paradigms and theoretical perspectives.

As for the first approach, the Commission for the Integration of Immigrants, as already mentioned, played indeed a crucial role in initiating a debate on the measurement of immigrants' integration, in line with previous initiatives undertaken by the Council of Europe (1997; 2000).[17] The first report of the Commission proposed an operational definition of »reasonable integration«, implying

---

17 More recently, literature reviews on indicators of immigrants' integration have been commissioned by the European Commission (Entzinger and Biezeveld 2003) and by the ILO in the context of the INTI project ›Managing equality in diversity‹ (Zincone, Caponio and Carastro 2006).

both nationals' and immigrants' physical and psychological well-being, on the one hand, and positive interaction between different groups, on the other (Zincone 2000). On this basis, in the second report a number of indicators on both dimensions were identified, taking into account for operationalisation the availability of official sources and administrative data (Golini 2005). Clearly, the Commission study looked at integration in aggregate terms, by considering immigrants either as a whole or as different national groups to be compared on a number of properties such as: long-term resident permits (higher rates indicating a higher level of integration), participation in the labour market or family reunions as far as the individual well-being dimension was concerned; or mixed marriages and criminal rates as indicators of positive interaction. Integration was essentially assumed as a process of gradual stabilisation into the Italian society and assimilation in the sense of becoming similar to the mainstream or reduction of immigrants' specific behavioural traits (such as remittances, endogamic marriages etc.).

A similar approach lies behind the regional indexes of social and labour market inclusion of third-country nationals elaborated since 2002 by the National Council for the Economy and Labour (Cnel) in order to »measure the potential for socio-economic integration of immigrants in the various areas, regions and provinces of the country« (Di Sciullo 2008, 6). A system of indexes has been constructed from a range of available statistical territorial indicators on the social and economic conditions of immigrants. In 2008, in the context of the EU INTI project ›Migrants' Integration Territorial Index‹ (MITI), such a methodological approach was applied to four more countries – France, the UK, Spain and Portugal – in order to allow for cross-regional and cross-country comparison at the same time.[18] Three indexes were identified: 1) the index of *absorptive capacity*, measuring the capacity of a local/regional area to attract and keep a sizeable foreign population; 2) the index of *social stability*, measuring the level of social inclusion and adaptation in each local area; 3) the index of *labour market*, concerning the level and type of inclusion of migrants in the local labour market. On each indicator, the situation of third-country nationals was compared with that of national citizens in order to identify the gaps between the two groups.

As is clear, such attempts to measure integration at an aggregate level look at inclusion as a ›capacity of the territory‹, thus implying that it is the product of specific structural factors. Among these, a prominent role is assigned to policies, of the efficacy of which some of the territorial indexes are considered to be a proxy (Pittau 2008, 12).[19] From such a structural approach a linear theory of integration follows: immigrants can be considered as integrated insofar as they acquire positions similar to those of nationals in access to health, school, housing, labour market etc.

---

18 For methodological problems and constraints faced by the research group see: Di Sciullo 2008, 7f.
19 This is the case for instance of indicators concerning housing conditions or access to health care.

A similar linear approach is shared also by the few research studies that have attempted to measure integration at an individual level through specific surveys. Blangiardo, Strozza and Terzera (2006), for instance, define integration as the product of five variables that are regarded as »objective« pre-requisites, i.e.: juridical status (ranging from the condition of naturalised Italian citizen to long-term resident, limited residence permit, no regular permit at all); registration at the municipal population register (yes/no); employment conditions (regular worker, family dependant, irregular worker, unemployed); housing conditions (ownership, rent of an apartment, sharing with others who are no family members, precarious solutions); family situation (living with the family/living alone or with friends). Integrated individuals are considered to be those who show the better positions on each variable, i.e. 1) have acquired Italian citizenship, 2) are registered at the municipality, 3) are regularly employed, 4) live in a house of their own property and 5) with their original or acquired family.[20]

It is not intended to enter here into a discussion of each indicator and its presumed ›objective‹ relevance in order to define integration. Yet, some of the chosen measures, such as for instance housing and family, clearly reveal that the benchmark of integration is the Italian social and cultural mainstream, notoriously characterised by high levels of house ownership and the crucial relevance of family for the sustenance of the individuals. The analysis does not only point out a linear conception of integration, but also a slightly assimilationist (in the classical Chicago School meaning) approach.

This can be said for the survey research carried out in 2000 by Recchi and Allam (2002). Actually, in this case the purpose was to account for the level of immigrants' cultural assimilation into Italian values and cultural orientations on the basis of a set of variables operationalising two competing perspectives, i.e. socio-economic integration[21] and immigrants' cultural background, with a particular attention to their religious affiliation and identification. Actually, the authors appear to be particularly concerned with Muslim religion regarded as a possible obstacle to adhesion to Italian cultural values and models of behaviour.[22] As is clear, integration as a socio-economic process is regarded just as a first step towards cultural assimilation, which is implicitly conceived as a linear, straight-line path of incorporation into mainstream Italian society and culture. The study points out that it is neither the ethnic background nor the religious affiliation *per*

---

20   The importance of other socio-cultural factors, not analysed by the survey, is also acknowledged, yet the socio-structural factors mentioned above are considered as ›objectively‹ more relevant.
21   This was measured by an index called ›level of integration‹, composed of a plurality of indicators such as: knowledge of the Italian language, stability of the housing conditions, social security position and legal residence status (Recchi and Allam 2002, 129).
22   The authors define cultural assimilation as a process implying three distinct dimensions, i.e.: socio-cultural practices (among the indicators considered: hang around with Italians, knowing about Italian news, supporting an Italian football team etc.); ethic values (indicators centred in particular on gender roles and the family, children education etc.); sense of national identity. For the full list of indicators see: Recchi and Allam 2002, 130f.

se to interfere with processes of assimilation but rather – Islamic – religious practice, clearly emphasising the authors' preference for a uni-dimensional theory of assimilation.

Such a straight-line assimilation theory does not seem to be shared by the first quantitative study on second generations' and foreign minors' school integration, the Itagen2 project, carried out during the school year 2005/06 to survey foreign pupils' school attainment in ten Italian regions (Casacchia et al. 2008). Actually, this research has adapted to the Italian context the questionnaire adopted by Portes and colleagues in their survey on second generations in Florida and California (Portes and Rumbaut 2001), thus sharing a view based on the concept of segmented assimilation. Immigrants' agency seems to creep in the analysis, or at least is somehow more considered than in the other surveys mentioned above.[23]

However, it is in qualitative studies that migrants' agency and their social relations have received greater analytical attention. Two perspectives can be regarded as particularly prominent today: the network approach, looking at opportunities and constraints of interpersonal solidarity ties; the transnational approach, considering also the links with the countries of origin and how these affect migrants' lives in their contexts of destination.

The first researchers adopting the network approach were concerned essentially with solidarity networks among foreign women and in specific communities such as the Senegalese one. Some analyses pointed out the intertwining of ethnic networks and host country institutions, as in the case of female migration from Catholic countries such as the Philippines and Peru (Ambrosini, Lodigiani and Zandrini 1995), which since the beginning could rely upon crucial resources of contact and mediation with the receiving society provided by Catholic parishes. Immigrants' networks have thus been regarded primarily as vehicles of social capital, providing crucial resources especially for the newly arrived, e.g. first job, a place to stay etc.

However, recent studies have assumed a somehow more critical stance, highlighting also the trapping effect of immigrants' networks into specific segments of the labour market, constraining possible trajectories of social mobility. This is clearly pointed out by the flourishing literature on immigrant female domestic workers (see contributions in Caponio and Colombo 2005; Andall and Sarti 2004; Catanzaro e Colombo 2009) and on ethnic entrepreneurship. In the case of Chinese businesses (Ceccagno 2003) for instance, among the ethnic resources mobilised by the community's network, the cheap labour of newly arrived illegal immigrants has to be considered, too. In the case of the Egyptians in Milan, along with the groups' social capital, also human capital – education, family's financial endowments etc. – seems to matter (Ambrosini and Abbatecola 2002; Codagnone 2003). Finally, opportunity structures may account for differences in groups'

---

23 It has to be pointed out, however, that not all research on the integration of second-generation immigrants adopts such an approach. Most of these studies are actually focused on accounting for gaps in school attainment between migrant and native children.

involvement in entrepreneurial activities in different contexts: Schmidt di Friedberg (2002) has pointed out how in the early 1990s Moroccans monopolised the sector of *halal* butcheries in Turin, while in Milan this sector was already occupied by Egyptians.

As is clear, from a first, a-critical enthusiasm for the network perspective in the analysis of immigrants' patterns of accommodation and integration in the Italian society, a more critical perspective prevails today.[24] Such a critical approach also characterises most of the more recent studies on immigrants' transnationalism. Actually, following developments primarily in the US migration studies, most Italian – younger – researchers seem to have adhered from the very beginning to the second-generation wave of studies, which, according to Rogers (2000), appear to be more aware of the structural and institutional factors constraining immigrants' agency, thus abandoning the somehow naïve and unconditionally positive stance of first accounts of immigrants' transnational practices. Studies have been carried out in Italy on transnationalism among Senegalese (Ceschi 2005; Riccio 2002), Peruvian (Caselli 2009), Rumanian (Cingolani 2009) and Ecuadorian (Boccagni 2009) immigrants. Moreover, a number of researchers have adopted a gender perspective to analyse transnational care practices and the changing social role of women in the countries of origin (Salih 2003; Baldisserri 2005).

In the context of this research stream, integration has been regarded as a multi-dimensional and interactive process, one that can actually follow a multiplicity of non-linear paths.[25] Transnational practices may well coexist and somehow reinforce successful integration, as pointed out by the study of Peruvian and Rumanian immigrants that have started their own businesses in Italy (Caselli 2009; Cingolani 2009). Yet transnationalism can also assume the form of nostalgia and pain for those women who left their family behind, or it can represent a symbolic dimension of positive identification to counteract perceived discrimination and marginalisation in the Italian society, as in the case of Ecuadorian and Eritrean second generations (Queirolo Palmas 2006; Andall 2002). In order to account for these different patterns of integration/transnational combinations, factors such as class, gender, age and migratory path appear to be crucial.

As is clear from this very brief literature review, it is difficult to identify a prevailing paradigm in contemporary Italian research on immigrants' integration. Whereas quantitative studies emphasise structural, and often also cultural, factors in accounting for immigrants' linear paths of integration, qualitative research pays greater attention to agency, social relations and transnational ties. The dialogue between these two perspectives appears scarce at the moment. if almost non-existent. Yet, the search for specific patterns of integration/assimilation cum transnationalism, following Morawska (2004), would indeed shed new light on

---

24 Actually, the concept of network has also been applied to the study of smuggling and trafficking as well as of deviant groups such as young Algerian migrants involved in illegal activities in Milan (Colombo 1998).
25 Such a conceptualisation is very close to Morawska's (2008) definition of assimilation in today's US migration studies.

how ›objective‹ structural conditions combine with immigrants' interpersonal relations, practices and orientations towards their countries of origin.

Italian Migration Studies Today. Gaps and Perspectives

As we attempted to point out, the developing of migration studies in Italy was characterised by the shift from one prevailing macro-structural paradigm embodying two alternative theoretical perspectives, Marxism and structural functionalism, to the emerging of a new, more agent-oriented perspective. Under this broad paradigm, different theoretical and methodological approaches can be found, i.e. segmented assimilation, network and social capital, transnationalism. Moreover, the structuralist paradigm, especially in its functional version, continues to be very vital and productive, as pointed out by the research stream on immigrants' integration indicators.

As a latecomer immigration country, research in Italy has been at the beginning almost exclusively concerned with making sense of new, unexpected, arrivals of foreign immigrants. Yet, throughout the 1990s and 2000s, thanks to the converging pressures of the research-policy nexus, on the one hand, assigning top priority to integration in the political agenda, and of the emerging of a new generation of highly internationalised scholars, on the other, Italian research on migration has started to characterise in the European context as path-breaking in some respect. In contrast to ›old‹ EU immigration countries, US literature seems to have exerted a stronger influence (Caponio 2008, 456), as emphasised by the success of the network approach among sociologists and of the policy approach among political scientists, as well as by the agent-driven version of transnationalism informing much of today's Italian – especially sociological and anthropological – research. Can we conclude that, from a latecomer position in international migration research, Italy has gradually reached a forerunner one? Let us try to find an answer by looking at potentialities and gaps in today's Italian scholarship.

A positive starting point is represented of course by the consolidation of the research infrastructure, with the emerging of new independent institutes such as the Forum Internazionale ed Europeo di Ricerche sull'Immigrazione (FIERI), founded in 2002 in Turin with the purpose of promoting research on the various aspects related with international migratory phenomena, e.g. inclusion in the labour market, social integration, transnationalism, policy-making etc., in collaboration with the main European research centres on migration.[26] More recent initiatives are those of Medì-Migrazioni nel Mediterraneo that started operating in Genoa in 2005[27] and of Scenari Migratori e Mutamento Sociale – Migratory Perspectives and Social Change (SMMS) promoted by the University of Trento in

---

26   FIERI is the only Italian member of the network of excellence IMISCOE (Immigration, Integration and Social Cohesion in Europe), funded by the EU in the context of the VIth Framework Programme and now self-financed by its members. This can be considered an indicator of such an increasing international profile of migration research in Italy.

27   It organises an annual summer school on Italian migration studies.

2008. In general, however, and with the exception of SMMS, migration studies are still poorly institutionalised in the Italian academic structure. This is particularly evident in the lack of PhD specific training programmes on migration of an interdisciplinary kind.

As a consequence, this results in a certain unevenness in terms of interest and level of research on migration in Italian social sciences: whereas sociology, anthropology and demography have already shown a considerable level of involvement in the field, other disciplines such as political science, juridical studies and economy have known an increasing interest only in recent years, while still others like psychology, geography and history lag behind. In particular, as far as this latter is concerned, much of the focus – with few exceptions of course – is still on the Italian emigration of the past, with rare parallels with contemporary immigration flows and patterns of integration.

Together with these lacks in the institutional research structure, other gaps at a more theoretical and substantive level have to be addressed. First of all, on the theoretical plan, a certain under-theorisation of the concept of ethnicity is evident. This is the case, for instance, of Italian studies on female domestic workers mentioned above, which so far have focused essentially on the functioning of foreign women's solidarity networks and on their differing levels of endowment with social capital. On the contrary, foreign scholars, especially British and American, have adopted a more critical and structural perspective, showing patterns of overlapping ethnic, racial, and social inequality in the employment of migrant women in the Italian domestic sector (see Andall 2000; Anderson 2000; Parreñas Salazar 2001). Dismissed as an old, in many respects highly ideological, Marxist perspective, critical social thinking seems to have almost disappeared from contemporary Italian migration research.

On the other hand, on the substantive plan, a major gap can be found in research on second generations. Today this represents a key challenge in southern Europe and in Italy in particular. So far, studies have concentrated on pupils' school attainment and, to a lesser extent, on foreign adolescents who were born in Italy or who joined their parents immigrated to the country, exploring their social relations and processes of identity formation. Far less attention has been devoted to processes of inclusion/exclusion from the labour market and post-graduate education, i.e. the key arenas for the second generations' social mobility. Research on factors accounting for social exclusion, particularly relevant in the ›old‹ European immigration countries, as well as studies on different patterns of immigrant youth's integration/assimilation, more developed in the US context, has still to be systematically pursued in Italy, especially in times when most of the foreign babies arrived or born in Italy in the late 1980s early 1990s are now in their early twenties.

These are just a few remarks showing that migration research in Italy, while far more developed and promising than two decades ago, still has to go some way to become a fully consolidated research field. As pointed out above, since the late 1990s Italian scholars have started to publish increasingly in English and chapters on the case of Italy have been incorporated in many comparative publications on immigrant and immigration policies.[28] Moreover, the younger generation of Italian researchers seems to be particularly influenced by US scholarship on assimilation and transnationalism. Still, a great deal of research is too often confined in Italian language publications and within strict disciplinary bounds. This does not go in the direction of strengthening the international profile of Italian migration studies.

References

Ambrosini, Maurizio, and Emanuela Abbatecola. 2002. Reti di relazione e percorsi di inserimento lavorativo degli stranieri: l'imprenditorialità egiziana a Milano. In *Stranieri in Italia: Assimilati ed esclusi*, ed. Asher Colombo and Giuseppe Sciortino, 195–223. Bologna: Il Mulino.

Ambrosini, Maurizio, Rosangela Lodigiani, and Sara Zandrini. 1995. *L'integrazione subalterna: Peruviani, eritrei e filippini nel mercato del lavoro milanese*. Milan: Fondazione Cariplo-Ismu.

Andall, Jacqueline. 2000. *Gender, Migration and Domestic Service: The Politics of Black Women in Italy*. Aldershot: Ashgate.

Andall, Jacqueline. 2002. Second Generation Attitude? African-Italians in Milan. *Journal of Ethnic and Migration Studies* 28 (3): 389–407.

Andall, Jacqueline, and Raffaella Sarti, ed. 2004. Le trasformazioni del servizio domestico in Italia: un'introduzione. *Polis* 13 (1): 5-16.

Anderson, Bridget. 2000. *Doing the Dirty Work? The Global Politics of Domestic Labour*. London and New York: Zed Books.

Baldisserri, Margherita. 2005. Relazioni famigliari nell'immigrazione delle peruviane a Firenze. In *Stranieri in Italia: Migrazioni globali, integrazioni locali*, ed. Tiziana Caponio and Asher Colombo, 89–116. Bologna: Il Mulino.

Barbagli, Marzio, Asher Colombo, and Giuseppe Sciortino, ed. 2004. *I sommersi e i sanati: Le regolarizzazioni degli immigrati in Italia*. Bologna: Il Mulino.

Barberis, Eduardo. 2007. Le politiche migratorie a Modena e a Vicenza. *Mondi Migranti* 3: 61–82.

Blangiardo, Marta, Salvatore Strozza, and Laura Terzera. 2006. Indicatori di integrazione degli immigrati in Italia. In *Il Mezzogiorno dopo la grande regolarizzazione – Immagini e problematiche dell'immigrazione, vol III*, ed. Gian Carlo Blagiardo and Patrizia Farina, 153–89. Milan: Angeli.

---

28 At the same time, the Italian case has started to become more and more a research field for an increasing number of foreign scholars, as pointed out by the researches on domestic workers in Italy mentioned above. This is the case also with researchers working on public policy, who have analysed Italian immigrant and immigration policy in comparison with other countries. See for instance Calavita 2005 on the cases of Italy and Spain, and Finotelli (2004) on Italy and Germany.

Blommaert, Jan, and Marco Martiniello. 1996. Ethnic Mobilization, Multiculturalism and the Political Process in Two Belgian Cities: Antwerp and Liège. *Innovation* 9 (1): 51–73.

Boccagni, Paolo. 2009. *Tracce transnazionali: Vite in Italia e proiezioni verso casa tra i migranti ecuadoriani.* Milan: Franco Angeli.

Bonifazi, Corrado. 2007. *L'immigrazione straniera in Italia.* 2nd ed. Bologna: Il Mulino.

Bosisio, Roberta, Enzo Colombo, Luisa Leonini, and Paola Rebughini. 2005. *Stranieri & italiani: Una ricerca tra gli adolescenti figli di immigrati nelle scuole superiori.* Rome: Donzelli Editore.

Calavita, Kitty. 2005. *Immigrants at the Margins: Law, Race, and Exclusion in Southern Europe.* Cambridge: Cambridge University Press.

Camozzi, Ilenya. 2008. *Lo spazio del riconoscimento: Forme di associazionismo migratorio a Milano.* Bologna: Il Mulino.

Campomori, Francesca. 2008. *Immigrazione e cittadinanza locale: La governance dell'integrazione in Italia.* Rome: Carocci.

Caponio, Tiziana. 2005. Policy Networks and Immigrants Associations in Italy: The Cases of Milan, Bologna and Napoles. *Journal of Ethnic and Migation Studies* 31 (5): 931–50.

Caponio, Tiziana. 2006. *Città italiane e immigrazione: Discorso pubblico e politiche a Milano, Bologna e Napoli.* Bologna: Il Mulino.

Caponio, Tiziana. 2008. (Im)migration Research in Italy: A European Comparative Perspective. *Sociological Quarterly* 49 (3): 445–64.

Caponio, Tiziana, and Asher Colombo, ed. 2005. *Stranieri in Italia: Migrazioni globali, integrazioni locali.* Bologna: Il Mulino.

Casacchia, Oliviero, Luisa Natale, Anna Paterno, and Laura Terzera, ed. 2008. *Studiare insieme, crescere insieme? Un'indagine sulle seconde generazioni in dieci regioni italiane.* Milan: Franco Angeli.

Caselli, Marco. 2006. *Le associazioni di migranti in provincia di Milano.* Milan: Franco Angeli.

Caselli, Marco. 2009. *Vite transnazionali? Peruviani e peruviane a Milano.* Milan: Franco Angeli.

Catanzaro, Raimondo, and Asher Colombo, ed. 2009. *Badanti & Co. Il lavoro domestico straniero in Italia.* Bologna: Il Mulino.

Ceccagno, Anna, ed. 2003. *Migranti a Prato: Il distretto tessile multietnico.* Milan: Angeli.

Censis (Centro Studi Investimenti Sociali). 1991. *Immigrati e società italiana* Conferenza Nazionale dell'Immigrazione. Rome: Editalia.

Ceschi, Sebastiano. 2005. Flessibilità e istanze di vita: Operai senegalesi nelle fabbriche della provincia di Bergamo. In *Stranieri in Italia,* ed. Caponio and Colombo, 175–204.

CeSPI. 2000. Migrazioni e politiche locali: l'esperienza italiana nel quadro europeo. In *Migrazioni. Scenari per il XXI° secolo*, 833–948. Rome: Agenzia Romana per la preparazione del Giubileo.

Cingolani, Pietro. 2009. *Romeni d'Italia: Migrazioni, vita quotidiana e legami transnazionali*. Bologna: Il Mulino.

Cocchi, Giovanni, ed. 1990. *Stranieri in Italia: Caratteri e tendenze dell'immigrazione dai paesi extracomunitari*. Bologna: Nuova Cappelli.

Codagnone, Cristiano. 2003. Imprenditori immigrati: quadro teorico e comparativo. In *Immigrati imprenditori: Il contributo degli extracomunitari allo sviluppo della piccola impresa in Lombardia*, ed. Antonio Chiesi and Eugenio Zucchetti, 33–85. Milan: Egea.

Colombo, Asher. 1998. *Etnografia di un'economia clandestina: Immigrati algerini a Milano*. Bologna: Il Mulino.

Colombo, Asher, and Giuseppe Sciortino. 2003. The Bossi-Fini Law: Explicit Fanaticism, Implicit Moderation and Poisoned Fruits. In *Italian Politics 2003*, ed. Jean Blondel and Paolo Segatti, 162–80. Oxford: Berg.

Colombo, Asher, and Giuseppe Sciortino. 2004. Italian Immigration: The Origins, Nature and Evolution of Italy's Migratory Systems. *Journal of Modern Italian Studies* 9 (1): 49–70.

Corti, Paola, and Matteo Sanfilippo. 2009. Introduzione. In *Storia d'Italia – Migrazioni*, ed. idem, 17–23. Turin: Einaudi.

Council of Europe. 1995. *Area-Based Projects in Districts of High Immigrant Concentration*. Strasbourg: Council of Europe.

Council of Europe. 1997. *Measurement and Indicators of Integration*. Strasbourg: Council of Europe.

Council of Europe. 2000. *Diversité et cohesion: des nouveaux défies pour l'intégration des immigrés et des minorités*. Strasbourg: Council of Europe.

Danese, Gaia. 2001. Participation beyond Citizenship: Migrants' Associations in Italy and Spain. *Patterns of Prejudice* 35 (1): 69–89.

Delle Donne, Marcella, Umberto Melotti, and Stefano Petilli, ed. 1993. *Immigrazione in Europa: Solidarietà e conflitto*. Rome: Cediss.

Di Sciullo, Luigi. 2008. The European Research Project: Migrants' Integration Territorial Index. In *Measuring Integration: The Italian Case*, 5–8. Rome: Idios.

Eggert, Nina, and Katia Pilati. 2007. Religious Cleavages, Organisations and the Political Participation of Immigrants in Milan and Zurich. Paper presented at the ECPR General Conference, September 6–8, in Pisa, Italy.

Entzinger, Hans, and Renske Biezeveld. 2003. Benchmarking in Immigrant Integration. Rotterdam, Ercomer/FSW, Report for the European Commission, http://www.uu.nl/uupublish/onderzoek/onderzoekcentra/ercomer/researchers/profdrhanentzing/29393main.html (accessed May 2009).

Fasano, Luciano, and Francesco Zucchini. 2001. L'implementazione locale del testo unico sull'immigrazione. In *Sesto rapporto sulle migrazioni 2000*, ed. Fondazione Cariplo-Ismu, 39–50. Milan: Angeli.

Fedele, Marcello. 1999. *Il ruolo del Parlamento nella riorganizzazione del governo centrale: il caso del Ministero del lavoro, della salute e delle politiche sociali.* Polity – Osservatorio istituzionale sulle politiche pubbliche, unpublished research report.

Finotelli, Claudia. 2004. A Comparative Analysis of the Italian and the German Asylum Policies. In *Migration and the Regulation of Social Integration* (IMIS-Beiträge 24), ed. Anita Böcker, Betty de Hart and Ines Michalowski, 87–96. Osnabrück: IMIS.

Golini, Antonio, ed. 2005. *L'immigrazione straniera: indicatori e misure di integrazione.* Bologna: Il Mulino.

Golini, Antonio, Salvatore Strozza, and Flavia Amato. 2001. Un sistema di indicatori di integrazione: primo tentativo di costruzione. In *Secondo rapporto sull'integrazione degli immigrati in Italia*, ed. Zincone, 85–155.

Lostia, Angela, and Grazia Tomaino. 1994. Diritti sociali e differenze territoriali. Appendix to: Giovanna Zinconce. *Uno schermo contro il razzismo*, 97–112. Rome: Donzelli.

Mantovan, Claudia. 2007. *Immigrazione e cittadinanza: Auto-organizzazione e partecipazione degli immigrati in Italia.* Milan: Franco Angeli.

Melotti, Umberto. 1993. Migrazioni internazionali e integrazione sociale: il caso italiano e le esperienze europee. In *Immigrazione in Europa: solidarietà e conflitto*, ed. Delle Donne, Melotti and Petilli, 29–66.

Morawska, Ewa. 2004. Exploring Diversity in Immigrant Assimilation and Transnationalism: Poles and Russian Jews in Philadelphia. *International Migration Review* 38 (4): 1372–1412.

Morawska, Ewa. 2008. Research on Immigration/Ethnicity in Europe and the United States: A Comparison. *The Sociological Quarterly* 49 (3): 465–82.

Morokvašić, Mirjana, ed. 1984. *Migration in Europe: Trends in Research and Sociological Approaches* (Current Sociology 32), London: Sage.

Mottura, Giovanni, ed. 1992. *L'arcipelago immigrazione. Caratteristiche e modelli migratori dei lavoratori stranieri in Italia.* Rome: Ediesse.

OECD. 1998. *Immigrants, Integration and Cities. Exploring the Links.* Paris: OECD.

Parreñas Salazar, Rachel. 2001. *Servants of Globalization: Women, Migration and Domestic Work.* Stanford: Stanford University Press.

Pastore, Ferruccio. 2000. Italy Facing International Migration: Recent Policy Developments. *The International Spectator* 35 (2): 29–40.

Pittau, Franco. 2008. Integration and Statistical Analysis in Italy. In *Measuring Integration. The Italian Case*, 9–13. Rome: Idios.

Ponzo, Irene. 2008. Quello che i comuni hanno in commune: Politiche locali di accoglienza per gli immigrati. *Polis* 3: 451–82.

Portes, Alejandro, and Rubén Rumbaut, ed. 2001. *Legacies: The Story of the Immigrant Second Generation*. Berkeley: University of California Press.

Queirolo Palmas, Luca. 2006. *Prove di seconde generazioni: Giovani di origine immigrata tra scuola e spazi urbani*. Milan: Franco Angeli.

Recchi, Ettore, and Magdi Allam. 2002. L'assimilazione degli immigrati nella società italiana. In *Stranieri in Italia: Assimilati ed esclusi*, ed. Asher Colombo and Giuseppe Sciortino, 119–42. Bologna: Il Mulino.

Rella, Piera, and Titta Vadalà. 1984. Sociological Literature on Migration in Italy. *Current Sociology* 32: 143–74.

Reyneri, Emilio. 1979. *La catena migratoria*. Bologna: Il Mulino.

Riccio, Bruno. 2002. Etnografia dei migranti transnazionali: l'esperienza senegalese tra inclusione ed esclusione. In *Stranieri in Italia: Assimilati ed esclusi*, ed. Asher Colombo and Giuseppe Sciortino, 169–94. Bologna: Il Mulino.

Rogers, Ali. 2000. A European Space for Transnationalism? Working paper for the Transnational Community Programme WPTC 2K-07, University of Oxford, www.transcomm.ox.ac.uk/working%20papers/rogers.pdf (accessed July 4, 2009).

Ruzza, Carlo. 2008. The Italian Antiracist Movement between Advocacy, Service Delivery and Political Protest. *International Journal of Sociology* 38 (2): 55–64.

Saint-Blancat, Chantal, and Ottavia Schmidt di Friedberg. 2005. Why are Mosques a Problem? Local Politics and Fear of Islam in Northern Italy. *Journal of Ethnic and Migration Studies* 31 (6): 1083–1104.

Salih, Ruba. 2003. *Gender in Transnationalism: Home, Longing and Belonging Among Moroccan Migrant Women*. London: Routledge.

Schmidt di Friedberg, Ottavia. 2002. Du local au transnational: Les réseaux économiques et les activités d'entreprise des Marocains à Milan et à Turin. In *La Méditerranée des réseaux: Marchands, entrepreneurs et migrants entre l'Europe et le Maghreb*, ed. Jacqueline Cesari, 27–62. Paris: Maisonneuve & Larose.

Sciortino, Giuseppe. 1999. Planning in the Dark: The Evolution of the Italian System of Migration Controls. In *Mechanisms of Immigration Control*, ed. Thomas Hammar and Grete Brochmann, 233–60. Oxford: Berg.

Sciortino, Giuseppe. 2004. Immigration in a Mediterranean Welfare State: The Italian Experience in Comparative Perspective. *Journal of Comparative Policy Analysis* 6 (2): 111–30.

Strozza, Salvatore, and Eugenio Zucchetti. 2006. *Il Mezzogiorno dopo la grande regolarizzazione – Vecchi e nuovi volti della presenza migratoria, vol II*. Milan: Franco Angeli.

Thränhardt, Dietrich. 1992. Germany: An Undeclared Immigration Country. In *Europe – A New Immigration Continent: Policies and Politics since 1945 in Comparative Perspective*, ed. idem, 167–94. Münster: Lit.

Tintori, Guido. 2009. *Fardelli d'Italia? Conseguenze nazionali e transnazionali delle politiche di cittadinanza italiane.* Rome: Carocci.

Triandafyllidou, Anna. 2003. Immigration Policy Implementation in Italy: Organisational Culture, Identity Processes and Labour Market Control. *Journal of Ethnic and Migration Studies* 29 (2): 257–97.

Zanfrini, Laura. 1998. *Leggere le migrazioni: I risultati della ricerca empirica, le categorie interpretative, i problemi aperti.* Milan: Angeli.

Zincone, Giovanna. 1994. *Uno schermo contro il razzismo.* Rome: Donzelli.

Zincone, Giovanna. 1998. Multiculturalism from Above: Italian Variation on a European Theme. In *Blurred Boundaries: Living with Diversity*, ed. Rainer Bauböck and John Rundell, 143–84. Aldershot: Ashgate.

Zincone, Giovanna, ed. 2000. *Primo rapporto sull'integrazione degli immigrati in Italia.* Bologna: Il Mulino.

Zincone, Giovanna, ed. 2001. *Secondo rapporto sull'integrazione degli immigrati in Italia.* Bologna: Il Mulino.

Zincone, Giovanna, ed. 2006. *Familismo legale: Come (non) diventare cittadini italiani.* Rome-Bari: Laterza.

Zincone, Giovanna. 2008. Italian Immigrants and Immigration Policymaking: Structures, Actors and Practices. IMISCOE working paper, http://www.imiscoe.org (accessed July 4, 2009).

Zincone, Giovanna, and Tiziana Caponio. 2006. The Multilevel Governance of Migration. In *The Dynamics of International Migration and Settlement in Europe: A State of the Art*, ed. Rinus Penninx, Maria Berger and Karen Kraal, 269–304. Amsterdam: Amsterdam University Press.

Zincone, Giovanna, Tiziana Caponio, and Rossella Carastro. 2006. Integration Indicators. Research report for the European project ›Promoting Equality in Diversity. Integration in Europe‹ (INTI), Turin, FIERI, http://www.fieri.it/2006/php (accessed July 4, 2009).

Zincone, Giovanna, and Luigi Di Gregorio. 2002. Le politiche pubbliche per l'immigrazione in Italia: uno schema d'analisi eclettico. *Stato e mercato* 66 (3): 37–59.

Zucchini, Francesco. 1998. L'implementazione della politica pubblica per l'immigrazione: i casi di Torino e Brescia. In *Terzo rapporto sulle migrazioni 1997*, ed. Fondazione Cariplo-Ismu, 173–89. Milan: Angeli.

Zucchini, Francesco. 1999. La genesi in Parlamento della legge sull'immigrazione. In *Quarto rapporto sulle migrazioni 1998*, ed. Fondazione Cariplo-Ismu, 61–72. Milan: Angeli.

Japan: A Non-Immigration Country Discusses Migration

By Takashi Kibe and Dietrich Thränhardt

> »We are having discussion on that issue. Since the population will start declining, some people are saying that some sort of immigration is needed, while others say that since the market is globalized, we don't need any immigrant population in this country. That discussion is continuing. I do not have a decisive opinion at the moment.«
>
> Heizo Takenaka, Japanese Minister for Internal Affairs and Communications, Newsweek, December 19, 2005

Abstract

Japan is the exception among the industrial countries, insofar as it did not organise or allow any large immigration and was able to control its borders. In the 1990s some rather small side- and backdoors were opened, for trainees, ethnic Japanese and students. They are kept in a legal limbo, largely work in low-paid niches and are confronted with thick stereotypes about criminality. The number of informal migrants has been reduced in the 2000s. In spite of the low numbers, immigration has long been debated in the Japanese public, with not much effect on the official policy. Dozens of plans have been developed over the years which mostly focus on guest worker schemes, to make labour available without having much immigration. Research highlights the precarious situation of many migrants, problems of cultural difference, xenophobia and the activities of local government and NGOs to assist with integration, working against the national government. The larger economic reasons for the precarious situation in the dual labour market and deregulation leading to outsourcing are not sufficiently addressed.

Japanese Exceptionalism

»Yet Japan remains an anomaly. It is the only industrial democracy that has not relied heavily on foreign labour to fuel economic growth in the postwar period« (Hollifield 1992, 15). Cornelius (1994, 383) describes Japanese women caring for their own children as an »anomaly«, thus making the US pattern of an immigrant and black household underclass a norm of international development. The usual prediction then is that Japan will follow the other rich nations in recruiting immigrants for »jobs like housecleaning, street sweeping, and garbage collecting« (ibid.). Other specialists choose to exclude the unfitting Japanese case from their reflections about a built-in tendency of liberal countries to become more and more open for immigration, in a sort of elite conspiracy against the poorer strata of society who bear the costs (Freeman 1995; Brubaker 1995; Perlmutter 1996). Neglecting Japan, they do not mention the decisive deviant case and fall in another trap of American-European parochialism. This makes any general theoretical approach less meaningful, as Japan constitutes one of the three grand centres of advanced development, with its specific mix of traditional and imported features. As Bartram (2000) suggests, studying »negative cases« of labour migration – notably Japan – can contribute to advancing theory, by accounting for variation in migration outcomes. In other words, simply excluding »negative cases« from theoretical analysis does not enhance its explanatory power, only narrowing the scope of theory application.

The Japanese exceptionalism is even more fascinating when we look into the Asian environment. In the last decades, South East Asia as well as the Middle East have become focuses of migration, on the same level as North America and Western Europe, mostly pursuing rotational and rather exploitative immigration systems, at tremendous human costs on the side of the migrants. Malaysia and Thailand alone employ more than one million foreign workers each. Taiwan and South Korea, Japan's former colonies, have officially started foreign worker programmes. South Korea has taken an important first step in integrating foreigners by giving them the right to vote in local elections. An important part of the Philippine national income originates in migrants' remittances. Moreover, China offers to send millions of redundant workers, who are looming around in search of work. Their numbers are calculated between 120 and 200 million, or 10 to 15 per cent of the population. Why then, does Japan not allow immigration? How should we evaluate Japanese policies in contrast to those of the other advanced countries?

Japan's Non-Immigration Policy

In its report to the OECD of 1995, the Japanese government stated in a rather diplomatic language:

»The official policy of the Japanese government is to allow entry to foreigners with technological expertise, skills or knowledge or who engage in businesses which require a knowledge of foreign cultures not possessed by Japanese. On the other hand, the entry of unskilled workers is not encouraged, because of the potential impact on industry, labour, education, welfare and public security as well as because of the absence of a national consensus on the issue.« (OECD 1995, 99; see also OECD 1997, 122; the official argument at length in Ministry of Justice 1990).

At the heart of this reference to Japanese bureaucratic pluralism lies a longstanding and ongoing disagreement between the Ministries of Labour and Justice. When the senior author interviewed the responsible officer in the Ministry of Labour in 1991, he was quite outspoken on the necessity of non-skilled labour immigration for the Japanese economy, and of the opposite view of the Ministry of Justice in this matter. This has not changed since, and the Ministry of Justice is keeping a watchful eye. Whereas up to 1993 Japan was not represented in the OECD immigration group at all – as it did not consider itself a country of immigration – since 1994 it has two representatives in contrast to all other countries: one from the Ministry of Labour, the other from the Ministry of Justice (OECD 1995, 243; OECD 2008, 392). In addition, the Ministry of Foreign Affairs and the Ministries and Agencies of Economy and Agriculture are also in favour of accepting foreign workers (Kajita 1995, 14; Chiavacci 2009, 328).

In Japan, we find continuity of the decisive ministries' views indicating that bureaucratic decision-making prevails (Pempel 1974), resting upon a conservative consensus about the upholding of cultural and »racial« homogeneity (Yamanaka 1993, 72f.). The economic crisis of 2008/09 makes any change extremely unlikely for the foreseeable future, even when the 2009 elections brought an end to the LDP's power monopoly.

As in other countries, economic interests are manifold. The construction industry is suffering from an intense labour shortage, despite massive investment in new technologies. Not only in the big cities but everywhere in the country you can easily detect South Asian men working on construction sites (Komai 1995, 100–8). The entertainment industry, which before 1970 used to take over poor Japanese peasants' daughters, is another special interest group. All the statistics available show that construction for men and entertainment for women have been the most important employers of legal and illegal immigrants for years.

On the other hand, the most influential bodies of Japanese industry have long been reluctant to lobby for foreign labour. The large companies found other sources of labour. First, they moved some of their new production facilities from the centres to the periphery of the Japanese archipelago. The next step was investment in South East Asia where some of the labour-intensive industries are concentrated, closely linked to Japanese companies. Indicative is the high percentage of imports in certain labour intensive sectors: 85 per cent for wristwatches, 55 per cent for TV sets already in the fiscal year 1993/94 (The Nikkei Weekly, 19 December 1994, 1).

In the present worldwide economic crisis, an opening for immigration is even more unlikely. The traditions of life-long employment for core workers in large companies are in disarray. Since 1998, the times of full employment are over. Japan has avoided the high immigration rates of Western Europe and North America in its high growth era. Whatever the future developments, immigration will be much lower than in other OECD countries. Bureaucratic stubbornness and isolationism have prevented an easy solution to the problems of the labour market. Moreover, Japan's position as a latecomer in industrial development, compared to

Britain, France, Germany, or the US, provides some explanation (Thränhardt 1996b, 7–9).

Japan lost its colonies in 1945. With the Peace Treaty of San Francisco in 1952, it discontinued the citizenship of its colonial subjects, including even those who had served with the Imperial army, had become victims of Hiroshima, or continued to live in Japan. In legal terms, Koreans constitute the largest category of ›foreigners‹ in today's Japan. They number 613,791 people or 32.1 per cent of all registered foreigners (Immigration Bureau 2004, 33). Most of these ›Koreans‹ were born in Japan, many of them from parents also born in Japan, since the immigration had started before World War I, and they speak Japanese as their first language (Weiner 1989, 1997b; Sik 1990). Eighty per cent of resident Koreans have married Japanese partners, and Japanese citizenship can be inherited from the mother as well as from the father since the early 1970s. As a result, the numbers of Koreans tend to decline in the Japanese statistics (Immigration Bureau 2004, 34). Intergenerational turnover to Japanese citizenship is made up by some new immigration. However, young people with two nationalities must opt for one or the other under Japanese law (at least in theory). More recently, the number of naturalisations has more than doubled from 5,767 in 1988 to 14,104 in 1995 (OECD 1997, 253). Thus, the naturalisation rate is now at 1.0 per cent of the foreign population living in Japan, which, however, is still somewhat below the natural reproduction rate of the ›foreigners‹ in the country.

If we compare immigration in Japan and in other countries, the group of ›Koreans‹ should not be taken into account. In any other country the bulk of this group (with the exception of some newcomers, often students) would be citizens. Their ancestors or they themselves have been Japanese subjects. However, the story of their immigration is bound to a culture of colonial discrimination and counter-hatred. Climaxes were the killings of Koreans after the great Kanto earthquake of 1923, the forcefully assimilationist policy of the 1930s aimed at suppressing the Korean culture, the post-war obligation to fingerprint every five years, and the anti-Japanese propaganda of both Korean governments, competing for the allegiance of the Koreans in Japan. In contrast to Europe, the US did not encourage or mediate a rapprochement between the two countries after the war, but tolerated the intense discrimination on the Japanese side and xenophobic propaganda on the Korean side. It is only in the last years that some kind of détente is coming about. Korea and the Koreans are valued higher in Japan, in connection with their economic success. The Seoul Olympics and the Japanese-Korean football championship were breakthroughs in this respect. Things have normalised somewhat in the last years, even with state agencies. It has become possible to award prices in national school contests, in literature and the like to people of Korean origin. Kimchi, the Korean national dish, and Korean pop stars have become popular in Japan. One reason for this upgrading of the Koreans is the existence and visibility of new immigration groups in Japan, triggering a shift of negative attitudes from an old outsider group to a new one. We know about the history of such shifts in the traditional immigration countries and also in Europe in the last decades. In this respect Japan has become a true immigration country.

The stereotypes against Koreans were developed in the context of colonisation, as a byproduct of learning from the West around 1900 (Gluck 1985; Armstrong 1989). Now these attitudes are being transferred to the new immigration from South and South East Asia. One striking example can be found in the representative ›Japan Almanac 1993‹, edited by the leading liberal daily Asahi Shimbun. It carried a special category ›International Crime‹, where rising figures are shown in impressive graphs. The comment says: »Crimes committed by foreigners have risen sharply, and they have become more violent. International crime has therefore come to be a serious problem.« The figures themselves, however, are very low, and amount to only 0.4 per cent of all Japanese crimes. This is less than half of the population proportion, the 3.8 million foreign tourists, business people etc. not even taken into account (Asahi Shimbun 1992, 210).

Thus, although the statistical data show that immigrants have much lower crime rates than the Japanese (and they again compared to the Europeans, and the Europeans compared to the Americans), there is a widespread coverage of criminal immigrants in the media, depicting them as a group bound to it (Herbert 1993). Since 1995, a general debate on criminality and insecurity in Japan has gained momentum, and it is often connected to immigrants (e.g. The Nikkei Weekly, November 3, 1997).

Japan still largely cultivates *Nihonjinron* or debate on ›Japaneseness‹ – the idea of national exceptionalism, peculiarity, and homogeneity (Dale 1988; Befu 1993; Yoshino 1992; Lipset 1994; Weiner 1997a). There are some older Japanese traditions of seclusion leading to such a concept, but essentially it is a variant of nationalism based upon the European nineteenth-century concepts of collective identity. The model of a *nation une et indivisible* these days is nowhere more entrenched and grounded – at least in the developed world – than in Japan. Helmut Schmidt, the outspoken former German chancellor, commented upon this with the uncharming phrase that »Japan has no friends«. At least in her immigration policy, Japan has behaved like this for a long time.

The Beginning: Entertainment and Undocumented Immigrants

Inside the traditional recruitment system of well-paid and respected foreign specialists of various kinds, the year 1979 saw the development of a new variety of immigrants. The *entertainment* category became more and more prominent, and in 1990 comprised 75,091 or 85 per cent of the officially recruited 87,969 foreigners. In the Japanese public, the phenomenon was discussed in the 1980s as »japayuki-san« (Japan goers, Kajita 1995, 2). The figures indicated a foreignerisation of prostitution in the years after 1979 when this group contributed the bulk of foreign workers in Japan, tolerated by the immigration control authorities (Komai 1995, 71–80). Another statistical indication is that most of the deported females were categorised as hostesses, prostitutes or stripteasers – 74 per cent in 1989. Up to 1988, most immigrants were female, from 1988 on we find more men who were working primarily in construction. In the 1990s, factory jobs became more important and the percentage of these two sectors decreased somewhat. In 1992, the percentage of hostesses plus prostitutes among the deported females was down to 45 per cent, and among men construction was down to 51 per cent. Factory work was up to 17 per cent among women and 28 per cent among men. In the mid-1990s, the Japanese authorities began to enforce stricter controls on the visas for entertainers, after the government and public of the Philippines had protested against the sexual exploitation of Filipino women in Japan, and passed a law on letting only qualified entertainment people out of the country (Republic of the Philippines 1995). The official government report to the OECD reads: »As a consequence of the stricter examination of entry based on this amendment and control over criteria for departure in sending countries, the number of these entries fell significantly from 91,000 to 60,000 in 1995.« (OECD 1997, 124).

As in other developed nations, the inflows have resulted in visa requirements for more and more poor countries, even distant ones. After visas had been introduced for Pakistanis and Bangladeshis in 1989, many Iranians came in as a substitute and were even more visible, as many of them convened on Sundays at two central parks in central Tokyo, one of which was nicknamed »little Teheran«. Iran faced economic downturn and isolation after the Gulf War at that time. As a consequence, Japan introduced visa controls for Iranians in 1992 (Fukawa and Vogel 1993, 8). Moreover, nationals of the main immigration countries have to produce invitation letters and guarantees from a Japan based host.

It is clear that controls against nearly all Asian countries are a problem for free trade and commerce. An open and prosperous Japan needs to let in more and more business people, tourists and the like, making control all the more difficult. The number of foreign visitors is rising every year. Most of them are Asians. Up to this day, however, the Japanese authorities are able to control every single passenger coming to the country. An efficient system of re-entry visas, financed by fees, enables them to control the movements of the foreigners inside Japan, and to calculate the number of overstayers. In addition, Japan's island status enables the authorities to protect against illegal arrivals. In the 1990s, detection of ships trying to smuggle foreigners into the country was a regular news item in the media. The Japanese police are famous for their ability to control people, and protection of personal data is not highly valued in Japan, particularly concerning foreigners, as demonstrated by the foreigners' obligation to carry registration cards.

Little Asylum in Japan

Although Japan signed the Geneva Refugee Convention in 1981, and a Japanese professor was a high profile UN High Commissioner on Refugees in the 1990s, the country has only accepted 200 refugees all in all. In addition, 9,200 refugees were taken in from Vietnam for long-term residence and another 4,500 received temporary protection in the 1970s (OECD 1995, 101), under American pressure.

The official policy is clearly directed against acceptance of any refugees, arguing that all those who arrive are economic refugees. Besides a general unwillingness to take in any foreigners that would bring costs instead of benefits, the problem in the background is always the possible extent of a refugee or migration stream, as many millions of Chinese, North Koreans, Burmese and Indochinese could claim to be the object of state repression, and many governments in the region would be happy to send some of their opponents or unemployed workers out of the country.

Concerning the few refugees that the country has taken in, there has been a well-organised integration process. A study comparing the integration policies for Vietnamese in Tokyo and Munich concludes that, on the whole, both programmes have been well administered, and that there is a great deal of functional integration and human understanding. However, in both cases there is some further migration to the United States where most of the relatives of the Vietnamese refugees live (Kosaka-Isleif 1991).

Intensity of Discussion

Japan has had little immigration, but much discussion about it. In the Japanese media and within academic circles, there has been a lively discourse about the issue. Shimada counted 46 proposals, reports and materials on migration between 1989 and 1993, originating from various governmental bodies, employers' associations, labour unions, political parties, and research and survey institutions (Shimada 1994, 50–54). This production has continued. Hundreds of articles have been published in journals, hundreds of conferences with international guests were held over the years. Experts went to Europe to look for experiences and they wrote dozens of books and articles on immigration policies in other countries. The Ministry of Labour conducted an extensive study of the French, British, Italian and German immigration policies. A dominant theory is that Germany – which many Japanese consider as nearly comparable – made a big mistake when it accepted so many Turks, and now has to deal with the consequences. We need not cite some of the dubious comments of several Japanese politicians like former prime minister Nakasone on the United States and particularly Afro-Americans to understand this point. Much to our surprise even noted historian Paul Kennedy, himself an English immigrant to the United States, wrote of the asset of »racial coherence« of Japan (Kennedy 1993, 34).

Consequently, the broad mainstream of Japanese specialists who are discussing regulated immigration at all conceive of various sorts of temporary schemes (an early systematic listing in Sekine 1991, 60–63). In short, Japan wants workers for time, but not immigration for good. Often this is linked to training or ›work and learn‹ programmes, which do not provide for full payment during the time of work in Japan. The most elaborate plan of this kind was outlined in Haruo Shimada's book *Guest Workers* – an expression that is no longer used in Germany or other European countries. Shimada was a rare exception among Japanese scholars when he argued that the inevitable consequence of a guest worker policy will be that some of the workers will stay on in the country (Shimada 1994, 155–7; 1990, 66–90). In addition, Shimada stated that a policy of openness is needed, and that the negative demographic balance necessitates a certain amount of immigration. All these discussions, including many critical articles on exploitation and human rights abuses, however, have not been able to change the laws. Nor did the many surveys have any influence, demonstrating that large majorities of the Japanese public were in favour of guest worker schemes, with percentages of 70 and 56 respectively (Prime Minister's Office 1991; Komai 1995, 217–32; Japan Institute 2004). This is a remarkable contrast to the regular majorities of people in Western countries claiming that there are too many foreigners.

Reacting to the desperate need of certain industries, like construction, health and old age care, and small companies which in the Japanese public are discussed under the ›3 K jobs‹ (in English the ›3 Ds‹: dirty, dangerous and dull), the Japanese government has altered the immigration law and the regulations to some extent in 1990. There was no amnesty in that context. On the contrary, the immigrants were under the impression that the policy would be stiffened (Komai 1995, 6). Whereas countries like Italy, Spain, France, the United States and Australia, upon reform of their immigration policies in the 1980s, granted amnesty to irregular foreign workers in the country, Japan's new law of 1990 led to the enforcement of expulsions. Many undocumented foreigners surrendered themselves to the authorities, and more than 30,000 people from developing countries were expelled in 1990. In the following years, the deportation numbers grew, and they are very high in relation to the declining numbers of undocumented workers in Japan, compared to those of other OECD countries. In 2005 the government stated the intention to cut the number of illegals by half (Ministry of Justice 2005).

Table: Numbers of Expelled People 1993–2007

Year	Number	Year	Number
1993	70,000	2003	41,935
1995	55,000	2004	45,910
1997	55,167	2005	55,351
1998	51,459	2006	56,410
1999	40,764	2007	45.502

Source: Immigration Bureau 2004; 2005; 2007.

These efforts, however, have not resulted in a Japan without foreign workers. Overstayers continue to work in the construction, entertainment and certain production sectors. At the same time as the regulations were tightened, the immigration law of 1990 has opened three channels of legal quasi-immigration. These programmes are administered through special organisations which are related to the ministries concerned. They provide a field for retired bureaucrats to hold lucrative posts with the practice of *amakudari* or »descending from heaven«, taking positions under or outside the ministries. Thus the problems discussed below do not simply result from negligence or maladministration but are related to deliberate intentions and interests. With respect to the »language students«, Komai (1995, 62f.) describes the education ministry's »hot pursuit« of the Ministry of Justice, to establish an agency under its umbrella. The government was able to formulate its regulations in such an unclear way that even specialists cannot be sure about the interpretation and therefore have to ask for advice from the administration – the typical Japanese ›administrative guidance‹.

After the economic slump of 1995–97, the discussion seemed to die down. In the whole year 1997, the leading paper *Nikkei Weekly* did not include any article on immigration. But public discourse about immigration has recently resurged, mainly due to concerns over the Japanese declining and rapidly ageing population. Considering the dire demographic prognosis of a declining working population and an ageing population, this would seem to favour a positive immigration policy. Given the very low fertility rate (1.2 children per woman), the percentage of the working age population (15 to 64 years) is expected to decline from 68.1 to 53.6 per cent from 2000 to 2050. The percentage of elderly people (over 65 years) is expected to increase from 17.4 to 35.7 per cent during the same period (OECD 2004, 200). In the face of this fact, the Ministry of Justice's ›Basic Plan for Immigration Control‹ – the second and the third editions alike – points to the need to review current migration policies including the issue of introducing foreign workers (Ministry of Justice 2000; 2005); two reports by government commissioned working groups – ›Japan's Goals in the 21st Century‹ (Kawai et al. 2000, 13) and ›A New Era of Dynamism‹ (Special Board of Inquiry for Examining »Japan's 21st Century Vision 2005«, 21f.) – share a positive stance towards accepting foreign labour force. Nippon Keidanren or Japan Business Federation (2004), which is the most influential organisation of business interests in Japan, urges the Japanese government to take measures to accept foreign workforces in order to counteract labour shortages due to the declining Japanese population.

We now approach the crossroads of a dilemma. The economy-driven concerns to overcome demographic problems by a positive immigration policy are compatible with the national concerns for economic prosperity but not with national notion for ethnic homogeneity and social stability based on it. This gives rise to the incoherent and halfway attitude of the Japanese government on immigration policy: it opens the door to immigrant workers in practice whereas officially denying this fact and taking no positive measures for integration policy at the national level (Morris-Suzuki 2002, 169).

Programme 1: Ethnic Japanese

People of Japanese origin down to the third generation (*Nikkeijin*) have been granted the right to live and work in Japan. This policy of preference parallels the approach of many other countries like Germany, Italy, Spain, Greece and Britain. It is founded on an idea of a shared cultural identity and homogeneity (Thränhardt

2000), and is also consistent with contemporary communitarian thinking. Although the *Nikkeijin* in this sense are »invisible« (Sellek 1997), ethnic Japanese from Latin America do have more cultural distance from the Japanese in Japan than East Asian immigrants, because of the deep influence of the Latin American way of life, religion, and their group migration to Japan, organised by brokers, in contrast to the individual and secluded migration of East Asians. However, since they are in Japan legally and enjoy educational and social services, it should be much easier for them to integrate in the long run.

Considering the tremendous per capita income discrepancies between Japan and Latin America, such new possibilities could probably lead to an uprooting of the Japanese communities in Latin America. The largest group of these immigrants lives in Brazil, and the second largest in Peru. Most of them being middle-class professionals, they usually work in factories around Tokyo when they migrate to Japan. In the early 1990s, the Japanese authorities reported that 40 per cent lost their jobs during the economic crisis, thereby underscoring their vulnerability to the business cycle (OECD 1995, 100; Komai 1995, 23f.). In the 2008/09 slump we see the same loss of employment.

The *Nikkeijins*' idea upon arrival is to stay for a limited time, and earn money to build up an existence at home. However, as happens in many migration movements, they then tend to stay longer and longer. They enjoy a safe status, and some observers predict that in the long run most ethnic Japanese from Latin America will migrate back to Japan. In contrast, there is no re-migration of ethnic Japanese from the United States or Canada, as living conditions in these countries are much better.

Another small group of ethnic Japanese sheds new light on the policy. In the early 1990s, an interest developed in Japanese children who had been left behind at the end of the war, and who were adopted and brought up by Chinese foster-parents. The daughter of former prime minister Tanaka, later herself foreign minister, built up personal prestige as a politician by organising a campaign to search for such lost children and bring them to Japan. In that way, the ethnicity and cultural identity of the Japanese were once again reaffirmed. In contrast to other countries, however, the Japanese authorities only accept these people if they can identify their relatives.

Programme 2: Trainees

The 1990 law introduced the status of ›trainee‹. Trainees are not defined as workers, and consequently official regulations make it unlawful to pay a full salary. Instead, a ›training allowance‹ shall be granted. These arrangements do not protect the trainee from hard work or long hours – as is common in Japan, and in particular for ›part time‹ workers who often work as long as regular employees, receiving however lower wages and fewer social benefits. The government has established the principle that at least one third of the trainees' working hours must be used for training, and that there must be a minimum ratio between Japanese workers and foreign trainees. However, such regulations cannot be controlled effectively, and the system favours the interest of the employer in cheap labour, backed by the desire of the foreign worker to save money to send home. In 1993, the system was changed to allow trainees to work full time for up to two years after the training period. In 1997, there was talk of extending the duration. Thus, the transition to a guest worker status has tacitly been made, and the companies as well as the government implicitly acknowledge the reality of labour recruitment through the trainee programmes (Kajita 1995, 10f.). Shimada is right to call the system »something of a charade« (Shimada 1994, 69, for examples of abuse see Komai 1995, 37–54).

The companies' responsibility to care for the trainees' housing can be considered a positive aspect of the scheme. At the same time, it enhances their dependence. When trainees are employed by small and medium firms, there is not much hope for a meaningful transfer of skills. This could only come about if the large transnational companies would adopt a trainee policy. They, however, do not need to employ unskilled trainees, and prefer to recruit Japanese, even to prepare tea for the staff. Furthermore, they could easily hire South East Asian specialists. On the whole, the trainee scheme makes it easy to exploit foreigners and difficult to receive a fair wage. The number of trainees entering Japan, which was only 40,000 in 1993 (OECD 1995, 100), increased to 75,000 in 2004 (GKMN 2006, 71). Most of them are working in small- and medium-sized firms of agricultural, manufacturing and construction sectors.

Programme 3: Language Students

The third and most problematic scheme is the ›language student visa‹ allowing to work for up to 20 hours a week. It is an outcome of former prime minister Nakasone's vision of attracting 100,000 foreign students to Japan by the 21st century. As a consequence, visa procedures were simplified for students in 1984 (Komai 1995, 54–70).

The students have to register at a language school. Most of them originate from poor Asian countries and are motivated to earn as much money as possible. In a vicious circle, they need the money to pay for the language school tuition even if the latter are ›front operations‹ without any quality teaching, or the students do not have the time to attend. Additionally, life in Japan is expensive. On the labour market, language students are unprotected. Consequently, the outcome of these institutional arrangements is cheap labour, and extra income for language schools. The total number of foreign students in Japan rose to 53,847 in 1995 and fell to 51,047 in 1997 (Monbusho 1997; Yamagiwa 1998).

To be certain, a more rational approach would be to organise courses in Japanese in the countries of origin where living costs are much lower than in Japan, one of the most expensive country in the world. Trainee programmes and language schools are planned and supervised by a new state agency, the Japan Immigration Association which also publishes nice booklets containing all necessary information (Japan Immigration Association 1990). This authority is also concerned with the immigration of skilled personnel.

Research Paradigms and National Context

In this section, we will characterise the Japanese paradigm of migration research by three features: (1) cultural approach, (2) human rights perspective, and (3) the focus on the local level. In doing so, we will relate them to a wide range of national contexts in which they are embedded. We will conclude this section with brief remarks on desirable directions of migration and minority group research.

Cultural Approach

A cultural approach focusing on ethnicity and identity is predominant among Japanese scholars studying migration and minority groups. This approach has encouraged scholars to engage in significant research questions: What kind of problems will emerge if immigrants with heterogeneous cultural backgrounds come to the supposedly homogeneous country (cf. Tsuzuki 2004)? What is necessary for a peaceful coexistence of culturally heterogeneous groups (cf. Miyajima 2003)? How does Japanese educational policy cause difficulties for children of immigrants (Miyajima 1999; Ota 2002)?

The predominance of a cultural approach can be understood in terms of four contexts. The first is the post-socialist context. After the collapse of Communist regimes, any overarching progressive social visions such as Marxism were discredited. Moreover, subsequent political and social conflicts such as the civil war in former Yugoslavia pointed to the importance of culture and ethnic identity. Thus, the post-socialist context, together with the influence of post-Marxist leftist thoughts such as cultural studies, has encouraged Japanese scholars to focus on cultural difference and ethnic identity that seemed to provide more plausible explanations than Marxist economic determinism. This is the Japanese version of the cultural turn.

Another, more directly national context is the common view of Japan as a culturally homogeneous country. While motivating scholars to show that Japan is not as ethnically, culturally, and linguistically homogeneous as the common view tells us (cf. Maher and Yashiro 1995; Maher and Macdonald 1995; Oguma 1995, 1998; Weiner 1997a; Denoon et al. 2001), this widely held view leads migration researchers to explore impacts on the supposedly homogeneous country by immigrant groups.

The third context is the existence of the long-established ethnic minority group of resident Koreans. Today, they enjoy civil and social rights almost on a par with those of Japanese nationals. Apart from the demand for local suffrage rights, their major claims are of cultural nature; specifically, they demand for institutional guarantee of ethnic education for Korean children to maintain their ethnic identity and pride – the demand for public recognition of cultural difference (cf. Kibe

2006). The precedent case of resident Koreans thus tends to strengthen an impression that the core of minority issues is always cultural in nature.

The fourth context is the popularity of multiculturalism. The Japanese version of multiculturalism is expressed by the idea of ›tabunka kyosei‹ (literally ›multiculturally living together‹). Roughly speaking, it designates a society in which diverse ethno-cultural groups can live together on the basis of mutual respect for cultural differences and reciprocal willingness to live in harmony. Gaining currency from the late 1990s as a key slogan of public discourse, it has been widely used by various groups such as local governments, NGOs (Komai 2004a), and business interest groups (Nippon Keidanren 2004) as well as scholars (Miyajima 1999, 2003; NIRA Citizenship Kenkyukai 2001). Practically, public policies based on this idea range from mere tolerance to active promotion of cultural differences. It is noteworthy that, contrary to American and European counterparts, the Japanese model of multiculturalism has not faced any serious nation-wide challenges related to concerns about social instability and disintegration. The widely accepted discourse of multiculturalism clearly shapes the social and intellectual context encouraging cultural approach.

It is not deniable that the cultural approach has largely contributed to exploring important issues of migration research. But there is a problem: If the cultural approach is deployed in a single-minded way – by regarding the core of migration issues as essentially cultural, and by ignoring a broad institutional, political, economic, and social framework in which they are embedded – it easily jumps into false conclusions. A case in point is the problem of conflicts between Japanese Brazilians and other residents in a community densely populated by the former group. A researcher, who has been long engaged in this case, finally blames Japanese Brazilians for bringing in their life styles indiscreetly into the community without complying with existent community rules concerning garbage disposal, car parking and so on (Tsuzuki 2004). As Kajita, Tanno and Higuchi (2005, 295f.) point out, however, this denunciation fails to identify the effects of structural factors and particularly the labour market: Japanese-Brazilian workers, used as flexible labour force, work in unstable employment conditions, so that they find it difficult to engage in community life.

Human Rights Perspective

This perspective is often deployed in Japanese migration research, which typically discusses whether and to what extent human rights of foreigners in Japan are guaranteed; what policy measures are needed for human rights protection of immigrants and other minority groups. As a matter of course, quite a few academic and practising lawyers actively engage in this field of research (for example Kondo 2002; Niwa 2003). The salience of human rights perspective is to be understood with respect to three contexts: (1) international human rights law, (2) local municipalities, and (3) the path dependency set by the case of resident Koreans.

As for the first context of international human rights law, it is clear that it has exerted a significant impact on the legal status of foreigners, by influencing public policies of the Japanese government. For example, Japan's ratification of the International Covenants on Human Rights in 1979 and the Refugees Convention in 1981 led to the elimination of the nationality requirement from social security laws, thereby making Koreans as well as settled foreigners eligible for the National Pension Law and the National Health Insurance Law (Iwasawa 1998, ch. 4; Kondo 2001, 17; Kim 2002). This clearly shows that Japan is another case of ›embedded liberalism‹ (Hollifield 1992), a liberal-democratic polity embedded within international and domestic rights-based regimes, although a regional human rights regime in Asia is yet to be established. Furthermore, the international human rights regime provides a legal and moral basis for Japanese NGOs working for human rights protection of foreigners (Niwa 2003).

The second context for the human rights perspective is the fact that it is a guiding principle for local governments. Indeed, it is not difficult to find local communities actively involved in improving human rights of foreign residents. The slogan of ›internationalisation‹, originally meaning efforts at building friendly ties with overseas municipalities, gradually shifted to ›inward internationalisation‹. This policy, aiming at accommodating various needs of visiting and living foreigners, has finally come to be coupled with public policies of human rights protection (Kashiwazaki 2002).

The third context is the precedent case of resident Koreans, who accounted for 80 per cent of resident foreigners up to the mid-1980s (Kim 2002, 259). First of all, most issues concerning them have been long discussed as »the problem of human rights of foreigners«. Resident Koreans, who were deprived of Japanese nationality by the Japanese government after the Second World War, had to struggle to acquire a set of human rights preserved only for Japanese nationals, while retaining Korean nationality (Onuma 1993). Due to this historical experience, one easily associates the foreigners' problem of rights with human rights problems. Furthermore, many local governments have endeavoured to accommodate human rights claims by resident Koreans. It is therefore no surprise that local municipalities committed to human rights protection of foreigners very often made the experience to have worked for the problem of resident Koreans (Kashiwazaki 2002). Thus, the case of resident Koreans has helped to focus on the human rights perspectives of immigrants and minority groups.

There is no doubt that the human rights perspective has contributed to advancing migration research. However, there is a caveat. Alan Patten and Will Kymlicka (2003, 34f.) point to a weakness of the human rights approach towards language rights of minority groups. Since human rights norms are universal and minimal standards applicable to all individuals regardless of differences, they cannot adequately address real policy questions without additional considerations of different needs, desires, and historical roots of ethnic groups. This argument applies to the human rights paradigm of Japanese migration research. For example, there exist different needs concerning cultural rights between children of resident Koreans, who normally do not have any difficulty with the Japanese language, and those of Japanese Brazilians, who often face diverse difficulties due to insufficient Japanese proficiency. Thus, human rights perspectives should aim at a view on ethnic minorities that is more attentive to their differences in important respects.

Focus on Local Municipalities, Communities, and NGOs

Japanese migration research is characterised by the local-level analysis that focuses on local municipalities, communities, and civic associations such as NGOs (e.g. Miyajima and Kajita 1996; Onai 2003; Komai 2004a). One can point to three contexts that encourage Japanese migration research to pay more attention to the local level than to the national level.

The first context is national in nature. As we observed above, the Japanese government has long clung to the position of non-immigration. Whereas there is no national systematic immigration policy, not to speak of integration policy, however, it is practically impossible to control migration perfectly, all the more because there are in fact ›back door‹ or ›side door‹ immigrants. In this context, local governments and civic associations have to play an important role in addressing problems and needs of immigrants. Furthermore, this tendency is reinforced by the recent neo-liberal policy orientation of the Japanese government. Neo-liberalism tends to shift costs and responsibilities for integration away from the central government into private agencies such as NGOs and charity organisations (Pellerin 2003, 188) and, especially in Japan, local governments as well. As a result, it seems quite natural for migration scholars to turn more attention to the local-level phenomena, and to accumulate case studies about them.

The second context is the fact that most significant efforts and policy innovations have been made mainly at the local level. It is understandable that, in the absence of nation-wide policy framework, local politics precedes national politics by dealing with various problems of resident foreigners, such as – to name but a handful – human rights protection, multicultural education, and political participation. Turning attention to municipalities thus provides scholars with an indispensable access to emerging problems and problem-solving attempts on the scene. For example, in the situation in which the Ministry of Education, Science and Technology has not taken any fundamental measures for multicultural education of minority children, Osaka City Board of Education (2001, 21) in the ›Basic Guidelines of Education for Resident Foreigners‹ explicitly acknowledges the task of cultivating ethno-cultural identities among minority children, notably Korean children, as an important goal of human rights-based education. A few local governments have hired part-time Portuguese and Spanish teachers to teach Nikkeijin children (Kondo 2001: 20). Concerning political participation, it is noteworthy that local municipalities such as Kawasaki, Shizuoka, Hamamatsu, and Mitaka have devised diverse consultative institutions comprising resident foreigners, providing important opportunities to integrate them into the political and social process (Miyajima 2003, ch. 8; Tegtmeyer Pak 2000a). According to an estimate in February 2005 (Mindan 2005), 177 local governments have granted various types of consultative bodies to resident foreigners. Finally, it is noteworthy that in 2001 thirteen municipalities with many foreign residents formed the ›Council of Cities with High Concentrations of Foreign Residents‹, to establish ties with each other and to make policy proposals to higher authorities (Komai 2004a). This potentially becomes an important pressure group to exert impact on national immigration policy.

The third context is the activism of civic associations and NGOs in particular. The NPO Law of 1998, which was driven by the Japanese experience with unexpectedly high numbers of active volunteers coming from throughout Japan to rescue the victims of the Hanshin-Awaji Earthquake of 1995, has eased the legal incorporation of NGOs, thereby helping them proliferate and take roots in Japanese society (Tegtmeyer Pak 2000b, 69–70). Today, there are more than one hundred NGOs involved in activities supporting migrant workers; the largest umbrella organisation of migrant support groups is the ›Solidarity Network with Migrants in Japan‹, comprising 88 groups (Okamoto 2004, 204). Moreover, local volunteer groups have emerged along with NGOs to help immigrants. For example, in Hamamatsu City, Brazilian Nikkeijin mothers and community members formed an association to meet the educational needs of migrant children (Yamanaka 2003). Studies on civic associations involved in immigrant groups can shed new light on important aspects of civil society in Japan that have not been well known.

One may be right to speak of ›local citizenship‹ for immigrant groups, considering institutions and practices to accommodate their needs (cf. Higuchi 2001). But ›local citizenship‹ must be a qualified notion, because any local approach is subject to methodological and practical constraints. From the methodological perspective of empirical analysis, it is problematic to ignore the broader national framework that possibly influences migration phenomena. As Kajita, Tanno, and Higuchi (2005) point out, if the macro-structural framework of the political economy – notably a labour market utilising flexible labour force through temporary work agencies – lies at the core of problems of Japanese Brazilians, it is very likely that any approach exclusively concentrating on local-level phenomena fails to reach a more appropriate understanding of immigration problems.

From a practical perspective, the local approach is prone to overstate problem-solving capacities of local actors, as if any issues of immigrants could be resolved only with the help of local actors. This line of thought is suggested by Hiroshi Komai (2004b, 20). He holds that non-state and non-profit organisations such as local municipalities and NGOs are the only agencies that can redress the immigrants' plight. It is impossible, he argues, to expect state and private enterprises to intervene on their behalf, since they are the very institutions that alienate immigrants from Japanese society and violate their human rights. Considering the macro-nature of the labour market, however, it is clear that local governments have only a limited set of policy measures to tackle problems emerging from it. As

Takeyuki Tsuda (2005, 275) points out, local citizenship is subject to regional contingencies and variation. Economically, the localities with immigrant labour are often rather weak, and thus not able to finance high-quality services. Moreover, a policy of clinging to local solutions without changing national policy would reinforce indirectly the neo-liberal policy orientation to shift the burden to local government and civil society generally.

Desiderata

The above considerations suggest two directions that possibly enrich the Japanese paradigm. One direction is to pay more attention to inter- and intra-group differences. We discussed this need with respect to the difference of needs between resident Koreans and Japanese Brazilians. Of course, we also need comparative approaches internationally. The other direction is to adopt a broader analytical framework comprising macro and micro levels of phenomena in order to capture the interactions of multiple factors. This direction encourages theory-guided approaches to compare the explanatory power of different theoretical approaches. Moreover, it contributes to practical and normative considerations on the issues of immigrants and minority groups. It would be impossible to make well-considered practical judgements without sound empirical knowledge.

This may be just a pious hope. But we would suggest that it is a possible move. Indeed, some studies have been done in line with the above directions. What we have in mind are studies by Kajita, Tanno and Higuchi (2005) and Oishi (2005). They are highly theory-guided, going far beyond the level of descriptive case studies. Kajita, Tanno and Higuchi analyse the case of Japanese Brazilians by focusing on labour market effects and network mechanisms. Oishi deploys an integrative approach to combine macro and micro levels to study female migration in Asia. This would demonstrate that Japanese migration studies can move from the stage of just accumulating case studies without drawing theoretical implications to the stage of advancing integrative, theory-guided studies.

Conclusions

All in all, the number of foreigners working in undesirable jobs was on the increase until 1995, and is slightly decreasing since that time. All indicators show this tendency. In contrast to other developed countries, most foreign workers do not get fully equivalent wages. Instead, they are held under carefully arranged systems of semi-legality that force them to give away part of their earnings to phony language schools, labour brokers, employers, or yakuza Mafiosi criminals, and to live in precarious situations quite often. Government policies further the emergence of such environments.

In Japan and in the countries of origin, migration has become big business. The Japanese state policy of non-immigration can be used by brokers, employers, or criminals as a ›big stick‹ in the background. If difficulties arise, workers demanding full wage or free time or women refusing to become prostitutes, these foreigners can be handed over to the authorities and are then deported. After deportation, it is extremely difficult to take any legal action. Moreover, in case of labour accidents or illness employers are unlikely to report to insurance agencies because they could face legal difficulties. Employer sanctions have been included in the law, following the German example. However, this has not resulted in severe punishment. Instead, Japanese employers turned to middlemen and brokers, and in that way skirted the law.

The official policy of denying immigration, combined with leniency towards unethical labour practice, has led to a foreign underclass in Japan that neither enjoys basic human rights nor gets an adequate salary. Furthermore, Japan's labour policy is largely patterned along the legal, social and economic discrimination of Koreans in the past. For Japan, and particularly for Japanese working in similar environments, this causes social problems. For many foreign workers, the situation leads to years of a precarious existence only to find in the end that an imagined return to their homeland as a wealthy person cannot be realised. As for the countries of origin, they do not profit by sending ambitious people, often with college qualifications, in their best working years, for jobs undesirable to Japanese, and getting in return little savings from abroad. For the relations between Japan and the Asian developing nations – many of them with memories of the Second World War – this practice of exploitation implies some problems of foreign relations. The situation can be summed up in seven points:

1. Japan's public opinion has broadly discussed the problem of immigration, but decision-making has been reserved to the Justice Ministry, based on a conservative consensus. A civil society unable to influence the government's decision-making is a typical feature of the Japanese decision-making process (Yamaguchi 1996). It should be pointed out, however, that there is a broad range of lawyers, humanitarian action groups, Christian parishes, trade unions and other concerned citizens that sympathise with the immigrants, provide help for them, and struggle with the authorities. They operate, however, on a local basis, without powerful nation-wide organisations.

2. Japan has largely been able to escape the worldwide flows of migration. The end of the high growth era and the rising unemployment rates in Japan, particularly among woman and young people (Terazono 1995), and the 1998 crisis of the East Asian economies, make it highly unlikely that Japan will opt for large-scale immigration in the foreseeable future. Thus – in contrast to Western Europe – the window of opportunity has never been opened. On the other hand, the sheer size of the Japanese economy makes Japan a rather important country of immigration, if we compare absolute numbers. The Japanese case demonstrates that large immigration flows are not an unavoidable fate for industrial democracies (Komai 1995, 247–51) – against the expectations of some foreign experts (Cornelius 2004, 375–410), and the ideas of a general opening of liberal countries (Freeman 1995).

3. Given the discrepancies in the socio-economic status between Japan and Latin America, the opening for ethnic Japanese from Latin America will result in a widespread re-migration that, however, would amount to only about 0,5 per cent of the Japanese population, in case all ethnic Japanese from Latin America return to the land of their forefathers.
4. The trainee and the language student schemes result in an organised exploitation of people from South East Asia. Only a tiny fraction of these foreign workers will become permanent residents. This rotational policy is largely due to the low level of judicial controls and legal rights for immigrants (Fukawa and Vogel 1993, 8) and a limited de-facto toleration of immigration, conforming with Japanese-style administrative guidance instead of legal instruments and judicial control.
5. In spite of the small numbers of immigrants, a negative stereotype has been created that is linked with the semi-legal and tenuous situation of the immigrants.
6. At present, these policy instruments serve the Japanese economy well. Migrants can be used as a buffer to avoid unemployment or other costs, and companies are forced to invest outside Japan. In the long run, however, the Japanese society is in a rapid ageing process, and will need immigration to fill certain positions, or it will be forced to take other groundbreaking measures to secure services like old age care, construction work or assembly line production.
7. When we try to evaluate Japanese exceptionalism in immigration policies, it is important to distinguish between the intentions and the policy outcomes. The often heard criticism against the exclusive and rigid character of the Japanese immigration policies and procedures may be well founded. The parallels in other countries, however, must not be forgotten – just to mention the US with its twelve million irregular migrants.

The policy outcomes are very close to an ideal Freemannian world (Freeman 1995). Here, a government protects the working classes against foreign competition. Arguing in market terms, it is likely that this had positive effects on the social situation of the vulnerable strata of society, particularly securing full employment, and opening more chances for women, less educated, and even outcasts. This is in sharp contrast to the American experience of the last decades where an ever available pool of immigrants made it unnecessary to employ the urban underclasses. Considering social cohesion, this policy can be considered successful.

The dark side of the policy, however, is the discrimination and semi-legality of many Asian immigrants in Japan, caused by the internal controls the state carries out, and the special quasi-immigration programmes. The existence of a grey area of non-legality and semi-legality constitutes the problem, whereas external controls at the borders and outside Japan seem to operate reasonably.

References

Armstrong, Bruce. 1989. Racialisation and Nationalist Ideology: The Japanese Case. *International Sociology* 4: 329–43.

Asahi Shimbun. 1992. *Japan Almanac 1993*. Tokyo: Asahi Shimbun.

Bartram, David. 2000. Japan and Labour Migration: Theoretical and Methodological Implications of Negative Cases. *International Migration Review* 35: 5–32.

Befu, H. 1993. Nationalism and Nohonjinron. In *Cultural Nationalism in East Asia: Representation and Identity*, ed. idem, 107–35. Berkeley: University of California Press.

»Bodyguard business booming as crime worries rise.« *The Nikkei Weekly* 1798, November 3, 1997.

Brubaker, Rogers. 1995. Comments on »Modes of Immigration Politics in Liberal Democratic States«. *International Migration Review* 29: 903–8.

Chiavacci, David. 2009. Japans neue Immigrationspolitik. Ostasiatisches Umfeld, ideelle Diversität und institutionelle Fragmentierung, Habilitationsschrift Freie Universität Berlin.

Cornelius, Wayne A. 2004. Japan: The Illusion of Immigration Control. In *Controlling Immigration*, ed. idem, Philip L. Martin and James F. Hollifield, 375–410. Stanford: Stanford University Press.

Dale, Peter N. 1988. *The Myth of Japanese Uniqueness*. Oxford: Routledge.

Denoon, Donald et al., ed. 2001. *Multicultural Japan: Palaeolithic to Postmodern*. Cambridge: Cambridge University Press.

Freeman, Gary P. 1995. Modes of Immigration Politics in Liberal Democratic States. *International Migration Review* 29: 881–902. Rejoinder: 909–13.

Fukawa, Hisashi, and Dita Vogel. 1993. *Japanische Zuwanderungspolitik im Zielkonflikt zwischen sozialer Homogenität, Beseitigung strukturellen Arbeitskräftemangels und Entwicklungspolitik: Ein Überblick*. Arbeitspapier 15. Bremen: Zentrum für Sozialpolitik.

GKMN (Gaikokujin Kenshusei Mondai Network), ed. 2006. *Gaikokujin Kenshusei: Jikyu 300 yen no rodosha [Foreign Trainees: Workers Paid 300 Yen an Hour]*. Tokyo: Akashi Shoten.

Gluck, Carol. 1985. *Japan's Modern Myths: Ideology in the Late Meiji Period*. Princeton, NJ: Princeton University Press.

Herbert, Wolfgang. 1993. *Die asiatische Gefahr. Ausländerkriminalität in Japan als Argument in der Diskussion um ausländische »illegale« ArbeitsmigrantInnen*. Vienna: Institut für Japanologie.

Higuchi, Naoto. 2001. Gaikokujin Sanseikenron no Nihonteki Kozu: Shiminkenron karano Approach [Japanese Configuration of Theories of Suffrage for Foreigners: Approach from Theory of Citizenship]. In *Tabunkashakai no Sentaku: Shitizunshippu no Shiten kara [The Choice of Multicultural Society: From a Perspective of Citizenship]*, ed. NIRA Citizenship Kenkyukai, 39–53. Tokyo: Nihon Hyoronsha.

Hollifield, James F. 1992. *Immigrants, Markets, and States. The Political Economy of Postwar Europe.* Cambridge, MA: Harvard University Press.

Immigration Bureau. 2004. *Heisei jyurokunendo jyuyo shutsunyukokukanri [Immigration Control of 2003].* http://www.immi-moj.go.jp/seisaku/index.html

Immigration Bureau. 2005. *Heisei jyurokunen niokeru nyukanhoihanjiken ni tsuite [Concerning the Violation Cases of the Immigration Control Law]*, http://www.moj.go.jp/PRESS/050328-3/050328-3.html

Immigration Bureau 2007. *Heisei 19 nen ni okeru nyukanho ihan jiken ni tsuite [Concerning the Violation Cases of Immigration Control Law]*, http://www.moj.go.jp/PRESS/070229-1.pdf

Iwasawa, Yuji. 1998. *International Law, Human Rights, and Japanese Law: The Impact of International Law on Japanese Law.* Oxford: Clarendon Press.

Japan Immigration Association. 1990. *A Guide to Entry, Residence and Registration Procedures in Japan for Foreign Nationals (Japanese/English).* Tokyo: Japan Immigration Association.

Japan Institute for Economic and Social Affairs. 2004. *Gaikokujin rodosha no ukeireni kansuru hokokusho [Survey Report on the Issue of Accepting Foreign Workers]*, http://www.kcc.or.jp /release/2004/rel0906.html

Kajita, Takamichi. 1995. Characteristics of the Foreign Worker Problem in Japan. *Hitotsubasi Journal of Social Studies* 27: 1–26.

Kajita, Takamichi, Kiyoto Tanno, and Naoto Higuchi. 2005. *Kaono mienai teijyuka: Nikkei Brazil jin to kokka, shijyo, imin network [Invisible Residents: Japanese Brazilians vis-à-vis the State, the Market and the Immigrant Network].* Nagoya: University of Nagoya Press.

Kashiwazaki, Chikako. 2002. Zaijyukaikokujin no zoka to jichitai no taio [The Increase of Resident Foreigners and the Responses of Municipalities]. In *Jichitai henkaku no genjitsu to kadai [The Reality and the Task of Municipal Reforms]*, ed. Shunichi Furuwaka and Toshihiro Menju, 142–72. Tokyo: Chuohoki.

Kawai, Hayao et al. 2000. *Japan's Goals in the 21st Century (English Version).* http://www.kantei.go.jp/jp/21century/report/pdfs/index.html

Kennedy, Paul. 1993. *Preparing for the Twenty-First Century.* New York: Random House.

Kibe, Takashi. 2006. Differentiated Citizenship and Ethnocultural Groups: A Japanese Case. *Citizenship Studies* 10: 485–502.

Kim, Dong-Hoon. 2002. Kokusai jinkenho to zainichi gaikokujin no jinken [International Human Rights Law and Human Rights of Foreigners]. In *Gaikokujin no Hotekichii to Jinkenyogo [Legal Status and Human Rights Protection of Foreigners]*, ed. Atsushi Kondo, 253–96. Tokyo: Akashishoten.

Komai, Hiroshi. 1995. *Migrant Workers in Japan.* London and New York: Kegan Paul.

Komai, Hiroshi, ed. 2004a. *Imin wo meguru jichitai no seisaku to shakaiundo [Policies of Municipalities and Social Movements concerning Immigrants]*. Tokyo: Akashishoten.

Komai, Hiroshi. 2004b. Jichitai no seisaku to NPO no katudo no seika to kadai [Achievements and Tasks of Municipal Policies and NPO Activities]. In *Policies of Municipalities and Social Movements concerning Immigrants*, ed. idem, 19–41.

Kondo, Atsushi. 2001. Citizenship Rights for Aliens in Japan. In *Citizenship in a Global World: Comparing Citizenship Rights for Aliens*, ed. idem, 8–30. New York: Palgrave.

Kondo, Atsushi, ed. 2002. *Gaikokujin no Hotekichii to Jinkenyogo [Legal Status and Human Rights Protection of Foreigners]*. Tokyo: Akashishoten.

Kosaka-Isleif, Fumiko. 1991. *Integration südostasiatischer Flüchtlinge in der Bundesrepublik Deutschland und in Japan*. Saarbrücken and Fort Lauderdale: Breitenbach.

Lipset, M. Seymour. 1994. American Exceptionalism – Japanese Uniqueness. In *Comparing Nations*, ed. Mattei Dogan and Ali Kazancigil, 153–212. Oxford and Cambridge: Blackwell.

Maher, John C., and Gaynor Macdonald, ed. 1995. *Diversity in Japanese Culture and Language*. London and New York: Kegan Paul International.

Maher, John C., and Kyoko Yashiro, ed. 1995. *Multilingual Japan*. Clevedon, PA, and Adelaide: Multilingual Matters.

Mindan. 2005. *The Current Situation of Legislations to Grant Referendums to Settled Foreigners*, http://mindan.org/sidemenu/sm_sansei28.php

Ministry of Justice. 2000. *The Basic Plan for Immigration Control* (2nd ed.), http://www.moj.go.jp/PRESS/000300-2/000300-2-2.html

Ministry of Justice. 2005. *The Basic Plan for Immigration Control* (3rd ed.), http://www.moj.go.jp/NYUKAN/nyukan40.html

Ministry of Justice: Study Group. Immigration Bureau. 1990. *Employment of Foreign Nationals, Questions and Answers*. Tokyo: Ministry of Justice.

Miyajima, Takashi. 1999. *Bunka to Fubyodo [Culture and Inequality]*. Tokyo: Yuhikaku.

Miyajima, Takashi. 2003. *Tomoni Ikirareru Nihonhe [Living Together: Policies for Foreign Residents in Japan]*. Tokyo: Yuhikaku.

Miyajima, Takashi and Kajita, Takamichi, ed. 1996. *Gaikokujin Rodosha kara Shimin e [From Foreign Workers to Citizens]*. Tokyo: Yuhikaku.

Monbusho. 1997. *Ministry of Education, Science, Sports and Culture*. Tokyo: Government of Japan.

Morris-Suzuki, Tessa. 2002. Immigrants and Citizenship in Contemporary Japan. In *Japan: Change and Continuity*, ed. Javek Maswood and Hideaki Miyajima, 163–78. London: Routledge Curzon.

Nippon Keidanren (Japan Business Federation). 2004. *Gaikokujin ukeire ni kansuru teigen [Recommendations on Accepting Non-Japanese Workers]*, http://www.keidanren.or.jp/Japanese/policy/2004/029/index.html; English version: http://www. keidanren.or.jp/english/policy/2004/02.html

NIRA Citizenship Kenkyukai, ed. 2001. *Tabunkashakai no Sentaku: Shitizunshippu no Shiten kara [The Choice of Multicultural Society: From a Perspective of Citizenship]*. Tokyo: Nihon Hyoronsha.

Niwa, Masao. 2003. *Minority to taminzokushakai [Minorities and Multiethnic Society]*. Osaka: Kaihoshuppan.

OECD. 1995. *SOPEMI: Trends in International Migration: Annual Report 1994. Continuous Reporting System on Migration.* Paris: OECD.

OECD. 1997. *SOPEMI: Annual Report 1996: Continuous Reporting System on Migration.* Paris: OECD.

OECD. 2004. *SOPEMI: Trends in International Migration. Annual Report 2003. Continuous Reporting System on Migration.* Paris: OECD.

OECD. 2008. *International Migration Outlook: SOPEMI 2008: Annual Report.* Paris: OECD.

Oguma, Eiji. 1995. *Tanitsuminzoku no Kigen [The Myth of the Homogeneous Nation]*. Tokyo: Shinyosha.

Oguma, Eiji. 1998. *Nihonjin no Kyokai [The Boundaries of the Japanese]*. Tokyo: Shinyosha.

Oishi, Nana. 2005. *Women in Motion: Globalization, State Policies, and Labour Migration in Asia*. Stanford, CA: Stanford University Press.

Okamoto, Masataka. 2004. Ijyusha no kenrio mamoru network undo no kiseki to kadai [The Footsteps and the Task of Migrants' Rights Protection Movement]. In *Imin wo meguru jichitai no seisaku to shakaiundo [Policies of Municipalities and Social Movements concerning Immigrants]*, ed. Hiroshi Komai, 203–39. Tokyo: Akashishoten.

Onai, Toru, ed. 2003. *Zainichi Brazirujin no Kyoiku to Hoiku: Gunmaken Ota Oizumi Chiku o Jireitoshite [Education and Childcare of Japanese Brazilians: The Case Study of the Ota and Oizumi Districts in Gunma Prefecture]*. Tokyo: Akashishoten.

Onuma, Yasuaki 1993. *Tanitsu Minzoku Shakai no Shinwa o Koete [Beyond the Myth of Monoethnic Japan]*, 2nd ed. Tokyo: Toshindo.

Osaka City Board of Education. 2001. *Zainichigaikokujin kyoiku kihonhoshin [Basic Guidelines of Education for Resident Foreigners 2001]*. http://www.korea-ngo.org/minzoku/4policy.htm

Ota, Haruo. 2002. Kyoikutassei niokeru Nihongo to Bogo: Nihongoshijyoshugi no Hihanteki Kento [Japanese Language and Mother Tongue in Education Achievement: Critical Examination of the Priority of Japanese Language]. In *Henyosuru Nihonshakai to Bunka [Japanese Society and Culture in Transfor-*

255

mation], ed. Takashi Miyajima and Hiromasa Kano, 93–118. Tokyo: Tokyodaigaku Shuppankai.

Patten, Alan, and Will Kymlicka. 2003. Language Rights and Political Theory: Context, Issues, and Apporaches. In *Language Rights and Political Theory*, ed. idem, 1–51. Oxford: Oxford University Press.

Pellerin, Hélène. 2003. Crisis? What Crisis? The Politics of Migration Regulation in the Era of Globalization. In *Globalization: Theory and Practice*, ed. Eleonore Kofman and Gillian Youngs, 172–92. 2nd ed. London: Continuum.

Pempel, T.J. 1974. The Bureaucratization of Policymaking in Postwar Japan. *American Journal of Political Science* 18: 647–64.

Perlmutter, Ted. 1996. Bringing Parties Back In: Comments on Modes of Immigration Politics in Liberal Democratic States. *International Migration Review* 30: 375–88.

Prime Minister's Office. 1991. *Public Opinion Survey on Foreign Workers: Summary*. Tokyo: Foreign Press Center.

Republic of the Philippines. 1995. Migrant Workers and Overseas Filipinos Act of 1995. *Asian Migrant* 8: 87–96.

Sekine, Masami. 1991. Guest Worker Policies in Japan. *Migration* 9: 49–70.

Sellek, Yoko. 1997. Nikkeijin: The Phenomenon of Return Migration. In *Japan's Minorities: The Illusion of Homogeneity*, ed. Michael Weiner, 178–210. London and New York: Routledge.

Shimada, Haruo. 1990. A Possible Solution for the Problem of Foreign Labour. *Japan Review of International Affairs* 4: 66–90.

Shimada, Haruo. 1994. *Japan's »Guest Workers«: Issues and Public Policies*. Tokyo: University of Tokyo Press.

Sik, Pak Kyong. 1990. Die Zwangsanwerbung von Koreanern für Japan während des Pazifischen Krieges. In *Japan zwischen den Kriegen*, ed. Masao Nishikawa and Masato Miyachi, 287–322. Hamburg: Lit.

Special Board of Inquiry for Examining »Japan's 21st Century Vision«. 2005. *A New Era of Dynamism: Closer Ties and a Wider Range of Opportunities*, http://www.keizai-shimon.go.jp/English/publication/index.html

Tegtmeyer Pak, Katherine. 2000a. Foreigners Are Local Citizens Too: Local Governments Respond to International Migration in Japan. In *Japan and Global Migration*, ed. Mike Douglass and Glenda S. Roberts, 244–74. London: Routledge.

Tegtmeyer Pak, Katherine. 2000b. Living in Harmony: Prospects for Cooperative Local Responses to Foreign Migrants. In *Local Voices, National Issues: The Impact of Local Initiatives in Japanese Policy-Making*, ed. Sheila A. Smith, 51–74. Ann Arbor, MI: Center for Japanese Studies, University of Michigan.

Terazono, Emiko. 1995. Jobseekers Find Their Work Cut Out. Culture Shock for Japanese Graduates. *Financial Times*, September 6.

Thränhardt, Dietrich. 1995. The Political Uses of Xenophobia in England, France and Germany. *Party Politics* 1: 321–43.

Thränhardt, Dietrich. 1996. Japan und Deutschland in der Welt nach dem Kalten Krieg. In *Japan und Deutschland in der Welt nach dem Kalten Krieg*, ed. idem, Münster: Lit, 15–59.

Thränhardt, Dietrich. 2000. Tainted Blood: The Ambivalence of Ethnic Migration in Israel, Japan, Korea, Germany and the United States. *German Policy/ Politikfeldanalyse*, no. 3. http://spaef.com/GPS_PUB/v1n3.html

Tsuda, Takeyuki. 2006. The Limits of Local Citizenship and Activism in Japan and Other Recent Countries of Immigration. In *Local Citizenship in Recent Countries of Immigration: Japan in Comparative Perspective*, ed. idem, 273–93. Lanham, MD: Lexington Books.

Tsuzuki, Kurumi. 2004. Gaikokujinshujyutoshi no genjitu kara [From the Reality of a City with Concentrated Foreign Population]. *Shimin Seisaku [Civic Policy]* 36, 44–50.

Weiner, Michael. 1997a. The Invention of »Self« and »Other« in Pre-war Japan. In *Japan's Minorities: The Illusion of Homogeneity*, ed. idem, 1–16. London and New York: Routledge.

Weiner, Michael. 1997b. The Representation of Absence and the Absence of Representation: Korean Victims of the Atomic Bomb. In *Japan's Minorities: The Illusion of Homogeneity*, ed. idem, 79–107. London: Routledge.

Weiner, Michael. 1989. *The Origins of the Korean Community in Japan, 1910–1923*. Manchester: Manchester University Press.

Yamagiwa, Kazuhisa. 1998. Japan Comes up Short of Foreign Students. *The Nikkei Weekly* 1817. 23 March.

Yamaguchi, Yasushi. 1996. Vom hegemonialen zum bipolaren Parteiensystem in Japan. In *Japan und Deutschland nach dem Kalten Krieg*, ed. Dietrich Thränhardt, 165–86. Opladen: Leske & Budrich.

Yamanaka, Keiko. 1993. New Immigration Policy and Unskilled Foreign Workers in Japan. *Pacific Affairs* 66: 72–90.

Yamanaka, Keiko. 2003. Feminized Migration, Community Activism and Grassroots Transnationalization in Japan. *Asian and Pacific Migration Journal* 12: 155–88.

Yoshino, Kosaku 1992. *Cultural Nationalism in Contemporary Japan: A Sociological Inquiry*. London and New York: Routledge.

Migration Research in a Transformation Country: The Polish Case

By Krystyna Iglicka

Abstract

This paper analyses open and hidden national and international agendas standing behind and influencing migration research in Poland. The author studies the period before the collapse of Communism in 1989, and the era after 1989, with special attention to the most recent events after Poland's accession to the European community. She reflects Polish research before the background of a radically changing emigration and immigration patterns.

Open and Hidden Agendas

In this paper I want to discuss in which ways migration research in Poland has been influenced by different national paradigms and ›hidden national agendas‹ in the two crucial periods: before and after 1989.[1]

Writing about international migration as it affects the territory of a given country is an extremely challenging and difficult task. It involves writing not only about the population flows from and into the country, but also about the country's history, geography, economy, internal and external policies, issues surrounding immigrants' integration or alienation, etc. Consequently, while trying to explain national paradigms of migration research one has to remember that the writer of this paper is in the same environment as the research she is referring to.

For years, researchers analysing international migration relied upon the ›pull-push‹ concept established by Lee (1966). The push-pull attributes of sending and receiving areas were considered as independent migration variables leading to the migration choices of individuals, households or certain communities. Although never stated explicitly, the nature of the factors considered in the push-pull model were always conceived as exclusively economic. This concept assumed that migration was driven by the differences between forces of economic growth and economic backwardness in different geographic locations (Arango 1998).

In the post-industrial period, however, restrictive migration policies (in pull-push models, they were accounted for merely as an *intervening set of obstacles*), though once virtually absent in the industrial era, have taken on extreme impor-

---

1 A first version of this paper has been published in Krystyna Slany (ed.), *International Migration. A Multidimensional Analysis*, Cracow: AGH, University of Science and Technology Press, 2005.

tance. Today, it is the state and its policies that are key elements in explaining contemporary migration, from both the theoretical and practical perspectives. Indeed, »it is precisely the control which states exercise over their borders that defines international migration as a distinctive social process« (Zolberg 1989, 405). This fact should be more fully acknowledged and taken into account by either developing new and better models of international migration or trying to build a general theory of this phenomenon.

Poland's geographic and political location predestined it to struggle and interplay between the West and the East, in both historical and cultural perspectives and economic and social contexts as well. Although, from the point of view of post-1945 population outflows, Poland gravitated undoubtedly to the Western European migration system[2], it was largely an outsider because of the one-way direction of movements. On the other hand, political circumstances pushed Poland into the Eastern European migration system, since flows between the former Communist block countries, albeit relatively moderate were mutual and quite diversified.

As already mentioned, this paper describes ›hidden national agendas‹ that have driven migration research in Poland before 1989 and during the transition period. Since, for centuries, Poland has been one of the major countries of emigration in the whole Central and Eastern European region we begin with a focus on the perception of emigration from Poland in both social and political contexts. After this I shall analyse national and international forces that are driving migration research in Poland on immigration issues.

The Social and Political Perception of the Phenomenon of Emigration

Before 1989

Although Poland, as a consequence in borders' changes, has experienced massive emigration and immigration fluxes immediately after the Second World, nearly no research was devoted to these phenomena until the late 1980s. Discussing ›national frames‹ of migration research in Poland and its ›hidden agendas‹ one has to remember that until the collapse of the Communist system, i.e. until the year 1989 official political propaganda did not acknowledge emigration or outflows from Poland as a fact. The problem was not that research was forbidden due to the

---

2 Migration systems can be defined in various ways. The most popular in the literature is a regional approach, a strategy effective inasmuch as geographical proximity is highly correlated with similar cultural and historical backgrounds. Flows of people between the countries belonging to one migration system occur »within a national context whose policy, economic, technological, and social dimensions that stem from the migration itself. Population exchanges within the system involve not only permanent migrants, labour migration and/or refugees, but also students, military personnel, businesspeople and even tourists since such short-term movements frequently set the conditions for subsequent long-term ones« (Kritz and Zlotnik 1992, 3).

›official political line‹ but rather that it was impossible to conduct research on phenomena of migration in Poland simply because there were no data collected on international population mobility on Polish territory. The Central Statistical Office published only the overall number of those who emigrated from Poland by basic demographic features. Therefore, more specific databases on international migration in Poland that had recently been created cover only the period beginning in the 1990s.

Migration research as such, in the sense of a research testing various theories and aspects of population mobility or creating new ones, did not exist during the Communist period in Poland. Selected studies, mainly anthropological, concentrated on research on conditions of Polish peasants' emigration prior to the Second World War and selected aspects of the old Polish diaspora spread all over the world (Slany 1991). Only a few others (mainly historical and descriptive) were conducted by researchers who were able to get access to archives of the Ministry of Foreign Affairs. This kind of research concentrated on the issue of the post-war repatriation of Poles from the Soviet Union, and the immediate post-war mass population mobility that took place on the Polish territory and its causes and consequences (Latuch 1961; Wasilewska-Trenkner 1973).

Looking at the problem of migration from Poland from another perspective we have, however, to acknowledge that, irrespective of political options during the Communist era, for more than a century Poland has been one of the biggest sending areas in Central and Eastern Europe and a vast reservoir of labour for many countries in Western Europe and North America. There were various reasons for migration from Poland in different periods. There were periods of massive politically indicated forced outflows (both to the West and to the East) and periods of massive economic oriented outflows, mainly illegal (to the West).

Generally the phenomenon of emigration, the phenomenon of Poles living somewhere abroad was extremely important for those who stayed in the country, which was during the last 200 years mainly either under partition or under political regimes imposed by stronger neighbours. In many periods Polish emigrants helped to maintain the national identity. This began with the elite ›Big Emigration‹ after the November uprising in 1830 that was popular all over Europe. More than hundred years later, the emigration during the Second World War which led to the creation of a Polish government in exile in England. These emigrations extended an idealistic portrayal of Polish migrants as martyrs fighting for, maintaining and spreading Polishness all over the world – an idea that had strong roots in the society and was still present when Communism collapsed.

After 1989

The year 1989 marks a turning-point in the migration process in Poland. Groundbreaking political, legal and institutional changes in the country brought about, *inter alia*, the opening of the borders and the freedom of movement. The visible arrival of various new categories of foreigners and their rising numbers created a qualitatively new migratory situation. At the same time, all the countries of Central and Eastern Europe were undergoing profound change. Possible East-West mass migratory movements were seriously considered in light of the break-up of the Soviet Union. There were fears of the eruption of ethnic conflicts and acts of violence, which could result in an exodus as well as large-scale returns of emigrant Poles to their homeland. The Polish State was neither prepared to that new migratory situation at the time nor able to render assistance and care for the asylum-seekers arriving in ever greater numbers. Accordingly, new structures and new mechanisms were being gradually built up within the state administration.

Migratory movements and their consequences raised concerns about state security in view of Poland's precarious geopolitical location, the absence of legal foundations for the policy on aliens as well as of effective state structures and procedures, aggravated by the shortage of funds and a relative lack of experience in dealing with problems of that kind. It was not the rapid rise in the number of border entries by the citizens of the USSR and later of the former USSR alone which fuelled such anxiety. Of greater concern was the onset of organised criminal activities, the smuggling of illicit drugs and other dangerous substances, car thefts, prostitution, illegal trade and related financial operations, document forgeries and arms trade on an unprecedented scale. The bazaar trade and the presence of foreigners on the Polish labour market also raised some controversy, reflected in the public opinions on migrations. The issue of limits on the arrivals of citizens of the former USSR was a permanent current in the debate. Several respected experts concurrently pointed to various public security threats and called for a state response.

These opinions, prevalent both in the public and among the experts, were taken up by the politicians. Clear expectations of law and order built a definite background to the legislative process. Polish authorities took a two-track approach to the migration policy. On the one hand, they aimed at settling the basic issues through international law and bilateral intergovernmental agreements. On the other hand, they set about adapting the national legal norms to the new political and social situation and establishing an institution responsible for the state's migration policy. Building and amending the Polish body of law on aliens ushered a debate on the model of the national migration policy. The political changes after 1989 brought also significant differences in the political perception of the phenomenon of emigration from Poland. Right at the beginning of the 1990s, a commission for contacts with the Polish diaspora was established in Senate (the upper chamber of the Polish Parliament) and Poles living abroad got some rights to participate in Polish elections. A new TV channel ›Polonia‹ was brought into existence and became accessible via satellite in the majority of the European countries, including the newly arisen countries of the former Soviet Union, and in North America.

The opinion that Polish communities and the Polish diaspora all over the world are very influential and strongly tied to Poland and that Poland has to take care of its offspring all over the world has become a common conviction among various political forces. Therefore a tendency in migration research to study Polish communities abroad (especially in the USA) arose with new strength after 1989 (Slany 1995). Several new research centres on ›Polonia studies‹ have also been created.

Additionally, after 1989, emotional feelings towards ›our forgotten‹ people living abroad arose with a new strength, and were invigorated and exploited by various parties. These feelings targeted mainly those Poles and their descendants who had been deported by the Tsarist or the Soviet regime to Russia (or the former Soviet Union). It has been a general point of view and a deep conviction that free Poland post-Communist has a historical mission to help those who still live in the former Soviet Union, either by spreading Polishness among them through financial or material aid or by creating a possibility of repatriation. At the beginning of the 1990s, Poland issued a new repatriation law. This law pertained to all Poles who – while living in the former Soviet Union – were able to prove their Polish origins. However, knowing that after EU enlargement Poland might have expected hundreds of thousands of applications for repatriation visas from neighbouring countries, particularly from Ukraine and Belarus, the repatriation law has been narrowed only to those from Asiatic republics and more specifically to Kazakhstan. Consequently, in the 1990s several field studies were conducted in Kazakhstan on ethnic Poles living there (Ciesielski 1996; Iglicka 1998; Kubiak 1997).

On the other hand, we have to remember that Polish emigrants were not perceived only as martyrs. In many periods remittances from abroad helped to invest and conspicuously enhanced a standard of living of migrants' families in Poland. In many periods a strategy to send a family member abroad was a strategy of survival for a household. In many cases it had tragic consequences because due to the restricted migration policy, those who left Poland had no chances to visit their motherland anymore. It was much better to leave once and forever than to struggle with the Ministry of Interior about the issuing of a passport.

Probably due to all these facts and experiences, the majority of the society generally still perceived emigration or possibilities of temporary migration from Poland as very sensitive issues, and politicians have to acknowledge this fact. In recent political negotiations between the Polish government and the EU concerning different aspects of Polish adaptation to the future EU enlargement it turned out that there are only two very hot, sensitive and emotional issues for Poles. One of them pertained to migration – a free access to the EU labour markets by Poles. The second one pertained to the access to Polish land by foreigners.

Research and studies that were conducted in the 1990s analysed trends and mechanisms of migration from Poland during the transition period and compared them to those observed in earlier periods. They were focused on a decline of migration from Poland and changes in migratory strategies of Poles: from settlement and long-term migration to short-term and shuttle mobility (Okólski 1994; Jazwinska and Okólski 1996).

Changes in Migratory Patterns into Poland after 1989

The dynamic relationship between the geopolitical shift and emerging migratory patterns and processes proved to be of extreme importance in post-Communist Poland and created great challenges for the migratory research and its rather inexperienced researchers.

Along with the dismantling of the Communist system, and subsequently with the collapse of the USSR, alarmist warnings began to be heard in Western Europe about the prospect of a mass population exodus from the former Soviet Union. In 1991 the most pessimistic scenario envisaged nine million citizens seeking work and living space among the ›well established‹ societies of Western Europe. Politicians, academics, journalists could not be persuaded that this exodus would not take place. And to some extent they were right. The exodus of citizens of the former USSR has not made itself felt thus in the countries of Western Europe, since it has manifested itself and been contained in the periphery – notably in Poland. In the 1990s two walls, which had divided Europe for several decades after the Second World War, ceased to exist. One of those was the boundary between the Socialist bloc and Western Europe. The other, far less often mentioned, was the strictly guarded border between the USSR and Moscow's satellite countries. As a result of these changes the most important inflow into post-Communist Poland was the short-term mass international shuttle movement of citizens of the former Soviet Union. This movement was already termed in the literature as ›primitive mobility‹ (Iglicka 2001). It is important to stress at this point that this kind of mobility had never before occurred anywhere. Therefore, we may say that Poland became not only a target area for ex-Soviets but also a laboratory of new population processes. ›Primitive mobility‹ means the new social phenomenon of people being systematically ›on the move‹ who often gave up their jobs or positions because shuttling across borders had turned out to be much more profitable for them. This kind of shuttle mobility stemmed largely from differentials in exchange rates and prices between Poland and post-Soviet countries compounded and magnified by a shortage of basic goods in the latter.

A strong demand and considerable financial resources from Western European countries were channelled into research on mobility of citizens of the former Soviet Union on Polish territory. Therefore, Polish research on the ex-SU citizens in Poland was driven at the beginning not that much by ›hidden national frames‹ but rather by ›hidden international frames‹ driven by ›jeopardised‹ security of Western societies.

Looking at the phenomenon of shuttle mobility from a Polish perspective alone, at first Poles perceived the *primitive mobility* mainly as a threat, like Western Europeans did. Eventually, however, that mobility revealed more positive aspects than negative ones. The enormous circulation of visitors from the former Soviet Union who came to Poland to buy products for export and re-export brought such benefits as: an inflow of foreign currency, partial mitigation of a chronically negative official balance of payments, local economic development in a number of regions, an increase in job opportunities, enhanced competition on labour markets, etc.

Therefore it may not be surprising that Polish migration policy has been to some extent in favour of this kind of mobility. For example, for the citizens of the main sending countries like Ukraine, Belarus and Russia, a visa regime was introduced by the Polish government on the very last moment before the enlargement, i.e. in autumn 2003. There are also some talks on high political levels about possibilities of issuing free or very cheap multiple entry visas for Poland's neighbours. Consequently, some research then focused on negative economic aspects of the implementation of the Schengen treaty for Poland's Eastern border lands and selected sectors of the Polish economy (Polska droga 2001; Kurczewska and Bojar 2002).

However, the new and widespread spatial mobility of citizens of the former Soviet Union was not only a social and demographic blip, but a harbinger of real immigration. Recently, after a decade of penetration of Polish merchandise and labour markets by petty-traders and seasonal workers from the East, one can observe that many of those people, having come to terms with the restrictions in Western Europe against mobility from the ›East‹, have started contemplating long-term or permanent residence in Poland. This is especially true for workers and traders who have already established networks in Poland.

One other development important in this analysis of national frames of migration research and hidden factors behind it, is a fact recently discovered by Poles: all Central European countries, and Poland among them, are now in the preliminary stage of an inflow of more stable immigration flows not only from the former Soviet Union countries but also from the Far East and from the West (managerial migration and return migration of Poles). During the 1990s one could observe the slow transformation of Poland from one of the biggest sending countries in the CEE region into a country of net immigration and transit. Completely new groups of foreigners, perceived as exotic, like, for instance, Vietnamese, Chinese and Armenians are rapidly forming. Their arrival takes all forms of inflow, from illegal entry, temporary stay and arranged marriages to the setting-up of business and permanent settlement. This is a beginning of processes of a ›new‹ ethnic diversity and also the creation of new ethnic consciousness.

Research on immigration, on different forms of arrival of foreigners and different aspects of their stay in Poland as e.g. possible modes of integration or a lack of integration is still almost not existing. If it is conducted, it is undertaken only by academic centres. However, since research approaches are not focused so much on the aspect of ›protection against‹ foreigners (which has occupied the state authorities until the present time) academic analyses on integration or discrimination issues have neither met with a meaningful response by state authorities so far nor are they adequately financed. The majority of studies and expertises conducted either by political centres or NGOs concentrate in accordance with the main political interests (both national and international) on EU enlargement and the consequences of the implementation on Schengen regime in Poland from a perspective of population mobility in the region.

References

Arango, Joaquin. 1998. New Migrations, New Theories. In *Worlds in Motion. Understanding International Migration at the End of the Millennium*, ed. Douglas S. Massey et al., 1–16. Oxford: Clarendon Press.

Ciesielski, Stanislaw. 1996. *Polacy w Kazachstanie w latach 1940–1946*. Wroclaw: W kolorach teczy.

Iglicka, Krystyna. 1998. The Migration of Ethnic Poles from Kazakhstan to Poland. *International Migration Review* 32 (4): 995–1015.

Iglicka, Krystyna. 2001. Shuttling from the Former Soviet Union to Poland: From Primitive Mobility to Migration. *Journal of Ethnic and Migration Studies* 27 (3): 505–18.

Jazwinska, Ewa, and Marek Okólski. 1996. *Causes and Consequences of Migration in Central and Eastern Europe*. Warsaw: ISS Press.

Kritz, Mary M., and Hania Zlotnik. 1992. Global Interactions: Migration Systems, Processes and Policies. In *International Migration Systems: A Global Approach*, ed. Mary M. Kritz, Lin Lean Lim and Hania Zlotnik, 1–16. Oxford: Clarendon Press.

Kubiak, Hieronim, ed. 1997. *Mniejszosci polskie i Polonia w ZSRR*. Wroclaw: Wroclaw University Press.

Kurczewska, Joanna, and Hanna Bojar. 2002. *Consequences of Schengen Treaty Implementation on Poland's Eastern Border*. Warsaw: ISP Press.

Latuch, Mikolaj. 1961. *Repatriacja ludnosci Polski w latach 1955–1960 na tle ruchow wedrowkowych*. Warsaw: SGPiS Press.

Lee, Everett S. 1966. A Theory of Migration. *Demography* 3: 5–18.

Okólski, Marek. 1994. Migracje zagraniczne w Polsce w latach 1980–1989 – zarys problematyki badawczej. *Studia Demograficzne* (3): 3–61.

Polska droga do Schengen. Opinie ekspertów 2001. Warsaw: ISP Press.

Slany, Krystyna. 1991. Emigracja z Polski w latach 1980. do glownych krajow imigracji zamorskiej i kontynentalnej: aspekty demograficzno-spoleczne. *Przeglad Polonijny* 4: 15–36.

Slany, Krystyna. 1995. *Miedzy przymusem a wyborem. Kontynentalne i zamorskie emigracje z krajow Europy Srodkowo-Wschodniej, 1939–1989*. Krakow: Jagiellonian University Press.

Wasilewska-Trenkner, Halina. 1973. *Ekonomiczno-spoleczne aspekty emigracji z Polski w latach 1960–1970*. unpublished typescript, Warsaw: SGPiS.

Zolberg, Aristide R. 1989. The Next Waves: Migration Theory for a Changing World. *International Migration Review* 23: 403–30.

Part IV:
New Nation States: Defining Nations and Their Migration Contexts

India and its Diaspora.
Changing Research and Policy Paradigms

By Daniel Naujoks

Abstract

In order to understand paradigms in migration research, one has to discern ›policy paradigms‹ on the one hand, and ›research paradigms‹ on the other. Often, research paradigms are manifestations of general policy paradigms, and the mutual linkage between both deserves attention.

Since the 1980s, India's diaspora relations have witnessed a major policy paradigm shift which we have dubbed as ›from the invisible diaspora to the diaspora empire‹ and ›from the traitor tune to a pride paradigm‹. This shift can be explained by two main factors. First, at a policy-related level, seminal changes in four policy sectors occurred, namely in the economic, foreign, cultural and home policies. Second, the modes of, and reasons for interaction between India and her diaspora changed with India's economic growth and the success of the overseas Indian community. Mutual mistrust changed into mutual pride and an increase in the personal intertwinement of the Indian thought-leaders with the diaspora as well as institutionalised ways of interaction contributed to a tectonic shift in the relationship.

The policy paradigm shift had implications for the Indian migration research agenda, affecting the institutional research set-up as well as the questions framed and the positions taken. Certain paradigms can be identified in all major research traditions in India, including research on the brain drain, migration and development, diaspora policies, ethnographic studies and temporary labour migration. The analysis is supplemented by a brief account of internal migration and related research.

Introduction

In a country of one billion people whose migrating descendants have established themselves in dozens of countries and regions of the world, discernible trends in the large-scale movement of people are a veritable treasure trove to researchers. International and internal migration processes are the main focus of interest and special emphasis lies on the multilayered relationship between international migrants and the Indian mother country. Over the last decades, India witnessed an interesting paradigm shift and it is of the utmost interest to ask the whys and hows of the change. Simplified one could think that it is a truth universally acknowledged that a country whose diaspora is in possession of a good fortune must be in want of closer links with its overseas community. As with Jane Austen's ›universally acknowledged truth‹, however, common beliefs and values about social phenomena have to be scrutinised critically in order to avoid traps and blind spots. As we will see, pride and prejudice play as important a role as changing economic and geo-political factors.

In order to understand research paradigms in social science research, it is necessary to have a dual view on the notion of ›paradigm‹. The ›research paradigm‹ as a general pattern of what is to be observed, what questions are asked, how these questions are structured, and how the results of scientific investigations should be interpreted – see Bommes and Thränhardt's introduction in this volume – is intrinsically intertwined with ›policy and societal paradigms‹ as well as with ways of social learning. Howlett (1994, 623) defines ›paradigms in policy research‹ as a »more or less consistent or coherent set of ideas about policies and policy problems [that] can be identified and analysed as distinct entities« whereas social learning is concerned with changes in »underlying beliefs, values, and attitudes towards the nature of social problems«. This notion of paradigm is thus somewhat related to Foucault's ›episteme‹ as a system of thought and knowledge (1980, 197). Often, ›research paradigms‹ are manifestations of general policy paradigms, and the mutual linkage between both deserves attention. We will try to shed light on several aspects of changing migration paradigms in this essay.

In order to frame the overall national migration context, ›minor‹ migration-related topics which are not a part of this analysis shall be briefly presented. Interestingly, regular immigration plays no significant role in Indian politics or public debate.[1] Research on immigration, integration and assimilation of foreigners in India is virtually non-existent. Although anecdotal evidence suggests that there are racial prejudices against foreigners in India, such as Africans, East Asians or ethnic Whites, their role and integration in the Indian society are not topics that attract much research. We will, however, not delve into this issue.[2] An anecdote from the ancient immigration to India might be of argumentative interest for researchers from other countries. When the Parsee community arrived from its Persian homeland in India around the eigth or ninth century, seeking refuge and admittance into India, the local ruler sent a bowl of milk full to the brim. ›As is this country with inhabitants‹ was the message. The Parsees, however, added sugar to the milk and sent it back. Their argument ›just as sugar mixes with milk, taking

---

[1] Less than 350,000 foreigners were registered in India as of December 31, 2007, equaling 0.03 per cent of the population. Students (8.2 per cent) accounted for the highest percentage followed by employees (5.3 per cent) (Ministry of Home Affairs 2009, 128). Although the 2001 census revealed that more than 6 million persons were born outside the country, 5.7 million alone originated from Bangladesh, Pakistan and Nepal. Subtracting persons born in Sri Lanka and Burma, a mere 230,000 individuals born outside of India remain, including many ethnic Indians who were born abroad (United Nations Global Migration Database 2009; Naujoks 2009).
[2] For more information on Indian immigration and refugee policies, see Naujoks 2009.

no additional space, but adding to its taste and flavour, so will we mix with the local people and be an asset to the kingdom‹ won them the right to establish themselves in India.³

Refugee and irregular immigration issues are two further topics that have to be mentioned briefly. The refugees residing in India are largely uncontentious and not overwhelming in numbers.⁴ More problematic is the constant inflow of irregular migrants from Bangladesh. As with most irregular migration phenomena, data on its extent is scarce. As of December 2001, the Home Ministry had announced the number of irregular Bangladeshi immigrants as 12 million, residing in 17 Indian federal states. However in February 2009, the Home Ministry withdrew these data as »unreliable« and based on »mere hearsay«, stating that it was not possible to indicate the exact number of undocumented Bangladeshi immigrants.⁵ Whatever the exact number be, it must be regarded as large-scale immigration. As recently as in April 2008 did the Indian Supreme Court direct the government to take all possible steps to prevent the »illegal immigration and infiltration« of Bangladeshis into India while approving of the government's ongoing efforts like fencing off the India-Bangladesh border.⁶ Due to the overwhelming importance of emigration from India for research and policies, we will not dwell on irregular migration or refugee studies in our further deliberations.⁷

The remainder of this essay is structured as follows: In the following section, we focus on the central topic of this essay regarding Indian out-migration and diaspora studies. We will try to shed light on the general policy paradigms, the research paradigms and the interplay between the two. In the final section, we add a brief account of *internal* migration and related research before we conclude with an outlook.

National Policy and Research Paradigms and the Indian Diaspora

The centre part of this analysis deals with paradigms regarding Indian migration and the ›diaspora‹.⁸ Before turning to the evolving paradigms, we will provide a brief overview of India's migration history. Thereafter we will illustrate a major

---

3   In a different version of the story the Parsee High Priest dropped his golden ring in the milk instead of sugar signifying that they will only add to the wealth of the kingdom, and never take it away.
4   There are about 110,000 refugees from Tibet, including the Dalai Lama, ethnic South Indians (Tamils) who fled from Sri Lanka in response to the ongoing civil war and refugees from Bangladesh (Ministry of Home Affairs 2009, 135f.). In addition, UNHCR protects and assists some 11,000 urban refugees, most of them from Afghanistan and Myanmar (UNHCR 2007). Interestingly, India is not a party to the 1951 Refugee Convention and its 1967 Protocol and has no national legislation on refugees or asylum seekers in place.
5   As reported in *Economic Times* (India), February 20, 2009.
6   *Indian Express*, April 26, 2009. See also Ministry of Home Affairs 2009, 29.
7   For an overview on the issues and research, see Ramachandran 2005; Naujoks 2009.
8   For now, we use the term ›diaspora‹ as an overarching concept to which all out-migration issues, the relationship of migrants and their descendants with the homeland and (potential) return questions are related. Below, some further thoughts on the notion and its limitations shall be provided.

paradigm shift in India's diaspora relations and shed light on the driving forces for the change. The subsequent section will connect the general paradigm shift to migration research paradigms.

Indian Migration History in a Nutshell

The first important wave of emigration from undivided India[9] followed the abolition of slavery by the colonial powers between 1833 and 1869.[10] Bonded contract labourers were shipped from British India to the Caribbean, Mauritius, South Africa, Fiji, Malaysia and Sri Lanka, in order to provide labour for sugar and rubber plantations. Such migration schemes, generally known as ›indentured labour‹ or kangani migration[11], have been described as a »new form of slavery« (Tinker 1974). Initially migrated on a temporary basis, a significant proportion of the labourers decided to remain in their new countries after the termination of their five-year contracts. The movement was supplemented by Indian traders, many of whom followed the bonded labourer as ›free‹ migrants or otherwise settled in countries of East Africa.

In 1947, the Republic of India gained independence from British rule. Post-Independence migration occurred in five broad patterns that are connected with distinct geopolitical and economic changes. Firstly, simultaneously with independence, British India was divided into the majority-Hindu India, and the predominantly-Muslim Pakistan. This *partition* led to an enormous migration of people, largely between the two newly independent countries, but also spilling over to other destinations. Secondly, the post-World War II reconstruction of Great Britain created a certain demand for Indian workers. Thirdly, from the 1960s and 1970s onwards, highly-skilled professionals from India started to gain access to the high wage economies of the US, Canada, Australia and Western Europe. At the same time, student emigration to those countries picked up. In the 1990s, a wave of Indian information technology professionals were recruited by companies in the United States and dominated the immigration pattern in Northern America.

Fourthly, in some of the African countries where ethnic Indians had settled under colonial rule, namely Uganda and Kenya, independence was closely followed by massive ›Africanisation movements‹ and anti-Asian agitations, causing many people of Indian origin to relocate, either back to India or to other countries. Conflicts with the indigenous population also caused such a movement of secondary migration in other countries of former Indian settlements, as in Fiji or some Caribbean countries. Finally, from the 1970s onwards, an increasing number of

---

9 ›Undivided India‹ refers to British India before the independence and simultaneous partition of the separate states India, Pakistan and later Bangladesh.
10 British Empire (1833), France (1848), Danish West Indies (1848), the Netherlands (1863), Portugal (1869). Slavery was abolished within Portugal by 1774, with slave trade in the colonies being banned in 1836, slavery as a status finally abolished in 1869.
11 ›Indenture‹ refers to the labour contract and was used for the migration to the Caribbean, Mauritius and Fiji while migration to Malaysia and Sri Lanka was organised by a system of local headmen, known as ›kangani‹ which was derived from the Tamil language *kankani* for overseer.

semi- and unskilled workers from South India went on temporary migration schemes to West Asia where the oil-driven economic development of the Gulf countries demanded labour in the oil industry, as well as for construction work and in the services industries.

The *Policy Paradigm* Shift – Changing Narratives and Themes

India's ›worldview‹ on her diaspora has undergone a tremendous change which is connected to changes in several beliefs and values. The old diaspora paradigm can be paraphrased as follows:

The diaspora consists of three elements: first, those who left under colonial rule and who live in remote places like the Caribbean, Africa and Fiji where they face significant social difficulties from the indigenous population, which is why India should not try to reach out to them. Second, there are mostly highly-skilled migrants residing in industrialised Western countries. Most of them obtained free education in India and deserted India for their personal benefit and without caring for the progress of the country. Third, there are labourers going temporarily to the Gulf countries, mostly from South India. As the High-Level Committee on the Indian Diaspora (2001, xi) concluded: »Barring some high profile names in the Information Technology and entertainment sectors abroad, the Diaspora has been largely out of public sight and awareness.«

This paradigm changed through a complex interplay of internal and external, objective and subjective factors to an episteme which can be described as follows:

The enormous Indian diaspora covers all continents and over one hundred countries. The diaspora in the Western countries is rich and makes India proud. Indians abroad are shining ambassadors of the great Indian civilisation. They are remitting money and are an asset to the country – they are a veritable ›brain bank‹ from which the country can make withdrawals. The perception of the temporary Gulf migrants has not changed significantly, although there is a greater awareness to safeguard their rights and working conditions.

The paradigm shift took place in many different strata of public life. The new views are expressed in statements from the political sphere, such as »if there is an Empire today on which the sun truly cannot set, it is the empire of our minds, that of the children of Mother India, who live today in Asia, Africa, Australia, Europe, the Americas and, indeed, on the icy reaches of Antarctica«[12] or »the BJP believes that the growing achievements of the vast Indian diaspora are a matter of pride and a source of strength for India.«[13] Since the early to mid-2000s, most important Indian print and online media have an ›Indian diaspora‹ news category and disseminate information on the glorified achievements of the brethren abroad.[14]

---

12 Prime Minister Manmohan Singh's inaugural speech at the Pravasi Bharatiya Divas, January 7, 2005.
13 2004 Vision Document of the National Democratic Alliance (NDA), the then-ruling Government coalition under the leadership of the Bharatiya Janata Party (BJP).
14 E.g. *Times of India* (Indians Abroad), *Hindustan Times* (Indians Abroad, Subcategory: Diaspora Diary), *Economic Times* (Pravasi Bharatiya), *Onlineindiannews* (NRI news).

Professional and industrial organisations (such as the Confederation of Indian Industries, the Federation of Indian Chambers of Commerce and Industry, and the National Association of Software and Services Companies) have departments or cells that focus on, and give legitimacy to diasporic claims. Indian movies and literature increasingly pay tribute to diaspora venues and concerns and finally, academic publications on the matter increased significantly and changed in focus, as we will see below.

This remarkable paradigm shift may be dubbed as ›from the invisible diaspora to the diaspora empire‹ and ›from the traitor tune to a pride paradigm‹. A closer look at the mechanics of the remarkable shift in the perception of, and approach towards the Indian diaspora reveals some interesting insights into homeland-diaspora relations. This section is intended as a general overview of the relevant changes.[15]

Significant changes at different levels led to the described paradigm shift. The most visible level is the realm of *policy-related ideas*, interests and factors which are displayed in four policy areas as discussed below. Further, less obvious factors at the individual level as vibrations and interactional elements played a role in the paradigm shift, too. A third level which regards political and other structural factors is neglected in this overview. Thus, changes of governments and different political approaches, issues of financial contributions from the diaspora to political parties, the importance for elections and political purposes, and other effects of overall diaspora relations does not constitute a focus of this analysis. We will limit discussion of the influences from this field to a few remarks at the end of this section.[16]

Major Changes in Policy-related Factors

From the home country's viewpoint there are four main policy fields that matter for the relation to its diaspora: (1) economic policies, (2) external affairs and related political interests, (3) cultural policies and lastly (4) convictions and goals in the field of home affairs. As figure 1 shows, each of the involved policy spheres is affected by internal and external factors. Since we are examining paradigms in the country of origin, ›internal‹ factors are related to its domestic matters while ›external‹ factors derive from circumstances from outside of the source country.

As we will see, in the Indian context major changes took place in all four policy areas, affecting substantially the national beliefs regarding the Indian diaspora. It deserves mention that the policy area structure outlined here does not represent a merely theoretically, inductively-derived set of possibilities; but is rather deducted from an extensive analysis of Indian diaspora polices and the concerned paradigms.[17]

---

15 For a detailed analysis of the paradigm shift and its factors, see Naujoks [forthcoming b].
16 For a detailed analysis of these factors, see ibid.
17 Based on the author's analysis of the Parliamentary debates, academic contributions, policy documents and media coverage as well as 50 interviews with key actors from the policy subsystem. See ibid.

Figure 1: Policy Sectors and Factors for Diaspora Relations

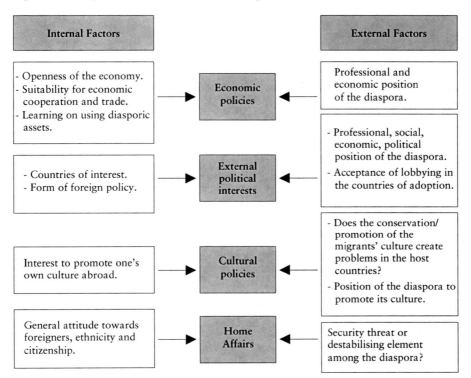

Economic Policies and the Diaspora

Before 1991, India pursued an economic policy which is commonly referred to as ›self-reliance strategy‹. Founded in a suspicion of international trade and private capitalists, self-reliance was a form of socialism involving complex industrial licensing requirements (the so-called ›license Raj‹) and predominantly public ownership of infrastructure and heavy industry. In order to attain national self-sufficiency India tried to produce everything within its national boundaries, while levying heavy customs duties in order to discourage imports (Acharya et al. 2003, 37; Tendulkar and Bhavani 2005).

In those days, India was neither looking much for foreign capital and investment, nor was it an interesting destination due to the many regulations and limitations on holding assets in India (Tendulkar and Bhavani 2005, 52f.). Given the small scale of foreign trade, as depicted in figure 2, the overseas community was not likely to be viewed as an important ›agent of trade‹. Particularly if one considers that the limited trade was rooted rather in a policy decision than in the lack of

Figure 2: India's Foreign Trade 1970–2007

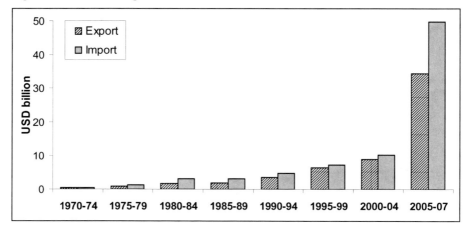

Source: Own calculations based on RBI (2003) for the period 1970–1989 and RBI (2008) for 1990–2007.
Note: The given years are fiscal years. Each figure represents the annual average for a five-year period, except for the three-year period 2005–2007.

trade and production capacities. Being focused on the ›development from within‹ India saw the emigration of highly-qualified professionals as a betrayal of the country's growth plans.

The seminal shift in India's economic policies started from 1991 onwards. Triggered by a double fiscal and external payments crisis[18], the government started liberalising the economy.[19] Reforms of India's trade, industrial and financial policies were geared towards opening up the market for foreign investment, allowing more private ownership in important economic sectors and reducing the required government permits and regulations (Acharya et al. 2003, 78f.). This process was an important precondition for the economic development that has been witnessed in India over the last ten to fifteen years. The greater integration with the world economy led to increasing foreign trade (see figure 2). Obviously, this was particularly true for countries with a significant diaspora population, like the United States, Canada and the United Kingdom. Also, with the opening up of the economy and consequent reduction of government spending, foreign direct investment from those countries, as from many others, became a major goal of Indian economic policies.

---

18 For accounts of the crisis see Acharya et al. 2003, Tendulkar and Bhavani 2005, or Government of India 1993.
19 As Tendulkar and Bhavani 2005 trace comprehensibly, the reform process was triggered by IMF and World Bank conditionalities agreed on in the bailout packages on short-term lending in the wake of the crisis. It continued, however, far beyond these conditionalities and was carried forward by all coming governments.

Meanwhile, the diaspora in many economically developed countries had arrived in decisive positions. It is obvious that a diaspora population which consists mainly of workers and blue collar workers cannot contribute extensively to the home country's search for large-scale economic cooperation and investment. The Indian migrants to the UK in the 1950s and 1960s belonged to a large extent to this category. The Indian diaspora in the Caribbean, South and East Africa, Fiji, Malaysia and other parts of the world, which traced its roots to emigration under colonial rule, was also less affluent and engaged in agriculture and petty trading rather than in investment-prone businesses (Naujoks 2009). The highly-skilled migrants who went to Northern America in the 1970s and 1980s, although comparatively affluent professionals such as medical doctors and engineers, were not often in a position to facilitate trade and investment. However, by the late 1990s, a critical mass of ethnic Indians had arrived in important positions in multinational corporations in the industrialised countries. Indian information technology workers in Silicon Valley owned many medium-sized IT companies. Thus the position of the Indian diaspora in terms of their potential impact on trade and investment had changed dramatically.

In addition, a global and national policy-learning process took place which recognised the diaspora as an economic asset and tool. We will deal with this learning process in more detail in the research paradigms discussed below. Suffice to say that due to the framing conditions of the Indian economy and the composition and position of the Indian overseas community, concrete benefits for India were not clearly visible up to the 1990s.

Figure 3: Inflow of Remittances into India 1970–2007

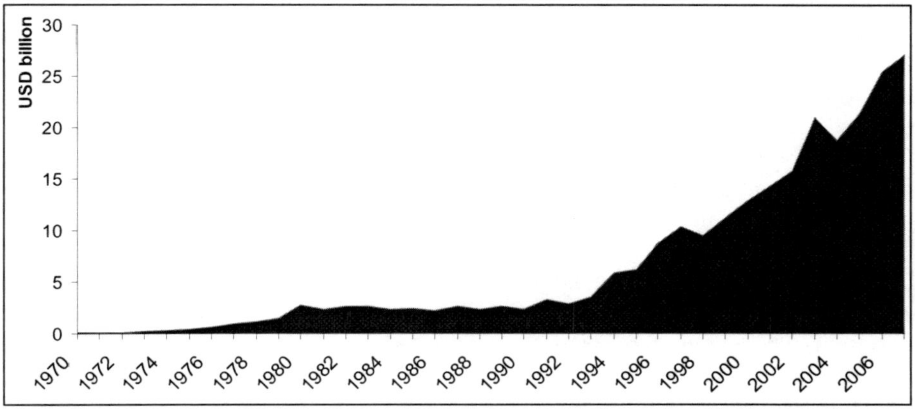

Source: World Bank estimates based on the International Monetary Fund's Balance of Payments Statistics Yearbook 2007.

Possibly the most oft-quoted and publicly discussed way for a source country to profit from its migrants is through the inflow of private transfers, so-called remittances. Since 2003, India is the world's largest recipient of private money transfers from abroad, at least in absolute terms. As figure 3 shows, India reached this position after a remarkable increase over the last one and a half decades. From a modest USD 2.1 billion in 1990/91, the inward remittances were pegged at USD 25.5 billion in 2006 and USD 27 billion in 2007. Another factor shaking the economic foundations of the ›brain drain‹ belief, was the visible involvement of the Indian diaspora in the country's rising IT industry which is widely recognised as a prototypical success story in the field of migration and development (Hunger 2004; 2005; Thränhardt 2005, 4; United Nations 2006, 7, 61).

Political and Strategic Interests Policies and the Diaspora

The domain of Indian international political and strategic interests also witnessed a tectonic shift. Having fought a long struggle for independence against the British colonial power, and witnessing the protective attitude of former colonial countries towards their ethnic communities that were still living in the former colonies, India wanted to pursue a distinct policy of empowerment and non-interference. This is one of the reasons India was at the forefront of the Non-Aligned Movement, which is often considered a brainchild of India's first Prime Minister Jawaharlal Nehru (Dubey 2003b). The Non-Aligned Movement is an international organisation of states which chose to align neither with the United States nor with the Soviet Union during the Cold War. Officially founded in 1961 after 15 years of increasing cooperation, the organisation's declared objective was to ensure »the national independence, sovereignty, territorial integrity and security of non-aligned countries« in their »struggle against [...] all forms of foreign aggression, occupation, domination, interference or hegemony» (Havana Declaration of 1979). A concomitant of such an approach was that India recommended to her diasporic communities not to look for help in their ancestral country, to be model citizens in their respective receiving countries and to promote the development of those countries (Bhat 2003, 15).[20]

A different explanation for the pursued policy, or another element underpinning it, would be that in many cases, Indian migrants were brought to those countries by the colonial power to serve as intermediaries between the indigenous population and the colonial power. Because of the consequent indigenous resentment against Indian communities, as well as the omnipresent xenophobia-based danger for newcomers to a foreign land, there were potential and actual threats from indigenous groups against the local Indian communities. The exodus of tens of thousands of ethnic Indians from Uganda in 1972 and hostilities against the Indian community in Fiji were only the obvious tip of the iceberg which shaped public thinking. Dubey (2003b, 133), too, states that India realised that including ethnic Indians in a policy framework would neither win them over for investment in India nor please African governments. In the years and decades after independ-

---

20 Dubey (2003b) provides several statements of India's first Prime Minister Nehru that confirm this policy attitude.

ence, India's economic, military and political power was limited. She was therefore not in the position to safeguard the interests of those people. In addition, there was a wide range of internal problems and no need for an increasing population. The possibility of hundreds of thousands of ethnic Indians searching for a safe haven in India in the aftermath of political problems in their countries of residence was not an attractive scenario to Indian policy-makers. Whatever the determining factors, reaching out to diaspora communities for political reasons did not seem to be a feasible or desirable policy option for India.

In North America, the community started growing significantly only from 1970 onwards. But it took some time before the community reached a certain threshold in big countries like the US and Canada. Although India was not formally aligned with the Soviet Union she had rather close ties with the USSR. India's diplomatic ties with the United States before the end of the Cold War are often described as strained. In this situation, with no major strategic interests in the US or Canada, the ethnic Indian community residing in, or holding citizenship of those countries, was unsurprisingly not perceived as a great asset.

By the late 1990s, the bi-polar Cold War lines of world politics had faded and India had abandoned her socialist self-reliance strategy, was gaining economic power and was beginning to assume a more active role internationally.[21] With the increased interest in assuming a more active role in international relations came an increased interest in India's relationship with the United States of America. By then, there was a critical mass of ethnic Indians with US citizenship. Well-off ethnic Indians were entering the political arena through their political contributions to election campaigns in the US and even, in rare but increasing cases, by running for public office themselves.

The growing community, its social and professional standing and its increasing awareness of its political influence led to the establishment of the ›Congressional Caucus on India and Indian Americans‹ in 1993, which was supposed to include 176 members or 40 per cent of all Congressmen in 2006.[22] As a senior observer of US politics notes: »It is as a foreign policy force that the caucus has become best known« (Hathaway 2001, 28). Besides a general shift in the policy-makers' idea and perception of India, the political lobbyists of Indian origin soon established their credentials through several successful involvements into Indo-American relations.

Their political weight and significance was felt first when India conducted nuclear tests in May 1998, which triggered international sanctions, most importantly from the United States.[23] Ethnic Indians in the US and the India Caucus were

---

21 For example, India started demanding a permanent seat in the United Nations Security Council; and instead of receiving, India began giving development aid, joining the ›club of donor countries‹ (Agrawal 2007; De la Fontaine 2008).
22 Information gathered at http://www.usindiafriendship.net (accessed April 10, 2009).
23 Apart from the US, Japan, Canada, Germany, the Netherlands, Sweden, Norway, Denmark, Switzerland and Australia imposed certain restrictive economic measures against India (Minister of State for External Affairs' answer to unstarred question No. 2086 in the Indian Parliament (Rajya Sabha), August 10, 2000).

vocal in explaining India's point of view and lobbying for the relaxation and removal of the sanctions. As India's then-External Affairs Minister said, »It was during those periods of negotiations and talks with the United States, I realised how valuable role [Indian-Americans] were playing and had played behind the scenes.«[24]

The most significant and highly-acclaimed success of the Indian-American lobbying efforts is widely seen in the context of the recent Indo-US civilian nuclear agreement. After the initial announcement to enhance Indo-US civilian nuclear cooperation in July 2005, several steps led to the final signature of the US-India agreement for civil nuclear cooperation in October 2008.[25] Recognising their efforts and contribution, Indian politicians publicly thanked the diaspora community as did India's Prime Minister: »I wish to record our special gratitude to the Indian community in the United States of America for the efforts made by them in mobilising support of the political leadership in that country for Indo-US cooperation in civilian nuclear energy.«[26]

It shall be added that also in other countries, such as the UK, Canada, Mauritius, Suriname, Malaysia and Fiji, ethnic Indian politicians held important positions in the government and parliament. The openness of US politics to lobbying efforts and the special interests of India in this country are the main reasons why mainly political efforts in the US contributed to the paradigm shift while the achievements in other countries are, at the best, acknowledged as a sideline issue.

Cultural Policies and the Diaspora

In the years immediately following Independence, India had no strong desire to promote her own culture abroad. The country had to confront the challenges of nation building, of dealing with its neighbours as a result of partition, and grave economic challenges. At the time of India's independence, the bulk of Indian migrants were residing as descendants of indentured labourers or traders in developing countries. In many cases, these populations were in a more vulnerable position than the indigenous population, and the promotion of Indian culture by them might have been interpreted as segregation by the indigenous population and provided an excuse for ethnic hostilities. However, by the mid-1990s, the cultural context had changed to a significant extent. India was older as a nation, economically on the ascent and also more outward-looking. No longer merely a vulnerable community in developing countries, Indian migrant communities were now also in economically and socially beneficial positions in industrialised countries. In those countries, they were often highly-skilled professionals with a good reputation and gave a good account of themselves as regards ›integration‹. There was no, or very

---

24 Interview by the author with former External Affairs Minister Jaswant Singh (BJP), July 30, 2008.
25 Momentous, but also contentious steps were the passing of the ›United States-India Peaceful Atomic Energy Cooperation Act‹ in December 2006 by the US Congress and Congress' approval of the agreement prior to its signing in July 2007.
26 Prime Minister Manmohan Singh's address at the Pravasi Bharatiya Divas, January 7, 2007.

limited, fear of racial hostilities if these communities promoted Indian culture. Also, several aspects of Indian culture had reached the mainstream in many Western societies: yoga, meditation, Ayurvedic medicine and lately, the so-called Bollywood movies, apart from influence on mainstream Western fashion and design. In this altered scenario, the diaspora was a welcome tool for India to promote certain aspects of her cultural heritage.

Another internal factor might be the change of the Indian government in 1998. The government elected that year was led by a nationalist Hindu party, the BJP, which had sustained cultural and religious connections with many parts of the Indian diaspora. More importantly, the BJP was more inclined to promote ›Indian culture‹ abroad and celebrate diasporic efforts and achievements in this regard.

Home Policies and the Diaspora

The fourth policy sector represents factors from the domain of home affairs. Domestically, India had a rather diffident approach towards the diaspora. One reason for this is that upon India's partition the massive *ex patriae* population was an uneasy fit into the new borders of India, Pakistan and later Bangladesh. Home affairs have always been dominated by fears and ideas regarding threats and security issues. In this regard, the diaspora faced negative publicity within certain domestic interest groups in a few cases. The most prominent negative diasporic involvement in internal affairs took place when Punjabi Sikhs put forth their demand for their own state, the independent Khalistan, in the 1980s. In order to achieve this goal, some militant groups pursued terrorist activities on Indian soil. Security agencies believed that much moral, personal and financial support for this struggle came from Sikhs abroad, especially those living in Canada and the UK (Singh Tatla 1999). It goes without saying that this did not make the diaspora appear in a favourable light to the Indian public and policy-makers.

By the 1990s, the Khalistan issue was no longer raised and there were no significant confrontational interferences by the diaspora into national politics.[27] However, the new concern to emerge was the abstract fear of Al Qaeda-like terrorism by the Muslim diaspora of Indian descent.[28] Not having been substantiated by any such actual activities, by and large, the diaspora has become much less of a security issue.

Interactional and Vibrational Changes – *Paisa*, Pride and Prejudice

Focusing on the rational, policy-oriented actor, most analysts do not pay significant attention to non-policy related factors in paradigm-shifts. We have described

---

[27] It has to be added though that liberal diaspora groups around the globe opposed some alleged ›Hindu-nationalist‹ projects and ideas of the BJP-led Government (1998–2004). Apart from ›confrontational‹ interferences, diaspora groups are said to finance political parties in India. Since this is not allowed under the Indian law, all political parties officially deny such contributions.

[28] In the 2005 London bombings, people of Pakistani origin were held responsible, which gave rise to a fear within the Indian security establishment, of PIOs infiltrating India with fundamentalist Islamic activities or supporting the existing domestic activities.

the popular attitude dubbing it the ›traitor tune‹. We have argued that the wealth of overseas Indians – or *paisa*, money in Hindi – is one element in the diaspora equation. However, there is another element, a mix of very human emotions, like envy and hurt self-esteem, pride and prejudice that should not be ignored. It appears that the negative school of thought which regarded emigrated (and educated) Indians as traitors who deserted their home country for their personal benefit and without caring for the progress of the country is founded largely also on this element.

With the emotional response to the situation comes an interactional element which deserves mention. When highly-skilled migrants returned for family visits to India, their interaction with their family, former classmates and friends was mostly of a private nature. The closed Indian economy provided few opportunities to leverage a private relationship to one of cross-border business. Further, barring some prominent examples, the bulk of the diaspora had not reached the highest levels of multinational corporations and thus was limited in its business interactions with India. Often, Indians returning from overseas complained about India and the backwardness of the country. During policy interviews the author conducted in 2008/09, many actors from the diaspora policy sub-system stated that overseas Indians had a tendency to complain about everything in India. As one interviewee put it »for NRIs, India was only dirt and filth and it was unorganised and chaotic«. Indians in India were overwhelmed by the harsh criticism and naturally developed an anti-attitude, regarding those who had left as condescending, abandoning their culture and roots.

As described above, India was not an important player in international relations. It was a country struggling heavily with its own economic challenges. The fact that the country's image abroad was one of snake-charmers, beggars and rural poverty did not help in the diaspora's interaction with the country. The diaspora, especially second-generation Americans of Indian descent felt the need to distance themselves from the country.

Once a certain negative attitude towards overseas Indians was established and displayed, it led to a negative cycle, because overseas Indians themselves felt unappreciated. Even those who did not complain about the country often received pre-emptive negative reactions from Indians in India, leading to a sense of discrimination. This led to a vicious circle of negative vibrations.

All these factors changed significantly with India's economic development. The reason for interaction, the context, the content and – importantly – the vibrations, have undergone a sea change.

A new platform for interaction between returning Indians and Indians in India was now to discuss business opportunities and ways in which the Indian corporate sector and the diaspora could collaborate. Politicians who went abroad were not necessarily supplicants for international and private aid, but rather messengers of great investment opportunities. This changed their role, their self-esteem and the entire mode of interaction. The vibrations changed too. First, Indians abroad perceived an improvement in the way they were esteemed as Indians. Thus, the country's economic boom had positive repercussions in their respective countries of residence. Second, they themselves saw a significant change in India. Although not everything was as they could have wished for, the change was discernable and tangible. They complained less in their interactions with counterparts in India. As previously pointed out, many interactions now took place for business purposes, in a relationship of equals. Also by then, many members of the Indian diaspora had reached prominent positions in the corporate sector, in academia, and even in politics in their countries of residence. Their reputation for hard work and smartness had earned India a new reputation. They were very successful brand ambassadors of the new, the emerging, the shining India. Indeed, the diaspora's role in promoting a different, successful image of India is one of the most invoked achievements of the diaspora. India's then-Home Minister opened the 2003 Parliamentary debates on Overseas Citizenship of India by stating that »Today the world over, India and Indians are viewed with respect, and one major factor contributing to this situation is the Indian diaspora settled abroad.«[29] The Deputy Chairman of India's Planning Commission confirmed that »Indians began to feel good about the fact that [Indians in developed countries] are doing well and that they are contributing to a perception of India, that Indians are very smart. And we Indians naturally loved that.«[30]

This naturally softened the way overseas Indians were perceived. Instead of complaints and arrogance on the one side and low self-esteem, envy and reproach on the other, one now witnessed a mutual shoulder patting: ›You have done well here. You have done well there‹. Mutual pride. And these positive vibrations shaped the entire interaction, and even the image of overseas Indians. In our view, this played a major role in overcoming the ›traitor tune‹ and reaching the ›pride paradigm‹.

With the broadening in membership of the great Indian middle class, and with a sharp increase in the number of overseas Indians, another factor that might have contributed to the change of attitude is the increasing intertwinement between the Indians at home and the diaspora. It is hard to find senior bureaucrats, politicians or other middle-class Indians who do not have a close relative abroad (Varma 2004, 204). As the Deputy Chairman of India's Planning Commission Montek Singh Ahluwalia said: »I think it's virtually impossible to move in professional circles without coming across a person who has some contact with the diaspora. It may not be his brother but certainly his cousin and so forth.«[31] This fact has been confirmed in many interviews the author held in the Indian diaspora policy subsystem. Though the conclusion we draw involves an element of speculation, we found that this close contact between policy actors and the diaspora naturally created more tolerance and a better understanding of their needs and attitudes. It

---

29 Statement by then-Home Minister LK Advani (BJP) in the Indian parliament (Rajya Sabha), December 18, 2003.
30 Interview by the author with the Deputy Chairman of the Planning Commission, Montek Singh Ahluwalia, June 6, 2008.
31 Interview by the author, June 6, 2008.

provided more opportunities for close interaction, first-hand information and – very importantly – the inclusion of those people in the notion of ›us‹ instead of ›them‹.

Once overcome, once the pride was displayed, overseas Indians obtained what many of them had longed for: recognition. And this recognition, together with the visible changes in the country, helped them to accept India as she is and to overcome their own critical attitude.

Finally, the relationship between the diaspora and India became institutionalised and this clearly had a positive effect on homeland-diaspora relations. Starting in 2000, a High-Level Committee on the Indian Diaspora was established, which went around the world and visited all major overseas Indian communities before it submitted its extensive and very influential report in January 2002.[32] Following one of the Committee's recommendations, from 2003 on the Indian government has been organising an annual diaspora conference, the Pravasi Bharatiya Divas, where diasporic and resident Indians as well as important members of the Indian establishment come together. In 2004, a special Ministry of Overseas Indian Affairs was established, easing the interaction with the diaspora and institutionalising the relationship. These means helped to establish better mutual understanding and contributed to the general paradigm shift.

Summarising Remarks on the Policy Paradigm Shift

To summarise the main driving forces of India's paradigm shift towards the Indian diaspora, we can say that at a policy-related level, before 1990, there was limited scope for extensive economic collaboration with the diaspora due to Indian economic policies, on the one hand, and the socio-economic-political position of the diaspora, on the other. Further, because of problems with indigenous populations in some countries and the diasporic involvement in terrorist activities on Indian soil, there was a tendency to view the diaspora rather as a liability than an asset. This changed with the U-turn in India's economic policy and the subsequent economic growth, as well as the emergence of a well-off diaspora in economically developed countries. Further, new political aims and tenets in international affairs rendered the diaspora, especially in the US, a very valuable partner.

On the interactional side of the diaspora equation, resident Indians used to perceive overseas communities as overly critical. Their modes of, and reasons for interaction changed with India's economic growth and the success of the overseas Indian community. Mutual mistrust changed into mutual pride and an increasing personal intertwinement of the national and local thought-leaders with the diaspora as well as institutionalised ways of interaction led to a tectonic shift in the relationship.

As mentioned in the beginning of this section, for the sake of brevity we have omitted an analysis of Indian politics and non-policy related factors. It may suffice to state here that although those factors played a role in the overall development,

---

32 The report is available at http://www.indiandiaspora.nic.in.

they were more important for the timing than for the paradigm shift itself. Especially the pro-active approach of the 1998 elected coalition government of the National Democratic Alliance acted as a time trigger for the shift. Further, the involvement of diaspora organisations such as the Global Organization of People of Indian Origin (GOPIO), a few policy entrepreneurs and the High Level Committee on the Indian Diaspora played a crucial role in the process.[33]

Paradigms in Indian Diaspora Research

In this section, we will present the manifestations and effects of the changing beliefs in and on migration research. After a short overview on Indian diaspora research, we will focus on the existing and changing paradigms.

Indian Diaspora Research: A Brief Overview

In analysing national research paradigms, we have to take the research landscape into consideration. With regard to cultural and ethnic background, research on the Indian diaspora is conducted by three genres of analysts. Apart from Indian scholars based in India, diasporic Indian and non-ethnic Indian researchers contribute to the academic discourse. Although all three bodies of publication are interrelated, we focus on research by Indian scholars based in India in order to identify the national research paradigms, while bearing in mind the impact of the international body of literature.

A second differentiation in the research landscape can be made with regard to the involved disciplines. Brettell and Hollifield (2000) remind us that migration research has not yet fully developed as a ›social science in its own right‹. Instead, the questions asked, the units analysed, the theories used and the hypotheses formulated, depend on the disciplinary canon of the different research traditions, such as sociology, history, economics, demography, anthropology, political science and law, to name only the most prominent disciplines. As we will see below, studies with regard to the Indian diaspora used to be largely ethnographic and historical, apart from economic research into brain drain. In recent years, political scientists and economists have increasingly found interest in the topic, while legal and demographic scholars seem to have not found their share in the research subject yet.[34]

A third way of assessing the research field is to examine the institutional establishments and affiliations. In India for example, quite a few of the publications are written by former bureaucrats or practitioners of diaspora relations rather than by career university professors (e.g. Kant Bhargava, J.C. Sharma and Muchkund Dubey). Within academia, few scholars focus entirely on diaspora studies. Often they cover regional studies and include diaspora relations in the respective region.

---

33 For a detailed analysis of these factors, see Naujoks [forthcoming b].
34 Legal contributions are, however, found on the questions of refugees and social and labour rights for internal migrants.

There are only three institutes at universities which formally focus entirely on diaspora studies. In 1996, the University Grants Commission established the ›Centre for Study of Indian Diaspora‹ at the University of Hyderabad's School of Social Sciences. The ›Centre for Indian Diaspora & Cultural Studies‹ at the Hemchandracharya North Gujarat University focuses rather on diaspora writers and according to its website, also contributes to some extent to research on »the patterns of migrations of various castes and communities from Gujarat to various parts of the globe.«

The ›Centre for Development Studies‹ in Kerala has focused on migration from Kerala and the related economic effects since the late 1990s. In 2006, the Ministry of Overseas Indian Affairs established a ›Research Unit on International Migration‹ within the centre. According to the unit's online self-description its purpose is to undertake studies on dynamics of migration, socio-economic impact of migration in different States of India, occupation-wise migration, remittances, investment and development. However, the South Indian state of Kerala seems to remain the main focus of the research activities. Further, in December 2007, the Organisation for Diaspora Initiatives (ODI) at the Jawaharlal Nehru University launched a six-monthly *Diaspora Studies* journal.

In addition, there are many influential migration scholars of Indian origin residing abroad; only some examples of which are the economist Jagdish Bhagwati (Columbia University, New York) and remittances-expert Dilip Ratha (World Bank), Devesh Kapur (Director of the Center for the Advanced Study of India, University of Pennsylvania), Brij V. Lal (Pacific and Asian History at Australian National University) and Mohan K. Gautam (anthropology and indology at Leiden University, the Netherlands).

Policy and Research Paradigms

In line with the conceptualisation by Bommes and Thränhardt in this volume, we consider social science research paradigms as a set of ideas and research beliefs that determines the framing of research questions and theory selection as well as research reception and appraisal. Such a scientific world (or problem) view has to be shared by a large majority in the scientific community, making it difficult to deviate from it. Analysing a wide spectrum of Indian migration studies, we find that the following research beliefs and elements of a general research paradigm can be discerned. It must be emphasised though that certain generalisations cannot be avoided in describing trends and patterns; we have tried though to do justice to the major research traditions, aiming simultaneously at a constructively critical assessment.

From Ethnographic Accounts to a Wider Diaspora Research Agenda

One of the side-effects of the general pre-1990s paradigm, labelled above as ›the invisible diaspora‹ and the ›traitor tune‹ was a lack of research interest. A senior researcher on the Indian diaspora writes in 1993: »The study of overseas Indian communities is a newly emergent field which has so far yielded only a few detailed monographs and comparative essays« (Jain, R.K. 1993, 52). Jain identifies two frameworks (or research paradigms) in the study of the Indian diaspora. The first examines cultural resistance and the second, adaptation of communities in their respective countries of residence (Jain, R.K. 1993, 52ff.; 2003, 1), although the latter is almost exclusively contributed to by scholars who do not reside in India. The state of research prior to 1990 focused to a vast extent on the ›old diaspora‹ and aimed at ethnographic accounts of their lives. An extensive bibliography is to be found in R.K. Jain (1993). As Sharma (2004, 45) and Jayaram (1998, 13; 2004, 32) observe, most of the research operates from within the parameters of conventional structural functionalism. Outside of India, Hugh Tinker's research (1974; 1977) is the basis for most studies on indentured labour migration and Stephen Vertovec conducted several influential and widely-quoted studies on the ›old‹ Indian diaspora and Hinduism.

With an increasing national interest in the diaspora, and the establishment of institutions on diaspora research, the scope widened and many more research questions appeared. Jayaram (1998; 2004) from the Centre for Study of Indian Diaspora at the University of Hyderabad is an example of the process of amplifying the research lens, including the following aspects in the possible study agenda: demography, the background of emigrants, the emigration process, social factors in the host country, social organisation of the diaspora community and its cultural dynamics, their question of identity, struggle for power and orientation towards India, as well as India's orientation towards the diaspora and secondary emigration. Apart from the thematic widening of the research scope, the regional focus also shifted from the Caribbean and Africa more towards the Western countries, especially the US. We assume that the growing interest of researchers in the well-off, highly-skilled migrants to industrialised countries is connected to the above-mentioned shift towards the ›pride paradigm‹. Also an increasing involvement of scholars with major diaspora organisations such as GOPIO has reportedly »influenced, enhanced, and sustained their interest in the Indian diaspora« (Assisi 2005).

Since the late 1990s, there is an increasing number of anthologies that try to cope with the diverse subjects and aspects of the Indian diaspora (e.g. Motwani, Gosine and Barot-Motwani 1993; Dubey 2003a; Daman Singh and Singh 2003; Lal, Reeves and Rai 2006; Singh 2007). It is therefore clear that the journey to a more comprehensive study of the Indian migration has just started – as it is true for much of the world's migration research. It goes without saying that migration research in general complains about the lack of reliable data and information. Having said this, it might be added that the bulk of publications on Indian migration is not based on genuine, primary research but on overviews of existing literature and anecdotes of persons who were involved in diaspora relations. This might be traced to the limited degree of institutionalisation, the restrained research interest of the Indian government, and the lack of adequate research funding in this sector.

Pride Paradigm

Although the ›pride paradigm‹ described above has led to greater awareness of the diaspora and, therefore, an expanded research interest, a certain pride of the diaspora can also narrow the view. As Varma (2004, 38) notes: »In India, the pendulum swings naturally to two extremes: adulation or rejection.« Instead of more objective research on the composition of the overseas Indian communities, their problems and their actual contributions, the ›pride‹ motive leads to a tendency to laud the greatness of the diaspora achievements, such as: »The ever-expanding and strengthening diaspora prides itself of the millionaire NRIs in UK, US, Canada and Australia« (Mulloo 2007, 26). It is not rare to find researchers listing Indian-American CEOs and raving about the high median income statistics. Despite the fact that anyone who has ever lived in New York thinks also of the taxi drivers as the prominent face of Indians in New York, this profession will hardly ever find its way into descriptions of the Indian diaspora in the US. One reason could be that those people do not fit in the glorious Indian diaspora picture sought to be fostered by some. Although it is true that many achievements of the community are amazing indeed, and stand out when compared to migrants from other origins, it is important that research takes a balanced look at the entire spectrum of the emigration. Some of the newer research by limiting its scope to a listing of the great achievements of Indians misses the opportunity to scrutinise the statistics and analyse the underlying trends. Obviously, this is not a blanket statement and there are critical and purely analytical accounts; however, a certain tendency in the other direction needs to be scrutinised and guarded against.

Brain Drain and Beyond

The ›traitor tune‹ was accompanied and fuelled by research on the brain drain. In research, the brain-drain belief is based on the economic new growth theory, which basically assumes a positive correlation between human capital and long-term economic growth (Straubhaar and Wolburg 1998; Straubhaar and Vadean 2006).

There is a vast body on Indian brain-drain literature from the 1960s and 1970s. However, most of the literature at that time does not represent ›migration research‹ in the proper sense. Rather, articles and monographs on the topic were comments from policy actors and scholars from fields that were not connected to migration research. The well-known Indian economist Dandekar (1968, 203) exemplifies the research questions: »Why do these people leave their home countries and seek employment elsewhere? Are the reasons ›normal‹ in any sense of the term? Is the migration inevitable or can it be prevented? Is it harmful to the developing countries? Will any measures to prevent it do even greater harm?« He states also that many explanations for the brain drain have »political, social, and cultural overtones. It is thus that passions, pride, and prejudice enter the discussion« (204).

Thus the focus of understanding the driving force behind highly-skilled migration and the retention of professionals are the key areas of interest. Consequently Dandekar (1968, 229) argues that »it will become inevitable to close the borders in order to prevent an accelerated drain on our personnel resources. [...] The legal opinion that the Fundamental Rights include the right to travel around the world is nonsense«.[35] Also Bhagwati (2008) quotes a nameless ›famous economist‹ in India who wrote that »no one under the age of forty should be allowed to emigrate.« Great popularity greeted Bhagwati's proposal for the taxation of skilled migrants through the country of residence, the so-called brain-drain or Bhagwati tax (Bhagwati and Partington 1976; Bhagwati and Wilson 1989).

In the mid-1980s, there was still discussion on the brain drain but the tone was milder and the focus was rather to understand how to use the resources abroad (Chopra 1986); although the understanding was still that »brain drain means that persons on whom society spends a considerable amount of money, ultimately give the benefit of their education to other countries« (Pant 1986).

Exemplary for researchers on India – and many other emigration countries – Bhagwati (2004, 215) clarifies that as of today researchers have moved on in the understanding of the phenomenon of out-migration of the skilled from the developing countries. The brain-drain worries apply only to countries »where the populations are small, the educational systems are inadequate, and the outmigration of the few skilled professionals they have is a *threat*« while for countries like India, the Philippines, and China »the outmigration of professional citizens is an *opportunity*« [emphasis in the original]. Thus in the last decade, research on brain drain has been to a very large extent replaced by discussions on India's endeavours to benefit from past migratory movements. This reflects a general trend from a problem-centric approach to a benefit-centric one in many countries (Thränhardt 2007; 2008). Driven by the investment of overseas Chinese and other ethnic communities, international research on the economic consequences and possibilities to benefit from former migration rose in extent and scope, giving policy-makers economic incentives to reach out to their respective diaspora communities. The narrow view that the emigration of skilled individuals is necessarily a loss for the country was gradually broadened and finally made way for a more differentiated approach. We have already stressed the impact and perception of overseas Indian involvement in the development of the Indian IT industry which in the international and Indian research context has been the much needed concrete example of positive migration effects for the source country (Hunger 2004; 2005; Thränhardt 2005, 4; United Nations 2006, 7, 61). Accepting migration as a fact, the new main focus is now what the positive contributions from migrants to the Indian development are. Khadria's monograph *The Migration of Knowledge Workers: Second-Generation Effects of India's Brain Drain* (1999) is a good example for the changing connotation and viewpoint.

As mentioned earlier, India is the world's largest recipient of remittances. There is, however, a glaring lack of research on remittances and their development

---

35 Dandekar (1968, 231) clarifies, however, that »there is no intention to isolate ourselves intellectually from the rest of the world. The doors have to be closed to protect ourselves from the lure of high living abroad [...] However, though the doors may be closed, the windows will remain open through which all knowledge may enter freely«.

impact. Again, the term *development* is not always self-explanatory. Largely it relates to economic development. Indicators are often searched at the macro-economic level (such as the impact on GDP, exports, foreign exchange rate and reserves) but the effects are of relevance also on the regional and household level. In international research there is a trend to seek also the impact on poverty reduction, be it regarding the depth, severity or the headcount of poverty.[36] In addition, social change as a consequence of migration and migrants' contributions to their home country can be in the research focus as well.

A researcher on remittances in India told the author that »everyone says: Look, we get more than China! But that's where the general interest stops.« There is a disturbing tendency to content oneself with looking at the big numbers. Billions of dollars worth of inputs must be good, is the common understanding. Although understandable, this tenet runs the risk of preventing critical research into the question and on the possible policy implications. A closer look at possible effects of remittances reveals that even at a theoretical level, there are several open questions and insecurities (Straubhaar 1988; Straubhaar and Vadean 2006; World Bank 2005, ch. 4–5; Ratha 2007).

Concrete economic research on the costs and benefits of migration has been largely limited to the South Indian state of Kerala, due to its dominant migration pattern, to effects of workers' migration to West Asia (e.g. Kannan and Hari 2002; Zachariah and Rajan 2007). There is growing research on the financial effects of internal migration in India (Srivastava and Sasikumar 2003; Srivastava 2005; Deshingkar, Khandelwal and Farrington 2008). Although this is a very promising topic, with significant implications for India, the findings are usually not applicable to the study of international remittances. Apart from obvious reasons like the fact that those flows will not affect the country's foreign exchange reserves, exchange rate and related factors, the migration patterns and the socio-economic conditions of the recipients are very different.

Research contributions on international remittances to India as a whole are rare and restricted to macro-economic effects (e.g. Nayyar 1994; Patra and Kapur 2003; Gupta 2005; Singh 2006; RBI 2006). Some of the general economic analysis of remittances and Indian migration in India are done by diasporic researchers (Ratha 2007; Chishti 2007; Desai et al. 2009).

Khadria (1999; 2002) has further drawn attention to what he terms ›backwash of remittances‹. This refers to the flows from Indian residents to migrants and the money transferred by migrants abroad. One explanation for this topic not having received much interest could lie in the newly-found ›pride paradigm‹. In order to show that the old negative school of thought is overcome, negative effects of migration do not seem welcome as a research topic.

---

36 ›Depth of poverty‹ is understood as the average shortfall below the poverty line expressed as a fraction of the poverty line (or the poverty gap ratio); and ›poverty severity‹ is the squared poverty gap ratio. Headcount, in contrast, displays how many people live below the poverty line (World Bank 2005, 129).

The More the Merrier – Defining the Diaspora

Some critics plead to regard ›the diaspora‹ not in substantialist terms as an entity or a bounded group which possesses countable, quantifiable memberships. Instead, it is prompted to analyse »diasporic stances, projects, claims« (Brubaker 2005, 10–13). For the field of research ›diaspora policies‹ it is in many respects of great interest to count the numbers. Counting sizes and assessing the diaspora's socio-economic characteristics are important elements of many analyses. However, we join Brubaker (2005, 3) in cautioning that the ›diaspora notion‹ must carry enough substance to differentiate phenomena in order to avoid becoming »stretched to the point of uselessness«.[37]

It bears mention that the bulk of the available literature on Indian migration and ethnic Indian communities refers to the Indian diaspora without any reflection on the scope of the term. Rarely are definitions provided, as P.C. Jain (2008, 161) defining it as »an ethnic minority group of migrant origins residing and acting in host country but maintaining strong sentimental and material links with its homeland.« Even rarer are critical assessments or discussions on the concept.

The government has its share in promoting this imperial diaspora idea. To quote India's Prime Minister Manmohan Singh, the Indian diaspora consists of »over 25 million overseas Indians, living in 110 different countries.«[38] Also, in computing the number of persons of Indian origin (PIOs)[39] the world over, the influential High Level Committee on the Indian Diaspora (2001, xlvii) was diligently listing four (!) persons of Indian origin in Cape Verde and five Indian citizens in Ecuador among other small groups of Indian descent. In Jamaica, there are supposed to be 60,000 PIOs. They intermarry with members of other communities and »all of them have assimilated themselves within the mainstream society of this country and do not have any direct links with India« (238). It is not our objective to argue that these groups should be omitted from the Indian diaspora count. But defining ›diaspora‹ solely on the basis of descent might be subject to scrutiny.

Oonk (2007, 11) remarks that the historical depth of interconnectedness, including the question of what structures the interconnectedness and what its limits are is often missing in the Indian diaspora discourse. While it appears to be a general feature of many ›diaspora studies‹ today and with regard to different ethnic groups, this seems also true in India where a certain tendency has developed to relish the idea of the empire of Indians abroad. We believe that the general ›pride motive‹ tends to cloud the objective view. The tendency to overestimate numbers or to unreflectedly argue on the basis of aggregate numbers is not neces-

---

37 For further discussion on the definitional elements of diasporas and ways to systematise the different forms, see Naujoks [forthcoming a].
38 Prime Minister Manmohan Singh's inaugural speech at Pravasi Bharatiya Divas, January 7, 2005.
39 Mostly, PIOs are defined as ethnic Indians who do *not* hold Indian citizenship, while Indian nationals abroad are referred to as ›Non-Resident Indians‹ (NRIs). Often both terms are used interchangeably by researchers and in the public discourse.

sarily ›wrong‹ but we think that a more reflected and differentiating use of the term would be fruitful for the discussion.[40]

The Search for ›Indianness‹ and the Segregated Diaspora

It is often noted that one of the few weaknesses of the Indian diaspora consists in its lack of unity. Instead of establishing strong ›Indian‹ groups and ›speak with one voice‹, diaspora associations form along regional, ethnic, linguistic or religious lines. As the entire country faces the challenge of ›nation-building‹ and the search for a national Indian identity, scholars on the diaspora look for the element of ›Indianness‹. On the other hand, there is a growing trend to examine and trace regional or religious diasporas as diasporas tracing their origin to Gujarat, or to Kerala, or the Sikh or Hindu diaspora.

Temporary Labour Migration

Temporary low-skilled labour migration mainly to the Gulf region but also to Malaysia and increasingly to other parts of the world has developed as a separate and important branch of Indian migration policies and research. The issues of pre-departure preparation of migrants, the licensing of agents and brokers, safeguarding the migrant's labour, human and social rights in the countries of temporary residence, maximising their remittance potential and facilitating reintegration upon their return are the key focus areas. Studies on this subject have increased significantly. But as P.C. Jain (2008, 184) notes, »one alarming aspect of the Indian diaspora in the Gulf countries however is the fact that relatively little research has been done on the subject.«

Diaspora Policies as Subject of Study

As concrete diaspora policies started to be formulated, Indian migration research obtained a further research topic: the policies themselves. Gradually, research developed a greater ›policy consciousness‹ and research contributions increasingly make policy recommendations.

Despite the increased policy-awareness of migration-related research, most of the publications remain in the Indian context and do not commonly refer to other countries' examples. The exception might be China which is often referred to, although detailed analyses of China's diaspora endeavours and tactics are hardly ever found. An interesting fact to note is that in the rare cases in which other countries' examples are invoked, it is for their ›diaspora policies‹, not for their attempts in the realm of migration and development. For example, the extensive study of the Jewish, Greek, Italian, Japanese, South Korean, Lebanese, Filipino,

---

40 For more reflections on the diaspora definition for research on migration and development, see Naujoks [forthcoming a]. The desire to expand the Indian diaspora empire is sometimes stretched beyond comfort. E.g. Lal (2001, 215) recounts that the major international Hindu organisation wrote in its publication that after the »Mahabharat War [i.e. a war in Indian mythology], our culture spread to China, Japan, and [the] Americas. The Red Indians of America are the descendants of Hindus who went there some 4000 years ago«.

and Irish diaspora by the High Level Committee (2001, ch. 23) interestingly does not include examples from Mexico, despite the fact that Mexico's attempts to make use of its *ex patriae* population in the US are one of the most prominent topics for research and policy learning in migration and development literature (P.L. Martin, S. Martin and Weil 2006).

Internal Migration

India covers a surface of almost 3.3 million square kilometres[41], almost as vast as the EU-15, with more than twice the population of the EU-27 and more than thrice the population of the USA. Economic opportunities vary significantly across states. For these reasons, there has always been a significant level of internal migration. Due to space constraints we can give but a brief overview of the existing challenges and research on the matter.

The Indian population varies substantially in ethnic, linguistic and religious characteristics. For this reason, migration from one state to another can have quite the same effects and challenges as international immigration in other countries. Local fear of job losses from internal migration as well as the impact on wages, together with a large number of immigrants from other states, often leads to xenophobic sentiments and also to inter-community violence. Recently, xenophobic violence broke out in early 2008, in the state of Maharashtra with its capital Mumbai (Bombay). As the Indian Supreme Court reportedly stated in response to the aforesaid violence: »India is not an association or confederation of states, it is a Union of states and there is only one nationality that is Indian. Hence every Indian has a right to go anywhere in India, to settle anywhere, and work and do business of his choice in any part of India, peacefully.«[42] Since the migrants are moving within ›their‹ country, the integration-assimilation perspective as well as research on xenophobic tendencies which has dominated migration research in immigration countries – as Bommes and Thränhardt in this volume show – is outside the research focus.

Research on internal migration currently focuses almost entirely on migrant labourers, and to a large extent, on the temporary migrant labour force (Srivastava 2005; Deshingkar, Khandelwal and Farrington 2008). This results from the magnitude of the migrant labour phenomenon, and from the research tradition of the base disciplines of most scholars who study internal migration. Most researchers have a background in rural development and thus focus on the strata of the migrant population which has more obvious impacts on rural livelihoods.

Mostly, international and internal migration are regarded as two separate topics and by different sets of researchers and policy actors (Skeldon 2003, 3). With regard to Indian research, however, there are some noteworthy exceptions (e.g.

---

41 The figure includes 121,000 square kilometres of disputed territories with Pakistan and China.
42 Reported in *Economic Times* (India), March 15, 2008.

Srivastava and Sasikumar 2003; Zachariah and Rajan 2008 for the state level in Kerala). Internal mobility is critical to the livelihoods of many people, especially tribal people, socially deprived groups and people from resource-poor areas. There is, however, a large gap between the insights from macro data and those from field studies (Srivastava and Sasikumar 2003, i).

Internal migration is often described as invisible migration. Thus researchers often attempt to make the invisible visible (Deshingkar, Khandelwal and Farrington 2008, 3). Obviously, public consciousness about the phenomenon and the associated problems and challenges form an important base in order to address these problems and to formulate and implement appropriate policies. Ten years from now, one might be able to discern and analyse a major paradigm shift in this so far undervalued and underresearched area.

Conclusions

In India, major paradigm shifts can be observed in the way the public and the political establishment look at the diaspora as well as in the national research agenda. We argued that both shifts are connected and in line with the general global trend which is changing from perceiving migratory phenomena in a negative light to positive connotations of the subject and its ramifications (Thränhardt 2007; 2008). We have identified several research beliefs and paradigms and pointed to lacunae in the research. Some of the lacunae in Indian migration research are no doubt connected to the lack of funding. There is hope that public funding will at least partially fill this gap. For example, the work of the Centre for Development Studies, as for the Migration Survey Kerala 2007, is financed by the Department of Non-Resident Keralite Affairs (NORKA) of the government of Kerala. As said above, since 2006, the Ministry of Overseas Indian Affairs supports a ›Research Unit on International Migration‹ within the centre. On the other hand, institutions like the ›Indian Council for Social Science Research‹ still have to develop greater awareness and research incentives – including funding programmes – on migration topics.

Borrowing from the Bridging Research and Policy Approach (Das, Virmani and Singh Laschar 2005, 57), the linkages between policy and research can mostly be seen in the following eight modalities: (a) research cited in official documents, (b) policy brief included in background materials; or an expert is (c) invited to express opinion, (d) to report before a committee, (e) commissioned to do research, (f) included in a task force, (g) hired to deliver training government officials, or (h) hired as government consultant. Based on this, the linkages between politics and research were not overwhelming. This might be one reason that academia and research have played a limited role in framing diaspora issues for collective debate. On the other hand, several former bureaucrats are actively involved in Indian migration research. Their contacts and experience in the Indian establishment might help academic opinion to gain easier access to decision-makers.

Although the interest at the political level to seek advice on its policies is currently limited, there seems to be a growing trend in this direction. In 2007, for example, the Ministry of Overseas Indian Affairs requested the Centre for Development Studies for a draft policy on International Migration which was delivered in 2008 (Kumar 2008; CDS 2008, 7).

As a conclusion on the significance and reach of ›research paradigms‹ we believe that in social sciences, paradigms are generally less rigid and absolute than in many natural sciences. This led Kuhn (1962) to the conclusion that there are no ›research paradigms‹ in social science. Even though in social science existing paradigms might not prohibit a certain research question or viewpoint, however, preconceived ideas, beliefs and values as much decide what researchers look at and how, as they influence what they do *not* look at. The omissions and ›blind spots‹ in a research community's approach are at least as interesting to examine as the actual foci. Apart from the general research areas, paradigms steer the research questions asked, as well as the ›direction‹ and ›tone‹ of migration-related research. Thus, those beliefs and values can, in fact, be considered ›research paradigms‹. We conclude by re-iterating Hirschman's (1970) caution that paradigms, unless constantly scrutinised and questioned, may become a hindrance to understanding. To search for some paradigms and to overcome others may be the dual, but crucial role of research.

References

Acharya, Shankar, Isher Ahluwalia, K.L. Krishna, and Ila Patnaik. 2003. *India: Economic Growth, 1950–2000. Global Research Project on Growth*. New Delhi: Indian Council for Research on International Economic Relations.

Agrawal, Subhash. 2007. *Emerging Donors in International Development Assistance: The India Case*. Ottawa: International Development Research Centre.

Assisi, Francis C. 2005. *Letter from the Centre for Study of Indian Diaspora on the Hyderabad Indian Diaspora conference*. http://www.gopio.info/indian-diaspora.htm (accessed April 18, 2009).

Bhagwati, Jagdish, and Martin Partington, ed. 1976. *Taxing the Brain Drain: A Proposal*. Amsterdam: North Holland.

Bhagwati, Jagdish, and John Wilson, ed. 1989. *Income Taxation and International Mobility*, Cambridge, MA: MIT Press.

Bhagwati, Jagdish. 2004. *In Defense of Globalization*. New York: Oxford University Press.

Bhagwati, Jagdish. 2008. *Skilled Migration. Introduction to Oxford University Press Volume 2008*. http://www.columbia.edu/~jb38/ (accessed April 10, 2009).

Bhat, Chandrashekhar. 2003. India and the Indian Diaspora: Inter-linkages and Expectations. In *Indian Diaspora: Global Identity*, ed. Dubey, 11–22.

Brettell, Caroline B., and James Hollifield, ed. 2000. Introduction. In *Migration Theory: Talking across Disciplines*, ed. idem, 1–26. New York: Routledge.

Brubaker, Rogers. 2005. The ›Diaspora‹ Diaspora. *Ethnic and Racial Studies* 28 (1): 1–19.

CDS (Centre for Development Studies). 2008. *Research Unit on International Migration: Annual Report 2007–2008*. Trivandrum: Centre for Development Studies.

Chishti, Muzaffar. 2007. *The Rise in Remittances to India: A Closer Look*. Washington, DC: Migration Policy Institute.

Chopra, S.K., ed. 1986. *Brain Drain – And How To Reverse It*. New Delhi: Lancer International.

Daman Singh, Sarva, and Mahavir Singh, ed. 2003. *Indians Abroad*. Kolkata: Hope India Publications/Greenwich Millennium.

Dandekar, V.M. 1968. India. In *The Brain Drain*, ed. Walter Adams, 203–32. New York: The Macmillan Company.

Das, Tarun, Arvind Virmani, and Tejinder Singh Laschar. 2005. *Linkages between Research, Policy Analysis and Reform Outcomes in India. Final Report of the Global Development Network Project ›Bridging Research and Policy‹*. http://www.gdnet.org (accessed January 10, 2008).

De la Fontaine, Dana. 2008. India as a Promoter of Regional Development and the Role of the EU. Conference Paper for the 12th EADI General Conference on Global Governance for Sustainable Development, June 24–28, Geneva.

Desai, Mihir A., Devesh Kapur, John McHale, and Keith Rogers. 2009. The Fiscal Impact of High-skilled Emigration: Flows of Indians to the U.S. *Journal of Development Economics* 88: 32–44.

Deshingkar, Priya, Rajiv Khandelwal, and John Farrington. 2008. *Support for Migrant Workers: The Missing Link in India's Development (Natural Resource Perspectives 117)*. London: Overseas Development Institute.

Dubey, Ajay, ed. 2003a. *Indian Diaspora: Global Identity*. New Delhi: GOPIO International/Kalinga Publications.

Dubey, Ajay. 2003b. Indian Diaspora in the Caribbean and Africa: Identity Issues and Responses of India. In *Indian Diaspora: Global Identity*, ed. idem, 117–45.

Foucault, Michel. 1980. *Power/Knowledge – Selected Interviews and Other Writings 1972–1977*, ed. Colin Gordeon. Brighton: Harvester Press.

Government of India. 1993. *Economic Reforms: Two Years After and the Task Ahead*. New Delhi: Ministry of Finance.

Gupta, Poonam. 2005. *Macroeconomic Determinants of Remittances: Evidence from India. IMF Working Paper 05/224*. Washington, DC: International Monetary Fund (IMF).

Hathaway, Robert M. 2001. Unfinished Passage: India, Indian Americans, and the U.S. Congress. *The Washington Quarterly* 24 (2): 21–34.

High-Level Committee on the Indian Diaspora. 2001. *Report on the Indian Diaspora*. New Delhi: Ministry of External Affairs, Government of India. http://www.indiandiaspora.nic.in

Hirschman, Alfred O. 1970. The Search for Paradigms as a Hindrance to Understanding. *World Politics* 22 (3): 329–43.

Howlett, Michael. 1994. Policy Paradigms and Policy Change: Lessons from the Old and New Canadian Policies Towards Aboriginal Peoples. *Policy Studies Journal* 22 (4): 631–49.

Hunger, Uwe. 2004. Indian IT-Entrepreneurs in the US and India: An Illustration of the Brain Gain Hypothesis. *Journal of Comparative Policy-Analysis* 6 (2): 99–109.

Hunger, Uwe. 2005. Vier Thesen zur deutschen Entwicklungspolitik für Indien. *Aus Politik und Zeitgeschichte* no. 27: 12–18.

Jain, Prakash C. 2008. Globalisation and Indian Diaspora in West Asia and North Africa: Some Policy Implications. In *India and West Asia in the Era of Globalization*, ed. Anwar Alam, 161–87. New Delhi: New Century Publications.

Jain, Ravindra K. 1993. *Indian Communities Abroad: Themes and Literature*. New Delhi: Manohar Publishers & Distributors.

Jain, Ravindra K. 2003. A Civilization Theory of Indian Diaspora and its Global Implications. In *Indian Diaspora: Global Identity*, ed. Dubey, 1–9.

Jayaram, N. 1998. *The Study of Indian Diaspora: A Multidisciplinary Agenda*. Occasional Paper. Hyderabad: Centre for Study of Indian Diaspora, University of Hyderabad.

Jayaram, N. 2004. Introduction: The Study of Indian Diaspora. In *The Indian Diaspora. Dynamics of Migration (Themes in Indian Sociology 4)*, ed. idem. New Delhi: Sage Publications.

Kannan, K.P., and K.S. Hari. 2002. Kerala's Gulf Connection: Remittances and their Macroeconomic Impact. In *Kerala's Gulf Connection: CDS Studies on International Labour Migration from Kerala State in India*, ed. K.C. Zachariah, K.P. Kannan and Irudaya Rajan, 199–230. Thiruvananthapuram, Kerala: Centre for Development Studies.

Khadria, Binod. 1999. *The Migration of Knowledge Workers: Second-Generation Effects of India's Brain Drain*. New Delhi: Sage Publications.

Khadria, Binod. 2002. *Skilled Labor Migration from Developing Countries: Study on India*. International Migration Paper (IMP) 49. Geneva: International Labour Organization (ILO).

Kuhn, Thomas S. 1962. *The Structure of Scientific Revolutions*. Chicago: University of Chicago Press.

Kumar, S. Krishna. 2008. *Policy on International Migration Reforms in India*. Thiruvananthapuram, Kerala: Centre for Development Studies.

Lal, Brij V., Peter Reeves, and Rajesh Rai, ed. 2006. *The Encyclopedia of the Indian Diaspora*. Singapore: Editions Didier Millet in association with National University of Singapore.

Lal, Vinay. 2001. The Politics of History on the Internet: Cyber-Diasporic Hinduism and the North American Hindu Diaspora. In *In Diaspora: Theories, Histories, Texts*, ed. Makarand Paranjape, 179–221. New Delhi: Indialog Publications.

Martin, Philip L., Susan F. Martin, and Patrick Weil. 2006. *Managing Migration: The Promise of Cooperation*. Lanham, MD: Lexington Books.

Ministry of Home Affairs. 2009. *Annual Report 2008/09*. New Delhi: Government of India.

Motwani, Jagat K., Mahin Gosine, and Jyoti Barot-Motwani, ed. 1993. *Global Indian Diaspora: Yesterday, Today and Tomorrow*. New York: Global Organization of People of Indian Origin.

Mulloo, Anand. 2007. *Voices of the Diaspora*. New Delhi: Motilal Banarsidass Publishers.

Naujoks, Daniel. 2009. *Emigration, Immigration, and Diaspora Relations in India*. Migration Information Source. Washington, DC: Migration Policy Institute.

Naujoks, Daniel. [forthcoming a]. *Defining ›Diasporas‹ for Development: A Theoretical Note on Defining and Systematising a Concept*.

Naujoks, Daniel. [forthcoming b]. *India's New Membership Concepts: Policy Change in the Light of Migration and Development*. PhD diss., University of Münster.

Nayyar, Deepak. 1994. *Migration, Remittances and Capital Flows: The Indian Experience*. New Delhi: Oxford University Press.

Oonk, Gijsbert. 2007. Introduction. In *Global Indian Diasporas: Exploring Trajectories of Migration and Theory*, ed. idem, 9–30. Amsterdam: Amsterdam University Press.

Pant, K.C. 1986. Brain Drain and National Development. In *Brain Drain – And How To Reverse It*, ed. S.K. Chopra, 30–37. New Delhi: Lancer International.

Patra, Michael Debabrata, and Muneesh Kapur. 2003. *India's Workers Remittances: A Users' Lament About Balance of Payments Compilation*. Paper prepared for the 16th Meeting of the IMF Committee on Balance of Payments Statistics, December 1–5, Washington, DC.

Ramachandran, Sujata. 2005. *Indifference, Impotence, and Intolerance: Transnational Bangladeshis in India* (Global Migration Perspectives 42). Geneva: Global Commission on International Migration.

Ratha, Dilip. 2007. *Leveraging Remittances for Development*. Policy Brief. Washington, DC: Migration Policy Institute.

RBI (Reserve Bank of India). 2003. *Handbook of Statistics on Indian Economy*. Mumbai.

RBI (Reserve Bank of India). 2006. Invisibles in India's Balance of Payments. *RBI Bulletin* November.

RBI (Reserve Bank of India). 2008. *Handbook of Statistics on Indian Economy.* Mumbai.

Sharma, S.L. 2004. Perspectives on Indians Abroad. In *The Indian Diaspora. Dynamics of Migration (Themes in Indian Sociology 4)*, ed. N. Jayaram, 44–65. New Delhi: Sage Publications. (Originally published in 1989 *Sociological Bulletin* 38 (1): 1–22).

Singh, Anand, ed. 2007. *Indian Diaspora – The 21st Century – Migration, Change and Adaptation.* New Delhi: Kamla Raj Enterprises.

Singh, Bhupal. 2006. *Cross-border Workers' Remittances: Transmission Channels and Measurement Issues in India.* Paper prepared for the International Monetary Fund (IMF)'s Remittances Statistics: First Meeting of the Luxembourg Group, June 2006 in Luxemburg.

Singh Tatla, Darshan. 1999. *The Sikh Diaspora: The Search for Statehood.* Seattle: University of Washington Press.

Skeldon, Ronald. 2003. *Interlinkages Between Internal and International Migration and Development in the Asian Region.* Paper submitted at the Economic and Social Commission for Asia and the Pacific's Ad Hoc Expert Group Meeting on Migration and Development, August 27–29, in Bangkok.

Srivastava, Ravi S. 2005. *India: Internal Migration Links with Poverty and Development.* Country paper submitted at the Regional Conference on Migration and Development in Asia, March 14–16, in Lanzhou, China.

Srivastava, Ravi, and S.K. Sasikumar. 2003. *An Overview of Migration in India, its Impacts and Key Issues.* Paper presented at the Regional Conference on Migration, Development and Pro-Poor Policy Choices in Asia, jointly organized by the Refugee and Migratory Movements Research Unit, Bangladesh, and the Department for International Development, UK, June 22–24, in Dhaka, Bangladesh.

Straubhaar, Thomas. 1988. *On the Economics of International Labor Migration.* Bern and Stuttgart: Paul Haupt.

Straubhaar, Thomas, and Florin Vadean. 2006. International Migrant Remittances and their Role in Development. In *International Migration Outlook: SOPEMI 2006*, 139–61. Paris: OECD.

Straubhaar, Thomas, and Martin Wolburg. 1998. *Brain Drain and Brain Gain in Europe: An Evaluation of East-European Migration to Germany.* Center for German and European Studies, Working Paper 4.16, Berkeley, University of California.

Tendulkar, Suresh D., and T.A. Bhavani. 2005. *Understanding the Post-1991 Indian Economic Policy Reforms.* The Global Development Network Project on Understanding Reform. http://www.gdnet.org (accessed November 15, 2008).

Thränhardt, Dietrich. 2005. Entwicklung durch Migration: ein neuer Forschungsansatz. *Aus Politik und Zeitgeschichte* no. 27: 3–11.

Thränhardt, Dietrich. 2007. *Entwicklung durch Migration: Globalisierung auch für Menschen.* Dossier Wirtschaftliche Potenziale von Migration & Integration. Berlin: Heinrich Böll Foundation.

Thränhardt, Dietrich. 2008. Entwicklung durch Migration. Ein neuer Forschungs- und Politikansatz. In *Migration als Entwicklungschance für Deutschland und für die Herkunftsländer. Jahrbuch Migration 2007/2008,* ed. idem, 102–28. Berlin: Lit.

Tinker, Hugh. 1974. *A New System of Slavery: The Export of Indian Labour Overseas 1830–1920.* London: Oxford University Press.

Tinker, Hugh. 1977. *The Banyan Tree. Overseas Emigrants from India, Pakistan and Bangladesh.* London: Oxford University Press.

UNHCR. 2007. *Global Appeal 2008–2009 – South Asia Subregional Overview.* http://www.unhcr.org (accessed April 18, 2009).

United Nations. 2006. *International Migration and Development, Report of the Secretary-General at the Sixteenth Session of the General Assembly.* New York: United Nations.

United Nations. 2009. *Global Migration Database.* United Nations, Population Division. http://esa.un.org/unmigration/ (accessed May 12, 2009).

Varma, Pavan K. 2004. *Being Indian: The Truth about Why the Twenty-first Century will be India's.* New Delhi: Penguin Books.

World Bank. 2006. *Global Economic Prospects. Economic Implications of Remittances and Migration.* Washington, DC: The World Bank.

Zachariah, K.C., and S. Irudaya Rajan. 2007. *Migration, Remittances and Employment. Short-term Trends and Long-term Implications.* Working Paper 395. Thiruvananthapuram, Kerala: Centre for Development Studies (CDS).

Zachariah, K.C., and S. Irudaya Rajan. 2008. *Kerala Migration Survey 2007.* Thiruvananthapuram: Research Unit on International Migration, Centre for Development Studies and Department of Non-Resident Keralite Affairs Government of Kerala.

The National Context of Migration Research in Malaysia. Which Nation, What State, Whose Migration?

By Diana Wong

Abstract

Foreign labour accounts for circa 25 per cent of the labour force in the developing economy of Malaysia, much of it comprising illegal labour migrants from Indonesia. The conventional paradigm in migration research based on the methodological individualism of the nation state sees the long and continuing presence of such an illegal labour force as symptomatic of a weak and incoherent state policy. The paper argues that the politics of ambiguity regarding the entry and deployment of illegal labour from neighbouring Indonesia stems from the unfinished character of the nation state itself. Recent shifts in the policy toward this group of migrants suggest that fundamental shifts in the identity politics of the nation state have since occured.

Introduction

Malaysia is the largest employer of foreign labour in Asia, with migrant workers, legal and otherwise, comprising some 25 per cent of the national labour market for the two decades from 1980 to 2000. In the plantation as well as in the domestic and construction sectors, their share of employment has amounted to 50 per cent, if not more (for accounts of the role of foreign labour in Malaysia, see Pillai 1992; Azizah Kassim 1996; Wong and Anwar 2003). Notwithstanding the scale and duration of this foreign immigrant presence, however, one is struck by the dearth of official migration data and a surprising paucity of research on migration by the research community in the country.[1]

Local migration research takes two distinct forms. The first is a fairly substantial reservoir of unpublished academic exercises plus a few MA and PhD theses by students of the local universities, some though not all replete with a wealth of rich ethnographic data. They are written in Malay and are generally (an exception is Darul Amin 1990) framed by two research concerns: the organisation of (illegal)

---

1 In a 1995 World Bank report on the labour market in Malaysia, it was noted that »most of the public and private sector people interviewed in 1994 had neither an estimate of migrant stocks and flows nor a proposed methodology to obtain data on migrant workers« (World Bank 1995).

entry, and/or the mode of migrant adaptation (this includes the investigation of labour market issues as well as migrant social networks). The second is a sprinkling of published journal articles, mostly written in English, by social scientists working in the local universities and think-tank research institutions in the country. The focus of these publications has been on government policy in the management of foreign labour (see Azizah Kassim 1996; Pillai 1999). Common to almost all such writing is the theme of *policy incoherence* on the part of the state. Pillai (1999) for example, refers to the »stop-go« character of state migration policy. Particular emphasis has been placed in this respect on the persistence of *illegal* migration (see Wong 2006). In general, the tone is critical of the country's heavy dependence on a foreign workforce, either in terms of the social (see Azizah Kassim 1996) or the economic (see Tham and Liew 2002) cost which state (mis)management of migration is seen to have generated.

Mode of entry, mode of adaptation and mode of governance – underlying all three concerns is not so much a ›national paradigm‹ as the unquestioned paradigm of the *nation state* in its modern territorial form. Constitutive of the very sovereignty of the nation state is its right – and its desire – to control the movement of populations within and without its borders. Border transgressions (mode of entry), self-sufficient migrant networks and settlements (mode of adaptation) and the sheer volume of the (illegal) foreign presence (mode of governance) are referenced, in both the above-mentioned forms of production, published and unpublished, to a nation-state paradigm of territorial sovereignty, based on its foundational distinction between nationals and aliens.

This ›national-territorial‹ framing of migration in both forms of production derives in large part from the standard comparative perspective which characterises research on ›international migration‹. Students pursuing academic qualifications have to explicitly refer to published research in metropolitan centres of scholarship as models for their own empirically-based micro-studies. Publications by established migration researchers are often commissioned as ›national‹ case studies in the context of comparative research projects on international or regional migration. This ›international migration‹ literature itself, much of it generated or commissioned by United Nations agencies such as the International Organization of Migration or the International Labour Organization, is entirely predicated on the ontological premise of a world of nation states, its conceptual apparatus consisting in the main of administrative categories deployed by state practice, such as the refugee/migrant/illegal migrant distinction.

The notion of ›methodological nationalism‹ (Wimmer and Glick Schiller 2002) builds on this assumption of a stable ›national‹ embodied in the state. In many contemporary countries of immigration which happen to be multiethnic states, however, as are indeed the vast majority of the nation states constituting the present international order, the question of the national is far from resolved and its status anything but stable. In many such states, the nation, the state, and the two in its conjoined double barrel form, remain highly fragile, unfinished projects. And indeed, they remain the object of vastly different projects. It is also such states, of which Malaysia is an example, which would appear to be experiencing inordinately high levels of migration in the contemporary world.

Central to this paper is the proposition that the ambivalent politics of migration in Malaysia, of which the excoriated ›policy incoherence‹ is the product, derives from the ambiguous and unfinished nature of the nation state itself. The corollary is that any comparative account of contemporary ›global‹ migration would have to begin with the substantive genealogy of the states concerned, rather than assume the comparability of their abstract territorial form. The unquestioning adoption of the nation-state paradigm in the policy-centred discourse of local academic production is not merely descriptive but also projective in nature, indicative of the engagement of the national academic elite in the on-going project of a territorially coherent nation and a modernising developmentalist state.

The paper is divided into four parts. The first part provides an overview of the current context of labour migration into the country. In the second and third, the ambiguous nature of the Malaysian nation state as evinced by its migration policy is discussed. The fourth part returns to the institutional and national constraints under which migration research operates in the country.

Contemporary Labour Migration to Malaysia

Before the country's constitution as an independent nation state in 1957, its demographic composition had been transformed by massive waves of immigration – primarily from China, India and Indonesia – under the aegis of British imperial rule. One of the first pieces of legislation passed by the new nation state was an Immigration Act (1959), which regulated the movement of non-citizens into its territory. This was followed in 1968 by an Employment Restriction Act which made access to the labour market for non-citizens contingent upon possession of a work permit. The institution of the nation state was thus made legally coterminous with that of a closed labour market; citizenship conferred the right of residence to a nationally-defined territory as well as the right of unhindered entry to the labour market. Non-citizens were excepted from both. In view of the then prevailing high rate of unemployment, these alienage distinctions were strictly adhered to. Migration came to a halt. Thousands of non-citizen workers, some of whom had been resident in the country for their entire lives, were repatriated. One telling exception, however, was made: immigrants from the neighbouring islands of the Archipelago, such as Sumatra and Java, did not fall under the legal category of aliens. In this, the new nation state merely followed the practice of the previous colonial state.[2]

The economic and political landscape of the country changed dramatically in the following decades. Following racial riots in 1969, a regime change saw the emergence of a highly interventionist, developmentalist state, bent on using the

---

2 When foreign immigration was stemmed in 1931 by the Aliens Ordinance Act, immigrants from the then Dutch East Indies were exempted.

state as a vehicle for economic growth and social engineering. In conjunction with changes in the regional division of labour in East and Southeast Asia associated with Japan's rise as a regional economic power, and as a result of the massive rural-urban migration which the state's New Economic Policy promoted, profound changes were effected in the country's labour market. By the mid-1970s, labour shortages had emerged in the rural sector, and by the end of the decade, half of the labour force in the plantation economy was estimated to have been migrants from Indonesia. The 1980 census was soon to confirm the significant shift in Malaysia's migrational history which had taken place in the decade of the 1970s: for the first time in its post-war and post-Independence history, a net migrational surplus was recorded, reversing the large net migrational deficits of the preceding decades (Saw 1988, 50ff). Malaysia had become a labour-importing country again.

This initial influx was to grow into a flood. In the 1980s, a construction boom in the urban centres of the country led to a frenetic demand for foreign labour in the construction sector. Similarly, urban double-income households began having to rely on foreign maids to manage the household chores. The migrant workers who came in to fill these new labour-market gaps were no longer confined to remote plantation sites. This move to the homes and construction sites of the growing metropolitan centres, however, infused a new quality to the phenomenon. The migrant presence became visible. So did popular hostility to their presence. As the mid-1980s crisis struck, this visibility was underscored by their emergence in the informal sector of services and petty trading in the main streets of Kuala Lumpur. And a further discovery was made: foreign labour had become localised. Recruitment was no longer merely confined to the arduous task of labour importation. By the late 1980s, over 12,000 Indonesians were living in 56 squatter settlements in Kuala Lumpur itself (Azizah Kassim 1996).

It was only then that the first attempts to regularise the importation of labour were undertaken (see below). Notwithstanding the various bureaucratic interventions, however, the size and scope of the foreign labour force continued to expand in the 1990s. The precipitous economic expansion of the early 1990s saw the entry of foreign labour into the manufacturing sector, as well as into broader domains of the service sector. Acute shortages of key personnel in the public service sector, in particular of health personnel, has led to the deployment of foreign labour in the public sector as well. The 1990s also witnessed the recruitment of migrant workers from countries other than Indonesia, including significant numbers of men from Bangladesh. By the end of the decade, the share of Indonesians had fallen, although they continued to predominate in the labour market.[3]

When the 1997 financial crisis struck the country, and induced a massive repatriation programme of foreign workers, the size of the foreign workforce was

---

[3] In a regularisation exercise in 1992, 83 per cent of those registered were Indonesians. Bangladeshis accounted for 5 per cent. In a similar exercise in 1992, the percentage of Indonesians was 63, that of Bangladeshis, 28 (Wong and Afrizal 2003, 174ff.)

estimated at 1.7 million out of a total workforce of eight million (Bank Negara Malaysia 1997, 63). Three years after the crisis, the size of the foreign labour force continued to be high. In the year 2000, 766,748 work permits were issued to foreign workers in the country, the majority of which were for the manufacturing sector (235,796), followed by the construction (176,218), plantation (135,787) and service sectors. In addition, an unknown number of foreign workers, with estimates varying from 300,000 to one million, were also working in similar sectors of the economy.

The above account of contemporary migration to Malaysia as market-driven labour flows is the standard starting point of migration research in the country. The severe labour shortage generated by the unrelenting economic growth of the past three decades, as well as the glaring wage differential between the labour market in Malaysia and that in the sending countries, have provided sufficient pull factors for labour flows to occur. Between 1987 and 1993 alone, 14 million new jobs were created, at the rate of 3.9 per cent per annum, in Malaysia, whilst the domestic labour force grew only at an annual rate of 3.1 per cent. The gap, as noted by the World Bank, was filled by immigrant workers (World Bank 1995, 58).

What has been omitted in this market-driven account is the role of the state and society. To this we now turn.

The Ambiguity of the Illegal

The theme of ›policy incoherence‹ in local academic production is largely centred around the figure of the ›illegal immigrant‹, and the seeming inability of the state to bring this intractable ›problem‹ under control. The issue first entered the public domain when it was raised in Parliament in 1976, followed by the introduction of the term ›*pendatang haram*‹ or illegal immigrant, into the Malaysian public vocabulary shortly thereafter. The subsequent explosive growth of a large pool of unauthorised and undocumented foreign migrant labour in the country has been accompanied by the use of an increasingly hostile vocabulary to describe their presence: illegal immigrants became *illegals*, a term which gained popular currency in the mid-1980s and is still widely used to refer to foreigners working illegally in the country. By the mid-1990s, the term *alien* was increasingly being deployed in public and academic writing on this issue.[4]

Seen as a mounting challenge to the ability of the nation state to enforce control of its borders in the face of the emergent forces of globalisation and transnationalism, the issue of illegal migration has also entered the international migration research agenda (see for example Jahn and Straubhaar 1998; Samers 2000). It should be noted, however, that in the developed economies of Western Europe, the United States and Japan in which illegal migration has now entered public debate

---

4 See for example the later work of Azizah Kassim, a leading researcher on foreign workers in Malaysia.

and academic discourse, illegal migrants, whose numbers are notoriously difficult to gauge, are likely to constitute only a fraction of the total national labour force. There were for example in 1991 an estimated 280,000 illegal aliens working in Japan (Morita and Sassen 1994). In Malaysia, an amnesty exercise in 1992 led to the registration of 442,276 hitherto undocumented Indonesian workers in the country, who accounted for almost 10 per cent of the then national labour force.

The sheer magnitude, the comprehensive scope (dispersal in all sectors as well as parts of the country), and the seeming intractability, of unauthorised and undocumented labour migration into Malaysia does indeed suggest a different policy context for the ›tolerance‹ of a phenomenon which challenges the integrity of the borders which define the sovereignty of the nation state. Whilst the lobbying pressure of market interests certainly have played a crucial role in the liberal recruitment of foreign labour in the past 30 years of economic growth (cf. Freeman 1995), it has not been the only determinant of policy. Labour is not a commodity like any other, and the dynamics governing its transnational mobility are subject to social, political and cultural constraints which, and that is the argument to be developed below, not only does ›the‹ state respond to, but which are constitutive of the very nature of the ›state‹ itself.

Four distinct phases of state policy toward foreign labour migration can be distinguished. The first, which lasted from the early 1970s until 1989, was manifested in the benign indifference to, if not tacit encouragement of, undocumented or irregular migration on the part of the state. The second, from 1990 to 1996, consisted in the various attempts at legalising the existing stocks of irregular migrant labour in the country, the third involved the parallel existence of an underground irregular migration system and a state-managed foreign contract worker system based on off-shore recruitment. The fourth, which took effect from 2002, marks the attempt to reduce the share of Indonesian labour in the foreign labour market. It is the fourth policy development which provides the perspective with which the relationship between the Malaysian nation state and migration will be read.

Central to this relationship is the fact that the contemporary wave of ›foreign labour‹, from the 1980s onwards, consists primarily of migrants from Indonesia. Neither the earlier pre-colonial or colonial state, however, had considered ›people from across the Straits‹ to be aliens. The movement of peoples across the Straits of Malacca, and indeed, throughout the Malay Archipelago, goes back several centuries to a pre-colonial past in which a vibrant network of busy trading emporias had constituted a shared cultural world and what was understood to be a common racial stock.[5] The British colonial state classified such migrants from the Indonesia of today as ›Malays‹ and they were as such exempted from the 1931 Aliens Ordinance which put an end to the open imperial immigration policy under which thousands of migrant labourers from India, China and the then Netherlands Indies had been brought to British Malaya. Not until the outbreak of military

---

5 The term *se-rumpun* is widely invoked to refer to this common racial stock.

hostilities between the two new nation states of Malaysia and Indonesia in the mid-1960s did this steady flow of people movement across the Straits come to a complete halt.

The resumption of migration across the Straits in the early 1970s can thus be taken to mark the commencement of a new chapter in an old migration history. It was treated as such, it would appear, by the Malaysian state authorities. Little effort was made to prevent the inflow of Indonesian migrants who gained access to work immediately upon entry into the country, and in countless instances, also acquired Malaysian permanent residential status within three months of their arrival (see Darul Amin 1990). Recognition of the market need for foreign labour, however, also resulted in a number of legal measures to establish an official channel of labour recruitment. This included the 1981 Act passed to allow for the establishment of legal recruitment agencies for foreign contract labour, the establishment of a Committee for the Recruitment of Foreign Workers in 1982 and the 1984 Medan Agreement signed with Indonesia for the government-to-government regulated supply of Indonesian labour for the plantation and domestic sectors. All were ineffectual. The market continued to be supplied by a largely ›free‹ flow of network-based chain migration, issuing in illegality, but with rapid and cheap access to legal settlement status. Children born of parents with permanent resident (PR) status are entitled to citizenship. By the mid-1980s, numerous Indonesian settlements had sprung up within the city quarters.

The practice of easy acquisition of PR status, which in effect transforms, in legal terms, migrant status to that of settler status, ended in 1989. This coincided with the initiation of what has been identified above as the second phase of migration policy. Indeed, it could be maintained that it was only then that a foreign labour policy as such came into being. In 1989 and subsequently in 1991, registration and amnesty exercises of illegal migrant workers were conducted, following which those registered were issued work permits as foreign contract workers. Supplementing this were enforcement exercises directed at preventing illegal landings on Malaysia's long coastline, as well as raids on work sites and squatter settlements to ›weed out‹ illegal workers. This attempt to regularise and contain the prevailing situation of de-facto undocumented migration was designed as an interim regime of five years, during which selected economic sectors were to be allowed on-site access to regularised illegal migrant workers.

In 1996, with the end of the interim five-year period, the stage was set for the third phase, the final eradication of the system of on-site illegal recruitment of labour, to be replaced by the implementation of an official migrant labour system of work-permit and contract-based off-shore recruitment. What emerged in effect was a parallel structure of labour importation – a foreign contract worker system based on off-shore recruitment, co-existing with a large reservoir of foreigners, in particular Indonesians, living and working outside of this formal system. This reservoir of foreigners was marked by a distinction of existential import – those in possession of PR status, and those who were ›illegals‹. ›Illegals‹ continue to be hounded by police raids and the occasional large-scale enforcement and deportation exercise. Underpinning the heightened frequency of such exercises was now a state-led discourse against illegal migration which emerged for the first time in 1996 at a party congress of the ruling party (see Pillai 1999) and which culminated in Prime Minister Mahathir's remark in 1997: »We have 20 million people and 1.7 million foreign workers. If we allow this to go on we would risk losing control of our country« (Bulletin Imigresen 1997).

The year 2002 marked one such major exercise. Again, the rhetoric of the country being held hostage to illegal migrants was aired, and again, the scale of the operation as well as the hardships encountered by those deported, attracted much media attention. In particular, the amendments to the Immigration Act, which introduced whipping for immigration offences, came in for much criticism. Of particular importance, however, and representing a major shift in policy, were the changes announced to the formal contract worker system. Circa 80 per cent of the contract workers originate from Indonesia, as would be the case for migrants in the informal sector as well. The formal system of labour recruitment, devised and implemented in the 1990s, had restricted labour recruitment to a few countries, with a definite bias for Indonesia. The government announced plans to diversify its source countries of recruitment, in order to reduce the share of Indonesians in this market. In fact, Indonesians were initially to be restricted only to the plantation and the domestic sectors. This regulation was later rescinded.

With this move, state policy toward foreign/Indonesian immigration into the country has come a full circle. From virtually unrestricted access to the labour market and even to the body politic, migrants from Indonesia appear now as unwelcome foreign nationals, both in the formal and informal labour markets. How is the remarkable trajectory to be explained?

The Unfinished State

The vocabulary of international migration studies, which frames the market-driven accounts of labour migration in Malaysia in which the inept efforts of the government to control illegal migration are highlighted, rests on the unquestioned binary between citizen and alien. This binary distinction, on the other hand, is based on the unquestioned assumption of equivalence between citizenship and nationality, as is indeed the case for multiethnic countries such as the United States. For the multiethnic state of Malaysia, however, the *disjunction* between citizenship and nationality in the context of contending notions of nationhood has been critical to the nature of the state and the migration policies it adopted.

Brubaker's work (1992) has drawn attention to two different notions of nationhood embodied in the French and German nation states, the one institutional, political and assimilationalist, the other Volk-centred, ethnocultural and differentialist. Other models of nationhood were also available in the marketplace of ideas to the would-be Malaysian inheritors of the colonial state. There was in particular the Western model of sovereign individual citizens constituting a libertarian state, and the Soviet model of equal rights of different nationalities qua collectivities within the institutional fold of the republic. As Tan (1988) shows, contending visions of nationhood, drawn largely from the above pool of ideas, accompanied the birth of nationalism(s) in the territory which was to become the state in 1957, with the result, as Muhammad Ikmal Said (1992) cogently argues, that the question of nationhood or the ›cultural form‹ of the nation, as he puts it, has, since the formation of the state, remained unresolved.

With the formation of the new postcolonial state in the former British Malaya, citizenship was granted to the substantial immigrant population, largely from China and India, but a crucial distinction was blurred over. This citizenship did not define nationality. It was understood to be »merely a legal guarantee of specified privileges« (Harper 2001, 350). At issue was, in Ikmal's words, »the cultural basis upon which the new state has to evolve« (Ikmal 1992, 278). The model of the modern nation state, in which citizenship is equated with nationality, would have all constituent population groups treated as ethnic groups »subject to the equal law of the modern nation state« (Harper 2001, 349). »Popular sovereignty« would decide on the cultural forms which the nation should acquire. As Ikmal notes, however, »in post-colonial societies, whether popular sovereignty should be based solely upon the colonised indigenous population or include the immigrant communities as well is an open question and is an object of struggle« (Ikmal 1992, 276). This model of the modern multi-ethnic nation state »transforms the Malay nation that seeks to become a sovereign nation among a community of nations into any other ethnic group in this country« (Burhanuddin, quoted in Ikmal 1992, 277).

These two contradictions, argues Ikmal, namely the transformation of the Malay nation into an ethnic group, on the one hand, and the integration of the immigrant communities within the historical evolution of Malay society and the new state, on the other, define the parameters of the unresolved character of the nationality of the state. It left open the question of the boundaries – political and cultural, and indeed, moral – of the ›people‹ of new state. The sustained tension between the two contradictions – of political vs. cultural nation – generate the ambivalent nature of the state and its policies.

An analytical parallel to Ernst Fraenkel's concept of the Dual State in his characterisation of the German national socialist state (Fraenkel 1941) is suggested here. In drawing upon this concept, however, it is not to two different spheres of state behaviour (the normative and prerogative, as intended by Fraenkel) that are referred to but to two different legitimising and legitimate models of the collective self as constituted by, and in, the independent, new, modern nation state. This duality was to have a crucial bearing on its migration policy.

The imaginary of the Malay (cultural) nation – as well as colonial immigration practice – was drawn from a vision of the past which encompassed the entire Malay-Muslim archipelagic world of Southeast Asia. This framed the unhindered entry – and more importantly, easy access to personal documents issued by the Malaysian state – in the first 30 years of its existence as a territorially sovereign nation state. It was only in 1989 that Indonesian migrants had their status ›regularised‹ as foreign contract workers, rather than as potential entrants to the body politic of the nation. It was only then that, as informants would say, »the door closed«.

Much research still needs to be done as to why this happened and what it signified. In light of the argument above, this virtually unnoticed (in the academic literature) but highly consequential policy shift would signal profound changes in the politics of nation and state and the resultant imagination of the national. And indeed, it was in 1990 that the concept of ›bangsa Malaysia‹ – Malaysian nationality – was first minted and popularised at the highest political level. A collective vision of the modernity of the future – fully industrialised status to be achieved by 2020 – was to be underwritten by »a nation at peace with itself, territorially and ethnically integrated, living in harmony and full and fair partnership, made up of one Malaysian race with political loyalty and dedication towards the nation« (Mahathir Mohamad 1991). The Malaysian economy was in transition, driven to new heights by dynamic market forces and the modernist leadership of a developmentalist state. The drive toward modernity required the harnessing of all national forces, and only those within the territorial jurisdiction of the state could be mobilised. The nation as a territorially delimited political community gained prominence in the imagination of the state.

But the door to labour migration, either through the newly-established formal contract labour market, or the ›back door‹ of nocturnal crossings into the informal labour market, remained wide open to Indonesians, especially with the economic boom of the first half of the 1990s. This decade witnessed the continued growth of widespread popular sentiment against immigrant labour, in particular among the urban Malay lower-income groups. This included migrants of Indonesian origin, now referred to by the derogatory term ›Indon‹, a reference to nationality, not ethnicity. Whereas public protest against the uncontrolled presence of illegal migrants from Indonesia in the 1970s came primarily from Chinese-based political parties such as the Democratic Action Party, popular sentiment against foreign labour, in particular ›Indons‹, legal or otherwise – in the 1990s emanated primarily from the Malay working-class public. In the increasingly tight urban market for jobs and land, local Malays were being pitted against migrant Indonesians, and ended up not infrequently as the losers. Indonesian migrant labour, for various reasons, was frequently the labour of choice, both in the formal and the informal labour markets. State policy, which acquiesced to employer demands for foreign labour recruitment in the context of its own developmentalist goals, came under increasing criticism for its neglect of the welfare of the nation.

In 2002, the decision was taken to reduce the share of Indonesian labour in the foreign workforce. Labour was to be recruited from countries such as Vietnam, which shared little cultural proximity with the Malay nation. Foreign labour was to remain transient and marginal, with no cultural affinities or social interaction with the local body politic. The aim was clearly a migration policy dictated purely by the national interest of a sovereign nation state, the stance taken in the official rhetoric of the state when this new policy engendered a diplomatic row with Indonesia.⁶

Conclusion

Academic production of migration research began in the second half of the 1980s, when the country was hit by a severe economic recession and massive job losses. It was also at the same time that urban Malay working-class resentment of their new co-residents (and old co-ethnics) in their midst first became apparent. Under those circumstances, the large stock of migrant labour from Indonesia already present in the country – until then, entirely undocumented – was framed by academic discovery as a ›problem‹. Working outside of the largely intransparent government decision-making machinery, but within the ambit of national institutions closely associated with the nation-building project of the postcolonial state, the academic framing of the problem was in terms of policy – and implicitly, in terms of state failure to defend the legitimate interest of the nation against territorial encroachments by foreign nationals.

The overwhelming concern with the territorial integrity of the nation state is reflected in the research focus on illegal migration, with the rhetorical figure of the ›illegal‹ taken to be paradigmatic of migrant workers *tout court*. Hardly any studies have been conducted on migrants with work permits working within the confines of the formal contract worker recruitment system, or on those migrants who have acquired permanent resident status in the country. This academic embrace of the territorial and political logic of the nation state is *itself* part of an ongoing profound struggle over the ›soul‹ (Harper 2001) of the nation and the form and identity of the state. Taking its invocation of this logic as issuing from a ›national agenda‹ or a ›national political tradition‹ may be misleading in the context of a postcolonial multiethnic state formation where the question of the ›national‹ has remained long unresolved.

At issue in the deployment of the concept of a ›national paradigm of migration research‹ in the Malaysian context, however, is not merely the (un)accomplished differentiation of state and society, it is also the negligible differentiation of science. In the absence of a robust national culture of research (the reasons for which lie beyond the scope of this paper), the institutional context for migration research in the country is in no small measure conditioned by the trans-national configuration of United Nations agencies and foreign foundations. That the twin issues of illegal migration and human trafficking loom large on the current research agenda of these institutions has been reflected in the production of migration research in Malaysia. The vocabulary of this genre of international migration research, grounded as it is on the assumption of the *sui generis* existence of nation states in

---

6 Indonesian protest included the invocation of the *konfrontasi* of 1965, when the Republic of Indonesia refused to acknowledge the legitimacy of the newly-formed Federation of Malaysia, and launched military hostilies against its territory.

the mould of the modern territorial state, has been as influential. It has been the argument of this paper that any reading of the migration literature in Malaysia has to question this assumption, and question why this assumption has been so readily accepted.

References

Azizah Kassim. 1996. Alien Workers in Malaysia: Critical Issues, Problems and Constraints. In *Movement of People within and from the East and Southeast Asian Countries: Trend, Causes and Consequences,* ed. Carunia Mulya Firdausy, 3–37. Jakarta: Indonesian Institute of Sciences.

Bulletin Immigresen. 1997. Department of Immigration, Kuala Lumpur.

Bank Negara Malaysia. 1997. *Annual Report.* Kuala Lumpur: Government of Malaysia.

Brubaker, Rogers. 1992. *Citizenship and Nationhood in France and Germany.* Cambridge, MA: Harvard University Press.

Darul Amin, Abdul Munaf. 1990. Pendatang Indonesia dan Implikasinya Terhadap Negara Malaysia (1970–1989): Kajian Kes di Kuala Lumpur. Unpublished MA thesis, Faculty of Social Sciences and Humanities, National University of Malaysia.

Fraenkel, Ernst. 1941. *The Dual State: A Contribution to the Theory of Dictatorship.* Translated from German by E.A. Shils, in collaboration with Edith Lowenstein and Klaus Knorr. New York: Oxford University Press.

Freeman, Gary P. 1995. Modes of Immigration Politics in Liberal Democratic States. *International Migation Review* 24: 881–902.

Harper, Tim. 2001. *The End of Empire and the Making of Malaya.* Cambridge: Cambridge University Press.

Ikmal Said, Muhammad. 1992. Ethnic Perspectives of the Left in Malaysia. In *Fragmented Vision: Culture and Politics in Contemporary Malaysia*, ed. Joel Kahn and Loh Kok Wah, 254–81. University of Hawaii Press.

Jahn, Andreas, and Thomas Straubhaar. 1998. A Survey on the Economics of Illegal Migration. http:/www.uni-Konstanz.de/FuF/ueberfak/fzaa/german/veranst/StraubhaarIllegalImmig.htm

Mahathir Mohamad. 1991. Malaysia: The Way Forward. Working paper presented at the Inaugural Meeting of the Malaysian Business Council, Kuala Lumpur, February, 28. Kuala Lumpur: Malaysian Business Council.

Morita, Kiriro, and Saskia Sassen. 1994. The New Illegal Immigration in Japan. *International Migration Review* 28 (1): 153–63.

Pillai, Patrick. 1992. *People on the Move: An Overview of Recent Immigration and Emigration in Malaysia.* Kuala Lumpur: ISIS.

Pillai, Patrick. 1999. The Malaysian State's Response to Migration. *Sojourn* 14: 178–97.
Samers, Michael. 2000. The Political Economy of Illegal Immigration and Informal Employment in the European Union. Paper presented at the conference ›International Migration: New Patterns, New Theories‹, Nottinghan Trent University, September 11–13.
Saw, Swee-Hock. 1988. *The Population of Peninsula Malaysia*. Singapore: Singapore University Press.
Tan, Liok Ee. 1988. *Rhetoric of Bangsa and Min*. Melbourne: Monash Asia Institute.
Tham Siew Yean, and Liew Chei Siang. 2002. Foreign Labour in Malaysian Manufacturing: Enhancing Malaysian Competitiveness? Unpublished paper presented to the international conference ›Globalization, Culture, and Inequalities: In Honour of the Work of the Late Professor Dr. Ishak Shari (1948–2001)‹, UKM, Bangi, August 19–21.
Wimmer, Andreas, and Nina Glick Schiller. 2002. Methodological Nationalism and Beyond: Nation-state Building, Migration and the Social Sciences. *Global Networks* 2 (4): 301–34.
Wong, Diana, and T. Afrizal. 2003. Migran Gelap: Irregular Migrants in Malaysia's Shadow Economy. In *Unauthorized Migration in Southeast Asia*, ed. Graziano Battistella and Maruja Asis, 169–228. Manila: Scalabrini Migration Center.
Wong, Diana. 2006. The Recruitment of Foreign Labour in Malaysia: From Migration System to Guestworker Regime. In *Mobility, Labour Migration and Border Controls in Asia*, ed. Amarjit Kaur and Ian Metcalfe, 213–27. Basingstoke: Palgrave Macmillan.
World Bank. 1995. *Malaysia: Meeting Labor Needs, More Workers and Better Skills*. Washington, DC: World Bank.

A Paradigm for Nigerian Migration Research?

By Dirk van den Boom

Abstract

This paper argues that there will be no significant paradigm within the public and academic discussion in Nigeria about migration policy as long as two major obstacles exist: One is the outward-orientation of the majority of the Nigerian academia, mostly forced by lack of funds for genuine research, which leads them to adjust to the paradigms of those countries who are able to provide financial means for research and publication; the second is the overarching paradigm of ›nation-building‹ which has been imperative especially in an extremely heterogeneous country like Nigeria and is still the transcending subject of social sciences in general, irrespective of the not very encouraging reality on the ground.

Introduction: Wrong Questions, Likely Answers

It is a common feature of the quite westernised academic discourse that it tries to develop questions and paradigms in regard to its own experience of reality and afterwards spreading the internally developed framework into the world, assuming that reality ›should‹ or ›will‹ be seen the same way and that research in regard to acute problems is as acute and as important in other areas of the world as in their own. It is obvious that 90 per cent of the migration debate is taking place in countries which are on the receiving end of mostly economic and job migration, and which are, for one reason or the other, regarding this process as a problem which has to be solved. This comes in congruence with the fact that most of these countries can parade a relatively ›strong‹ state which tends to assume responsibilities everywhere, surely often in response to sometimes sudden public sentiment, sometimes irrespective of rationales and realities. ›Strong‹ states – i.e. states with a relatively effective administration and a relatively high degree of internal legitimacy, therefore a wide area of influence and a variety of more or less well financed ways of political intervention – tend to define political and social phenomena indirectly through their actions. And the academic discourse – sometimes more, sometimes less willingly – takes these actions as proof of fact that there is a problem to be observed, analysed and solved, be it practically or with a more philosophical approach. On the other hand, in ›weak‹ states – and the Federal Republic of Nigeria, which is in the focus of this contribution, is generally regarded as such – the ›agenda setting‹ of both the academic discourse and the identification of political and social problems is more simple and more complex at the same time. It is more simple in regard to the fact that academic discourse is really mostly confined to the academia, the linkage between public sentiment or opinion and the academic scene is weak, corresponding to the gap between the rulers and the ruled. The academic system, heavily dependent on the government resources to survive, orients itself according to the agendas set by the rulers, and if they do not set them, there is hardly any reaction. It is more complex in the regard that because of the quite limited resources, some professional researchers are outward oriented, perceiving and internalising the discourse in the ›strong‹ states and, with the inherent desire to be part of a worldwide academic community, they are therefore developing access to research funds. The inherent danger is that the content of the discourse is simply copied, only some terms are exchanged and the needed empirical research is only done in regard to questions which have been formulated somewhere outside. Sometimes luck is with the research and the foreign discourse has asked the right questions. Some other times the linkage between the question and the expected answers is weak because of quite different circumstances. Asking for a paradigm of migration research in Nigeria – a country with considerable migration experience both as recipient and source of migrants – is possibly just such a question no one in Nigeria really bothers about – if not for someone from the outside who will ask it. The author of this contribution is from the outside and therefore in an awkward position. He has to find an answer to a question he possibly considers ill-placed. There is, however, an answer and it will be given. Nevertheless one has to take into consideration that it might be possible that the answer is – for the Nigerian research community – as irrelevant as the question.

Paradigms in Nigerian Research Discourse

Academic discussions in Nigeria – and their linkage to government policies – have always been full of paradigms. Many of them were quite superficial, trying to introduce the author into the research mainstream by using certain ›buzzwords‹ which would cause automatic acclaim and acceptance without much regard to the quality of the work actually done. Questions of ›identity‹, ›ethnicity‹ and ›religion‹ have been abundant, and two general trends in the analysis emerged: First, the evident desire to use these topics to mould an academic foundation for the ›multi-ethnic society‹ members of the Nigerian elite proclaim as the ideal for the crisis-ridden country. Therefore, the research done, a lot of it in a rather essayistic form, had primarily a political goal, not an empirical or scientific one. Second, other scientists made their point by proving through their analysis that there are needs to rethink and reform the Nigerian polity state as such to have any chance to survive as one. This more critical attitude again had a primarily political goal. The question of ›nation building‹ – one or the other way – can be described as the paramount paradigm in the political discourse in Nigeria, and all other issues generally submit to it. Paradigms in regard to what – in reference to the British discussion – might be called ›race relations‹ are part of the general discussion about the »reality of the Nigerian nation« (Uwazie 1999, 2), or, to be more precise, about the question if there is or ever will be something like a Nigerian nation. To this day, this general question is highly disputed in the country itself, not only among the academia. So if we talk about paradigms in a national discourse on a certain matter, we might come back to the remarks of one of the foremost Nigerian politicians after independence, Obafemi Awolowo, who wrote in 1947: »Nigeria is not a nation. It is a mere geographical expression. There are no ›Nigerians‹ [...]. The word ›Nigeria‹ is merely a distinctive appellation to distinguish those who live within the boundaries [...] from those who do not« (Awolowo 1947, 47f.). If there is no nation, there will be no national discourse. If every Nigerian, as Awolowo surely expected, identifies himself primarily through his primordial group, how should the scientific community, the amalgamation of scientists from all these different ethnic groups, be able to develop common paradigms? In fact, accusations of ›ethnic bias‹ in regard to certain political matters are easily traded against each other in Nigeria. Nevertheless, the amount of research done under the paradigm of ›nation building‹ within a ›multi-ethnic society‹ is considerable (despite the fact that nearly none of it concentrates on the question of international migration). Be it from conviction or by force, to please and further the official ideology of the nation state, the paradigm exists. Whether it is always taken seriously, is a totally different question.

In this context the question of religion comes to the forefront automatically. It has strong linkages to the discussion of migration as well, because governments and moderate religious leaders have always been quick to condemn ›foreigners‹ to incite religious turmoil and clashes when violence erupted. Besides that, the ›nation-building‹ paradigm and religion are heavily intertwined in the academic discussion. There is no paper about ethnic relations within Nigeria that does not emphasise the influence of the great divide of religions in Nigeria, i.e. between the Muslim and Christian faith. Despite the fact that different religious beliefs transcend ethnicity – best illustrated by the second largest ethnic group, the Yoruba, which is roughly equally divided among Muslims and Christians – the discussion sometimes gives the impression that followers of religions are themselves some kind of an ›ethnic group‹ and that both of them try to use ›foreigners‹ to pursue their interest – be it missionaries, money from Saudi-Arabia or illegal migrants from predominantly Muslim neighbours who are ›permitted‹ to enter the country without proper procedure. But this is primarily a matter of public, political discourse, not of the scientific one. When it comes to the subject of religion and migration, science has been reluctant and careful to point fingers. Too much damage can be done if caught up in the overheated, highly politicised and often violent religious discussions in Nigeria. In this context it is worth to note one utterance by one of the foremost Nigerian researchers – in fact, teaching and publishing in the United States – by the name of Toyin Falola. In reference to the situation in Nigeria, he said: »Pluralism endangers political stability« (Falola 1997, ix). Again, the paradigm of ›nation building‹ shows up, as political stability, the continuity of the existence of the Nigerian state project, is seemingly of higher interest than the pursuit for a viable pluralism. Migrants may or may not be a danger for this goal but the historical evidence shows that the political elite has played this card repeatedly in times of crisis. In summary, all political, philosophical and sociological discussion in Nigeria has always returned to one basic question, which still awaits a definite answer. To use the words of Crawford Young, who has published widely on questions of culture and politics in Africa, it is all about »how to define a new cultural identity linked to the dimension of the polity and related to commonalities among the polity's populace, while eschewing identification of the state with any one of the cultural segments within it, which would immediately threaten the identity of other collectives.« (Young 1976, 93). If there is a possible paradigm for migration research in Nigeria, that would fit the description. But is there any?

Migration Policy in Nigeria: A Short Survey

The Federal Republic of Nigeria enjoys a special status in Africa, mostly because of the fact that it is the most populous nation and – before Angola took over recently – the biggest exporter of crude oil on the continent. The development of migration policy in Nigeria has always been highly dependent on the economic status and the political framework, which, for most of the time, has been shaped by military governments.

During the 1970s and early 1980s, the Nigerian labour market attracted a huge number of foreigners because of the oil boom, the resulting earnings in hard currency and, in parallel, the economic downturn of many of the neighbouring countries, especially anglophone Ghana. Generally, in terms of receiving migrants, Nigeria has been quite a ›late-comer‹ in West Africa. In the 1960s countries like the Ivory Coast, Senegal and Ghana have been the preferred goals for especially labour migration. The collapse of the Ghanaian economy during the 1970s and the search of the anglophone population for new opportunities, the economic dependence on Nigeria by the francophone countries Benin and Togo, the increasingly difficult ecological situation in neighbouring Sahel countries – like Niger and Tchad, in the latter case intensified by civil war – lead to a massive, mostly illegal labour migration to Nigeria. The migrants were easily absorbed especially in the booming construction industry, the emerging harbour facilities along the coastline and in those jobs the average Nigerian was not willing to do anymore, especially unqualified manual work and services (Afolayan 1988, 13). With the collapse of the oil boom in the beginning of the 1980s two historical political decisions in regard to migrants were taken: The extradition of illegal migrants, mostly Ghanaians, in 1983 and 1985. About two million people were affected. This internationally reported action caused a short-lived ›flash attraction‹ for Nigeria in international migration research as well.

Of generally greater importance – in the academic field as well – was the problem of internal migration. Beside the common problem of migration from the rural areas to the urban centres, labour migration within the country (mostly from the north to the south) and forced internal migration under the continuity of oppressive military dictatorships have been a regular feature of Nigerian politics (overview: Dare 1997). During the civil war between 1967 and 1970, more than one million Ibo were internally displaced. During the 1980s and 1990s internal displacement because of mostly ethnic and religious violence was abundant. In 2000, more than 50,000 mostly Christian Nigerians had to leave their places of residence in the north because of religious turmoil after the introduction of sharia law in many northern federal states. Internal displacement has always been high on the agenda in regard to political management, despite the fact that the reaction of the political leadership mostly remained to be helpless or oppressive.

Another important feature of Nigerian migration policy was the management of the phenomenon of illegal migration of Nigerians to the US and Europe. Especially the new democratic dispensation since 1999 – the IV. Republic – has seen it necessary to engage in crisis management in this regard.

In congruence with nearly all other African countries, Nigeria has always been open to refugee migration caused by crises in neighbouring countries. There has never been a significant quantity of refugees, aside from a limited number of war refugees from Liberia and Sierra Leone.

Shaping and Agenda Setting in an Autocratic Democracy

Paradigms in Nigerian research are, as we have seen, mostly set by two sources: The government policy of the country itself and, to a lesser degree, the academic interest of the international research community. It is therefore necessary to point out some underlying features of government policy in Nigeria to be able to understand why – until now – no national paradigm specifically in regard to migration policy has been developed, despite a variety of visible migration phenomena in the country.

As mentioned above, the political history of Nigeria is a continuous succession of military dictatorships, only interrupted by short periods of civil rule (overview: Osaghae 1998). Despite the fact that Nigeria has called itself a democracy since 1999, political decision-making is still centred around autocratic and dictatorial traditions (some scholars call it the ›military psyche‹ of Nigerian politics), making the single person in the centre of power – in this case the president of the Federal Republic and, more recently, the governors of the 36 federal states – the only legitimate source of agenda setting in Nigeria. Evidently, during its 40 years of existence, no Nigerian president has found it useful to develop anything like a migration agenda or political doctrine dealing with this area. As politics only starts ›when the president arrives‹, areas of political intervention are totally left in limbo as long as the single source of legitimacy is not willing or capable to or interested in attaching itself to the problem. There have been small exceptions: The politics of indigenisation during the 1970s with the aim to incorporate more able Nigerians into internationally owned enterprises had a certain strategy and limited e.g. the influx of highly qualified management staff from outside the country. The recruitment of teachers from Ghana during the 1970s to bolster the rapidly growing Nigerian education sector is another instance of government initiative in regard to labour migration. But these single decisions were not put in any comprehensive political framework. Migration policy in Nigeria has always been and is likely to remain an example of ›patchwork policy‹ which reacts – more or less blessed with insight and ability – to occuring problems, following a ›fire-brigade approach‹ (reacting to political crises with sudden force but without any long-term strategy) which is a familiar feature of internal politics not only in Nigeria.

In addition, the state apparatus and administration, heavily affected by widespread corruption, is by no means a good tool to put a possible migration policy effectively into place. There are many ways, mostly greased by money, to avoid any legal requirement in regard to immigration in Nigeria. The basic illness of a rent-seeking state, more interested in the distribution of the oil wealth than in effective service-delivery, is therefore hampering any earnest effort in creating an agenda for migration policy. Often, the immediate management of migration is left to the federal states. In fact, the wide and mostly deserted borders of Nigeria make any effective border regime a logistical nightmare. Migration takes place permanently and is mostly recognised only when the migrants have already arrived where they wanted to go to.

In these conditions, where there is no agenda set by any government in regard to migration policy, it is quite obvious that the average Nigerian researcher tends to look into problems which seem to be of higher interest – either in attaining the favourable acknowledgement of the government or funds from the international community. Questions like the ethnic relations in the oil-producing areas of the Niger Delta have prominence, as well as religious relations since the introduction of sharia. Migration to and from Nigeria does, until now, not belong to this category.

A Basis for Research: The Nigerian University System

If we deal with the Nigerian situation, we have to take into account the current state of university research, especially its material and logistic framework. Despite the fact that Nigeria has over the last 30 years developed one of the most dense university systems in Sub-Saharan Africa – with more than 40 universities and technical colleges, not to count the numerous private institutions – the current state of affairs can best be described as a relative decay. During the boom period of the 1970s, increasing oil revenue made it possible to rapidly expand the system. In addition to that, following British traditions, the higher education concentrated on ›soft sciences‹. Political science, sociology and related subjects featured and feature prominently in Nigerian universities. Unfortunately, since the beginning of the 1980s the university system has been consistently neglected by various military governments, not only because they were known as breeding grounds for political opposition, but also because of either dwindling or misused state resources. At the beginning of the 1990s, the universities in Nigeria were in a catastrophic condition, marred by permanent strikes, sometimes lasting for years, by the university teachers union ASUU. Research facilities were chronically underfunded, salaries not forthcoming, many researchers either tried desperately to leave the country or had to revert to additional jobs to make a living – be it taxi driving. In this environment, only few Nigerian researchers have been able to develop and maintain a distinct record of independent and worthwhile research. Since the inauguration of the IV. Republic, small reforms have taken place which might finally lead to university-autonomy and the end of tuition-free higher education.[1] They might also facilitate the renewal of university research in Nigeria. It is obvious that Nigeria does not generate a conducive environment for migration research, taking all problems and obstacles into consideration.

Conclusive Remarks: If there is none, do we need one?

In final consideration, one might come to the conclusion that the apparent absence of profound migration research, the problematic circumstances under which Nigerian researchers still have to struggle and the lacklustre approach by consecutive Nigerian governments towards the issue do not give sufficient reason to believe that either a research paradigm will develop itself or is even needed. In the current state of affairs in Nigeria, where problems of internal cohesion, distribution of wealth, economic development and perseverance of peace and stability are on the forefront of issues to be tackled, it is in fact quite obvious that the overwhelming paradigm of Nigerian research – ›nation building within a multi-ethnic society‹ – will continue to overshadow everything and everyone. Furthermore, it is these pressing issues of national survival and meaningful development which have to be addressed first and foremost, before migration will even be perceived as a vital problem. As long as official politics will not concentrate considerable resources towards the phenomenon of especially labour migration to Nigeria, it is not to be expected that Nigerian research will spearhead any development in this area. This does not mean that international migration research will be as negligent. In the course of the observation that those willing to travel from the rural area to the urban area, and then from one country to the neighbouring country, are most likely those willing to take another step and leave the continent altogether, it will be interesting and worthwhile to examine labour migration in West Africa thoroughly. Current research especially in the ›remittances‹ issue, closely linked to development policy, points into that direction. These migrants are likely candidates for illegal labour migration e.g. to Europe, their biographies, their motivations, their experiences and their strategies for survival are of high interest if we want to understand migration to Europe better. In the end, migration research regarding this specific area will be led by another paradigm of the north, or otherwise it will not be done for the foreseeable future. Keeping that in mind, and

---

1 Including some problems of its own, see: *Re-Engineering Nigerian Universities*, in: Vanguard (Lagos), 5 June 2003.

with all apprehension, well-developed research may have some helpful insights for the situation in Nigeria as well, if the right questions are asked and the right approach is used. For a start, the lack of a Nigerian paradigm in migration research might even prove to be helpful in the search of open-minded Nigerian colleagues who might be activated to participate in this context. Whatever the case, Nigeria will remain an important country for migration both as a recipient and a source. Migration research should have that in mind, wherever in the world it is done.

References

Afolayan, A.A. 1988. Immigration and Expulsion of ECOWAS Aliens in Nigeria. *International Migration Review* 22 (1): 4-27.

Awolowo, Obafemi. 1947. *Path to Nigerian Freedom*. London: Faber.

Dare, Leo. 1997. Political Instability and Displacement in Nigeria. In *Displacement and the Politics of Violence in Nigeria*, ed. Paul E. Lovejoy and Pat A.T. Williams, 21–30. Leiden et al.: Brill.

Falola, Toyin. 1997. Foreword. In *Religious Pluralism and the Nigeria State*, ed. Simeon O. Ilesanmi. Athens: Ohio University Center for International Studies.

Osaghae, Eghosa E. 1998. *The Crippled Giant: Nigeria since Independence*. Bloomington, IN: Indiana University Press.

Uwazie, Ernest E. 1999. Inter-Ethnic and Religious Conflict Resolution in Nigeria: An Introduction. In: *Inter-Ethnic and Religious Conflict Resolution in Nigeria*, ed. idem, Isaac O. Albert, and Godfrey N. Uzoigewe, 16. Lanham et al.: Lexington.

Young, Crawford. 1976. *The Politics of Cultural Pluralism*. Madison: University of Wisconsin Press.

The Authors

Sigrid Baringhorst holds a Chair in Political Science and is currently Dean of Faculty at the University of Siegen, Germany. She works on comparative integration and migration policies, political communication and in the field of social movement studies. She is author of *Fremde in der Stadt* (1991), *Politik als Kampagne* (1998), co-author of *Protest Online/Online* (2009) and co-editor of *Politische Steuerung von Integration* (2006), *Herausforderung Migration* (2006), *Politik mit dem Einkaufswagen* (2007), and *Political Campaigning on the Web* (2009).

Michael Bommes, Dr. phil. habil., is Professor for Sociology/Methodology of Intercultural and Interdisciplinary Migration Research at the Institute for Migration Research and Intercultural Studies (IMIS), University of Osnabrück, Germany. He studied sociology, linguistics and philosophy in Osnabrück, Marburg and Birmingham. His research fields are: migration and political system, migration and organisation, migration and social theory, methodological problems of interdisciplinary and cross-cultural research. Among his recent publications are: *International Migration Research: Constructions, Omissions and the Promises of Interdisciplinarity* (ed. with Ewa Morawska, 2005); *Illegalität: Grenzen und Möglichkeiten der Migrationspolitik* (ed. with Jörg Alt, 2006); *Migrationsreport 2008. Fakten – Analysen – Perspektiven* (ed. with Marianne Krüger-Potratz, 2008).

Tiziana Caponio, Ph.D. in Political Science, University of Florence, 2003, teaches Political Sociology and Sociology of Migration at the University of Turin, Italy, Faculty of Political Science. She collaborates with FIERI (Forum for International and European Research on Immigration, based in Turin) and is co-leader (together with Giovanna Zincone) of the IMISCOE network Cluster C9 on ›The Multilevel Governance of Migration‹. Her research interests are in policy-making of immigrant and immigration policy, with a focus on the city level, as well as on immigrants and second generations' integration processes.

Krystyna Iglicka, economist and social demographer, Professor at the Lazarski School of Commerce and Law, Warsaw, Poland; Polish government expert on migration policy. Ph.D. in 1993 (Warsaw School of Economics), habilitation degree in Economics (University of Warsaw) in 2003. She was a Fulbright Fellow at the University of Pennsylvania in 1999/2000 and a Polish Science Foundation, British Academy and Foreign and Commonwealth Office Fellow at the University of London, 1996–1999. She published eleven academic books, forty research papers and articles in academic journals in the USA, the UK and Poland and numerous policy-oriented reports and analyses.

Takashi Kibe, Professor of Political Science at International Christian University, Tokyo, Japan; Dr. rer. soc., University of Tübingen, Germany. His research interests are egalitarianism, multiculturalism, citizenship, migration politics, philosophy of social sciences, and history of political thought. He published *Frieden und Erziehung in Martin Luthers Drei-Stände-Lehre* (1996). His last publication is: Differentiated Citizenship and Ethnocultural Groups: A Japanese Case. *Citizenship Studies* 10 (2006), 485–502.

Daniel Naujoks is an attorney at law and a doctoral research fellow at the Migration Research Group, Hamburg Institute of International Economics (HWWI) and at the Institute of Political Science, University of Münster, Germany. He has been engaged with the International Labour Organization and the United Nations Population Division. His forthcoming doctoral dissertation is on *India's New Membership Concepts: Policy Change in the Light of Migration and Development*. He has written several analyses of dual citizenship policies as well as on terms and systematisations of diasporas.

Bernhard Perchinig, Dr. phil, is a faculty member of the Department for European Integration and Law of the Danube University Krems and a lecturer at the Institute for Political Sciences at Vienna University, Austria. His main research interests are citizenship policies, antidiscrimination policy, European migration policies and urban integration. He has served as a consultant to the European Commission, the Council of Europe, the Fundamental Rights Agency, the Migration Policy Group and the International Organisation for Migration (IOM).

Baukje Prins is Associate Professor for Citizenship and Diversity at the Hague University of Applied Sciences, The Netherlands. She is the author of *Voorbij de onschuld* (2004), a study on the debates on immigrant integration in the Netherlands which also appeared in Czech (*Konec nevinnosti*, 2005). Recent articles appeared in the *European Journal of Women's Studies*, *Social Theory and Practice*, and *Ethnicities*. She is currently working on a book on inter-ethnic relationships through the life-stories of her former Frisian and Moluccan classmates in the 1960s.

Oliver Schmidtke is Associate Professor and a European Studies Scholar in the Department of Political Science at the University of Victoria, Canada, where he also holds the Jean Monnet Chair in European History and Politics. He received his Ph.D. from the European University Institute in Florence, worked at the Humboldt University in Berlin in the late 1990s and spent a year as a research fellow at the Center for European Studies at Harvard University before coming to UVic in 1999. In 2007 he was a Fernand Braudel Senior Scholar at the EUI and currently acts as leader of the domain ›Citizenship and Social, Cultural and Civic Integration‹ for Metropolis BC. His research interests are in the fields of citizenship, the political sociology of immigration and ethnic conflict, the role of identities and the transformation of the nation state.

Karen Schönwälder is Research Group Leader at the Max Planck Institute for the Study of Religious and Ethnic Diversity in Göttingen, Germany. She previously worked at the Social Science Research Center (WZB) in Berlin, the University of London and at several German universities. Her current project investigates issues of diversity and inter-ethnic interaction in European cities and the political incorporation of immigrants. She has published widely on migration and integration policies and processes, with a focus on Germany and Britain. A detailed list of her publications can be found at www.mmg.mpg.de

Dietrich Thränhardt is Professor emeritus at the University of Münster, Germany, where he was Dean of the Philosophical Faculty and Director of the Institute of Political Science. He was a fellow at the Transatlantic Academy, Washington DC, at the Netherlands Institute for Advanced Study (NIAS), and he served as a guest professor at the International Christian University, Tokyo. Among his books are *Europe – A New Immigration Continent* (2nd ed. 1994), *Geschichte der Bundesrepublik Deutschland* (2nd ed. 1996), *Migration im Spannungsfeld von Globalisierung und Nationalstaat* (2003) and *Entwicklung und Migration* (2008).

Dirk van den Boom, Dr. phil., works as consultant with the Association of Experts in the Fields of Migration and Development Cooperation (AGEF), lecturer of Political Science at the University of Münster. Publications in regard to Subsahara-Africa and development policy, e.g.: *Bürgerkrieg in Liberia* (1993), *Afrika: Stagnation oder Neubeginn?* (1996, ed. with Paul Kevenhörster), *Regionale Kooperation in Westafrika* (1996), *Probleme der Süd-Süd-Kooperation* (1997, ed.), *Tiger, Jaguare und Elefanten. Politische und ökonomische Aufstiegsprozesse sich entwickelnder Staaten im Vergleich* (2001, ed.), *Nigeria-Jahrbücher 2000, 2001, 2002*.

Diana Wong is currently working as Research Coordinator on a Social Science Research Council (New York) project on ›The Religious Lives of Immigrant Communities‹. She obtained her first degree in sociology from the University of Singapore and her Ph.D. from the University of Bielefeld. She was previously teaching in Germany, Singapore and Malaysia. Her current research interests are in the area of international migration and other transborder issues.